Watercolor

DREAMSCAPES

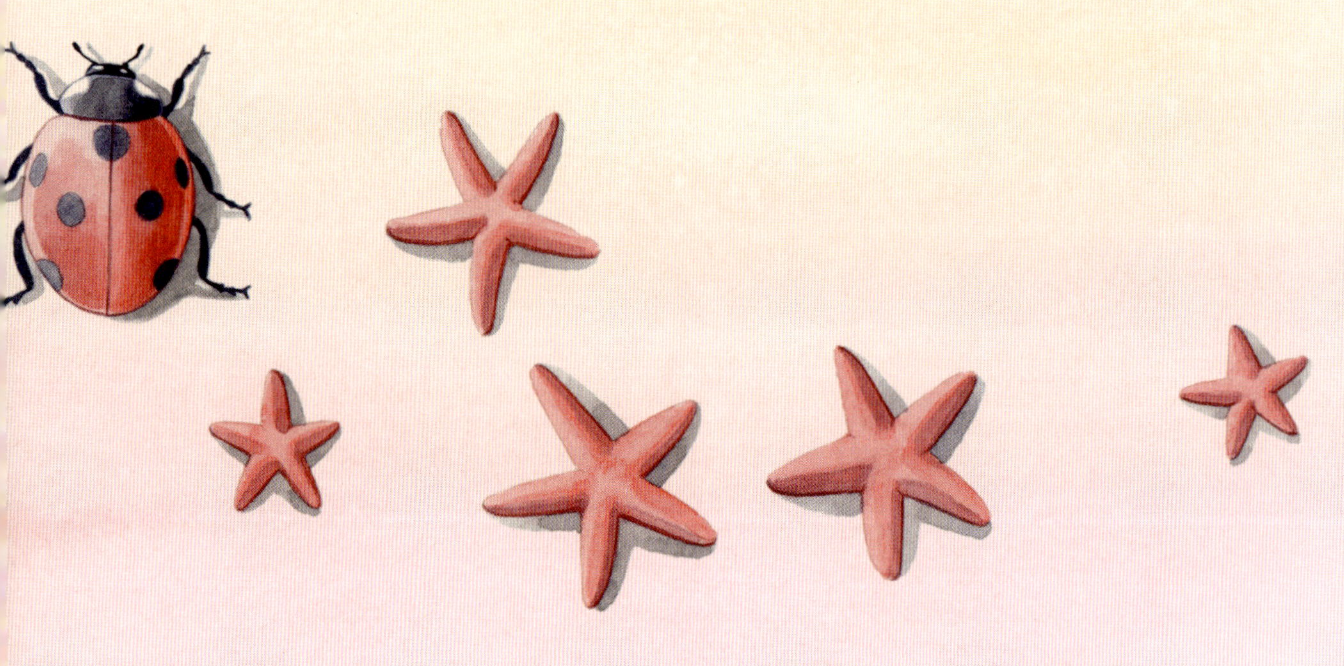

Watercolor

DREAMSCAPES

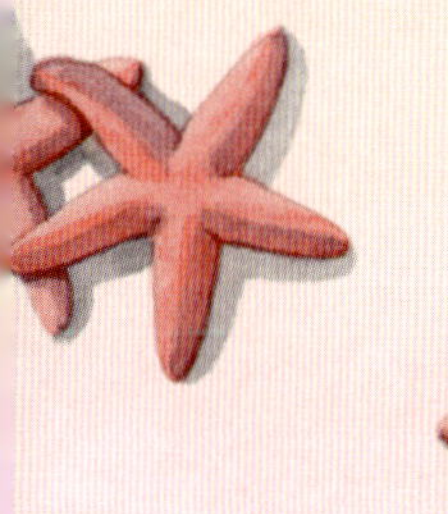
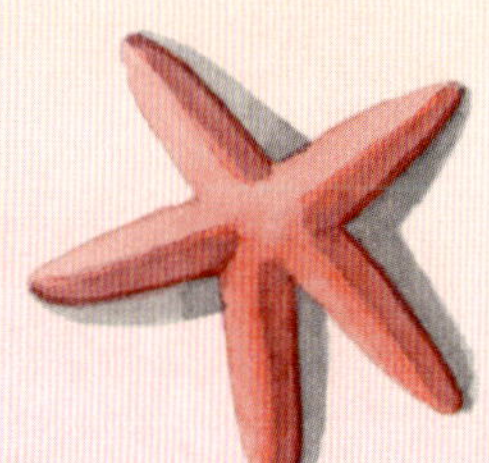

20 Whimsical Projects to Create
Otherworldly Creatures and Surreal Scenes

CHRISTOPHER MAXWELL

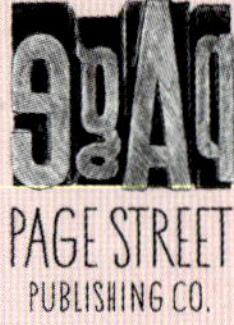

PAGE STREET
PUBLISHING CO.

First published in 2025 by

Page Street Publishing Co.

27 Congress Street, Suite 1511

Salem, MA 01970

www.pagestreetpublishing.com

Distributed by Macmillan, sales in Canada by The Canadian Manda Group.

29 28 27 26 25   1 2 3 4 5

ISBN-13: 979-8890032782

Library of Congress Control Number: 2024945233

Edited by Sadie Hofmeester

Cover and book design by Elena Van Horn for Page Street Publishing Co.

Artwork by Christopher Maxwell

Printed and bound in China

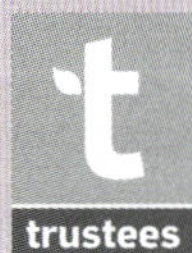

DEDICATION

To my loving Mum and Dad, who bought me my first watercolor set
and enrolled me in weekend classes.

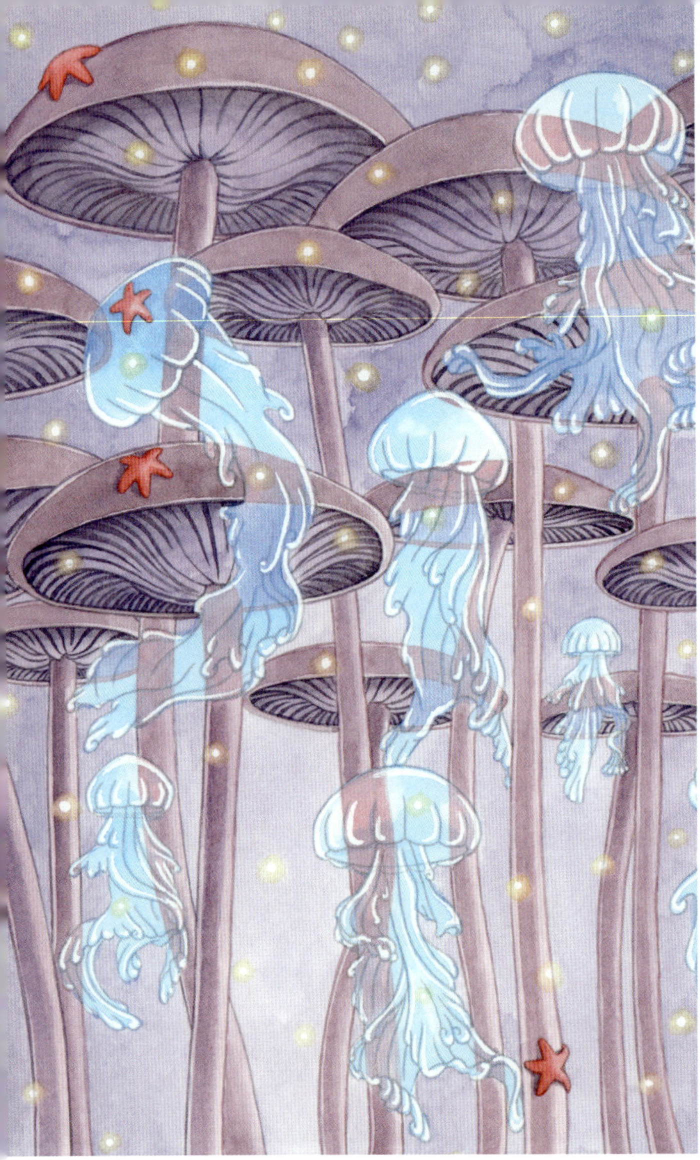

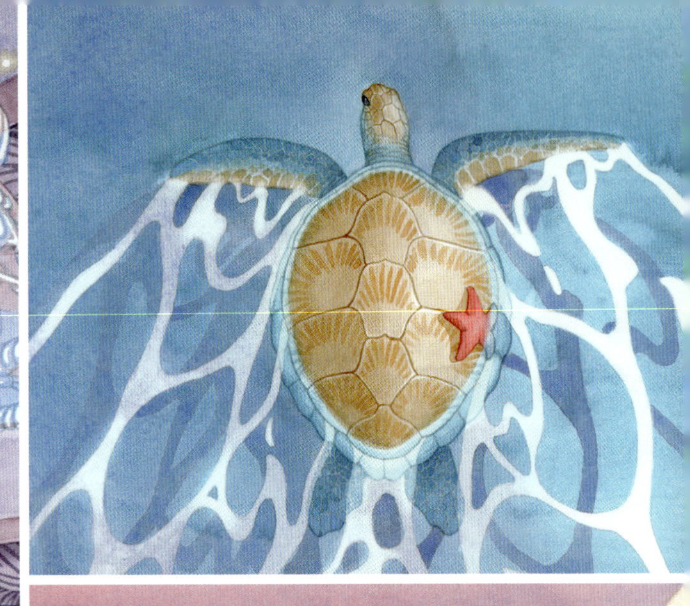
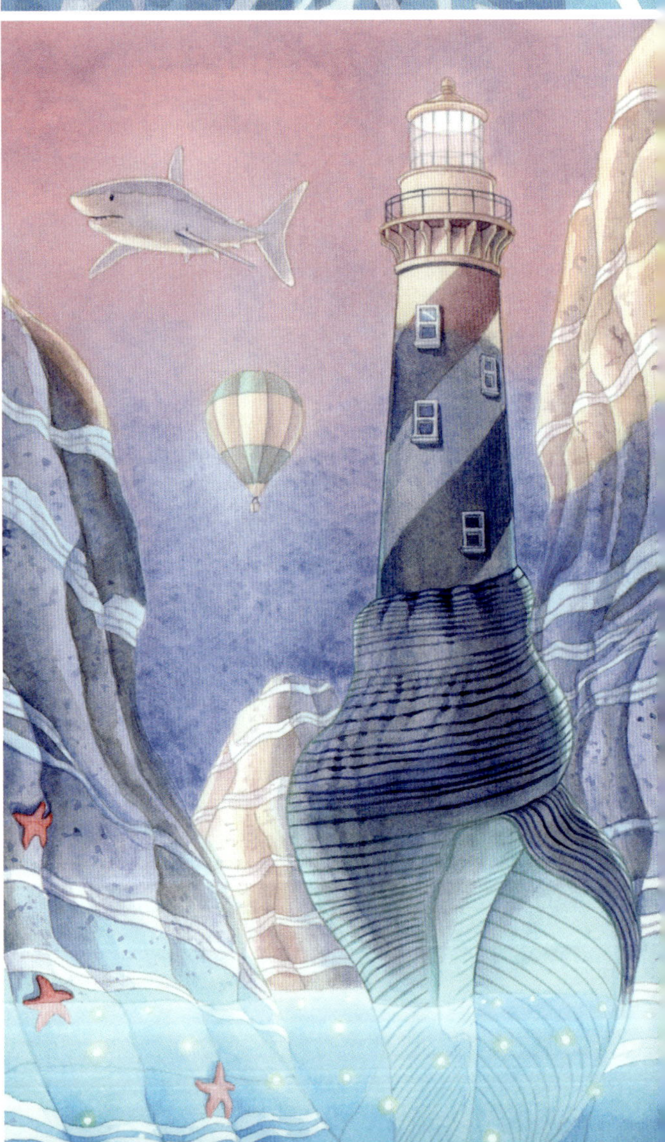
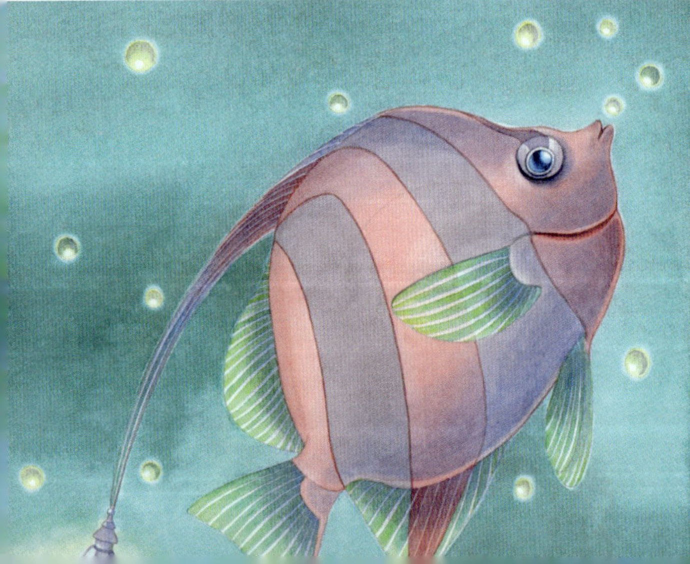

Contents

INTRODUCTION

Making this book accessible was my top priority—I wanted it to be something anyone could follow, no matter their skill level. In today's world, information on any topic is more readily available than ever. With that in mind, I aimed to move away from the more tedious, repetitive aspects of watercolor instruction and instead create something unique: a book filled with engaging illustrations that readers could re-create while learning important techniques and processes. My goal was to spark inspiration and encourage readers to develop their own imaginative scenes.

This book is all about trying something new and having fun along the way. You don't need to master every aspect of watercolor to produce great results. What matters most is being open to the process and giving yourself the freedom to experiment. Not everything will come easily, and that's okay. Sometimes, it takes persistence and a positive attitude to keep moving forward.

Take me, for instance—writing isn't my strongest skill. I usually teach through visual formats like videos, which is also how I prefer to learn. The thought of putting my ideas into written form felt a bit overwhelming. But I've come to appreciate the unique benefits of learning from a physical book with clear, step-by-step instructions. Stepping out of my comfort zone to take on this challenge is what led to this book you're now holding. It's a practical, enjoyable workbook packed with insights and lessons I've learned—ones I believe every watercolorist can benefit from.

I want to personally thank you for purchasing this book. Your support means a lot to me. While it's impossible to please everyone, my hope is that this book inspires you and helps you discover new things about this beautiful medium. Watercolor can be challenging, but having a positive mindset will go a long way toward helping you grow. Don't be too hard on yourself if things don't turn out exactly how you imagined right away. It's a journey, and everyone progresses at their own pace—sometimes in weeks, months, or even years. What truly matters is that you're enjoying the process and finding joy in your creative exploration.

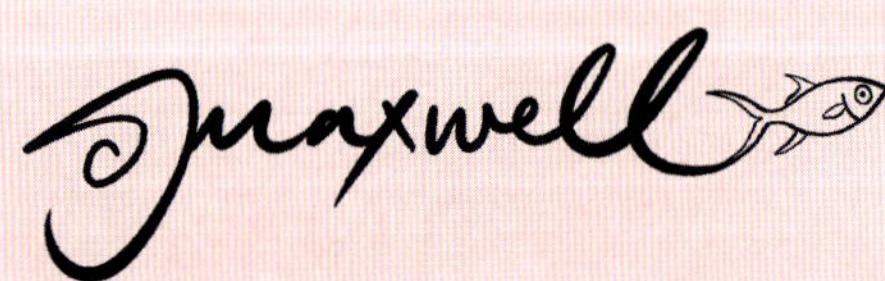

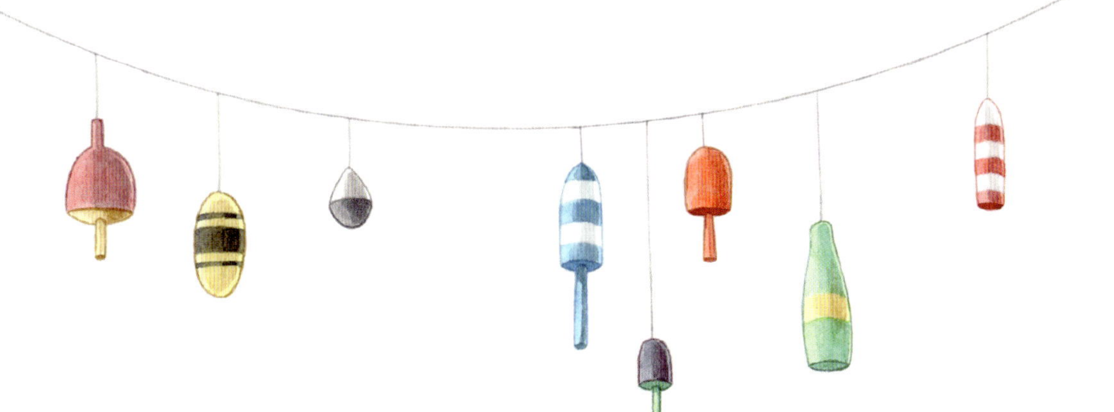

HOW TO USE THIS BOOK

The best part about this book is that you can use it however you like. There's no right or wrong way—it's all about enjoying the learning process and only doing what feels comfortable for you. Chapter 1: Wooden Voyage (page 17), which has four projects, is designed to be done in sequence, but there are no rules. Feel free to explore the book in your own way! All the project sketches (page 193) are provided as tear-outs, making it easy for you to trace each illustration multiple times onto your watercolor paper of choice. I've also included the sketches for the whimsical filler illustrations sprinkled throughout the book on pages 235 through 239. I hope they inspire you to create your own unique compositions and have fun!

Even if you don't want to follow the steps right away, you can use the designs as a coloring book and paint watercolor washes to fill them in. Simply trace them on your preferred watercolor paper and dive in. This can be a relaxing approach that helps you build confidence in your brush control before moving on to the more detailed steps. By removing the pressure, you'll likely find yourself achieving better results and feeling more open to tackling the challenging projects.

If you're feeling particularly ambitious, all the projects in this book can be taken to the next level by increasing depth and using dramatic lighting to enhance the mood. If you'd like to explore even more possibilities, come say hi! You can find me at christophermaxwellart.com and on Instagram, YouTube, and TikTok @christophermaxwellart.

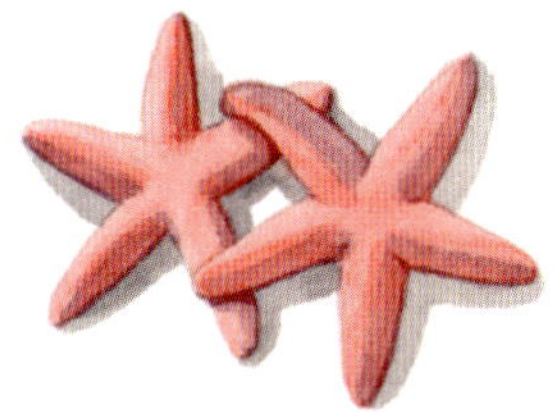

7 VALUABLE POINTERS

Invest in Yourself

Invest in 100% cotton, high gsm watercolor paper to prevent warping and achieve smooth washes. Often, a beginner's frustration stems not from their ability but from the limitations of the paper they are using.

Glaze to Win

These thin, translucent layers increase luminosity and allow for more complex color mixing directly on the paper, creating a vibrant, glowing effect. Keep in mind that whenever you glaze, you will partially reactivate the color beneath, shifting some pigments around and mixing them with your new color.

Patience of a Monk

Watercolor painting takes time! You build your painting from light to dark, often layering over areas multiple times to create tonal variation and depth. It's not until the end of the process that you'll see everything come together, so trust the journey and give your eye time to assess what the painting needs. You will achieve better results when you don't rush this process or become frustrated by the unpredictable flow of watercolors.

Think in Reverse

Unlike other art mediums, it's helpful to consider your lighting first. Light areas in watercolor cannot be easily recovered, so plan your highlights and negative space beforehand. Build up your painting gradually, starting with light washes and layering darker tones.

Avoid White

Using white watercolor paint reduces the transparency that makes watercolor painting unique, giving your colors a cloudy, dull appearance. Also, avoid yellows that contain a lot of white. Instead, for large highlights, leave areas with minimal pigment or untouched completely. You can always use white gel pens or white permanent ink for small finishing details.

No to Premixed Blacks

Premixed blacks tend to give a dull and flat appearance. You can equally mix all three primary colors together or use colors like French Ultramarine and Burnt Sienna to create blacks with more depth and dimension.

Pans for Beginners

Mixing colors in smaller quantities with less pigment is easier, which is why I recommend watercolor pans for beginners. Transferring paint from your pan to a mixing palette allows for a more gradual process. In contrast, paint from tubes is highly concentrated when first squeezed onto your palette, making it more challenging to control color ratios during mixing.

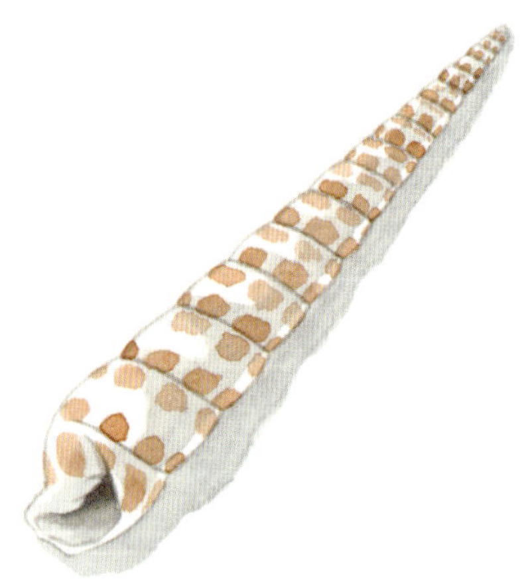

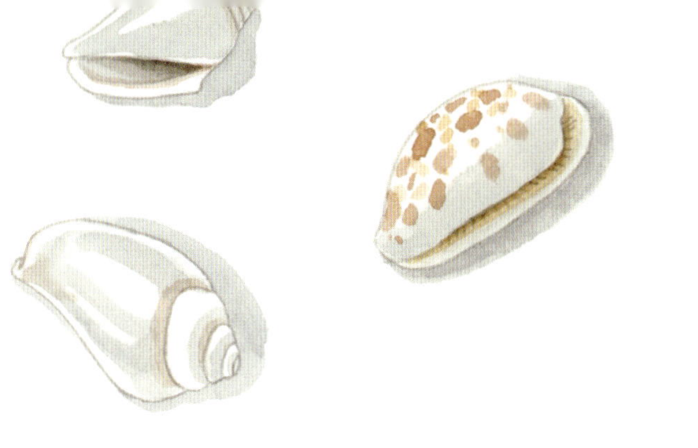
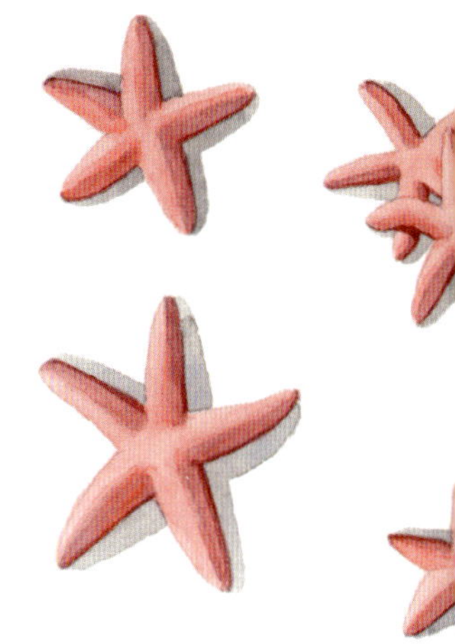
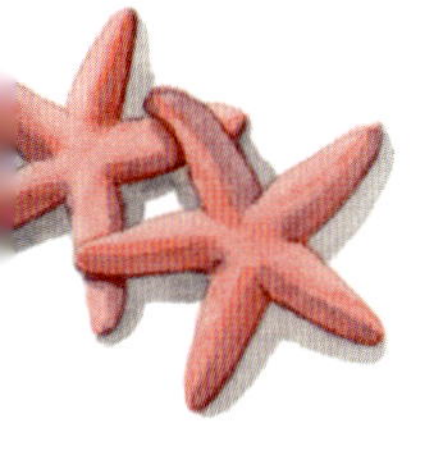

"There are no mistakes
when you are having fun."

- CHRISTOPHER MAXWELL

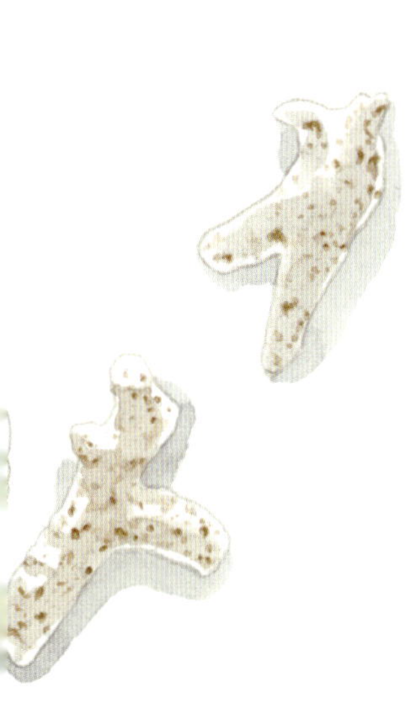

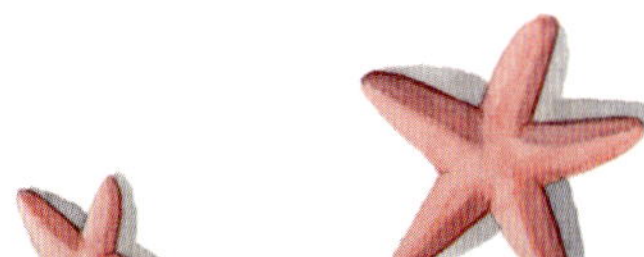

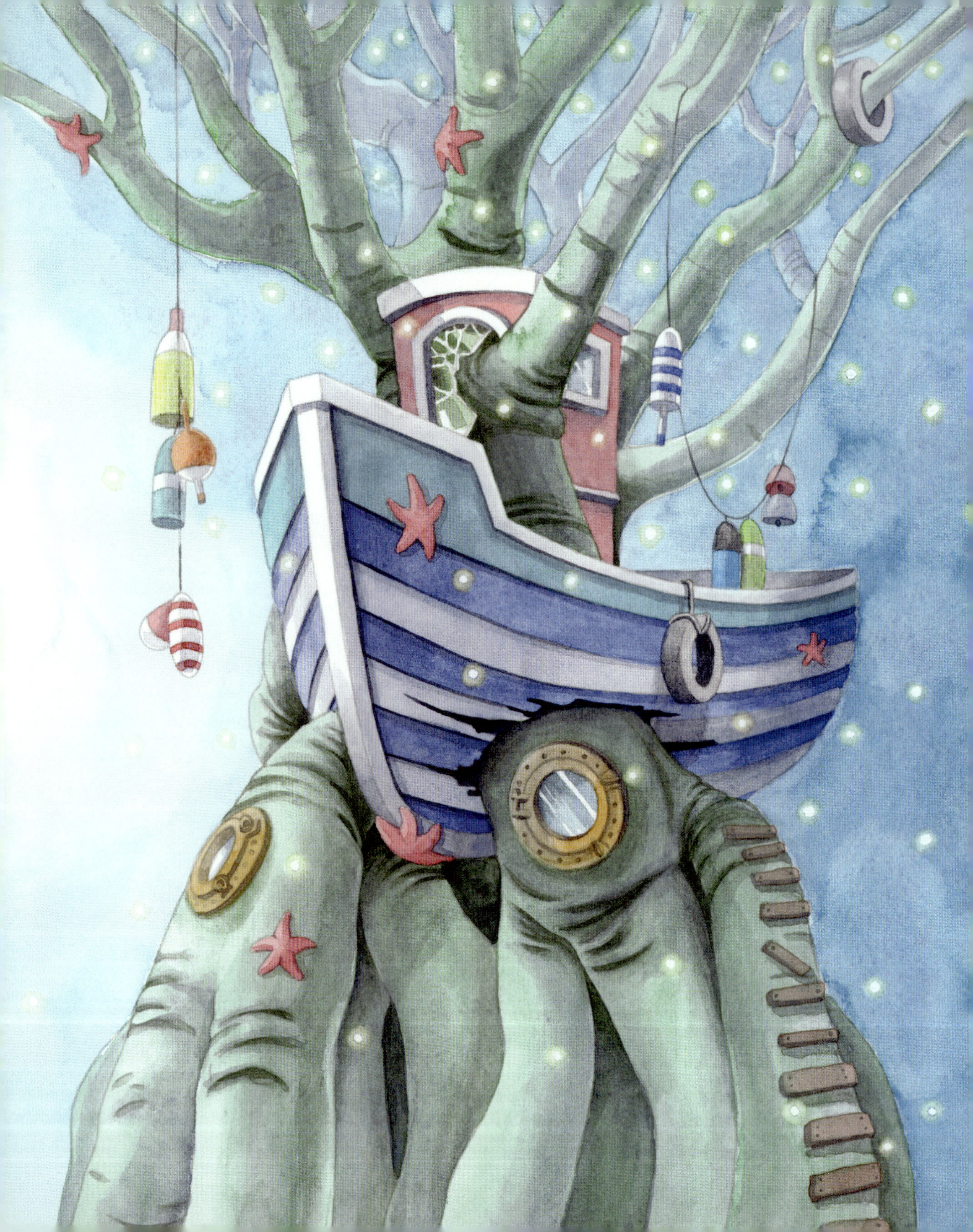

Wooden Voyage

In this chapter, you'll embark on a creative journey, illustrating the evolution of a charming wooden fishing boat while exploring essential watercolor techniques. Through these projects, you'll focus on building your artwork in layers, a process that gradually adds depth, texture, and vibrancy. Layering and glazing—two fundamental techniques—bring your paintings to life by creating richness, glowing colors, and a luminous quality. They allow you to build tones smoothly and blend seamlessly while preserving watercolor's signature transparency. Designed to be completed in sequence, the four projects in this chapter will steadily enhance your skills and lay the foundation for success throughout the book.

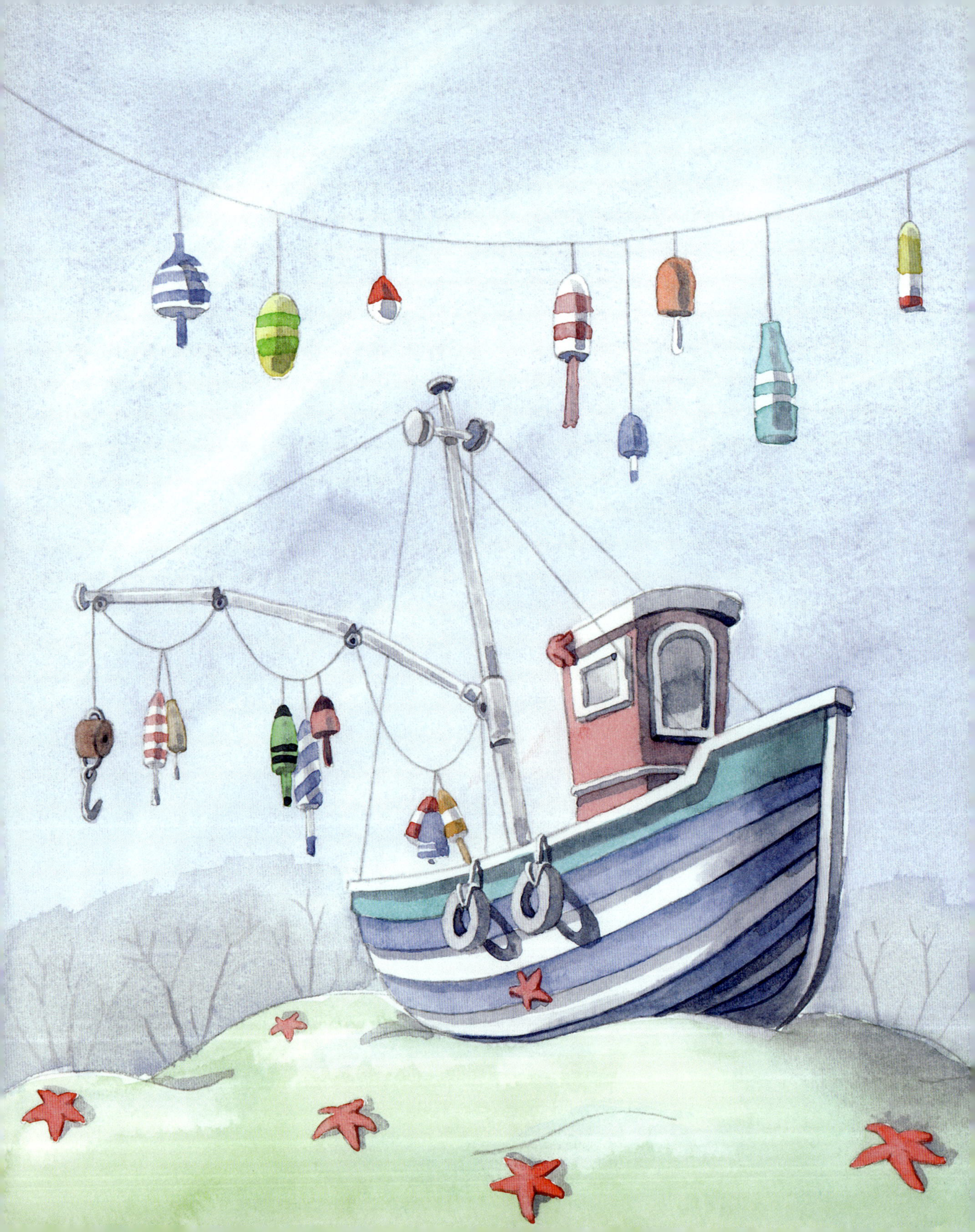

ENCHANTED TRAWLER

In this introductory project, we're keeping things simple so you can get familiar with some of the most common watercolor techniques, like wet-on-dry, wet-on-wet, washes, and glazing. You'll find yourself using these techniques often in your future creations.

Why a boat, you ask? Well, besides being perfect for practicing watercolor techniques, I've always loved old-fashioned fishing boats and tugboats. They've been a source of inspiration in my art for years, so I couldn't resist making them the starting point for this book. Even now, I still enjoy discovering different boats during my travels, especially in small coastal towns. Some of my favorites have been found in Greece and Italy. I'm not entirely sure what draws me to old wooden boats, but I think it's the craftsmanship, the bright colors, and the unique designs that give each one its charm. This charm is even more captivating on a sunny day, with crystal-clear water and fish swimming just below the shimmering surface.

Now that you know why, let's dive into painting!

Sketch

Draw the trawler freehand or trace the sketch template on page 195.

Step 1

Using a round brush or ball stylus, fill in all the small details, such as the mast, buoys, starfish, and tires with masking fluid. This will make painting the background and the boat quick and easy, and it will also help you achieve an even finish with the paint. If you don't have masking fluid, you can skip this step and paint around the shapes you would have masked, leaving them blank. This method is more time-consuming, and you may encounter more texture, such as bleeding or staining, as your paint dries at different rates.

However, don't be discouraged by this; simply embrace the unpredictability and the beautiful patterns that emerge.

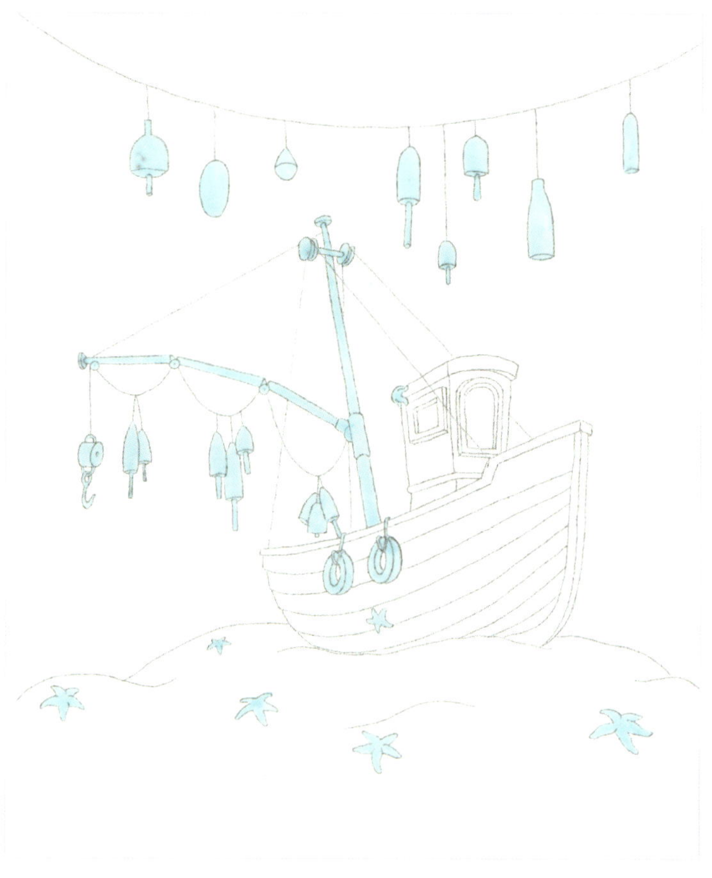

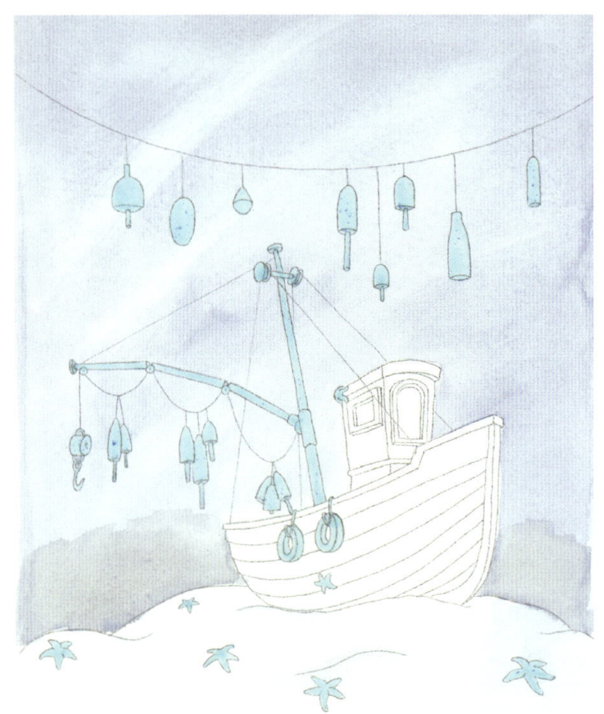

Step 2

We are going to use the wet-on-wet technique (page 12) to fill in the background and some light shadows in the foreground. Start by using a ½-inch (1.3-cm) flat brush to apply clean water to the entire background and foreground. Be careful to paint neatly around the boat so no paint flows into that area later. While your paper is damp, mix two separate watered-down bodies of paint:

> **French Ultramarine** – for the sky and foreground shadows
>
> **French Ultramarine + Raw Sienna** – for the distant tree line

French Ultramarine	French Ultramarine	Raw Sienna	Tree Line

The paper should still be damp. You can now fill in the entire background and some foreground shadows with the first mixture. There is no rush or strict rule for this, so just fill the area with color; the damp surface will help pull and distribute the pigment evenly over the background. While the paint is still wet, use a tissue to remove water and pigment from the paper with diagonal sweeping movements to represent clouds. You can also dab the tissue if you want rounder clouds.

Lastly, use a ½-inch (1.3-cm) flat brush to apply the second mixture to the horizon. The idea is to create a tree line in the distance, so no detail is required—just block in the color and it will naturally blend with the French Ultramarine. Once the paint has fully dried, use an adhesive eraser to remove the masking fluid from the mast and buoys. If you don't have an adhesive eraser, you can try using your finger.

Step 3

Imagine that the main light source is coming from the top left of the picture; this will be the basis for our shadows. Mix **French Ultramarine** with **Burnt Sienna** to create a blue-gray. If your mixture looks too gray, simply add more French Ultramarine to increase the blue. Using a size 4 round brush, start painting in the shadows. Try to visualize where you think the shadows would be cast and follow along with my example.

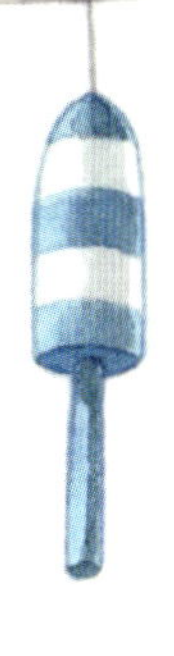
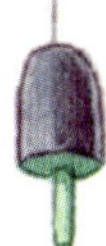
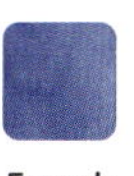

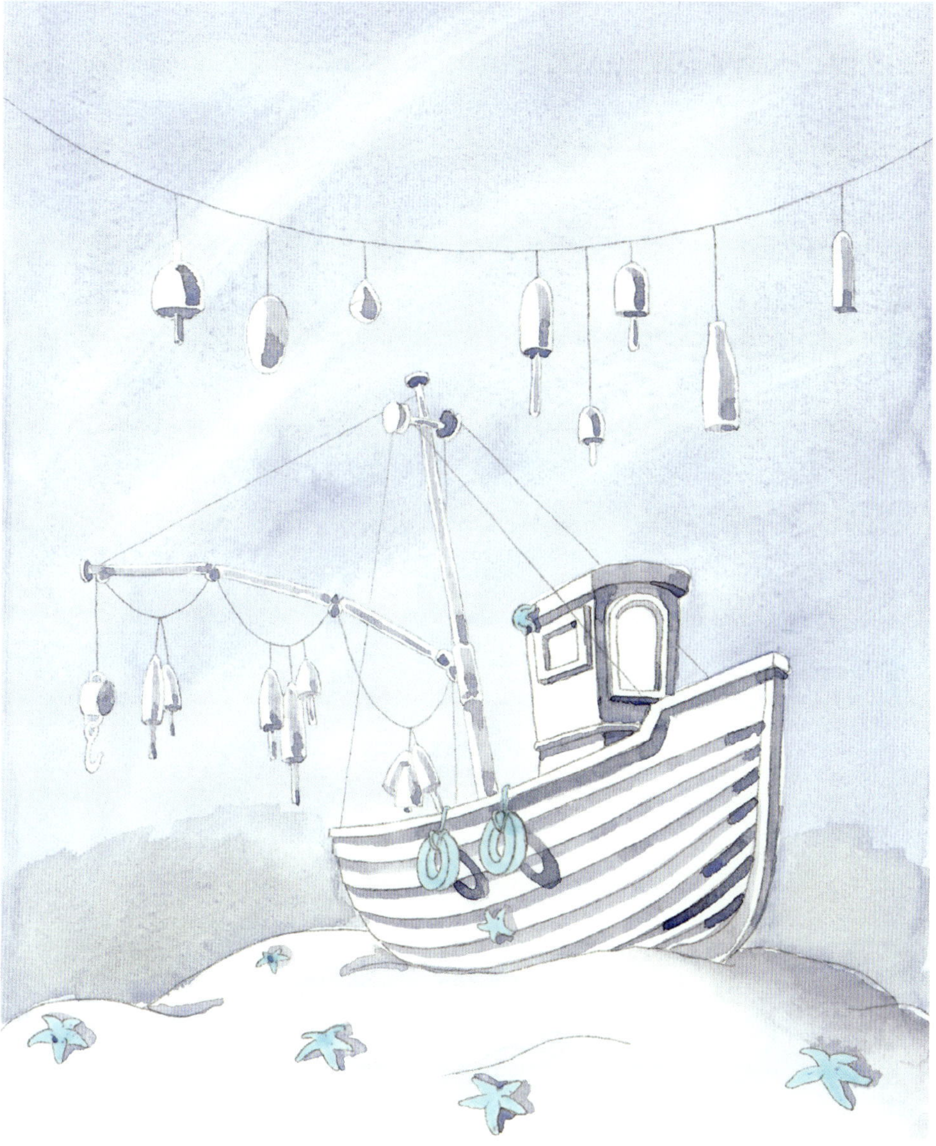

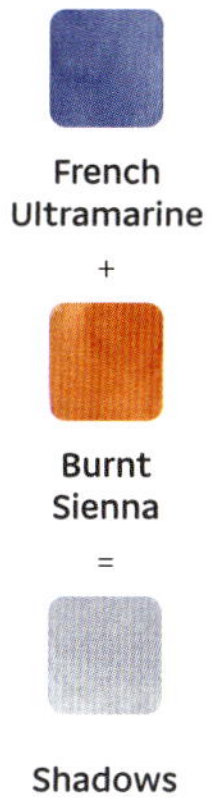

French
Ultramarine

+

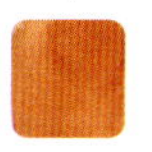

Burnt
Sienna

=

Shadows

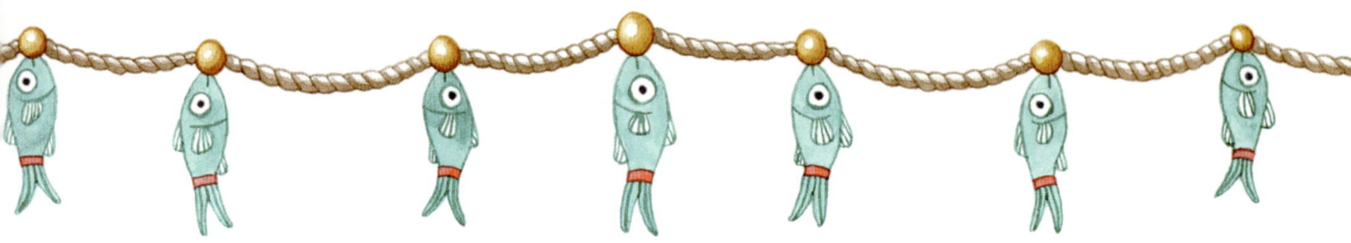

Step 4

This step is all about filling in the blank areas with color. All the different color mixtures should be quite watery; we do not want heavily pigmented paint at this point. The colors you choose for the boat are entirely up to you, but I will share the three I used, as well as what I used for the grass:

Winsor Red – for the boat cabin

French Ultramarine (more pigment than in the sky mixture) – for the boat stripes

Winsor Blue + **Permanent Sap Green** – for the top teal stripe on the boat

Permanent Sap Green + **Yellow Ochre** – for the foreground grass

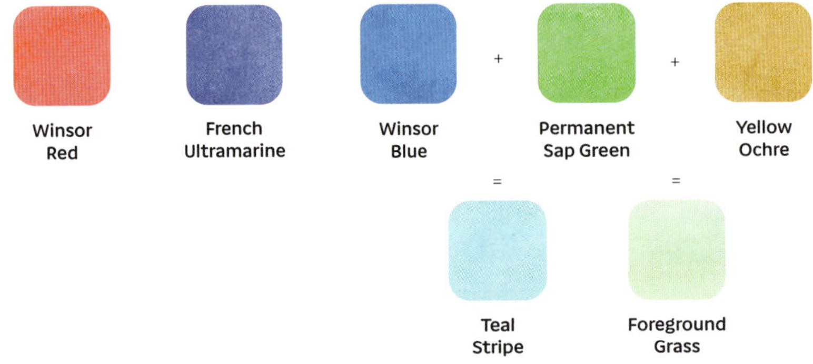

While filling in your colors, you will occasionally use the glazing technique (page 13) by applying a transparent color over an existing dried color (the blue-gray shadows). Throughout this process, apply your paint evenly and avoid multiple passes over the same area. The goal is not to overwork the areas where you have already painted your shadows; you will develop a feel for this as you go. I encourage you to practice mixing as many different colors as you can to decorate the buoys, and also try adding different patterns to them. Once you have painted all your beautiful colors, let them dry completely before removing the remaining masking fluid from the starfish and tires.

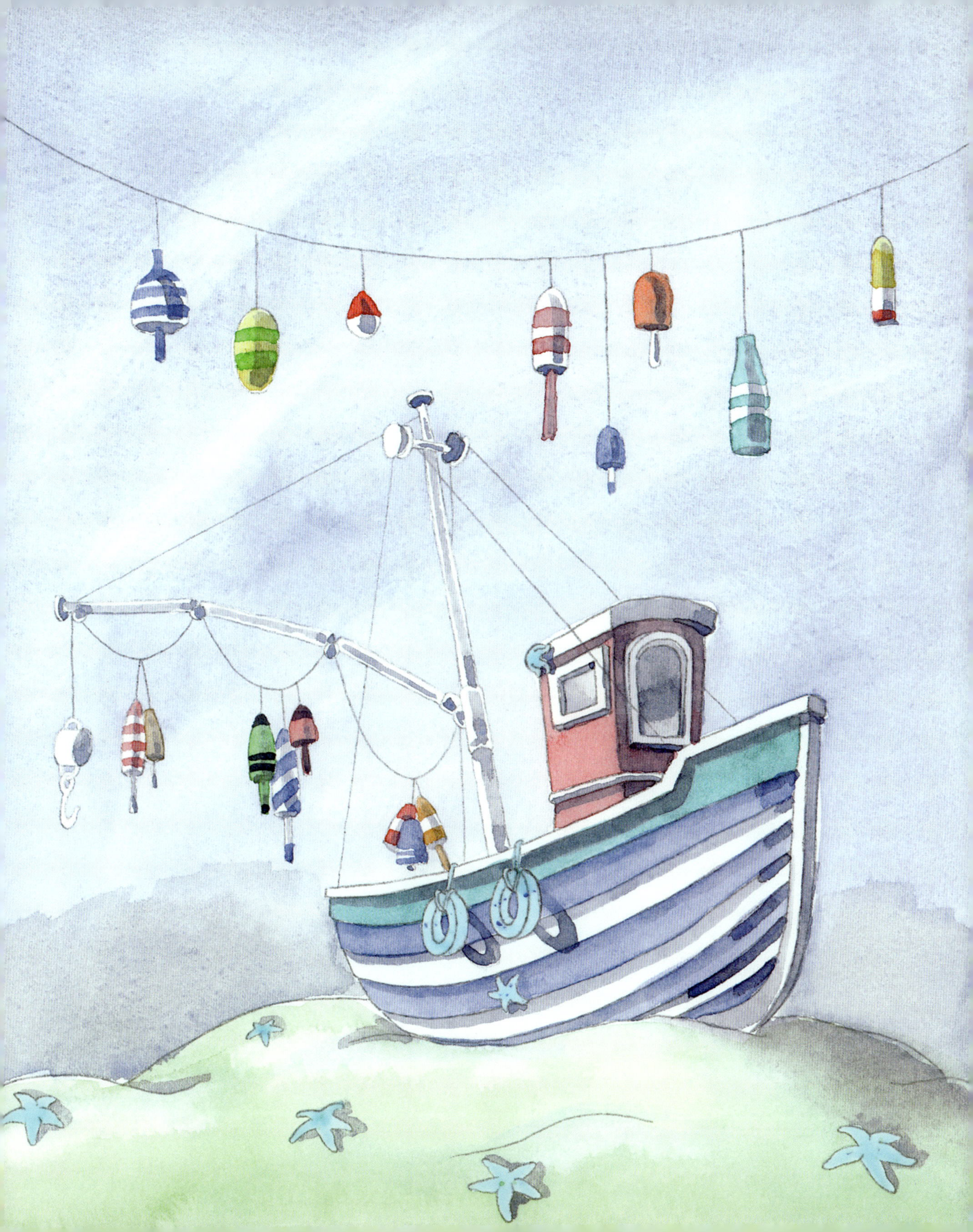

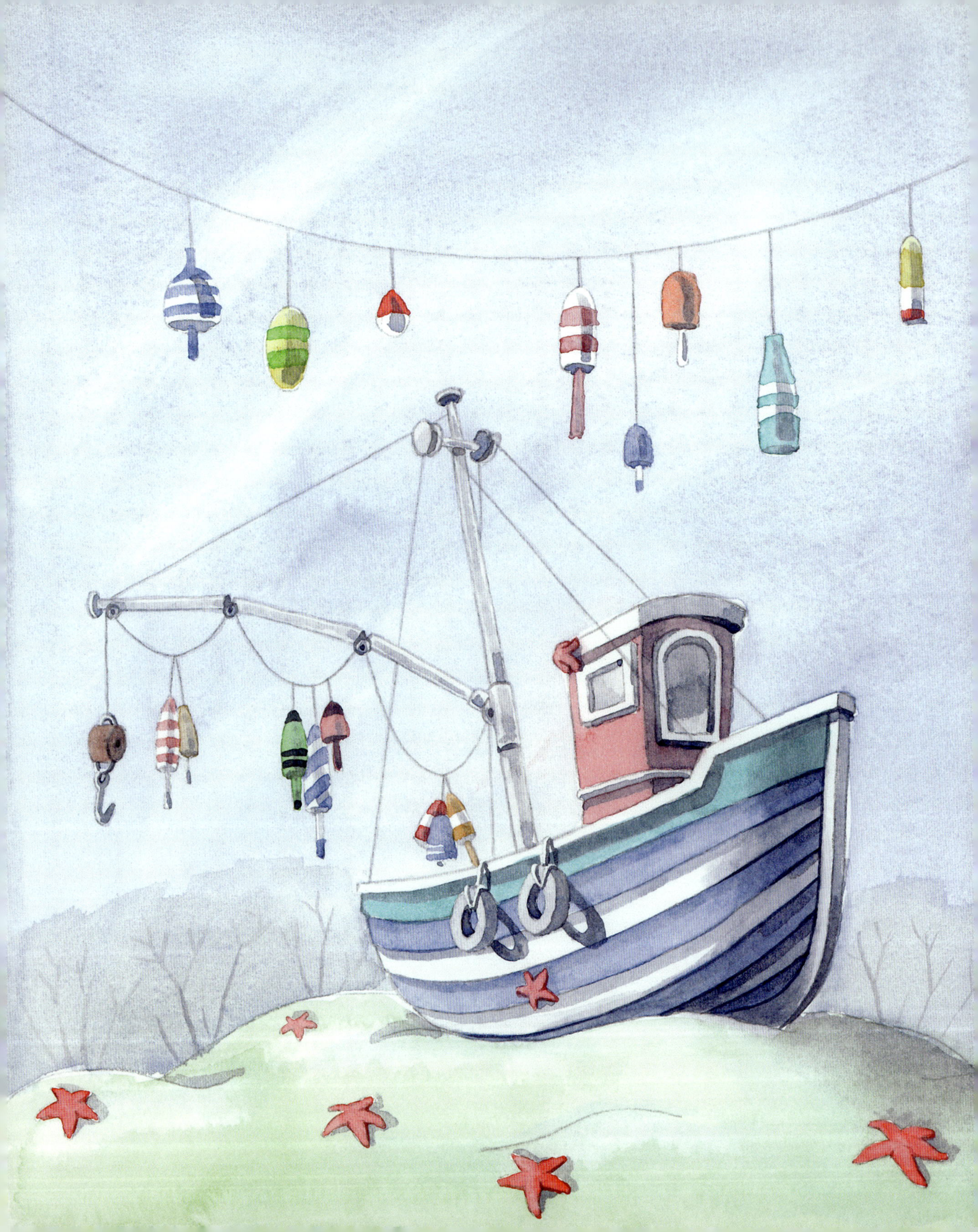

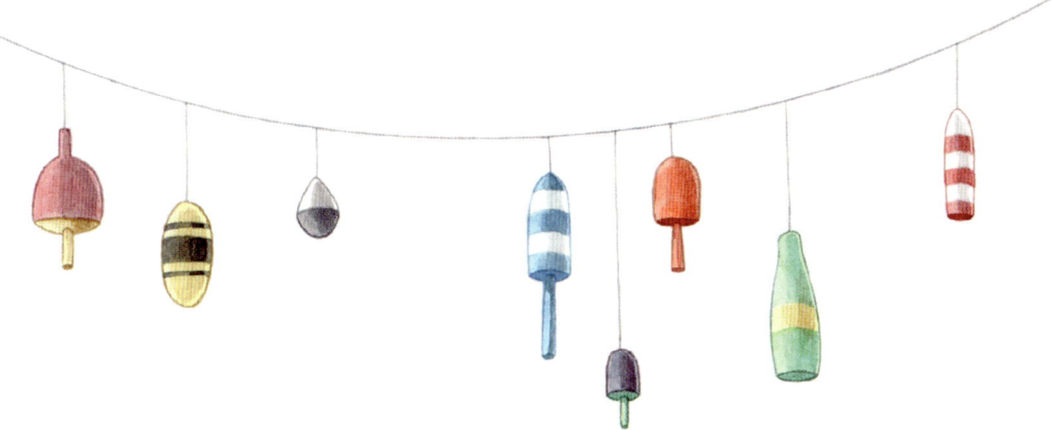

Step 5

It is time to finish this painting by focusing on details and adding one more layer. To complete the details, outline the areas you want to draw attention to, such as the mast and its features, the tires, and the ropes holding them up. You can also lightly paint the rope lines and subtle branches within the tree line. Use a size 0 round brush for all these details. If you have leftover paint from your shadow color from Step 3, use that and add some more **Burnt Sienna** to make it grayer. Don't forget to paint the starfish; I used **Winsor Red** for them, but you can choose something different if you prefer.

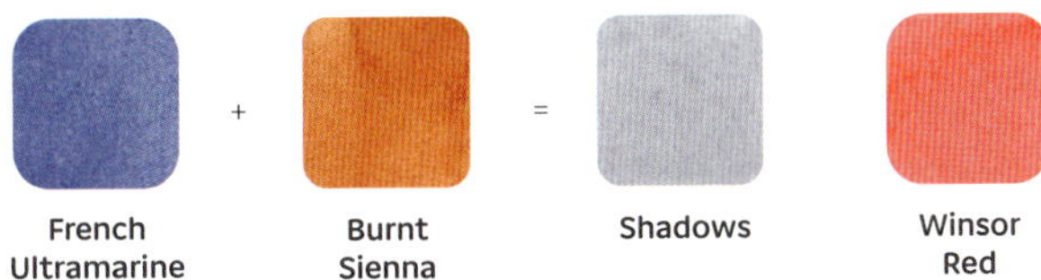

French Ultramarine	Burnt Sienna	Shadows	Winsor Red

To create our last shadow, we can use the same color we originally mixed in Step 3 and glaze it over the front of the boat to help create a cured look for the hull. Painting over what you have already done can be intimidating, but trust me, it will make a huge difference in the overall appearance. The boat is made up of bands of color (teal, blue, and white) and horizontal lines that show the hull's curves. When glazing over them, follow the direction of these lines, and feel free to glaze each band of color individually. If you paint your shadow through these bands, it will pull the blue into the white, causing the colors to mix. If you lose detail in your linework after glazing, simply add it back in with a size 0 round brush.

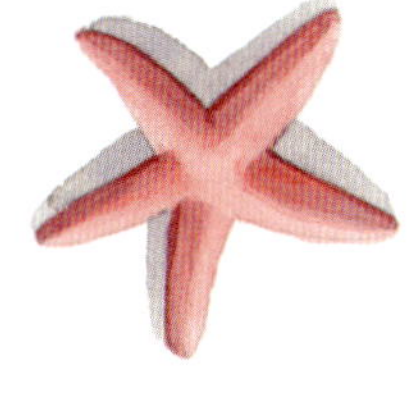

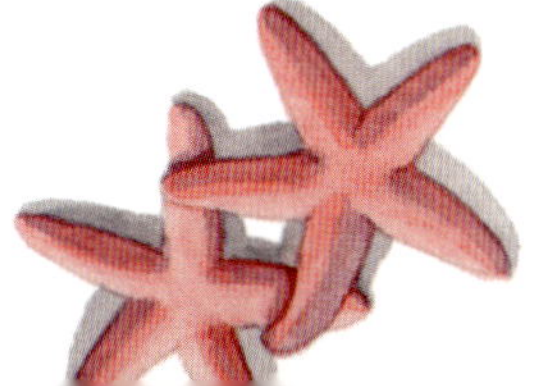

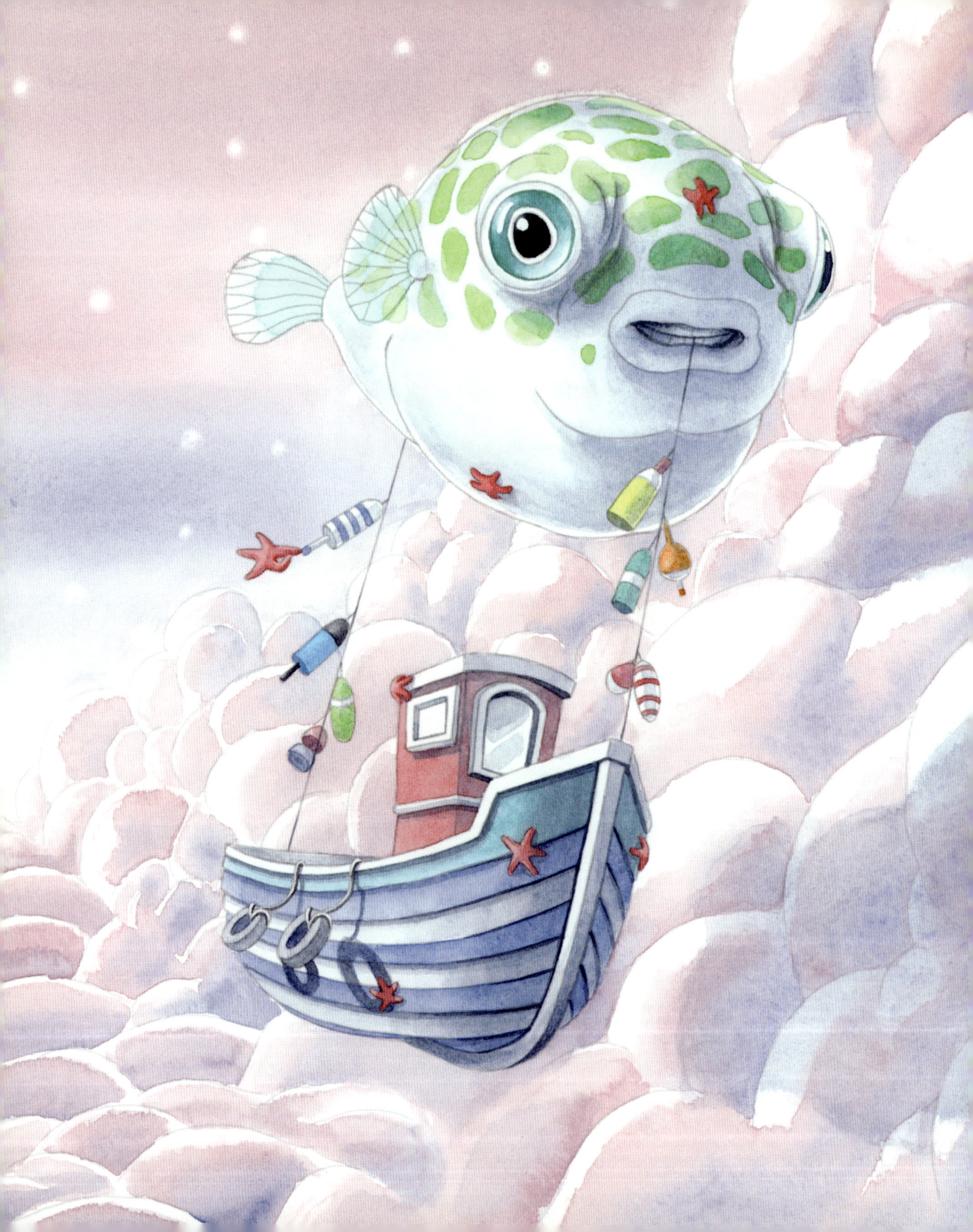

THE PUFFED-UP ADVENTURER

We will continue with the boat theme, taking the Enchanted Trawler (page 19) and the skills we've learned to new and interesting heights (pun intended). Regardless of what you're painting, it's always good practice to paint the same object multiple times. Of course, you can change small details with each attempt to keep it interesting, but the goal is to reinforce the skills you've learned and gain a better understanding of the object's form. With each painting, you'll see improvement and develop your own streamlined approach.

This picture may seem quite random, with a pufferfish carrying the old fishing boat through the clouds. But like everything I paint, the subject matter is more deliberate than it appears. The most obvious reason for the pufferfish is the visual link between a hot-air balloon and the inflated body of a pufferfish. However, this picture is actually a tribute to a cute little pea pufferfish that lived in my studio aquarium. Sadly, he passed away after launching himself out of the tank. I realized it too late, but I was amazed by how far he got. For a short time, he was actually flying! That moment, combined with the image of him bursting out of the water, inspired me to imagine him flying through the clouds.

Inspiration truly is all around us—you don't have to look far to find it.

Sketch

Draw the scene freehand or trace the sketch template on page 197.

Step 1

In this step, we will begin to consider how to layer the picture. Masking fluid isn't always necessary, but it's a great starting point. This is because it encourages you to think critically about your painting and create a clear order of approach. This step is also used to mask areas that may be difficult to paint around or that you might want to keep clear until the final layer. With a ball stylus or old brush, mask the stars in the sky, starfish, tires, and buoys. This will make painting around these areas much easier and preserve the white of the page. Let the masking fluid dry completely before moving on.

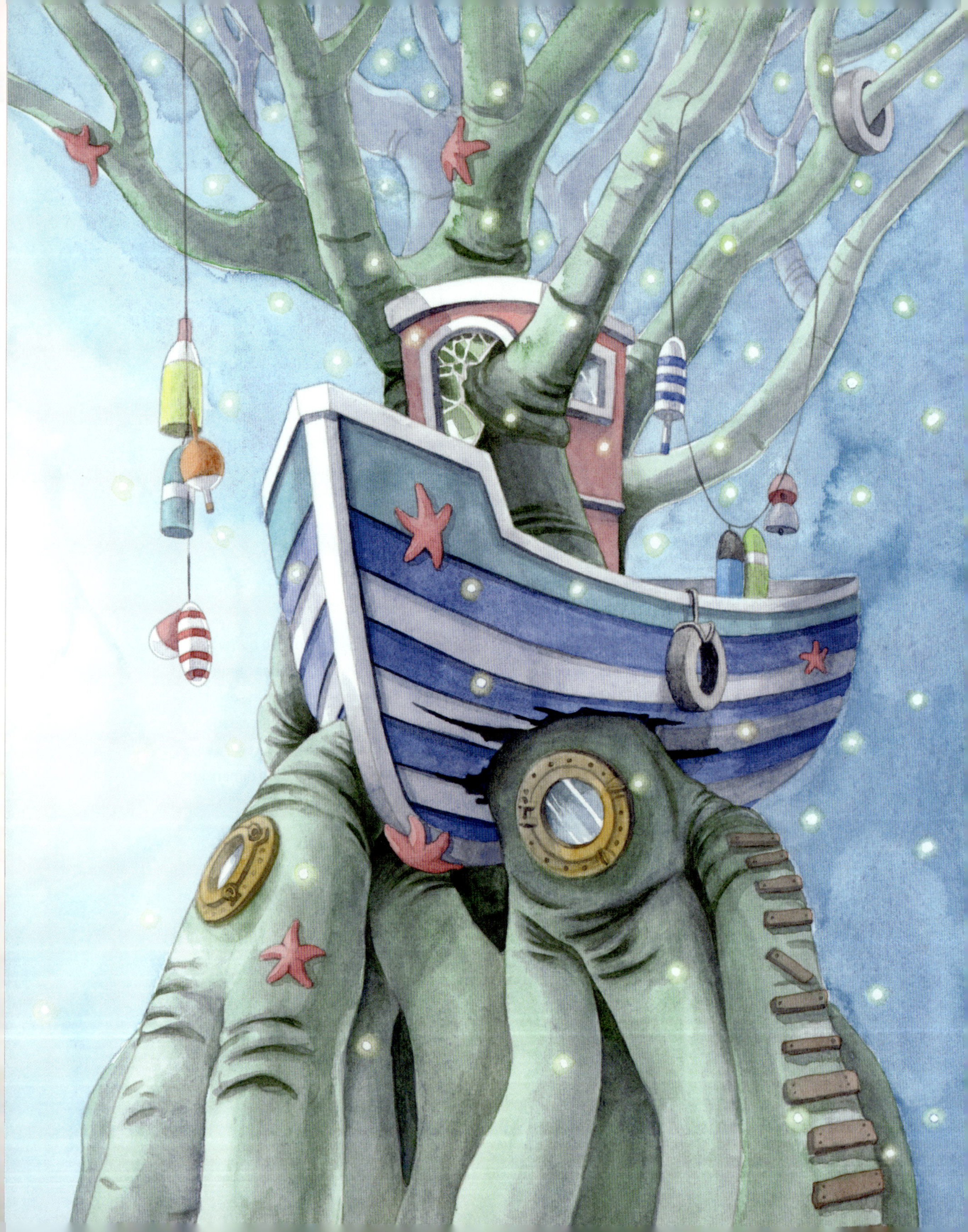

GNARLED NAUTICAL NEST

Now, after a couple of attempts at painting boats, you should feel more confident with the techniques and processes being used. I want you to reinforce this further in this project. One of the things I love exploring in my work is playing around with objects, like a fishing boat, and placing them in locations where they typically wouldn't be found. You can easily apply this simple concept to anything you may be interested in. It's all about creating a visual story or scene that is unconventional and full of mystery. You can even tell a story over multiple paintings.

Let's look back at what we have completed so far. Firstly, we had the old Enchanted Trawler (page 19) that had passed its service life, sitting on a grass mound, begging to be brought back to life. Just when it seemed like all hope was lost, it was reborn in The Puffed-Up Adventurer (page 27), flying through the air and adventuring around the world. Finally, in this painting, the beloved fishing boat rests deep in the forest, weathered and decayed, slowly being consumed by nature.

This simple idea or story has allowed us to practice painting something multiple times without losing interest. It has also been enhanced by personal touches, like the inclusion of the pea pufferfish, the tree inspired by a desert rose from my plant collection, and my love for all things nautical, as well as treehouses and clouds. Like the paintings themselves, you can layer your inspiration to create something you can't wait to paint.

With that being said, let's paint!

Sketch

Draw the scene freehand or trace the sketch template on page 199.

Step 1

The masking fluid step in this painting is straightforward and minimal. This is because the sketch mostly consists of large curved lines that are easy to paint around. As in the previous two paintings, mask the starfish, buoys, tire, and light orbs with a ball stylus or old brush. Even though the wooden steps on the tree root are fiddly to paint around, we won't mask them because both the tree and the steps will be predominantly green.

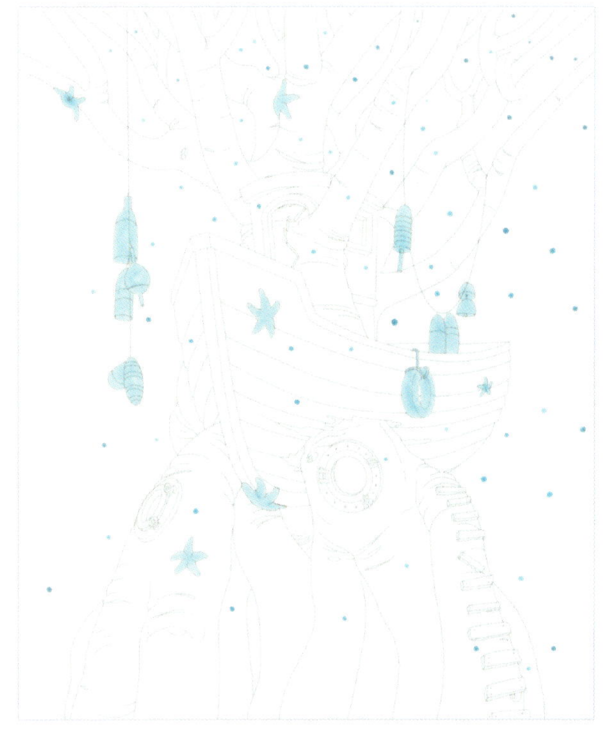

Step 2

This time, we will try the wet-on-dry technique (page 12) for the background to create some texture. You will want to paint at a steady pace to avoid going over areas that are fully dried. As with the wet-on-wet technique (page 12), it's always helpful to mix your colors first on a palette, ensuring you have plenty to paint the entire background in one go. The background color is made up of equal parts **French Ultramarine** and **Winsor Blue** with some **Raw Sienna** to create a bluish-green hue.

Since the light source will be coming from the left-hand side, start painting the color on the right first with a size 0 quill brush. The reason for this is that the pigment in your mix will be most concentrated at this point. As you dip your brush into the water and use more paint, you'll gradually dilute what remains on your palette. The diluted paint will be perfect for when you reach the other side, allowing you to effortlessly create transitional glow. You should clearly see the contrast between the two sides when you're finished. You can always darken areas further if needed.

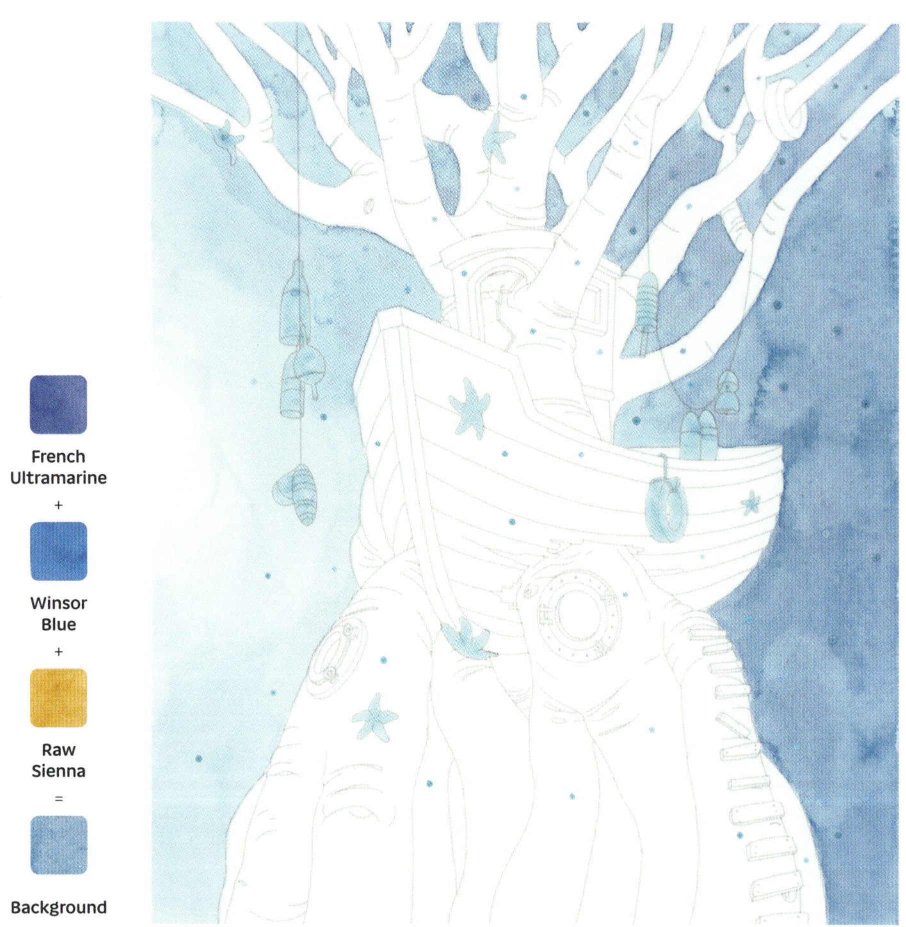

French Ultramarine

+

Winsor Blue

+

Raw Sienna

=

Background

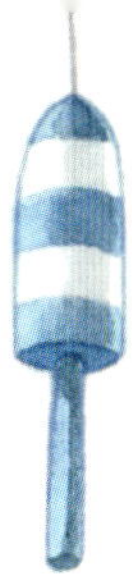

Step 3

Now that the background is complete, remove all the masking fluid from the buoys. We have already considered our light source while applying the background, so it's now time to take that a step further by adding shadows. Use a size 2 quill brush and a mix of **French Ultramarine** and **Burnt Sienna** to do a general wash over the main shaded areas, referring to my image as a guide. Once dry, come back in with a size 4 and size 0 round brush, depending on the area you're working on, to further establish deeper shadows with the same shadows mix. Focus on areas like where the tree root breaks through the boat's hull, the deepest crevices in the roots, and all the overhangs on the boat. You will build up a few layers with this process, which is fine as long as you ensure your paint isn't heavy with pigment, as we will be glazing color over these areas in the next step.

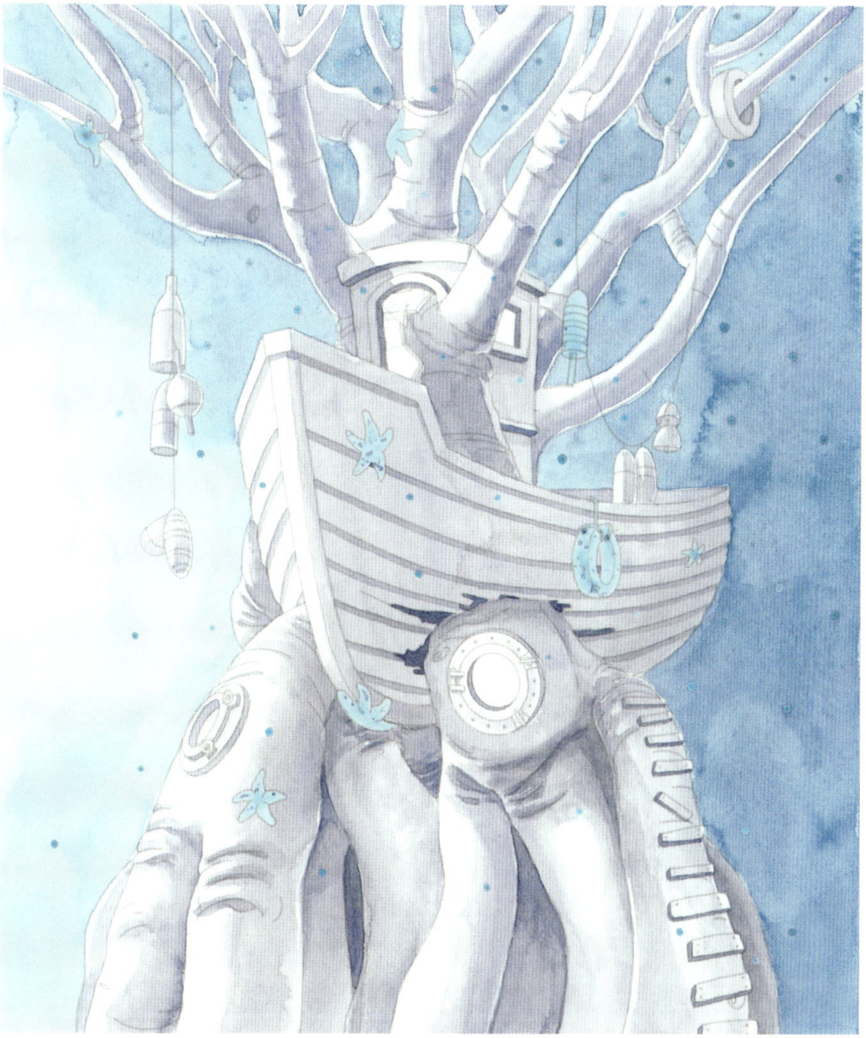

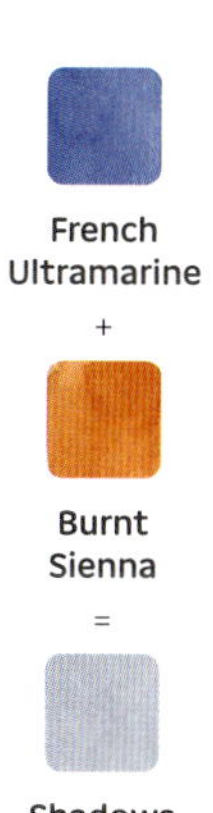

French Ultramarine

+

Burnt Sienna

=

Shadows

Step 4

Mix **Permanent Sap Green** and **French Ultramarine**. Use this color to paint the tree roots, covering the steps at the same time. Continue with the tree branches above, but only paint the foreground branches. The goal is to apply one even glaze over these areas. Once dry, apply another glaze over the deepest recesses in the tree roots to darken them.

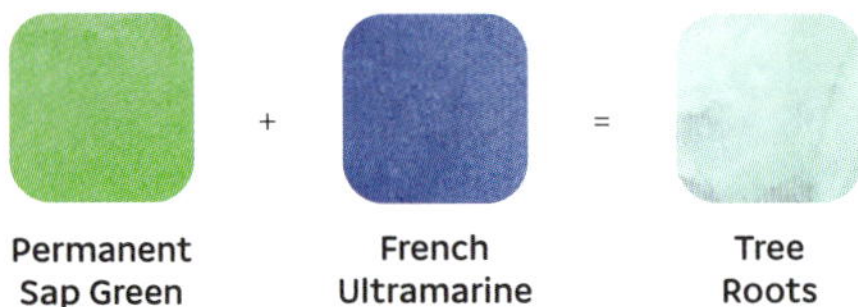

Permanent Sap Green + French Ultramarine = Tree Roots

Next, mix some **Winsor Blue** into the remaining paint on your palette and use this to glaze over the background branches that were left unpainted. This will create the impression of depth, making those branches appear farther away.

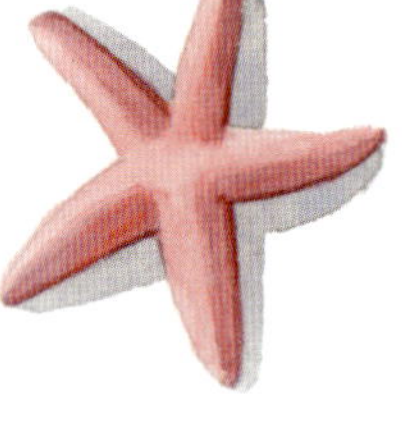

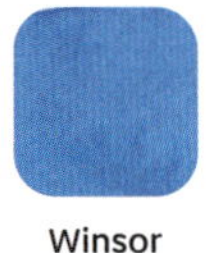

Winsor Blue

For the boat, use the following colors as previously shown:

Winsor Red – for the boat cabin

French Ultramarine – for the boat stripes

Winsor Blue + **Permanent Sap Green** – for the top teal stripe on the boat

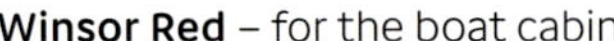

Winsor Red   French Ultramarine   Winsor Blue + Permanent Sap Green = Teal Boat Stripe

To mix the color for the portholes, combine **Permanent Sap Green**, **Winsor Yellow**, and a little **Burnt Sienna** to create a brassy bronze tone. Green is always important when mixing yellow metals. For the wooden steps, mix **Alizarin Crimson** and **Permanent Sap Green**.

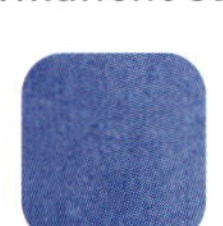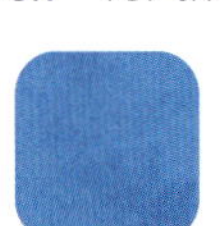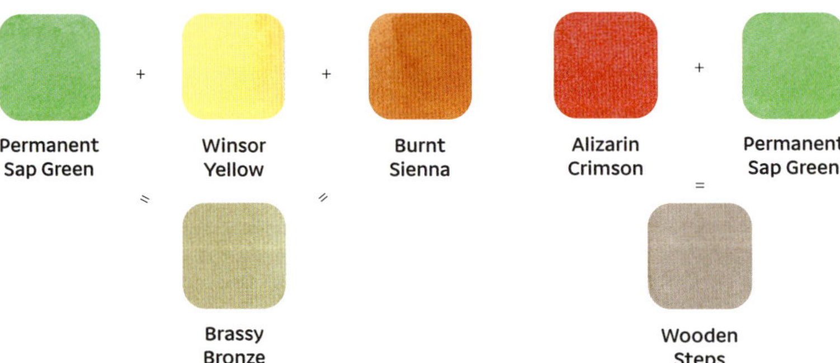

Permanent Sap Green + Winsor Yellow + Burnt Sienna   Alizarin Crimson + Permanent Sap Green

Brassy Bronze   Wooden Steps

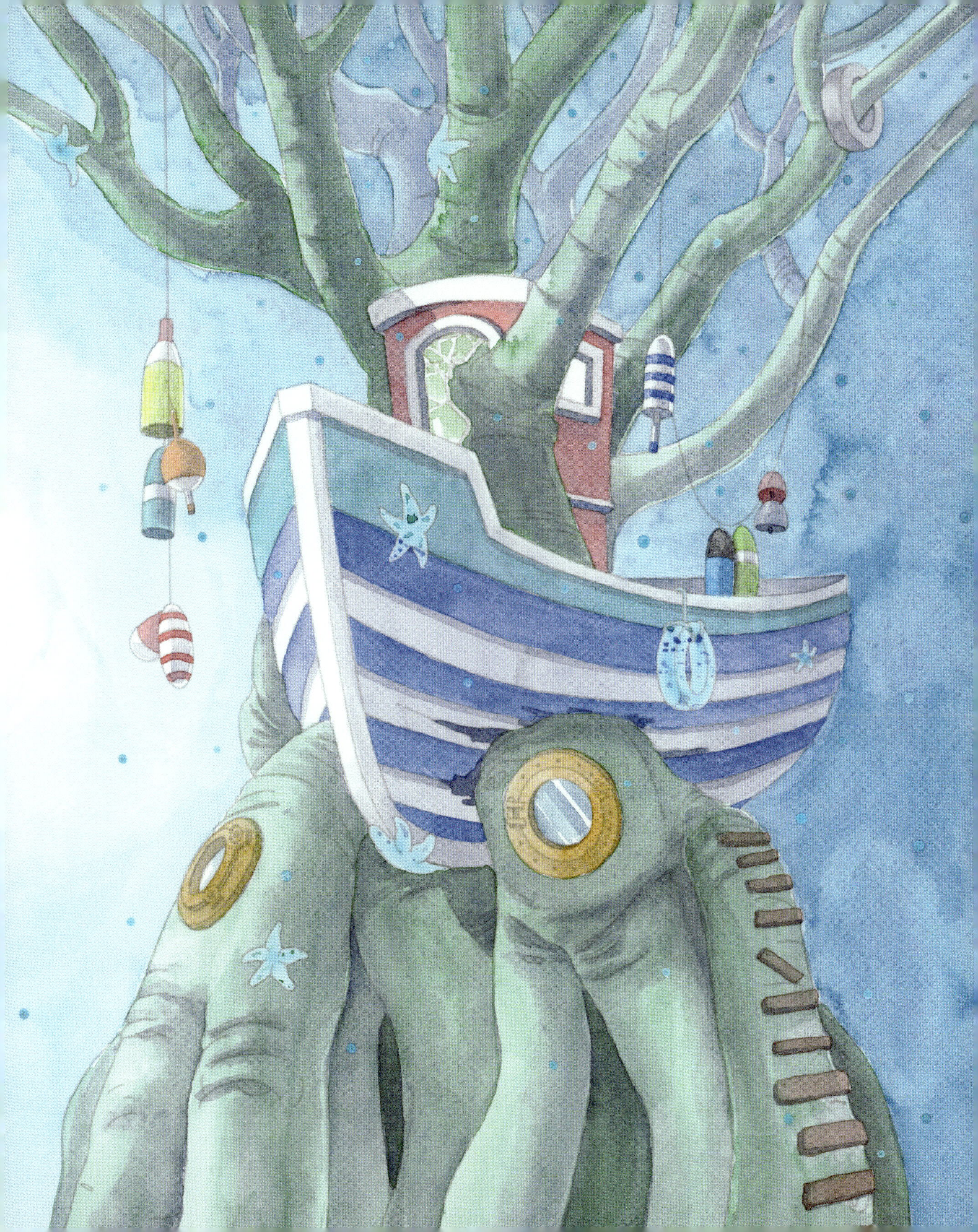

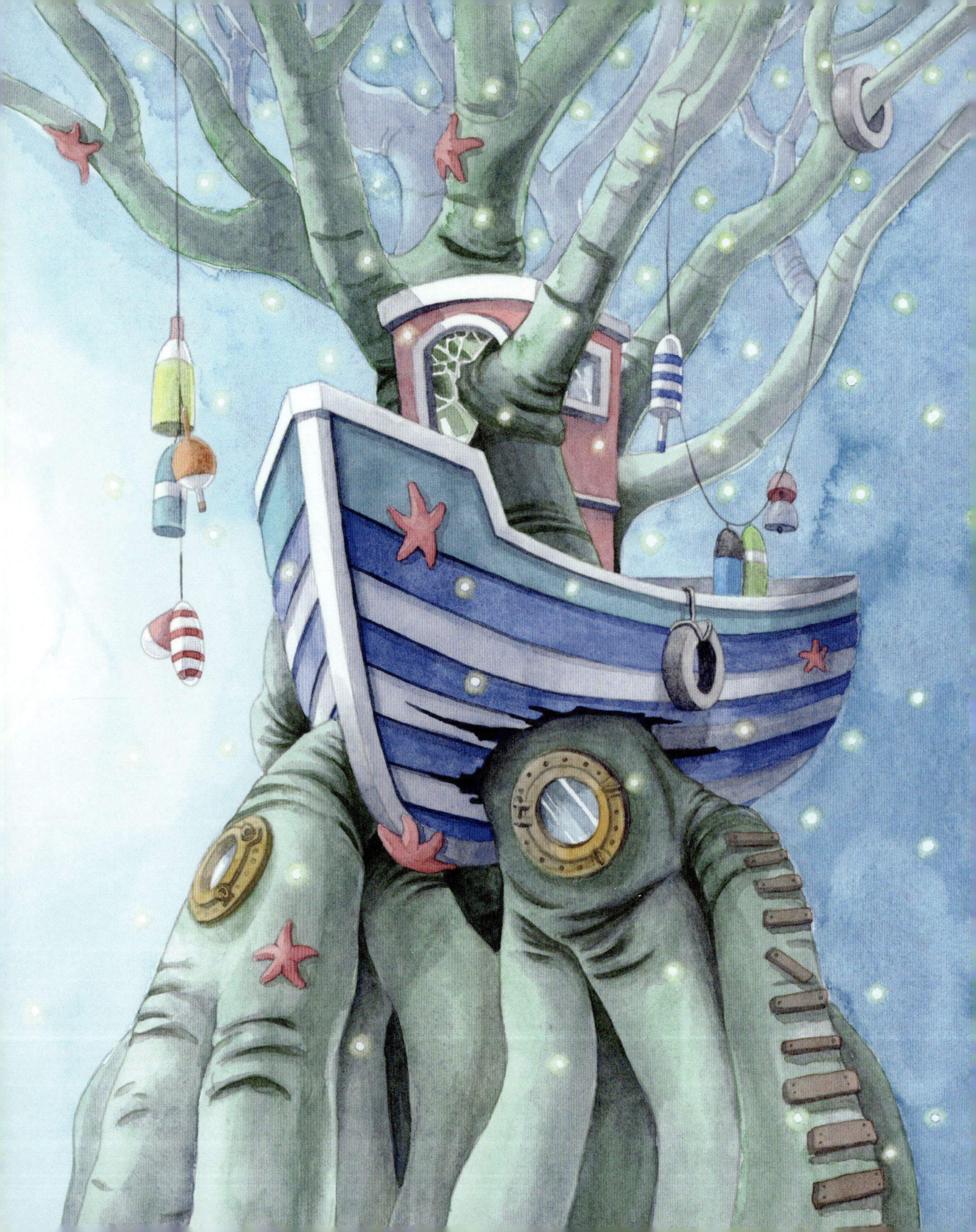

Step 5

Now that all our main colors are blocked in, it's time to focus on the details. You should still have colors on your palette, and it's always good to work with what's already there to avoid waste. When paint dries on your palette, the water evaporates, leaving concentrated pigment. By using small amounts of water and a small brush (I used a size 0 round brush), you can reactivate this paint to achieve a strong pigment for crisp, dark details.

You can also mix the shadow color (**French Ultramarine + Burnt Sienna**) with the tree root color (**Permanent Sap Green + French Ultramarine**) to darken any creases and folds in the tree. Use any remaining French Ultramarine and Burnt Sienna with minimal water to paint sharp details on the boat.

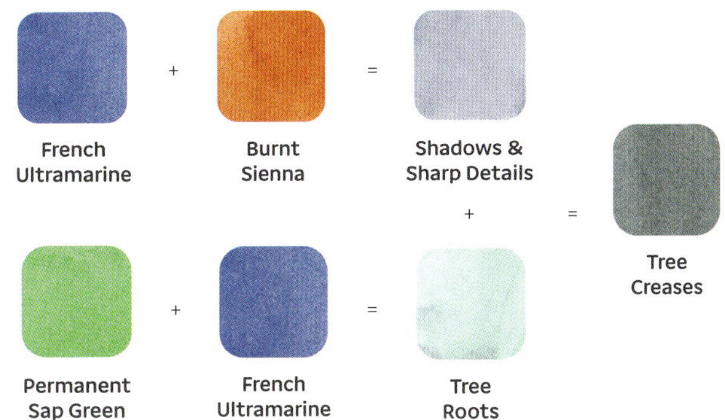

Lastly, lift some paint around each masking fluid dot using clean water and a brush, and then glaze over with diluted **Winsor Yellow**. Once dry, remove all the masking fluid and paint the starfish and tire.

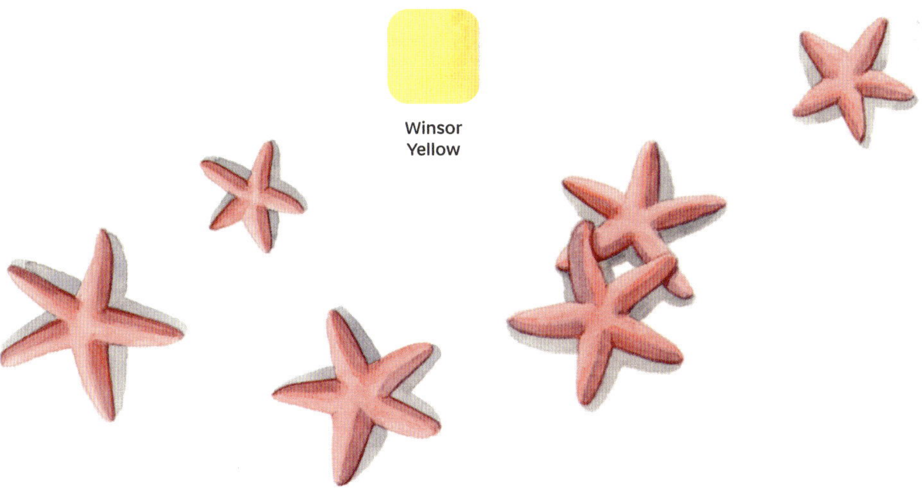

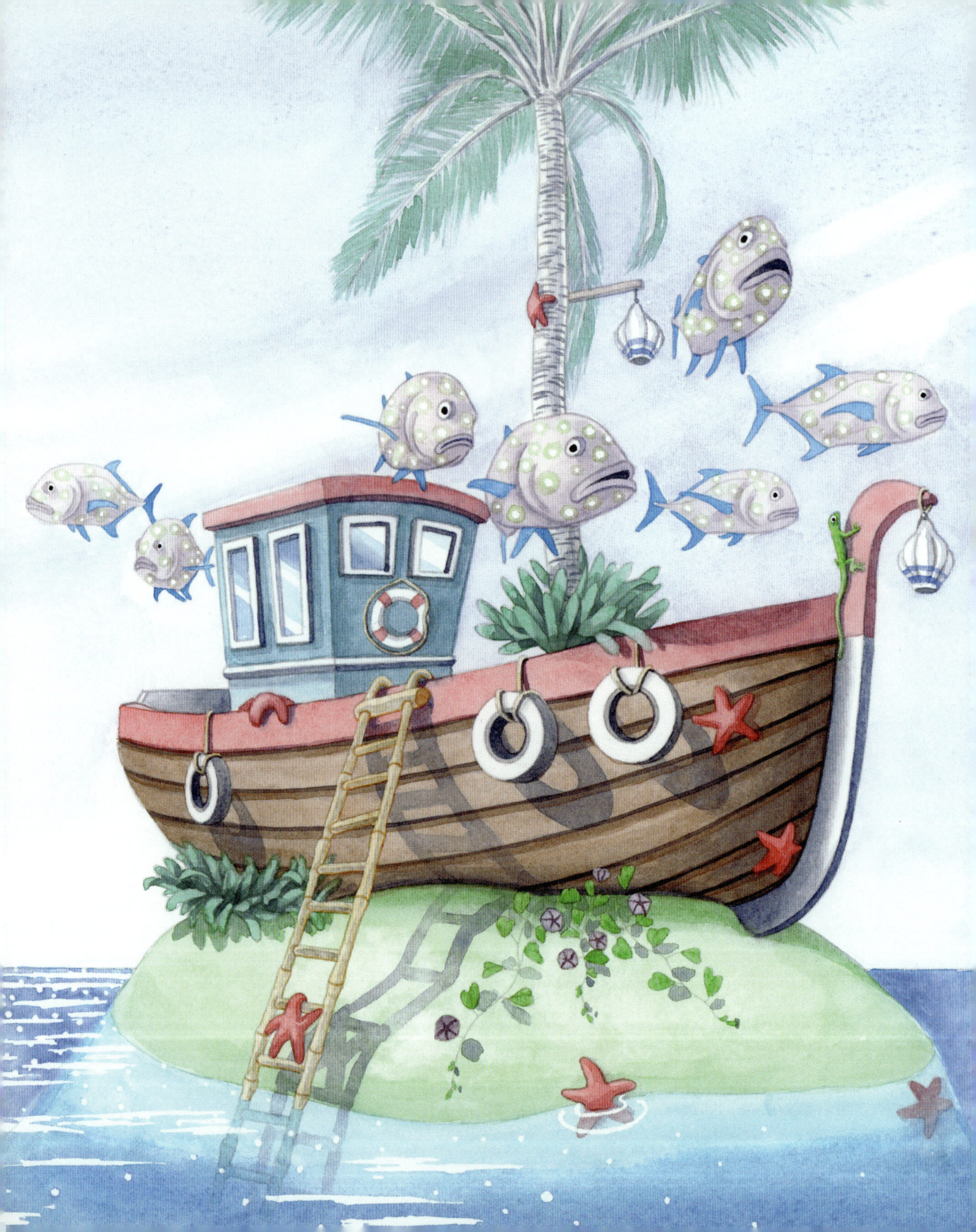

AQUATIC DREAM

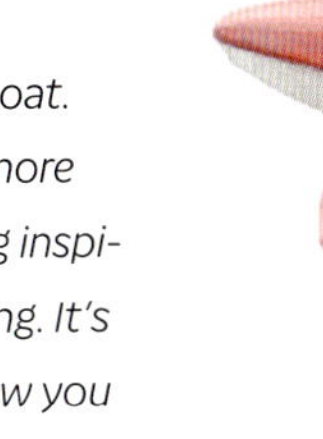

So far, we've been on a creative journey, exploring key moments in the life of a little fishing boat. Now feels like the perfect time to revisit the original project, especially since you've gained more confidence and experience with various colors and techniques. For many new artists, finding inspiration can be a challenge, but you don't always need to reinvent the wheel with every painting. It's incredibly valuable to revisit ideas and concepts you've already explored and think about how you can improve or expand them. This often rekindles the joy you felt when creating the original piece.

That's exactly what this project is about. I've taken the original concept of the boat on the grass mound and amplified it in every way—with more details, more elements, richer colors, and a more engaging composition. Incorporating personal elements into your work helps enhance a deeper connection, adding both meaning and purpose to your creative process. This new version was inspired by a trip to the Maldives, where I got engaged, so there are a lot of fond memories attached to this picture for me.

Sketch

Draw the scene freehand or trace the sketch template on page 201.

Step 1

When it comes to watercolor, if you find yourself repeatedly lifting your brush off the paper and restarting while painting around an area, your paint will dry at different rates. If a smooth finish is what you require, this method is not desirable. So, like the masking we have done in the other projects, you should fill in any small areas with masking fluid and a ball stylus or old brush. This will allow you to apply large continuous brushstrokes over areas like the boat hull and the grass mound, achieving a consistent finish. Additionally, use your masking fluid to add broken lines and dots to the left-hand side of the water. This will represent light reflecting off the water once it is painted in and the masking is removed.

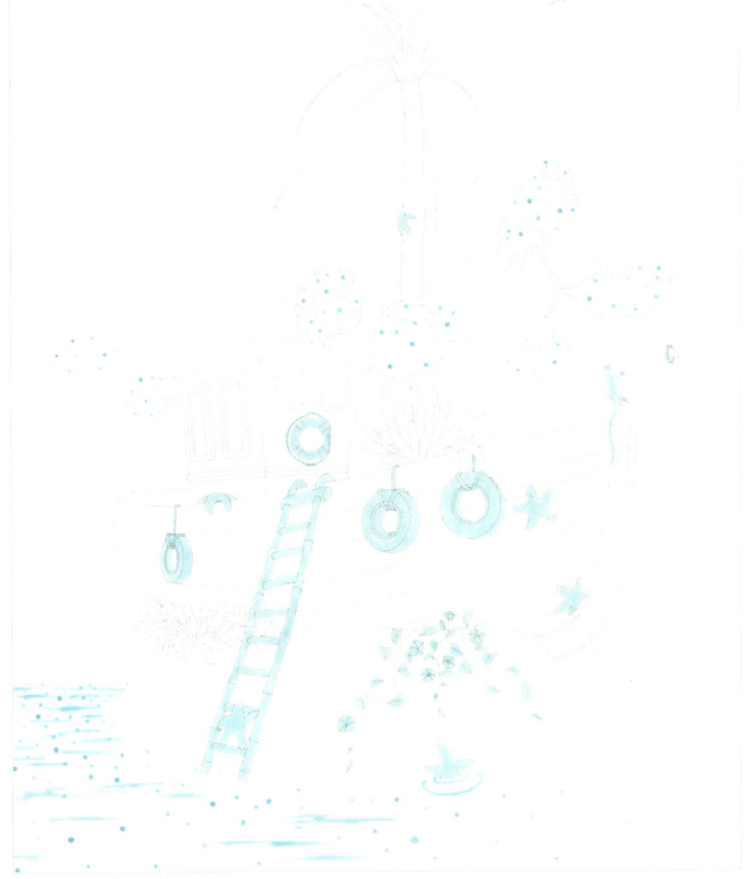

Step 4

It's time to start mixing and painting the main colors for the picture. Here's what you will need:

Burnt Sienna with a touch of **French Ultramarine** + **Alizarin Crimson** – for the brown color of the boat

Permanent Sap Green + **Yellow Ochre** – for the grass mound

Add **Winsor Blue** to any leftover grass mixture to create a darker, deeper green – for the bush under the boat and deck as well as the palm fronds

Winsor Red – for the trim on the boat

Winsor Blue + **Permanent Sap Green** – for the boat cabin

Alizarin Crimson + **French Ultramarine** – for the bodies of the fish

Winsor Blue – for the fins on the fish

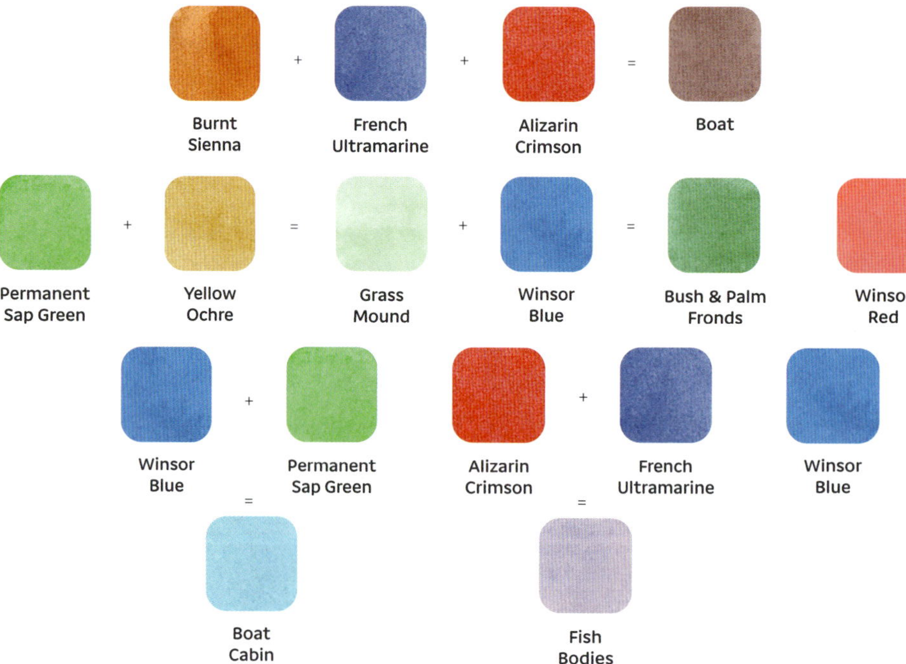

Lastly, paint the water in the background using mainly **French Ultramarine** with a hint of **Winsor Blue**. Also, glaze this color in the foreground, fading up into the previous color.

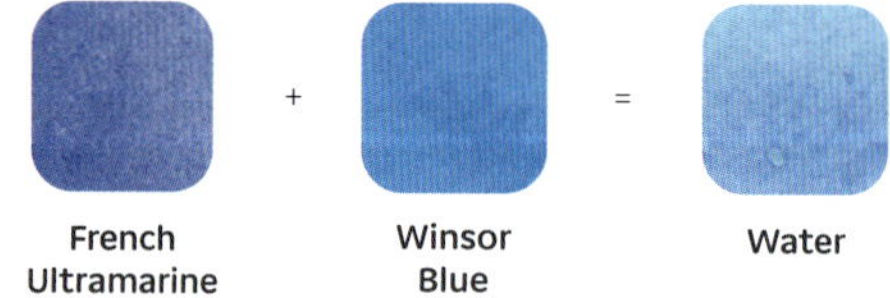

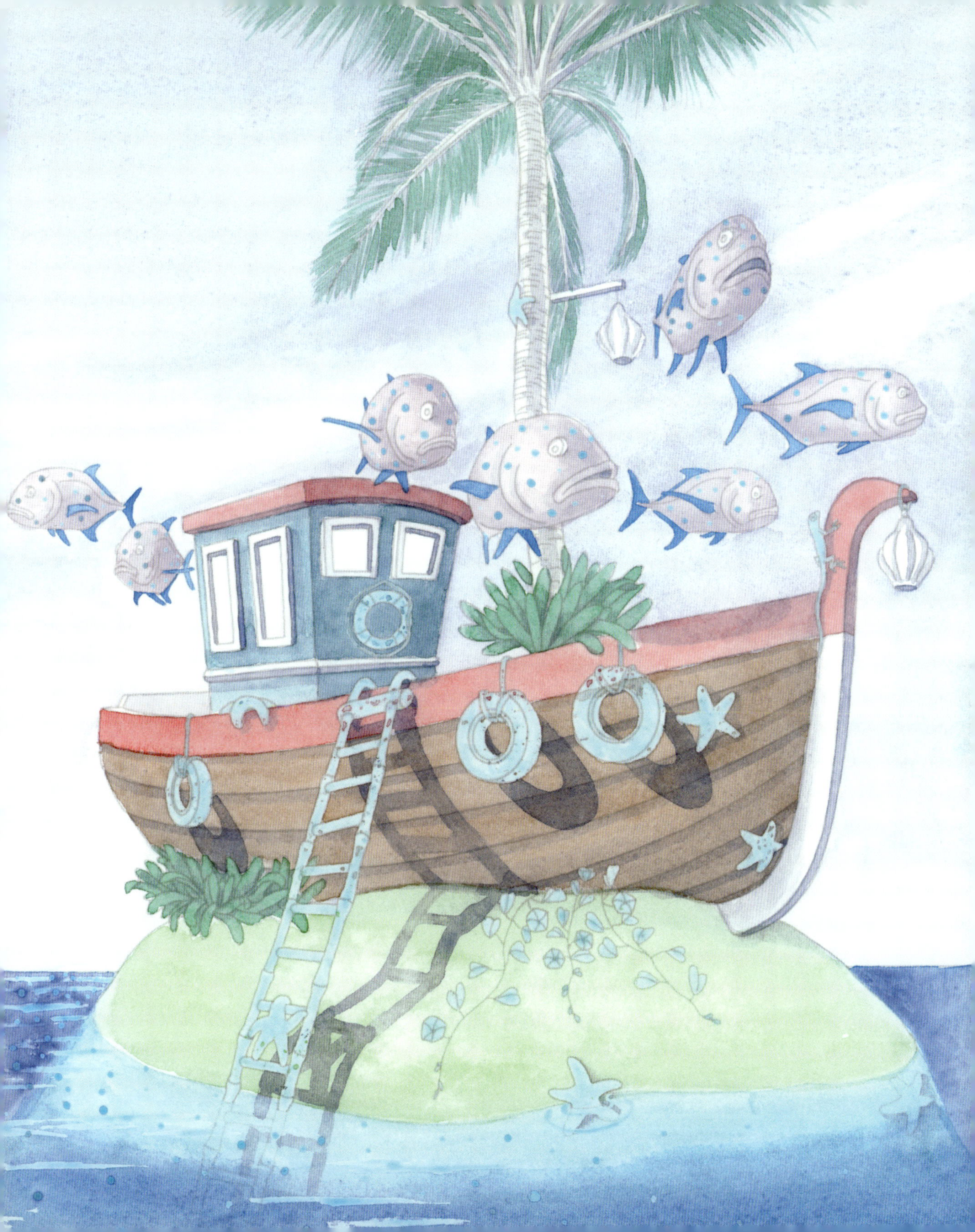

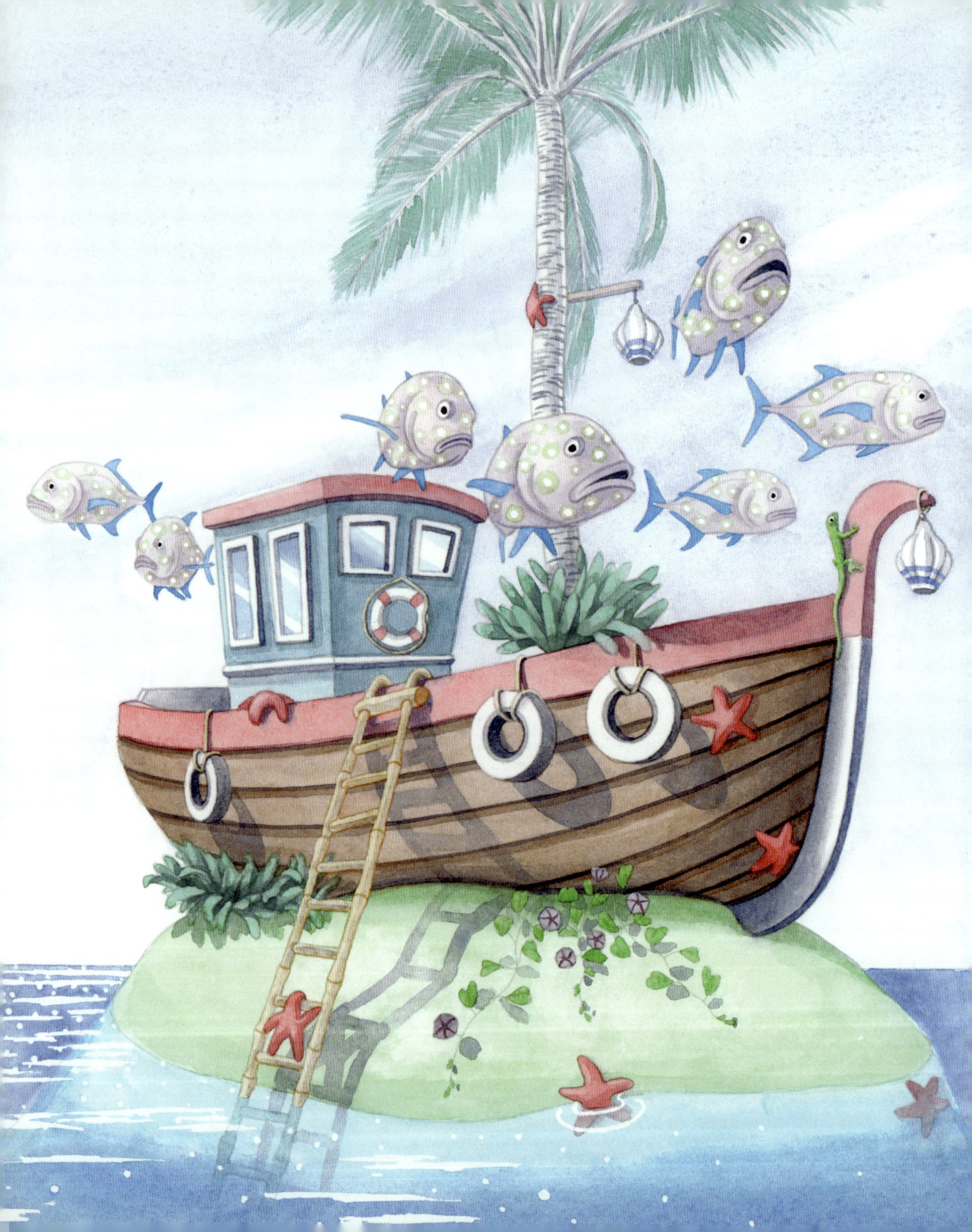

Step 5

In this final layer, there are many details to define, but the areas around the masking fluid need to be addressed first. Use a size 0 round brush and the original brown color from Step 4 for the boat to darken some areas further, such as the underside of the boat, the nose, and the panel overhangs. You can also do this on the grass mound with a green already on your palette, focusing on areas like below the boat and brush.

The only other step before removing the masking fluid is to glaze a mixture of **French Ultramarine** and **Burnt Sienna** on the front of the boat to emphasize its curvature, as you practiced in previous projects. Once everything is dry, remove the masking fluid. Paint the bamboo ladder with **Yellow Ochre**. Then, paint shadows on the bamboo ladder using the same mix of French Ultramarine and Burnt Sienna.

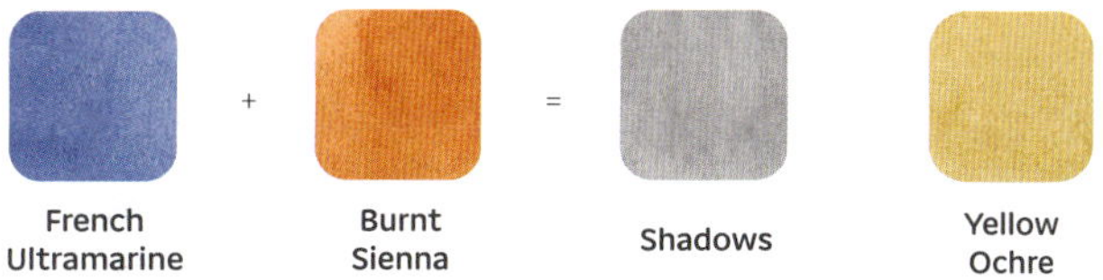

| French Ultramarine | + | Burnt Sienna | = | Shadows | Yellow Ochre |

Once dry, paint over the shadows with a mixture of **Yellow Ochre** and **Burnt Sienna**.

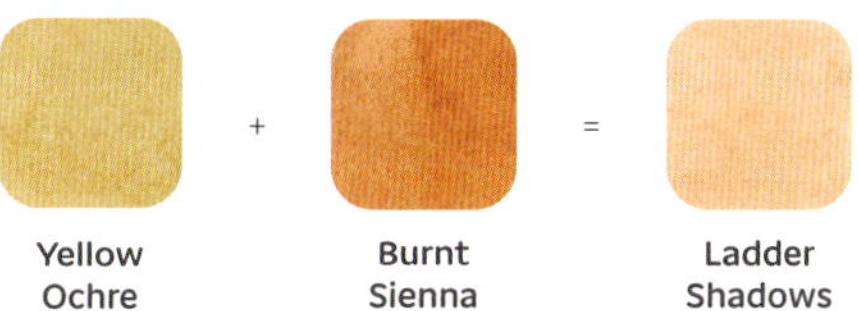

| Yellow Ochre | + | Burnt Sienna | = | Ladder Shadows |

The other main elements to address are the tires. Paint the sides and center with the same gray shadow mixture shown above. Keep the facing surface of the tires in negative space to draw the viewer's eye toward the center of the composition. Once dry, paint the ropes with **Yellow Ochre**. Now, go around the painting and fill in any areas that haven't already been completed. You can mix a combination of colors that you already have on your palette to create new subtle variations in color. Use my reference image as your guide.

Yellow Ochre

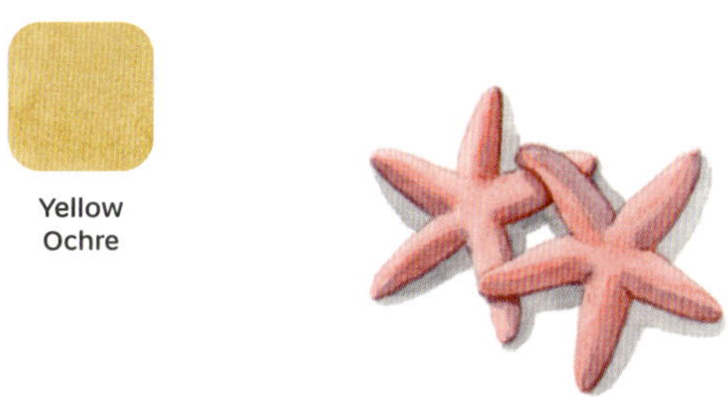

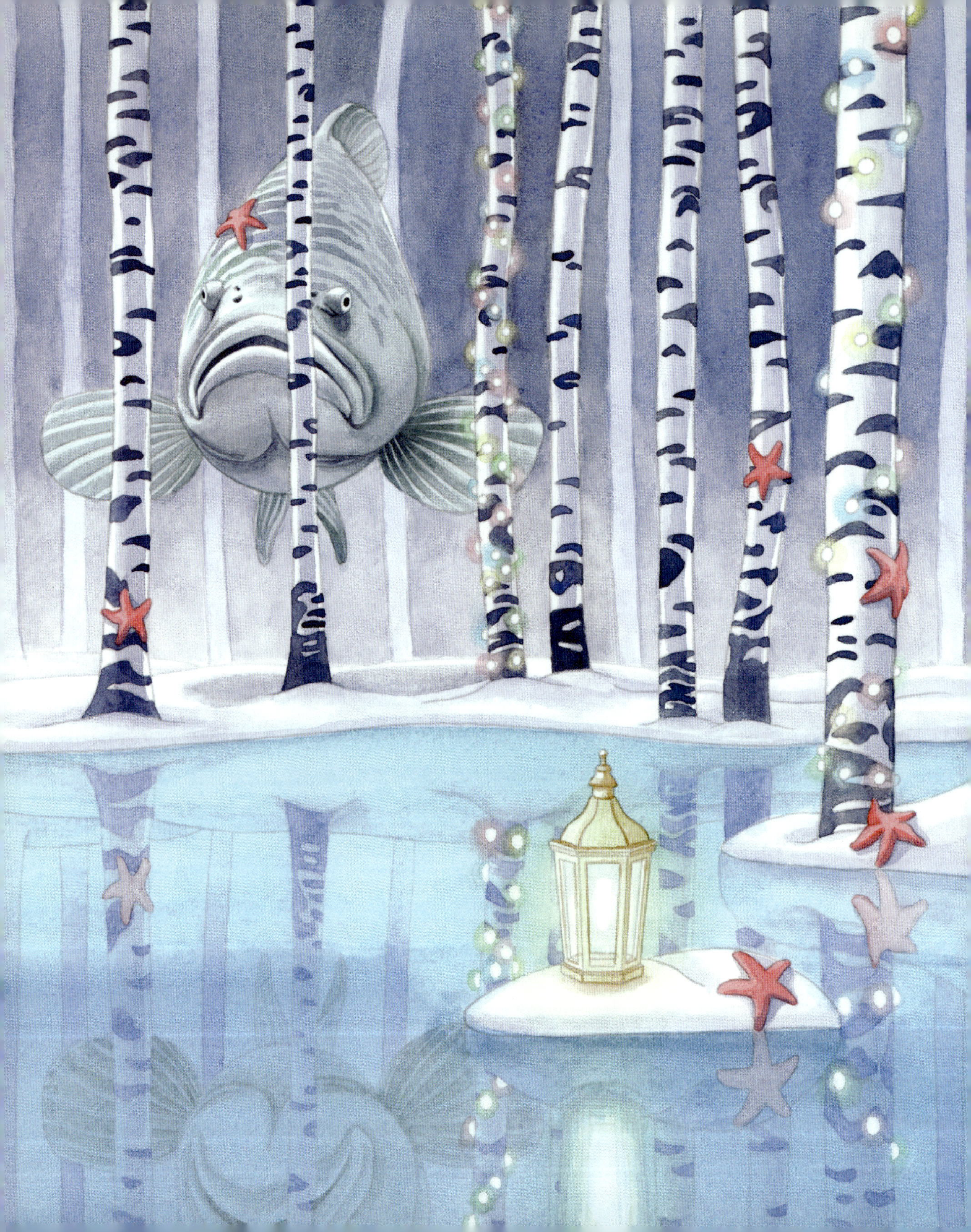

Wondrous Whisper of *Light*

When beginning any watercolor painting, one of the most important elements to consider is lighting. Every layer you add will be influenced by the lighting decisions you make. Whether your light source is artificial—such as from a lamp, lantern, or bulb—or natural, like sunlight, moonlight, or light reflected off surfaces, lighting dramatically shapes the mood and tone of your painting. The direction, intensity, and color of the light all play significant roles in creating atmosphere and depth.

In this chapter, you'll explore how various lighting scenarios can transform your work. By practicing how to build layers that capture different lighting effects, you'll learn how light can guide the viewer's eye and evoke distinct emotions. These three projects will help you deepen your understanding of how to use light as a powerful storytelling tool in your paintings. As you practiced in the previous chapter, layering and glazing are key skills that will assist you in achieving depth and subtle lighting effects in your work.

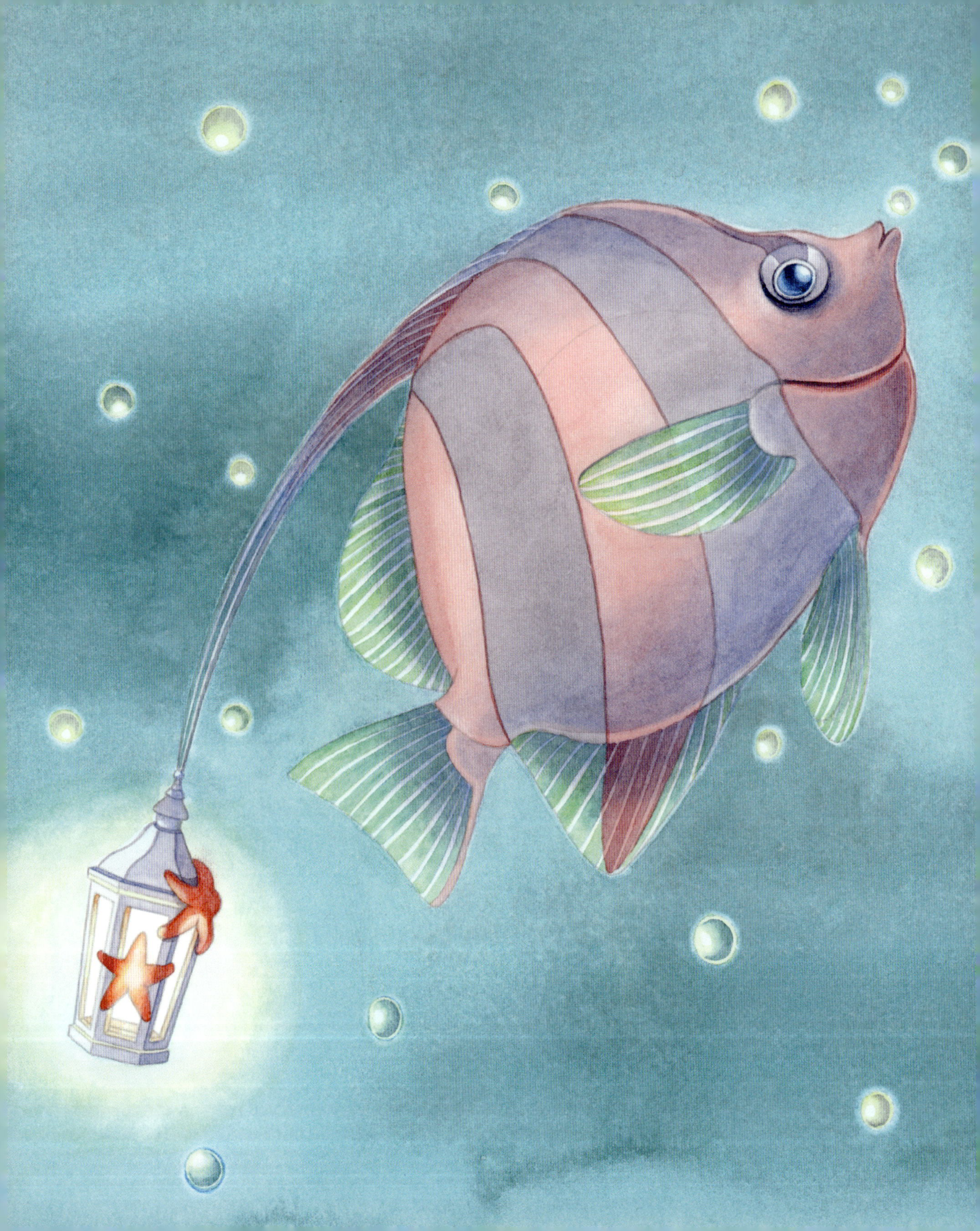

LANTERN-FINNED LUMINARY

This lantern-finned fish draws inspiration from the anglerfish, especially its distinctive glowing lure. While anglerfish are often seen as intimidating due to their large teeth and fearsome bite, I wanted to create a friendlier version. My design features a fish inspired by the schooling bannerfish, which carries a lantern, casting a warm light in the water. This gentle glow acts as a guiding beacon, offering comfort and direction to any fish that may have lost their way. By reimagining the anglerfish in this manner, I aim to highlight the beauty and wonder of the underwater world, promoting a sense of safety amid the depths.

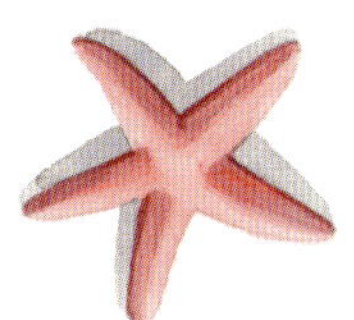

Sketch

Draw the lantern-finned fish freehand or trace the sketch template on page 203.

Step 1

Apply masking fluid to all the bubbles in the water, both starfish, the highlights on the eye, and the dorsal fin. Masking the fin will make painting the background a simpler process. Otherwise, it may be noticeable that you have separately painted on either side of the shape.

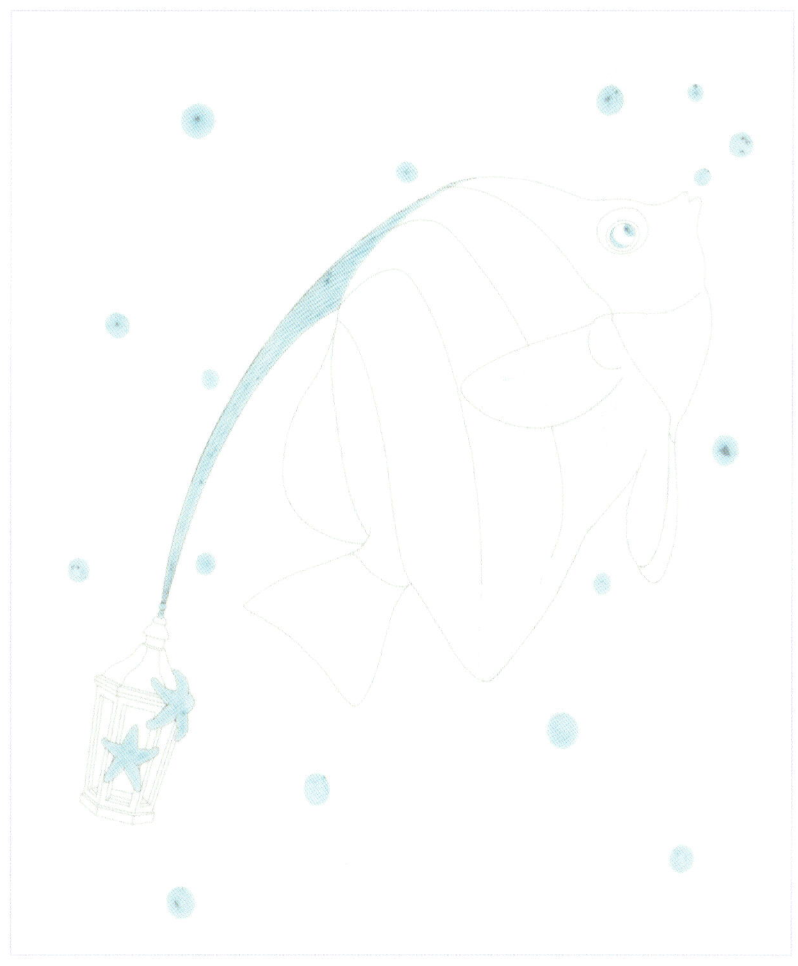

Step 2

On a clean palette, mix **Winsor Blue** and **Permanent Sap Green** with a small amount of **Burnt Sienna** to create the background color. Adjust the ratio to make it either more green or blue, depending on your preference. Use the wet-on-wet technique (page 12) to apply color across the entire background, gradually fading out around the lantern. Alternatively, you can paint right up to the lantern and use a tissue to remove some pigment, creating a glowing effect— just don't wait too long to do this. Once the background is completely dry, use an old brush to lift some paint around the masked bubbles, softening the edges. When it's fully dry, remove the masking fluid from the bubbles and fin. Finally, use a small amount of the background color to paint the fish's eye.

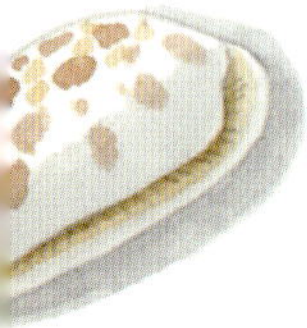

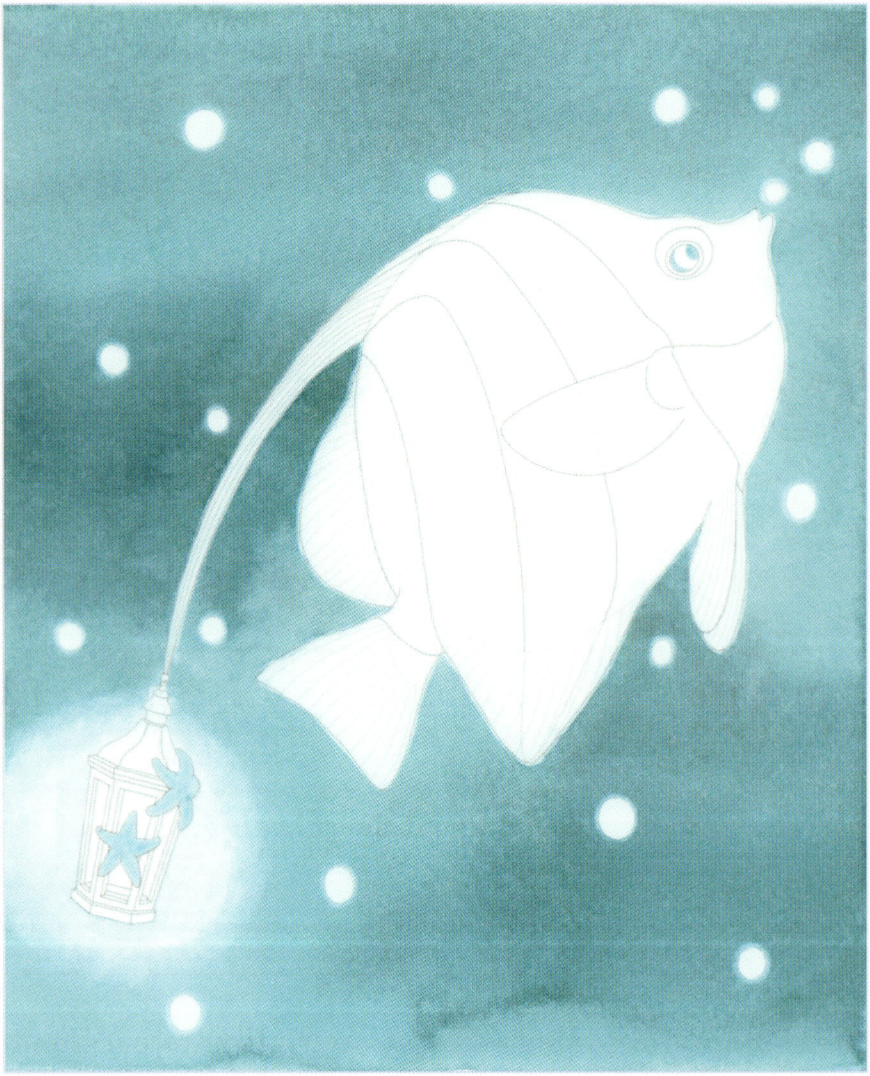

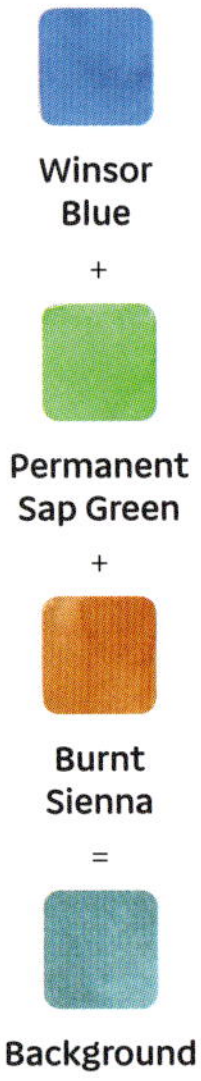

**Winsor
Blue**

+

**Permanent
Sap Green**

+

**Burnt
Sienna**

=

Background

Using **French Ultramarine** mixed with plenty of water, apply the paint to all the areas where shadows would fall. As you paint the shadows, use additional water to dilute the pigment, gradually fading it into the body of the fish and the fins. Also, add shadows to the bubbles by painting a crescent shape on the side farthest from the lantern. Finally, use heavily diluted **Winsor Yellow** to paint the warm glow around the lantern, including its inner surface.

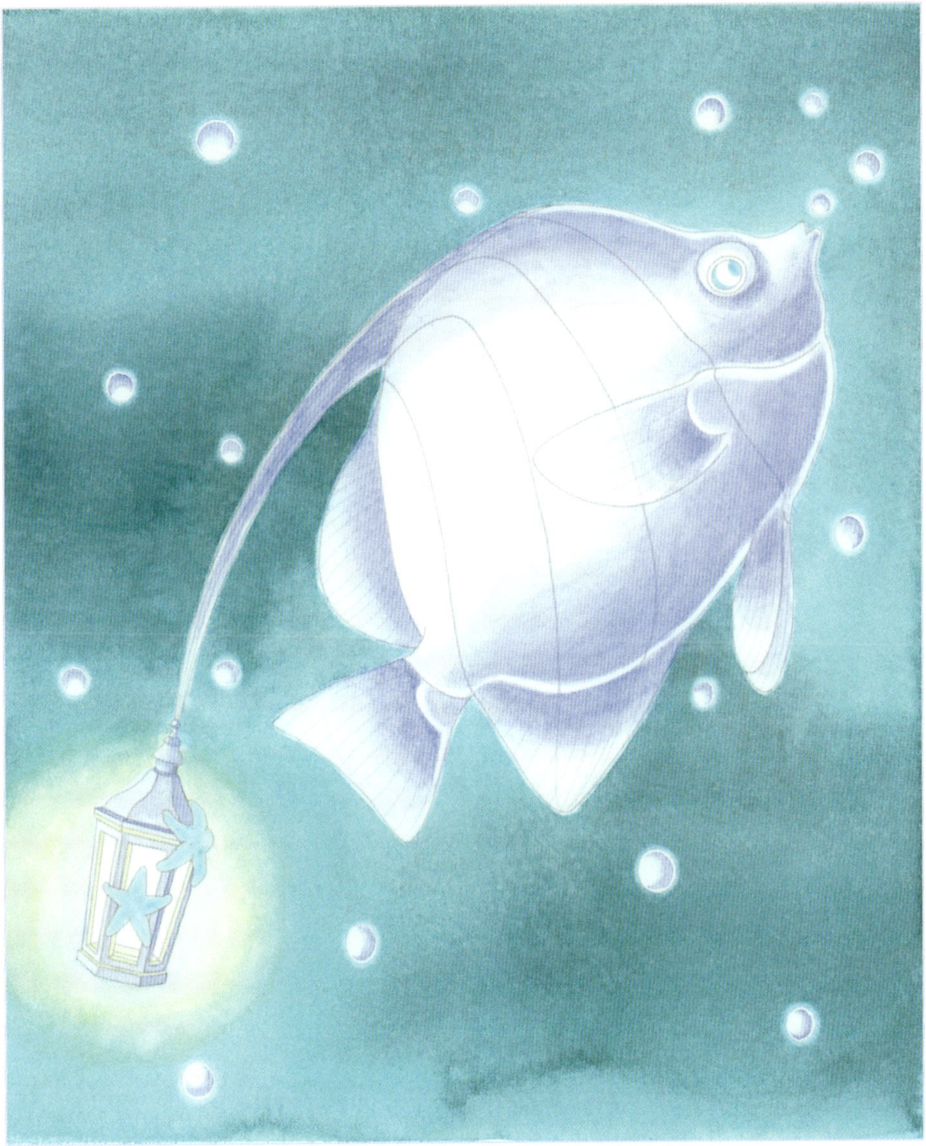

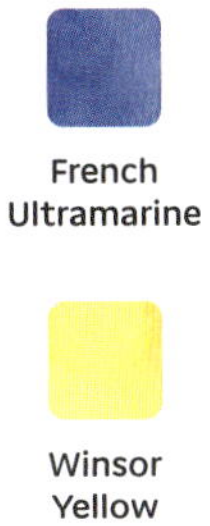

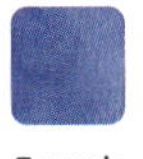

French Ultramarine

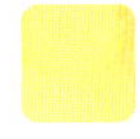

Winsor Yellow

Step 4

This is the fun layer where you get to paint all the bright colors and start bringing the fish to life. When mixing the colors, don't use too much pigment in each mix and apply them using the wet-on-dry technique (page 12). The fish's body consists mostly of bands of color, so start at the top of each section and work your way down. Apply the paint evenly by not going back over areas you've already brushed; this will help achieve a smooth finish.

Alizarin Crimson – for the head and alternate body stripes

French Ultramarine + **Winsor Red** – for the remaining stripes

Winsor Yellow – for the fins and bubbles (leave a thin gap between each stripe on the fins)

Winsor Blue + **French Ultramarine** – for the center of the fish's eye

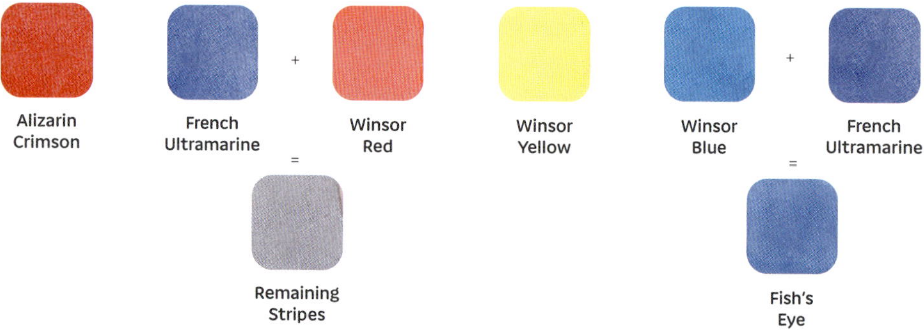

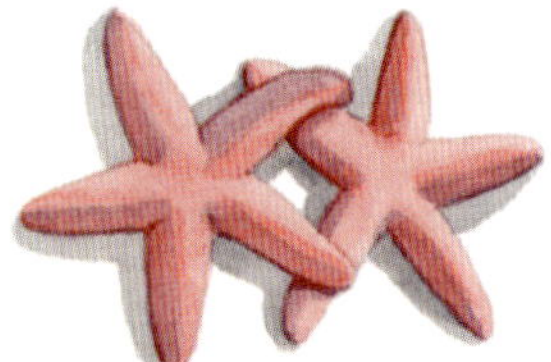

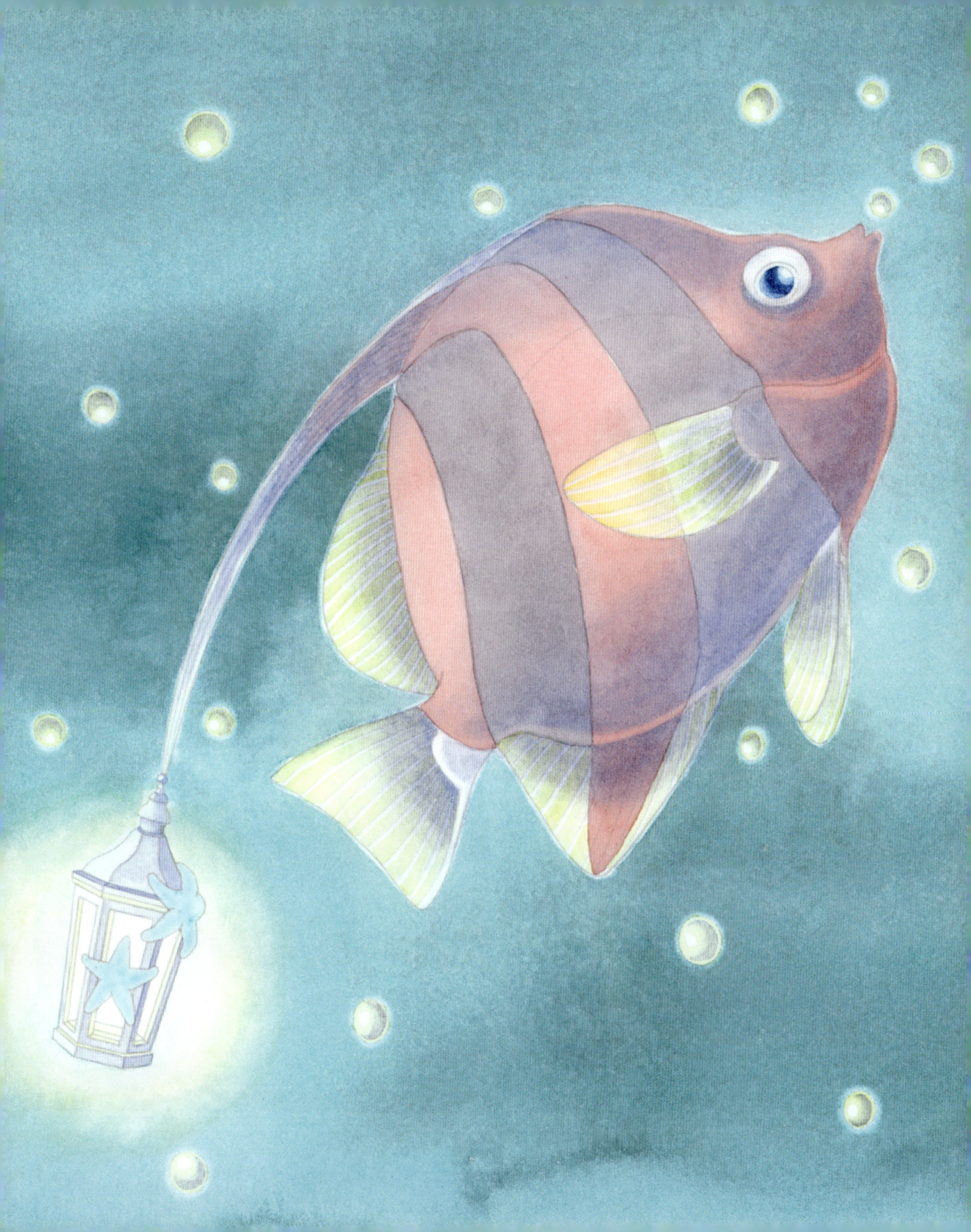

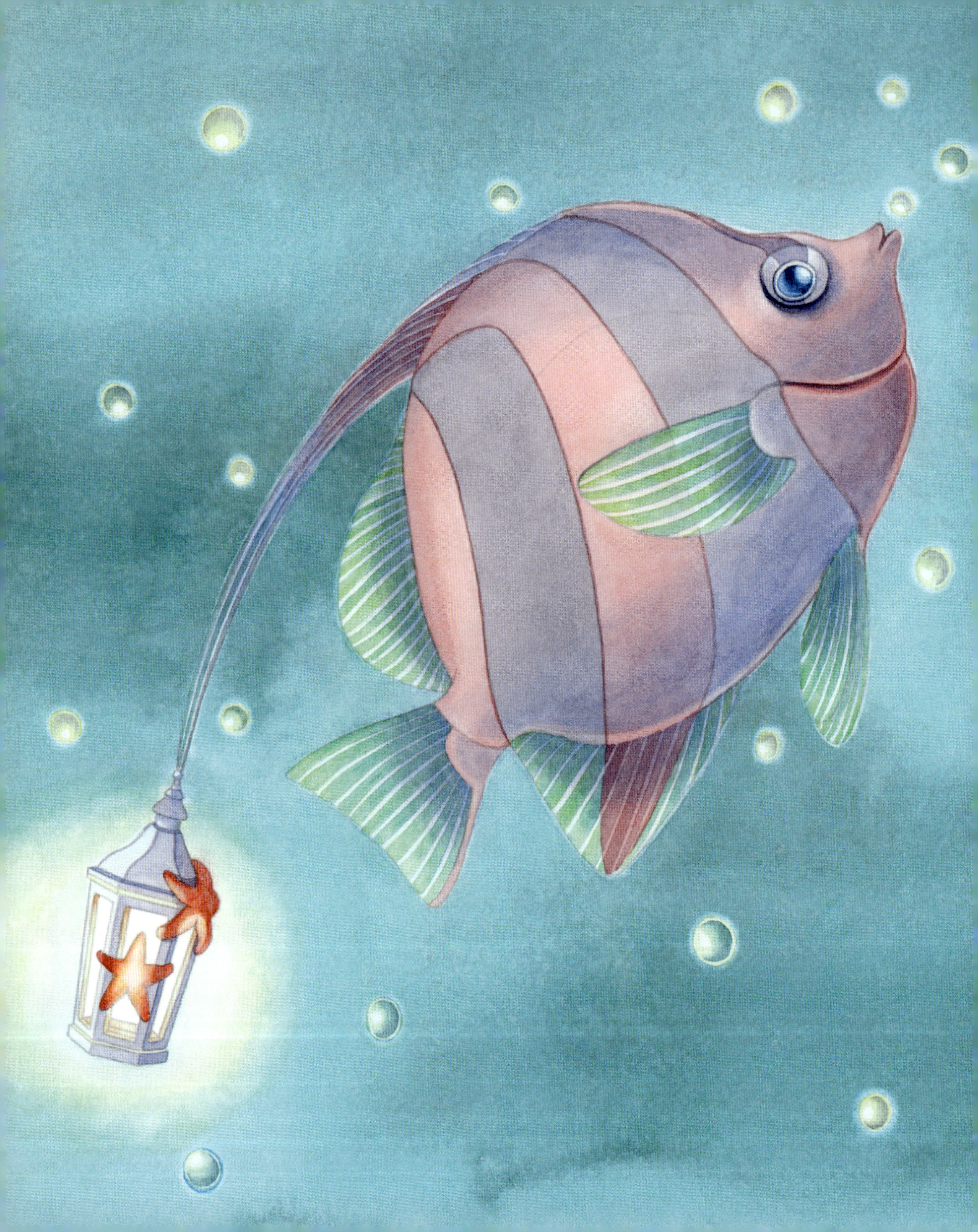

Step 5

Remove the masking fluid. In this layer, you won't be introducing many new colors. Start by using **Winsor Red** for the majority of the starfish body, mixing in a little **Winsor Yellow** to create an orange for the highlighted areas. While you still have some Winsor Red activated, glaze a small amount into the gill opening. Next, shift your focus to the fins. Take some diluted **Winsor Blue** and glaze it directly over the yellow fin stripes you previously painted. This is a cool technique, as you will see the two translucent colors come together to create the green color for the fins. For the remaining details throughout the painting, use colors that are already on your palette, but apply them in a more concentrated manner (meaning less water and more pigment). You can also mix **French Ultramarine** with **Burnt Sienna** to create a dark color for around the eye and gill. Feel free to blend this color combination with any of the other colors on your palette to achieve the desired darkness.

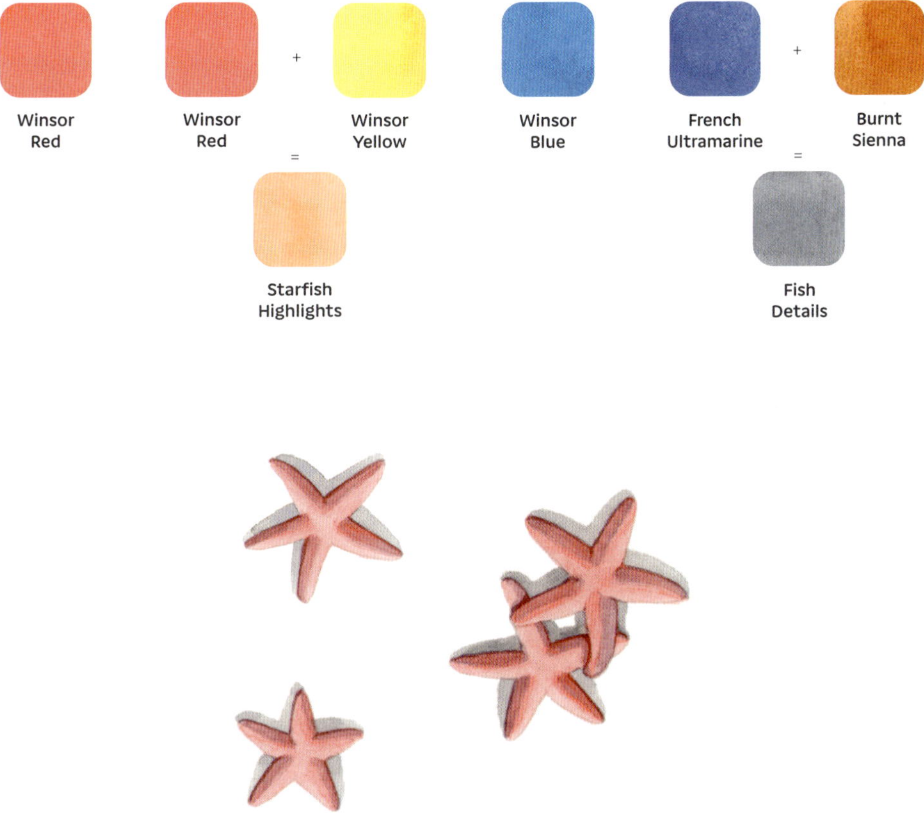

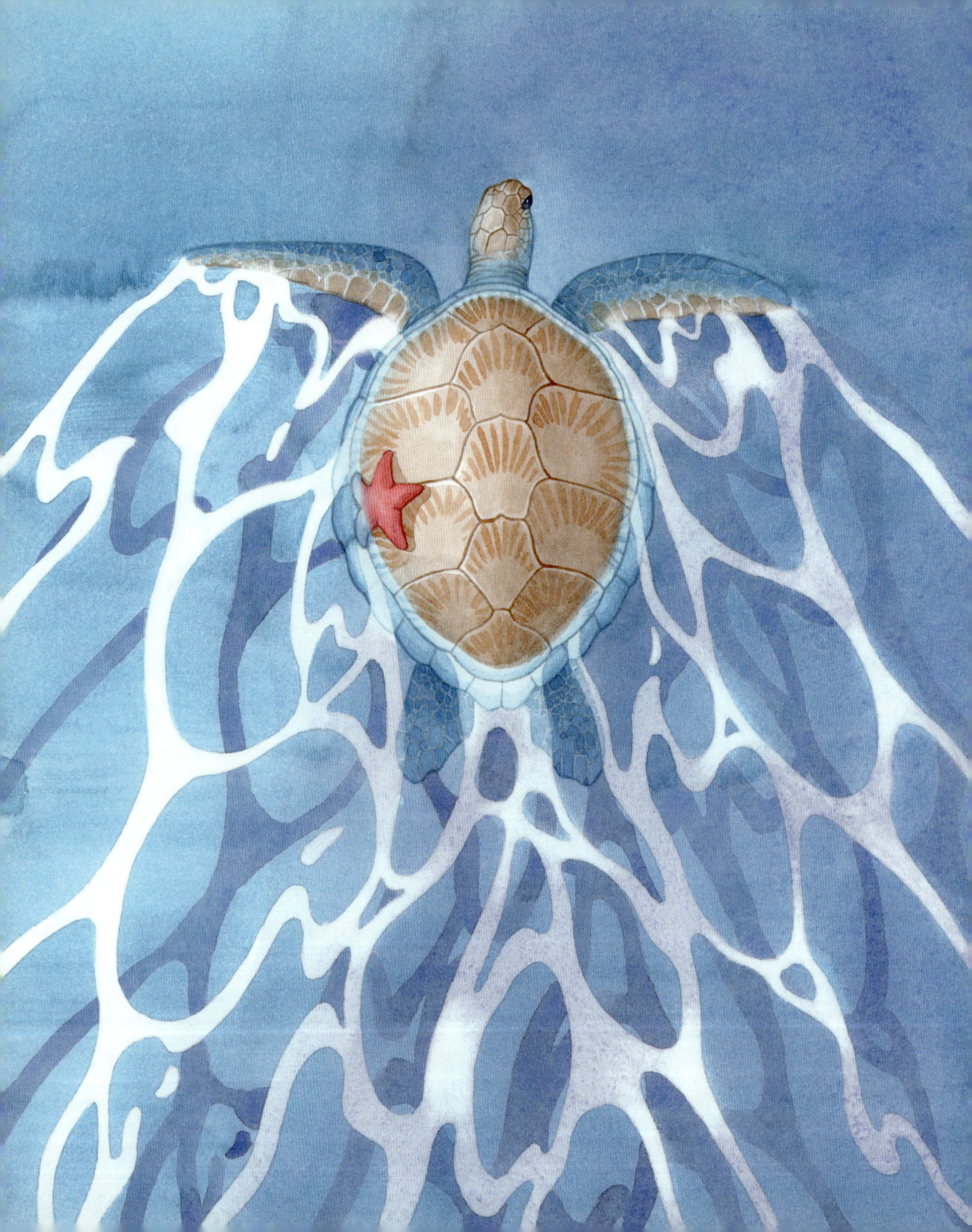

PATH OF THE SHELL-BEARER

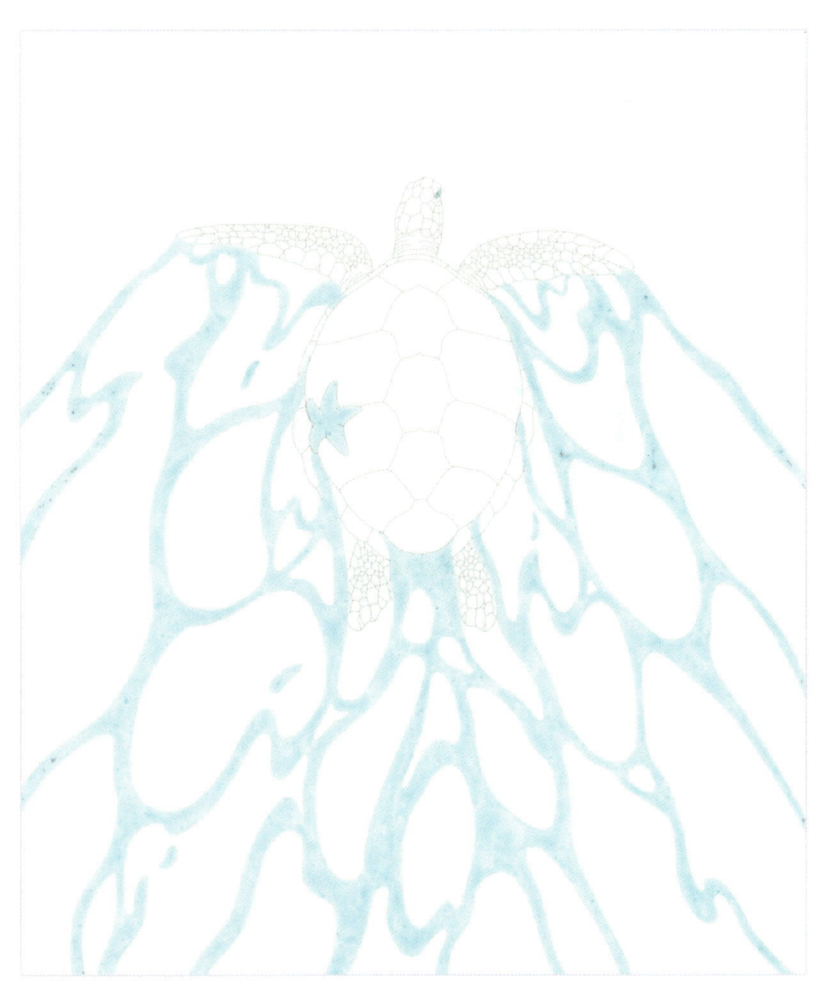

Turtles are not only majestic and peaceful creatures but also captivating subjects for painting. Their intricate markings beautifully contrast with their simple, streamlined bodies. In this project, you will follow a step-by-step process for painting water, learning how to capture its movement and reflectivity in an engaging way. You'll experiment with various techniques and layers of color to create a dynamic water scene that is vibrant and enhances the serene beauty of the turtle.

This picture is seemingly simple but is a great example of how to achieve depth by having a structured layering process.

Sketch

Draw the turtle freehand or trace the sketch template on page 205.

Step 1

Use your masking fluid to fill in all the areas representing seafoam trailing behind the turtle. This may be quite time-consuming, but doing so will save you time in the later steps and make them much easier. Also, fill in the starfish and the turtle's eye.

Step 2

On a clean palette, mix a combination of **French Ultramarine** and **Burnt Sienna** to create a shadow beneath the seafoam. You have used this shadow color combination before; however, this time, add more pigment to the mix. The idea is to paint the same shapes that you masked in, only shifted to the right. Don't worry if you don't replicate it perfectly, as it's just about being suggestive with the shadow. Neatness isn't that important either, as you'll be glazing over these shadows multiple times in the next few steps. Every time you glaze a new color over a previous one, you reactivate what is already there, slightly shifting those pigments as they mix with your new color. This shifting of pigment will even out minor inconsistencies.

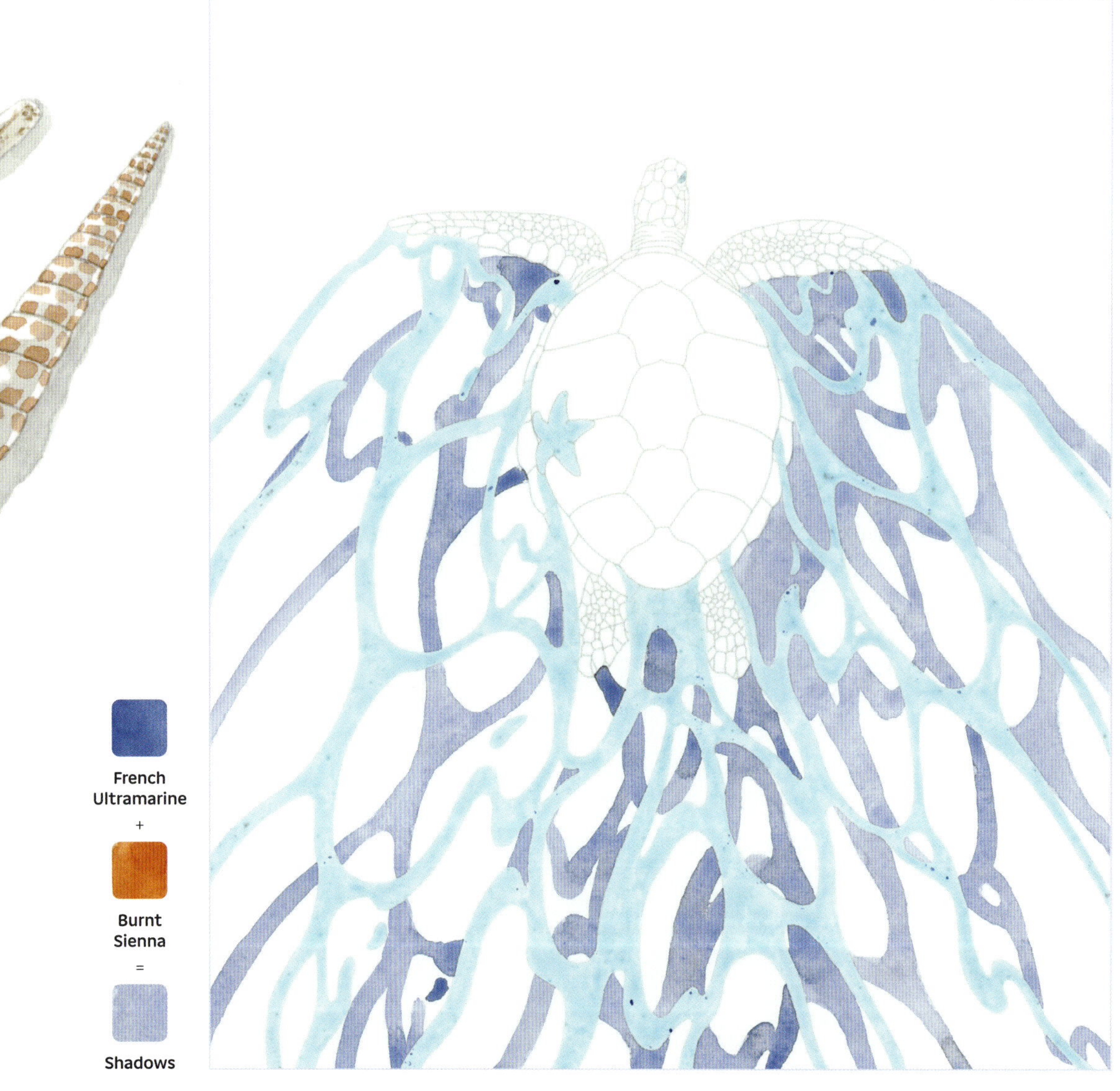

Step 3

Mix a generous amount of **Winsor Blue** with a small amount of **Permanent Sap Green**. You'll need enough of this mixture to cover the entire background, and it should be diluted with plenty of water. Use the wet-on-dry technique (page 12), and remember that using a larger brush will help create a more seamless finish by minimizing any disruption to the previous layer. Paint the background color up to the borders of the turtle. Once the paint is completely dry, apply the same color within the turtle's shape. As you paint, fade the edges to create a gradual transition, leaving the top of the head, shell, and the back edge of the front flippers blank—this will represent the part of the turtle that is above the water's surface. If you're confident in painting quickly, you can combine both the background and the turtle painting in one step.

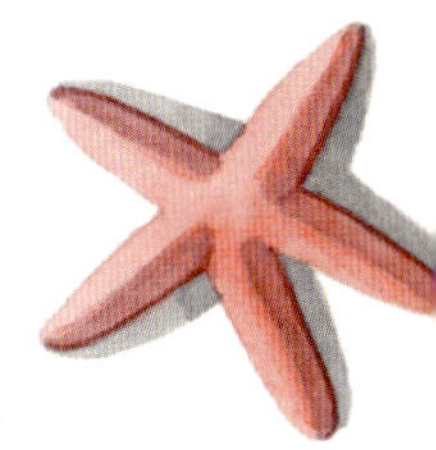

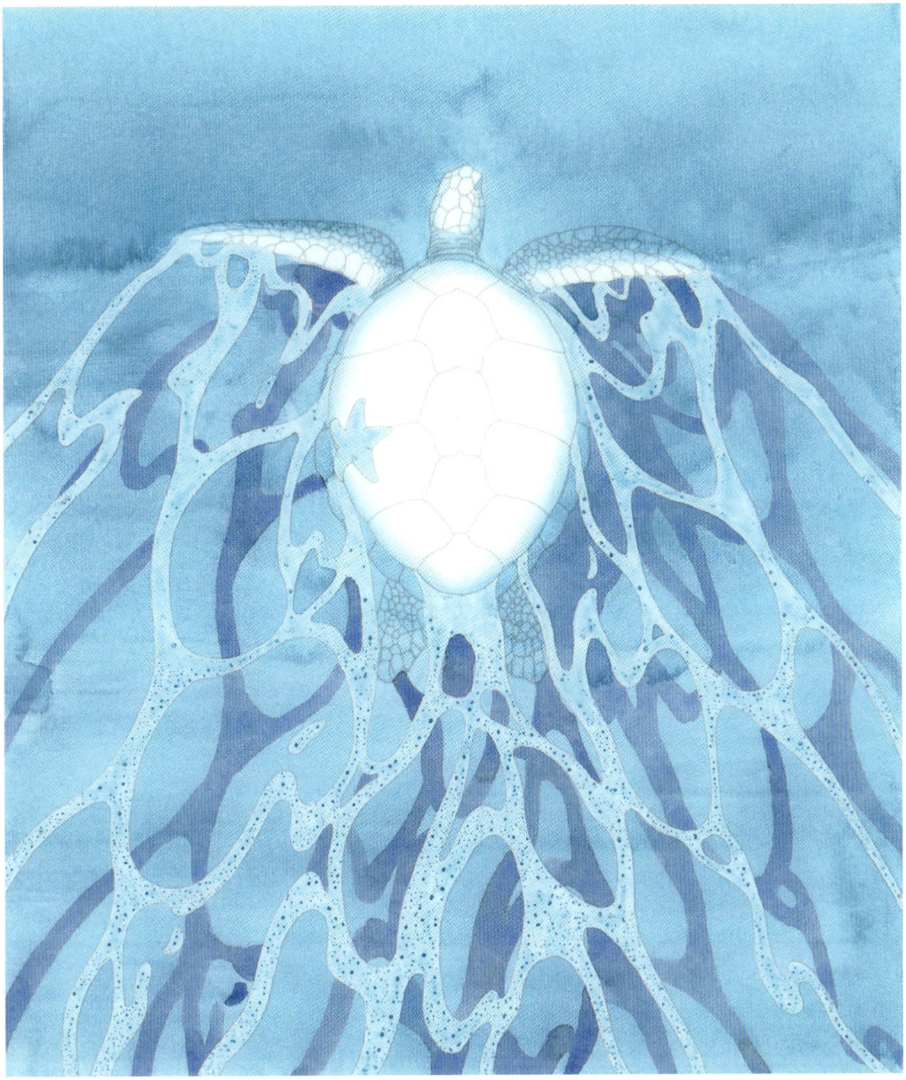

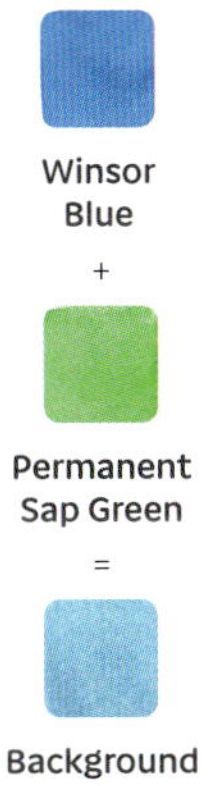

Winsor
Blue

+

Permanent
Sap Green

=

Background

Step 4

Once everything is completely dry, remove all the masking fluid from the seafoam. Once that's done, further dilute some of your background color from Step 3 so you can paint over any areas of the turtle visible through the translucent seafoam. Next, mix **Yellow Ochre** and **Raw Sienna** to paint each individual segment of the shell, head, and flippers. By painting each part separately, you'll create subtle variations in tone and add interest to the shell. Embrace blooming and texture, but be sure to leave an even gap between each segment. Use **Winsor Red** to break up the blue and paint the starfish, except for the tips of the lower arms beneath the water's surface.

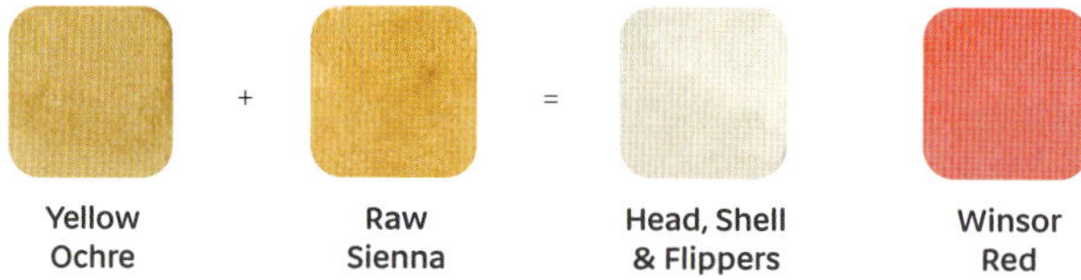

Yellow Ochre + Raw Sienna = Head, Shell & Flippers   Winsor Red

Finally, mix **French Ultramarine** with a small amount of **Burnt Sienna** and glaze it over the entire right side of the water. As you do this, paint directly over the previously masked areas, including the shadows, creating a gradual transition to the lighter left side. Before the paint dries, use a tissue to blot random areas of watery pigment on the seafoam to help create a more realistic water surface.

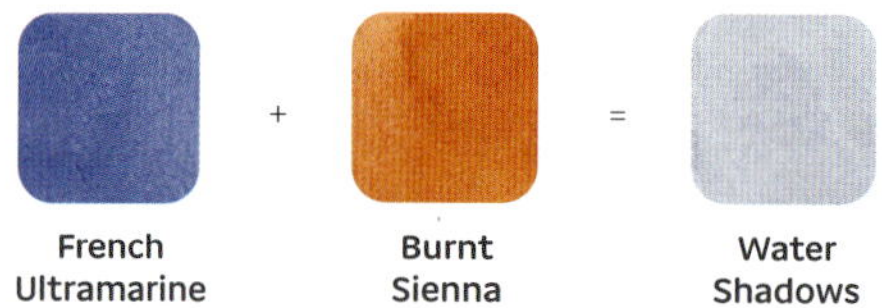

French Ultramarine + Burnt Sienna = Water Shadows

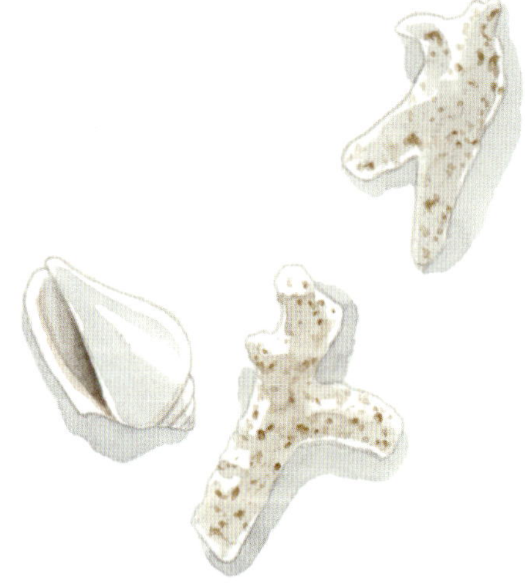

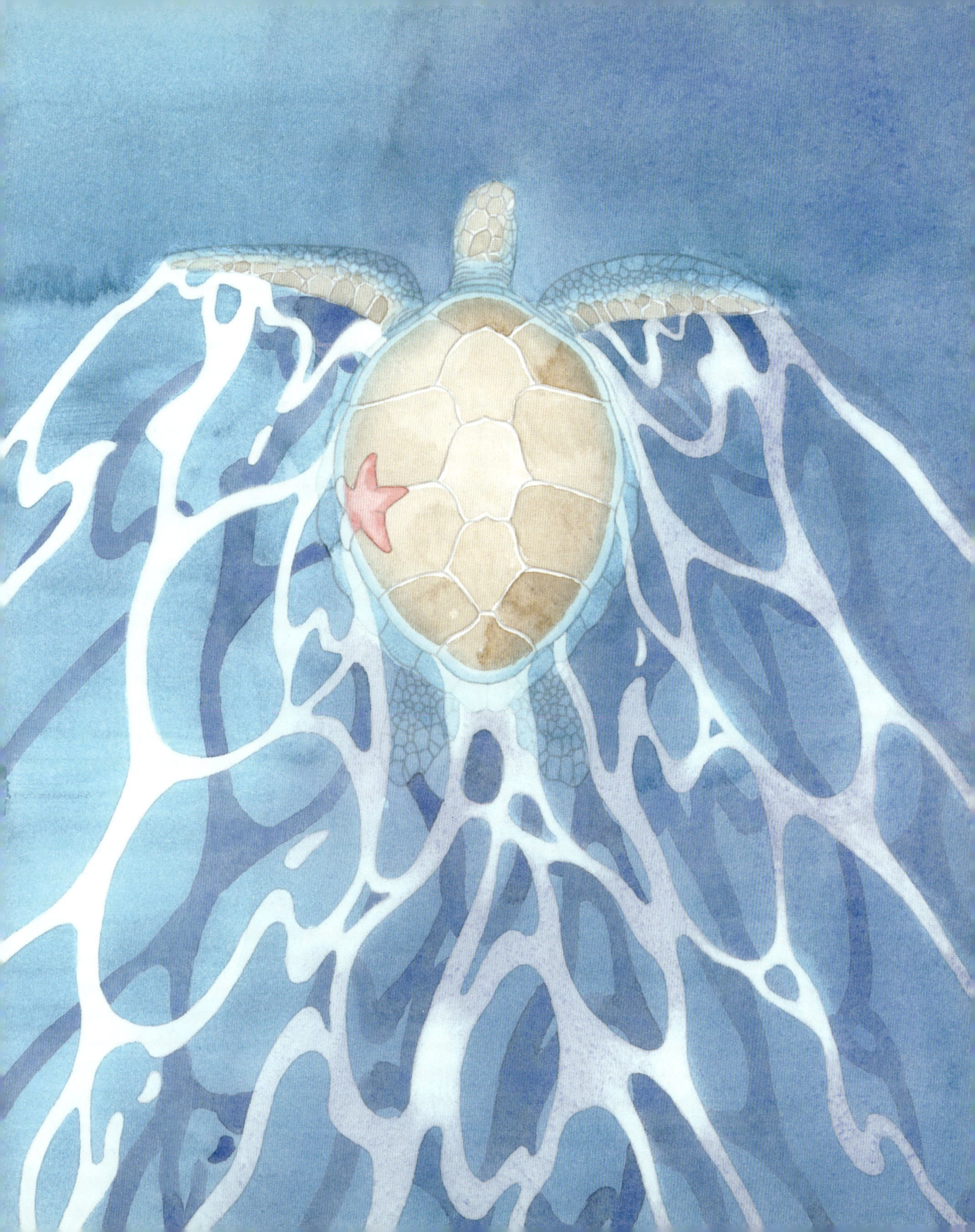

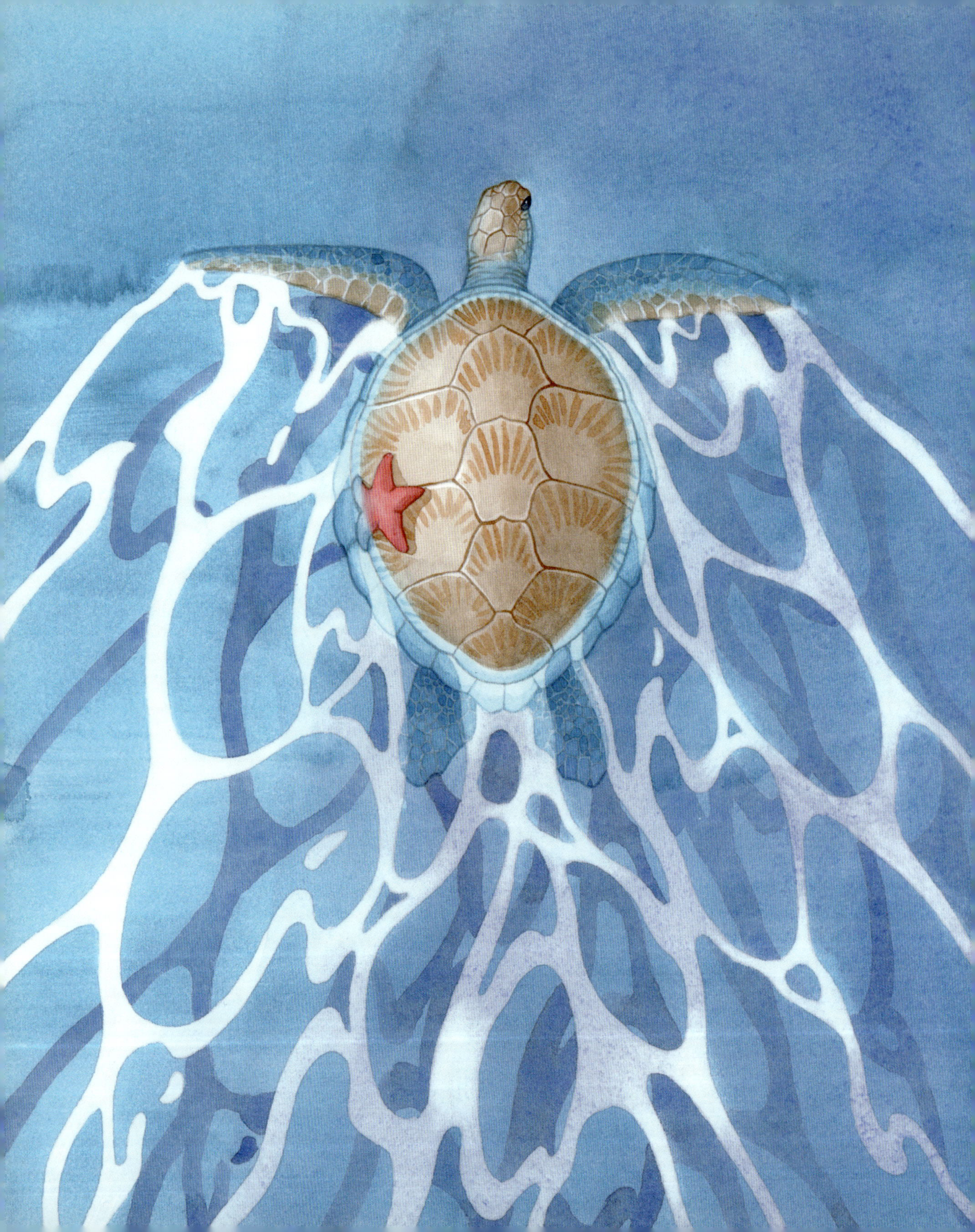

Step 5

Before you start painting all the details, mix some **French Ultramarine** with a hint of **Alizarin Crimson** to darken the color used for the turtle. Use this darker shade to glaze the right side of the turtle's shell and head and to add a shadow for the starfish.

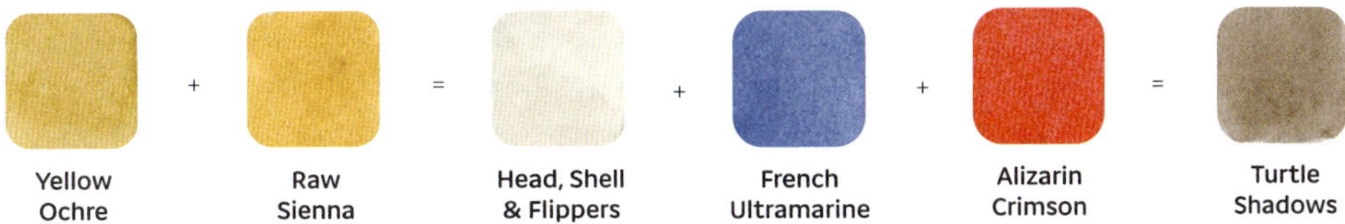

<table>
<tr><td>Yellow
Ochre</td><td>+</td><td>Raw
Sienna</td><td>=</td><td>Head, Shell
& Flippers</td><td>+</td><td>French
Ultramarine</td><td>+</td><td>Alizarin
Crimson</td><td>=</td><td>Turtle
Shadows</td></tr>
</table>

Once this is dry, use some diluted **Burnt Sienna** to paint a textured pattern on each shell segment. Now, all that's left are the crisp line details. Define any part of the turtle that is underwater by adding some **Winsor Blue** to your shadow color used under the seafoam. For the deeper markings on the shell, use the brown mixture you created for the shell's shadow, but apply it more concentrated.

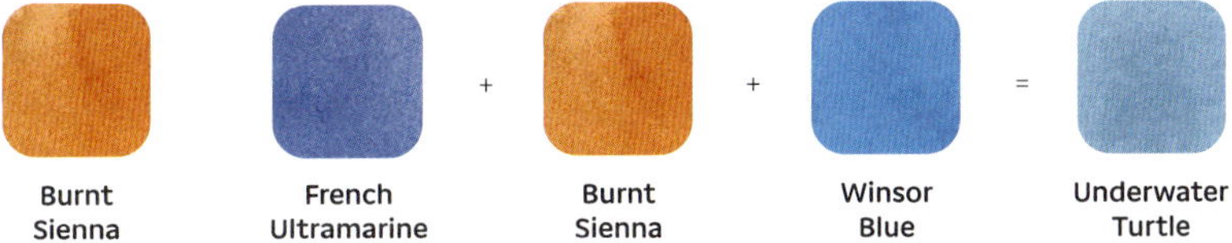

<table>
<tr><td>Burnt
Sienna</td><td>French
Ultramarine</td><td>+</td><td>Burnt
Sienna</td><td>+</td><td>Winsor
Blue</td><td>=</td><td>Underwater
Turtle</td></tr>
</table>

Finally, intensify the starfish with **Winsor Red** mixed with a little **French Ultramarine**, and increase the pigment ratio in the water shadow color from Step 4 for the turtle's eye.

<table>
<tr><td>Winsor
Red</td><td>+</td><td>French
Ultramarine</td><td>=</td><td>Starfish</td></tr>
</table>

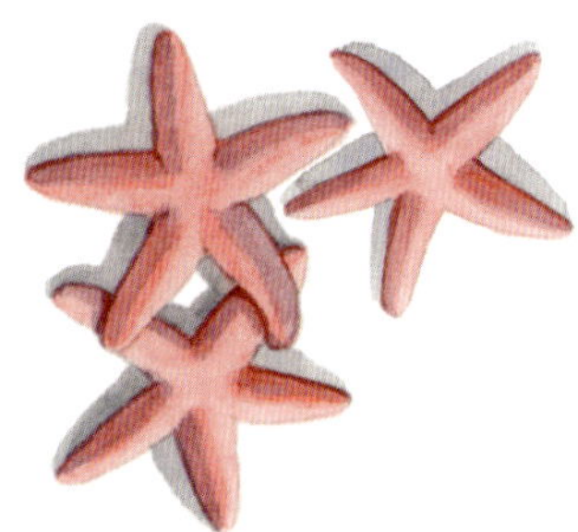

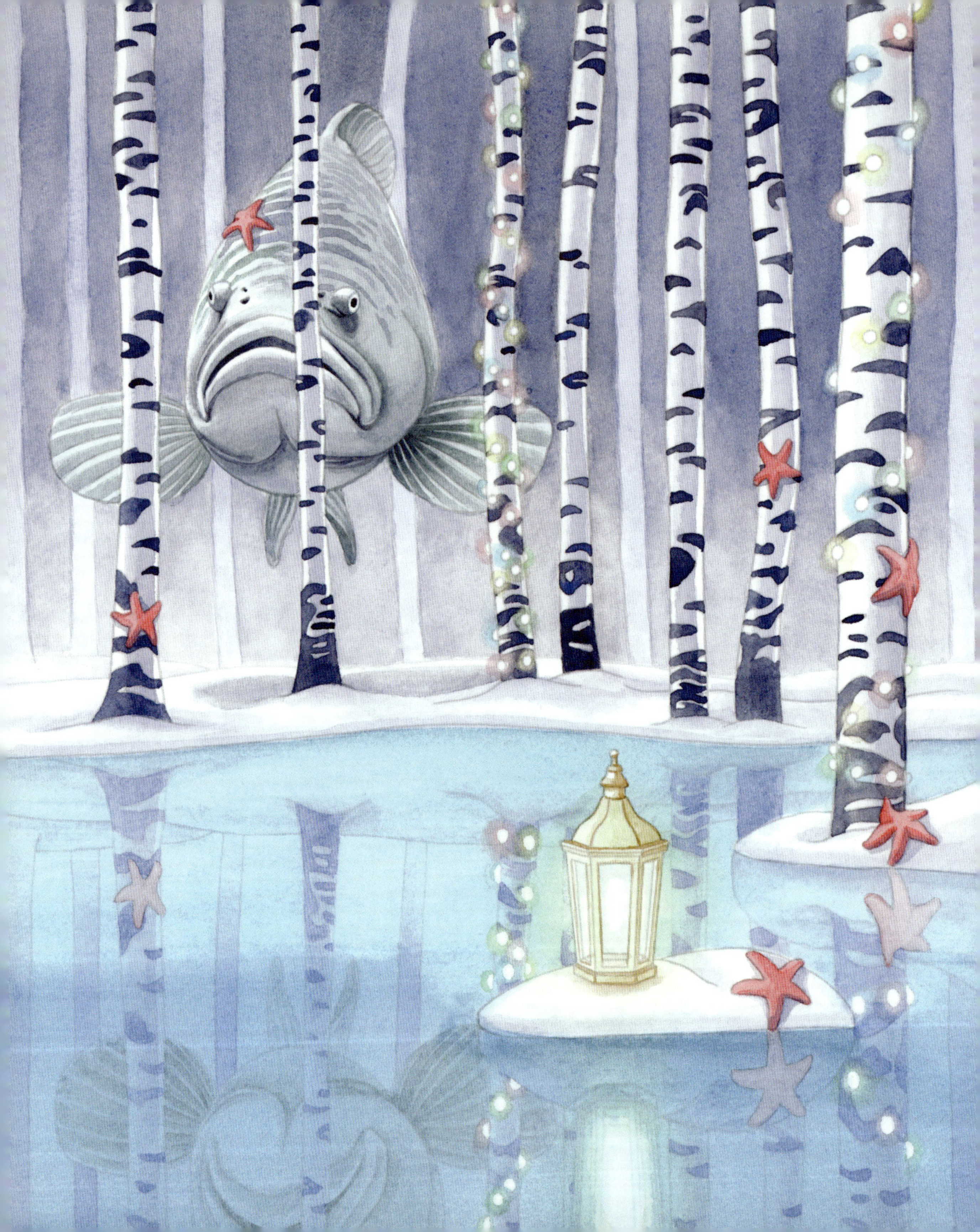

MIRRORED MIRTH

The grouper is my favorite fish, captivating me with its mysterious appearance and stunningly beautiful markings. There's something about their prehistoric look that fascinates me; I often imagine them having a grumpy attitude, as if they've seen it all before and are simply uninterested in the world around them. This project centers on the concept of reflections and how they can add an entirely new dimension to your artwork. You will learn a straightforward-yet-effective approach to creating natural-looking reflections that enhance the vibrancy and brightness of your picture.

Sketch

Draw the scene freehand or trace the sketch template on page 207.

Step 1

As in previous paintings, the masking fluid step is the starting point for building up layers. Mask all the starfish, the entire lantern, the fairy light globes, and the grouper's eyes. The lake in this scene has a mirrorlike surface, which can be easily achieved after masking the lantern. This allows you to paint over areas instead of around them, helping to avoid potential blooming and unwanted texture.

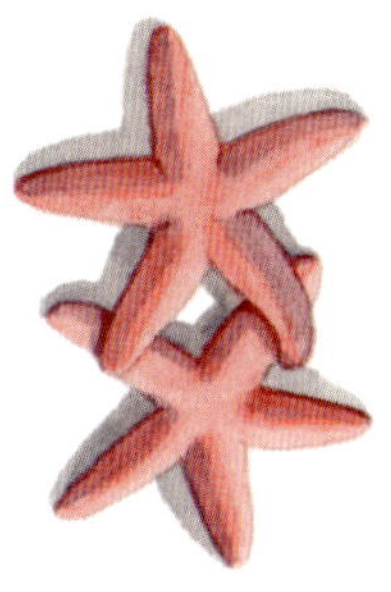

Step 2

Mix a generous amount of **French Ultramarine** and **Burnt Sienna**. You'll use this mixture and its variations frequently throughout the painting process. With your paint ready, fill the gaps between the trees using the wet-on-dry technique (page 12). Before the paint dries, gently dab the lower portion with a clean tissue to lighten it. Work on a few areas at a time, focusing on what feels manageable. Use **French Ultramarine** to paint the background trees, fading them toward ground level. Mirror this effect in the trees' reflection on the lake.

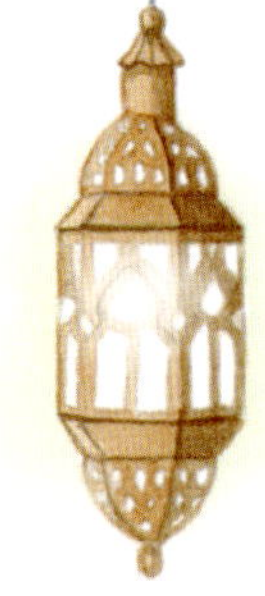

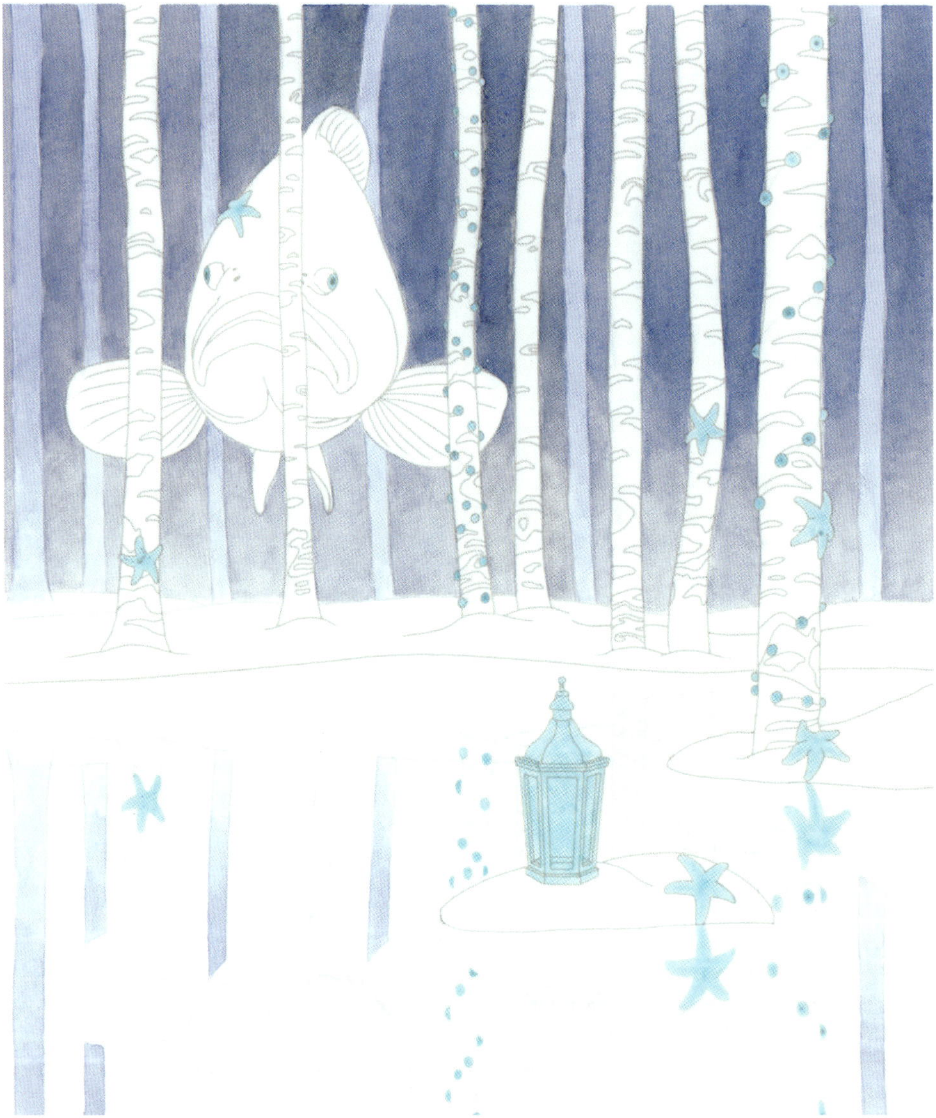

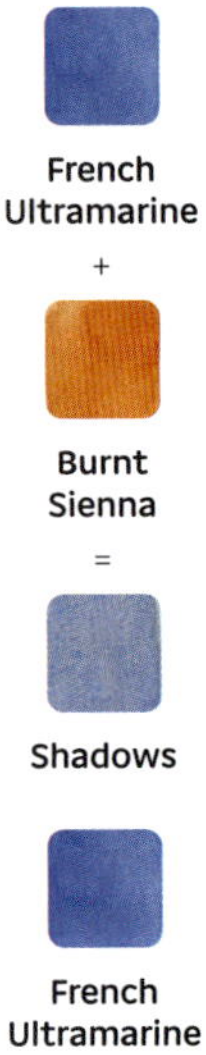

French
Ultramarine

+

Burnt
Sienna

=

Shadows

French
Ultramarine

Step 3

Using the **French Ultramarine** and **Burnt Sienna** mix on your palette, paint all the shadows on the foreground trees, snow, and their reflections in the water. Now, add a small amount of **Permanent Sap Green** to your mixture to create a green-gray color for painting the shadows on the fish and its reflection.

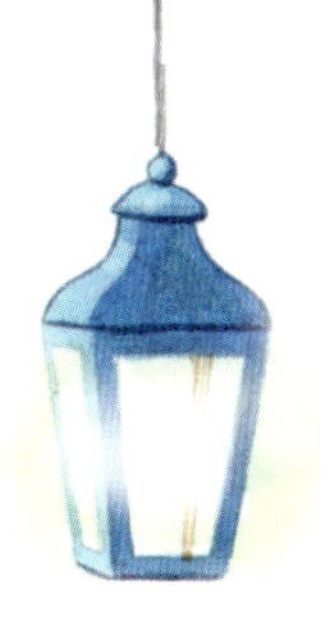

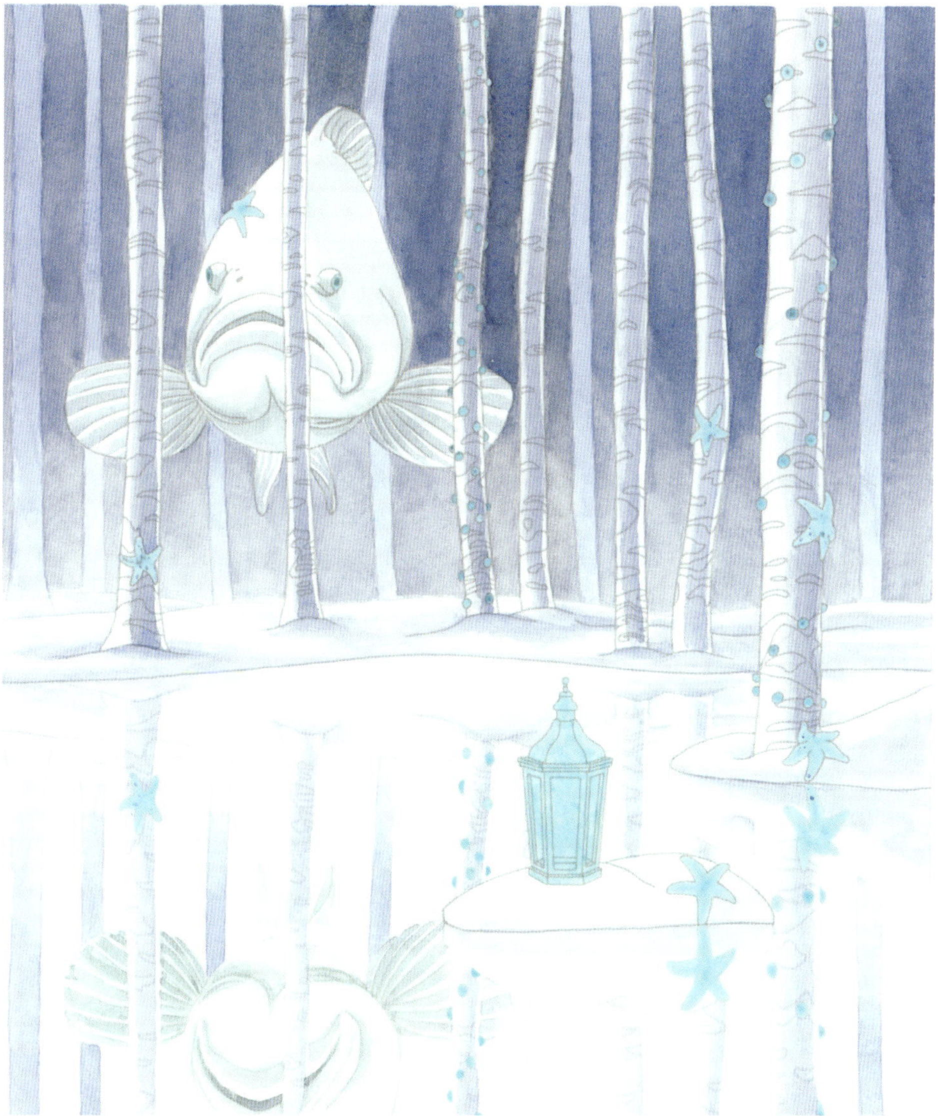

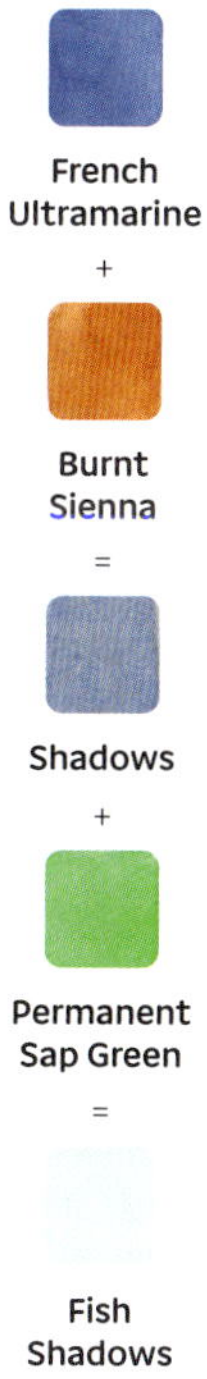

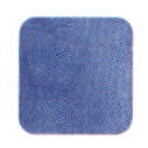

French Ultramarine

+

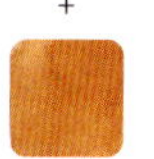

Burnt Sienna

=

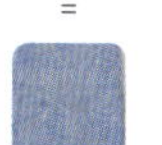

Shadows

+

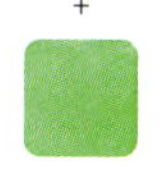

Permanent Sap Green

=

Fish Shadows

Step 4

There are a few parts to this step, and the order is particularly important. First, let's address the water. Using **Winsor Blue**, paint all the tree patterns reflected on the lake. Don't worry if it looks too bright at this stage.

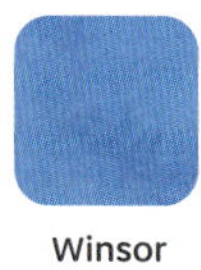

Winsor
Blue

While the paint dries, mix **Winsor Blue** with **Permanent Sap Green** to create a cool, icy color—leaning more toward green. Once the paint is dry, use a decent-sized flat or quill brush to gently apply an even coating of clean water over the lake, excluding the lantern's reflection. Let the water soak into the paper for a bit, but don't wait too long before applying the icy green-blue to the lake. After everything has dried, remove the masking fluid from the starfish reflections and lightly paint them in with a light value of **Winsor Red**. This completes the lake portion for now.

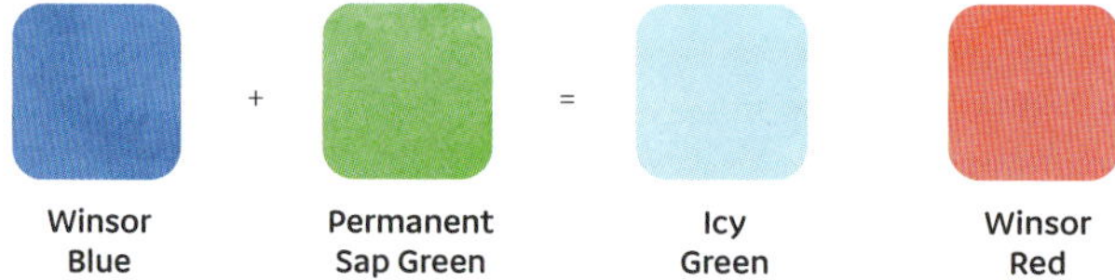

| Winsor Blue | + | Permanent Sap Green | = | Icy Green | Winsor Red |

Next, the **French Ultramarine** and **Burnt Sienna** mix you made in Step 2 is probably dry, so reactivate it with a little water and begin painting the markings on the foreground trees. The two colors in your shadow mix may have separated slightly while drying—don't worry, just re-mix as you go. This will add some natural color variation to the pattern of the trees, which is a nice touch.

French
Ultramarine + Burnt
Sienna = Tree
Markings

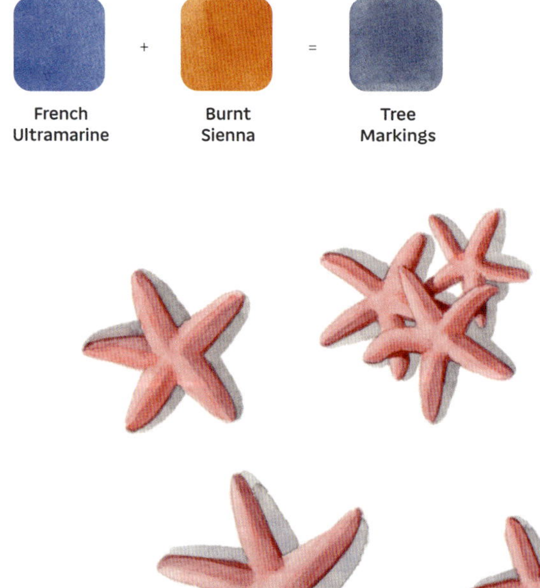

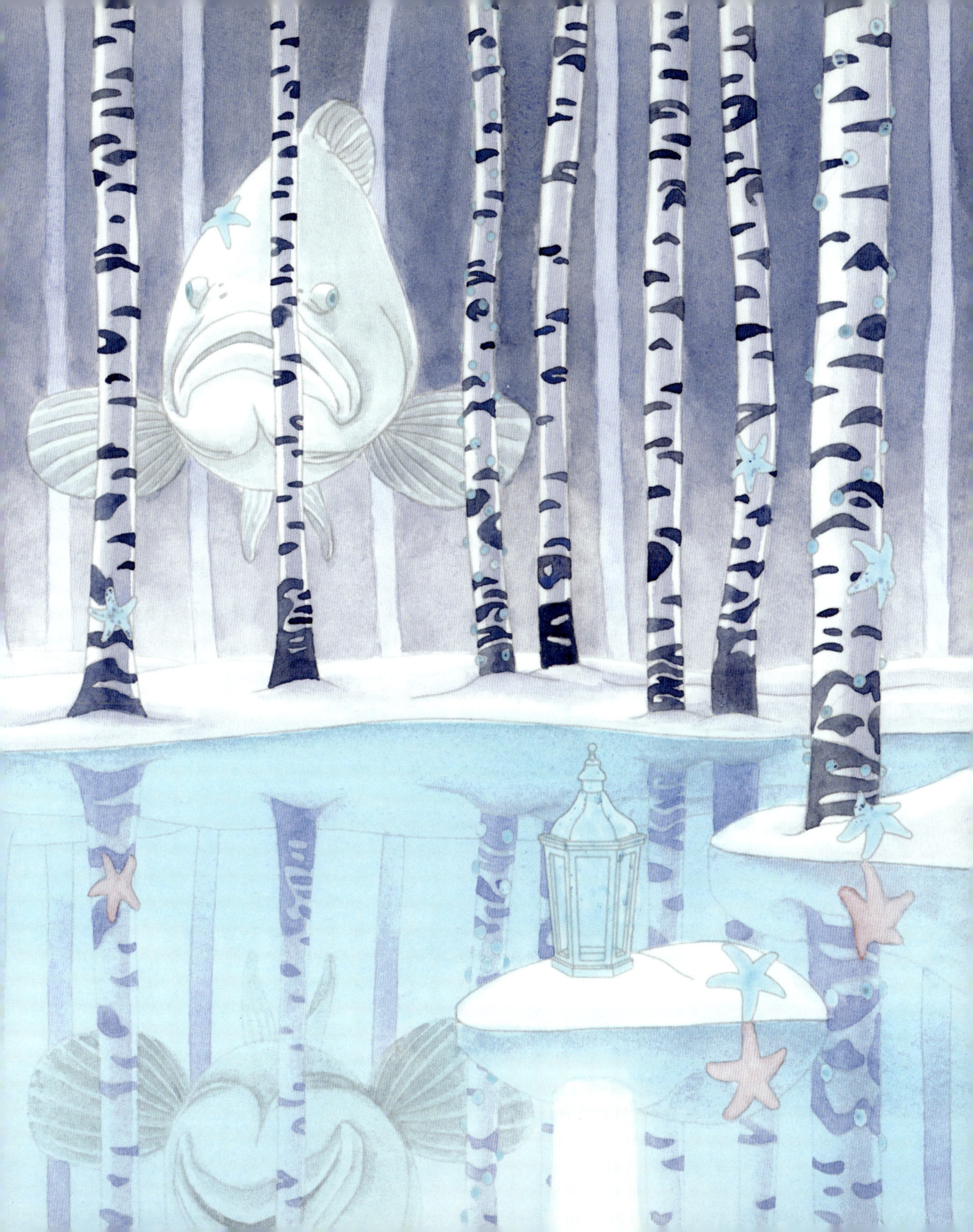

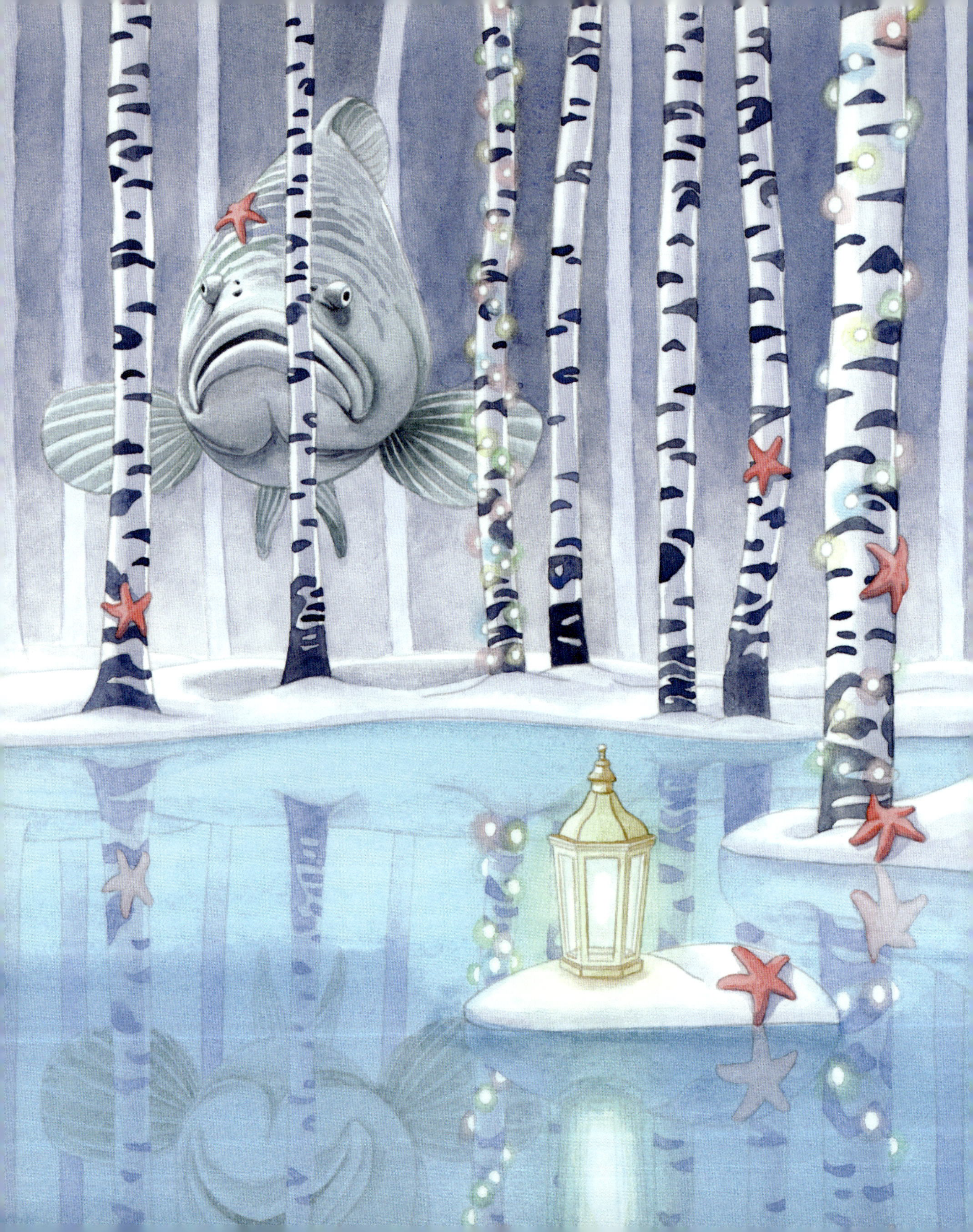

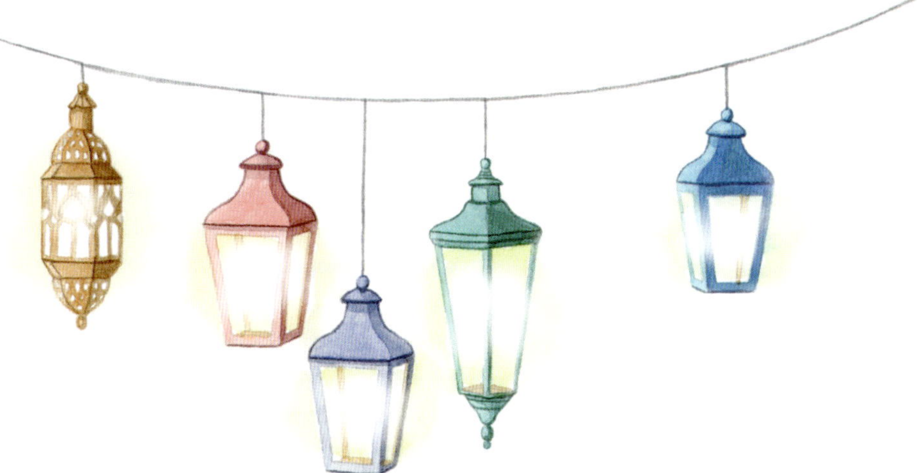

Step 5

Take a large brush and apply clean water to the lower half of the icy lake. It's important not to overwork this step. While the paper is still damp, use some diluted **French Ultramarine** from your palette and apply it to the entire area. Before the paint dries, use a tissue to soak up some of the pigmented water where the lantern reflection is.

French Ultramarine

Once everything has dried, remove the masking fluid from the lantern so you can paint it with **Yellow Ochre**, **Burnt Sienna**, and a small amount of **Permanent Sap Green**. Further dilute this color to glaze the lake around the lantern and its reflection to create a warm glow. Now, start softening the edges of all the light globes using the lifting technique (page 13). Use whatever bright colors you want for the globes, and once dry, you can remove the remaining masking fluid. Lastly, use the colors already on your palette to enhance the shadows and details on the grouper, using the reference image as your guide. Don't forget to add some **Winsor Red** for the starfish.

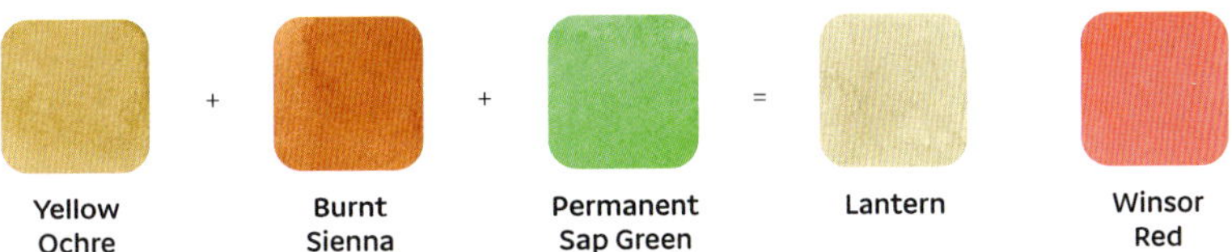

| Yellow Ochre | + | Burnt Sienna | + | Permanent Sap Green | = | Lantern | | Winsor Red |

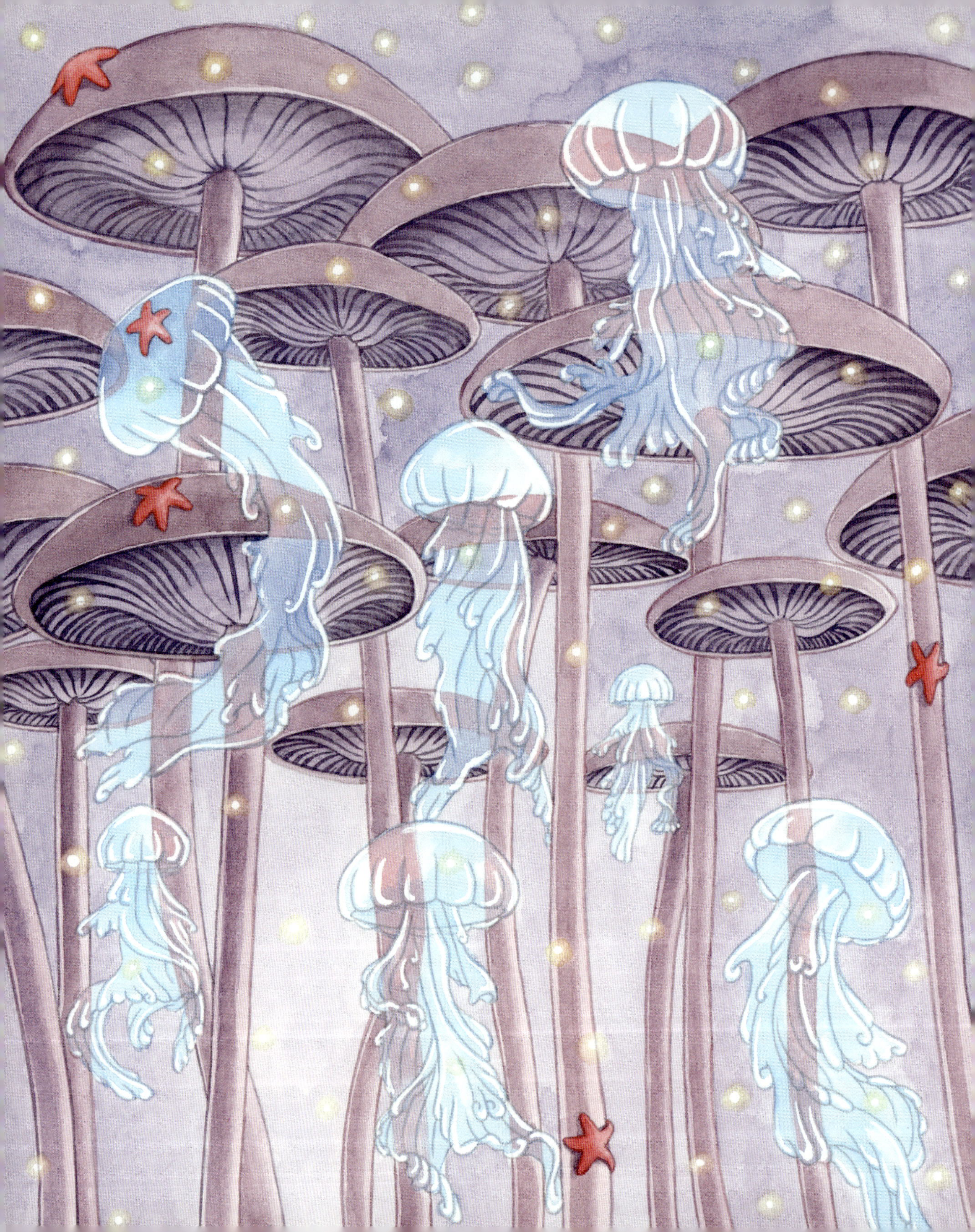

Mysterious Realms Above & Below

Watercolor's unique characteristics make it the perfect medium for capturing the essence of transparent objects. The way watercolors blend and flow allows you to achieve a sense of luminosity that is difficult to replicate with other mediums. This aspect of painting can be an incredibly enjoyable area to explore, opening a new dimension for you to push your creative boundaries.

If you have a fondness for mushrooms and jellyfish, this chapter is for you! Their otherworldly traits and delicate structures harmonize perfectly, enhanced by the fluidity and luminosity of watercolors. You will learn to observe the subtleties of light as it passes through and reflects off different materials, allowing you to convey depth and dimension in your work.

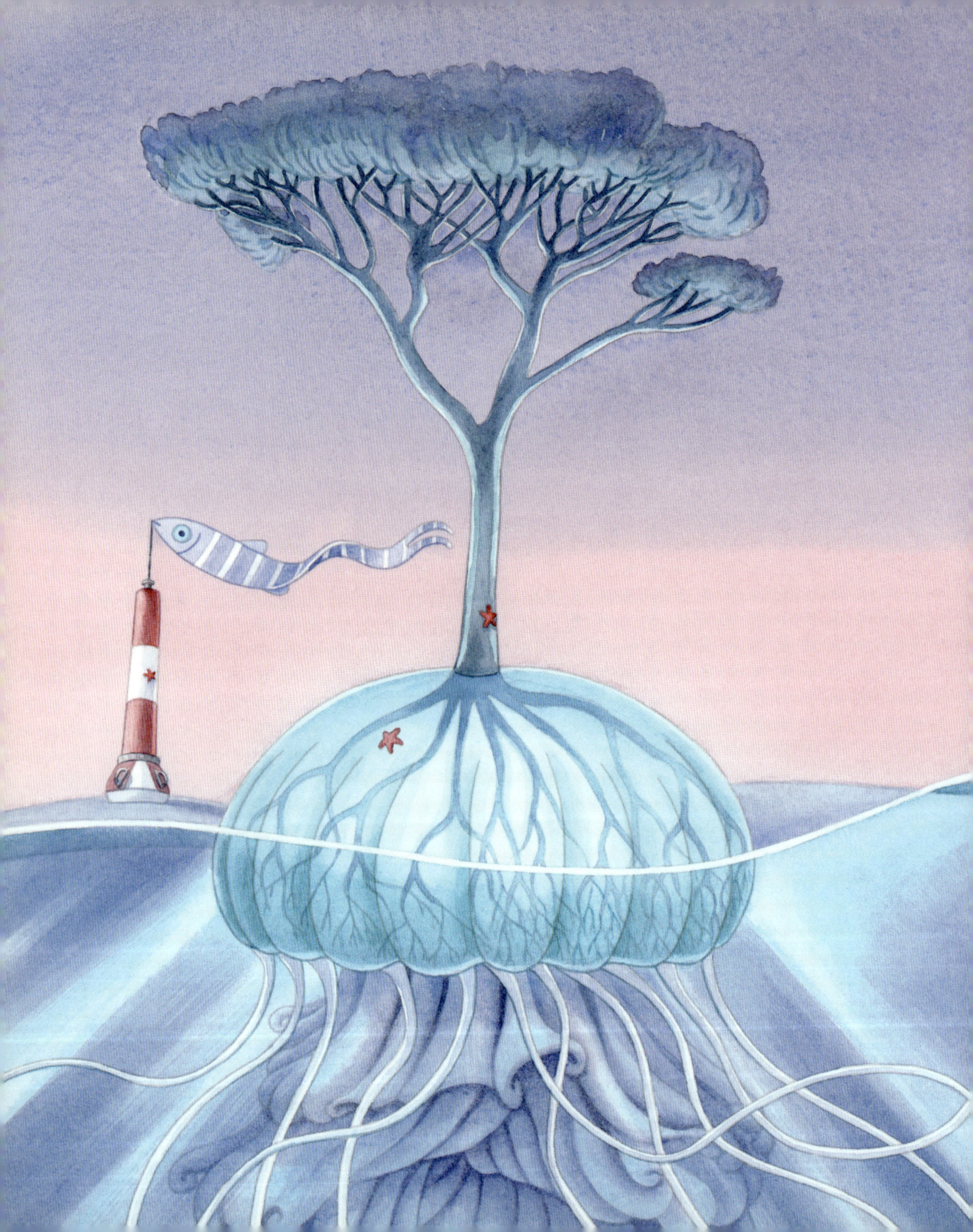

LUMINESCENT ARBOR

I have always been fascinated by merging the forest and ocean into a single ecosystem. This picture captures that idea, featuring a tree growing from a floating jellyfish, creating a striking juxtaposition between land and sea. It's intriguing to envision thousands of jellyfish drifting through the ocean, forming a forest that flows with the currents. This concept allows exploration of what lies above and below the water, revealing exciting possibilities for interesting lighting effects. In this project, you will learn how to re-create a captivating lighting scenario, hopefully inspiring you to incorporate similar effects in your own artwork.

Sketch

Draw the scene freehand or trace the sketch template on page 209.

Step 1

The most important areas to apply masking fluid to are the tree trunk and branches, the entire buoy in the distance, the jellyfish tentacles, and the line that separates the view between above and below the surface. Don't forget to mask the starfish on the jellyfish as well.

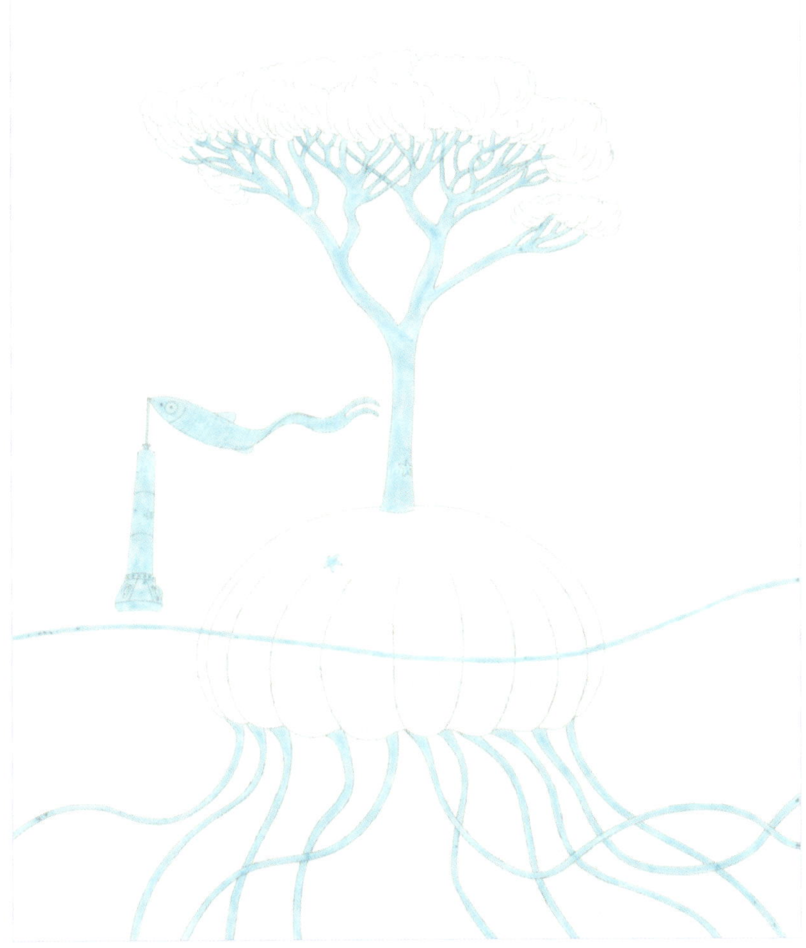

Step 2

The goal of this step is to create a gradual transition between two colors in the sky to represent a sunset. You'll need **Alizarin Crimson** and a separate mixture of **French Ultramarine** and **Alizarin Crimson** on your palette. Now that your two colors are ready, prepare the entire background sky, including the tree canopy, with clean water to use the wet-on-wet technique (page 12) to blend the colors on the paper. While the paper is still damp, apply Alizarin Crimson to the bottom half of the sky. Without any delay, apply the mixture to the top half of the sky, passing directly over the top of the tree canopy. Work evenly from one side to the other, blending downward just past halfway. Before the paint dries, use a tissue to absorb any water or pigment that has pooled over the tree canopy, focusing more on the underside.

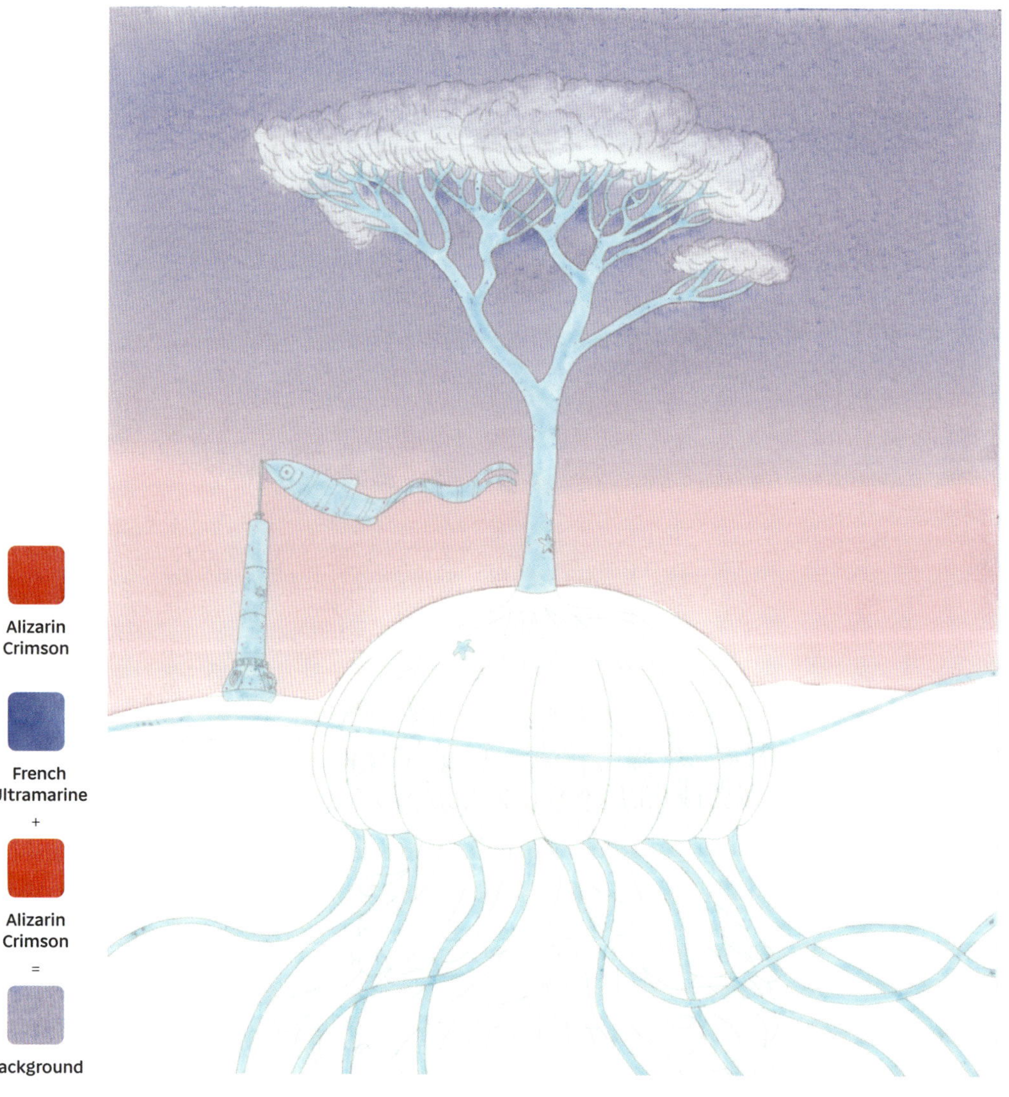

**Alizarin
Crimson**

**French
Ultramarine**

+

**Alizarin
Crimson**

=

Background

Step 3

Now that the background is completely dry, remove the masking fluid from the tree and the flagged buoy. Like in the previous step, you need to prepare two new color mixtures:

French Ultramarine + Alizarin Crimson – for the shadows and jellyfish oral arms

Winsor Blue + **Permanent Sap Green** – for the tree; mix a decent amount of this color as it will be used repeatedly throughout this project

Use the second mixture to paint the entire tree, including the canopy. Before it dries completely, add some of the first mixture (French Ultramarine and Alizarin Crimson) to the top side of the canopy and the inner parts of the tree trunk and branches. The goal is to create a glowing reflection from the water.

Next, use **French Ultramarine** and **Alizarin Crimson** to shade and define the oral arms of the jellyfish. You can build up the tonal value and depth with multiple layers, using more concentrated pigment for finer details. Some of these details will be softened later when you glaze over the area.

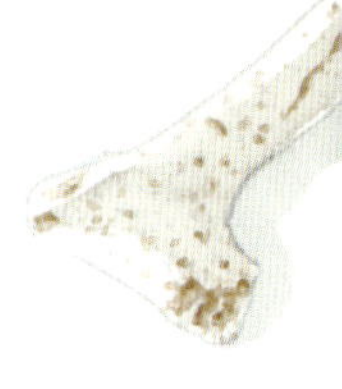

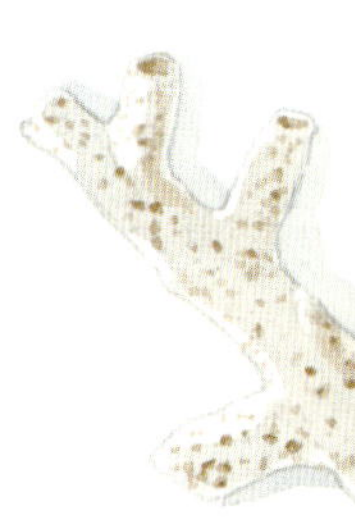

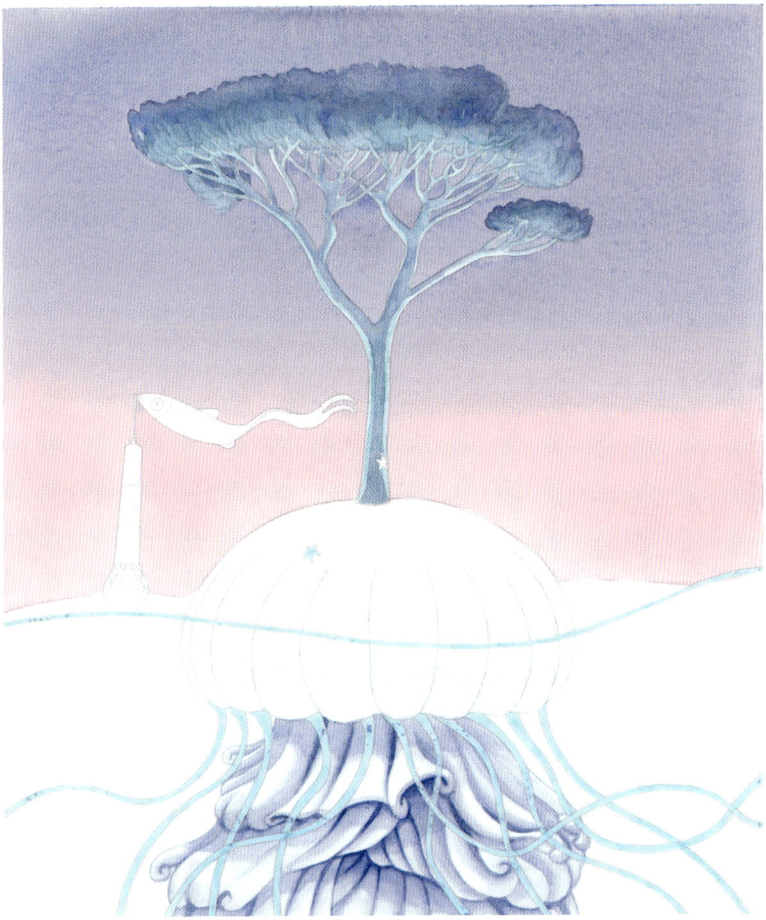

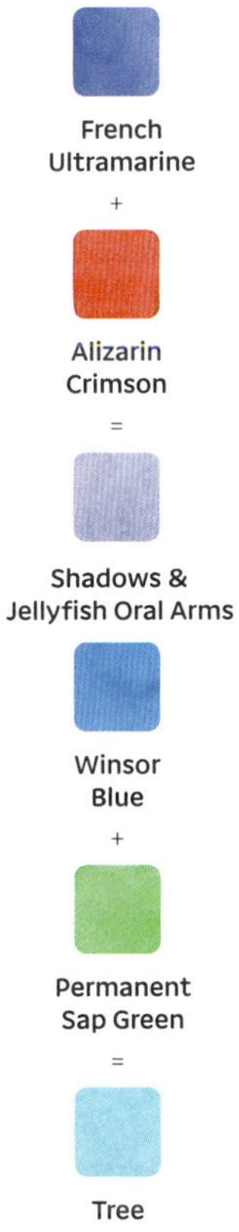

French
Ultramarine

+

Alizarin
Crimson

=

Shadows &
Jellyfish Oral Arms

Winsor
Blue

+

Permanent
Sap Green

=

Tree

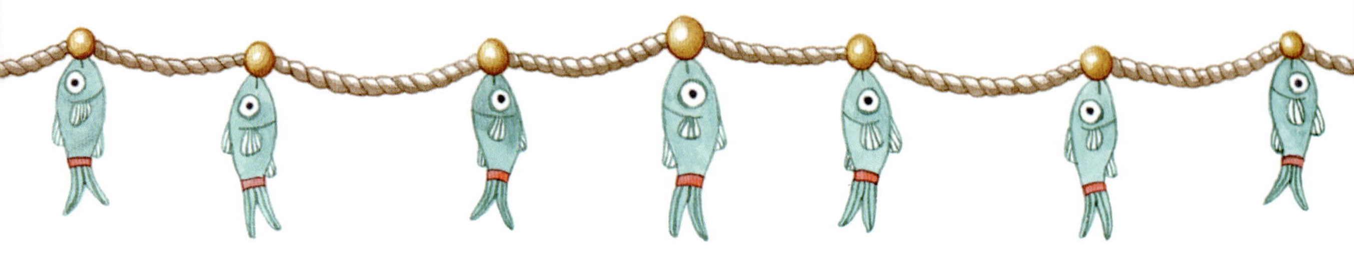

Step 4

Apply the **Winsor Blue** and **Permanent Sap Green** that you mixed on your palette in Step 3 to the entire body of the jellyfish. Once dry, use the same mix to darken the lower part of the jellyfish and between each indent. Now, using **French Ultramarine** and a flat brush, create stripes of color angling away from the jellyfish. The goal is to depict light rays passing through the water. Use the reference image as a guide.

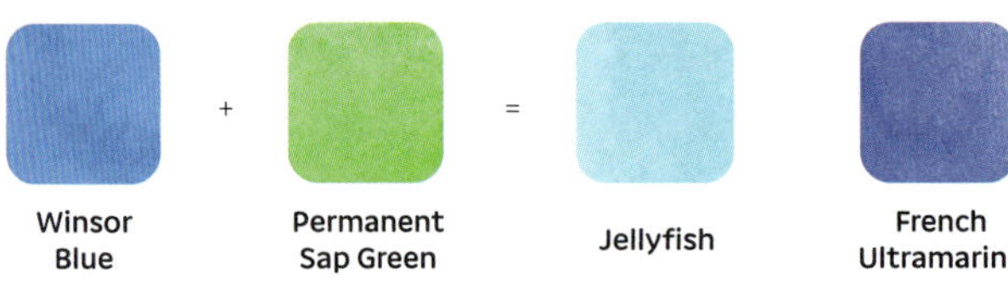

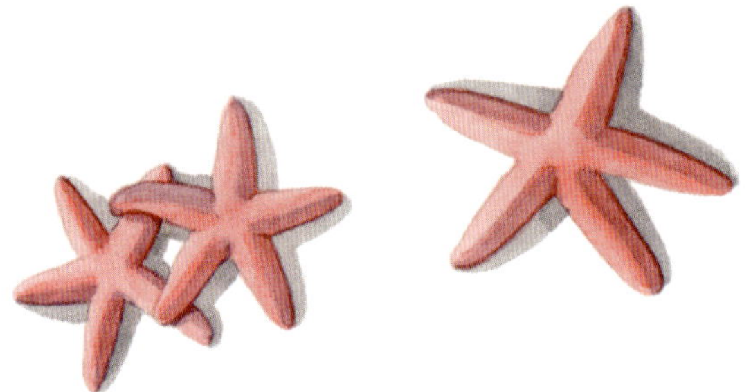

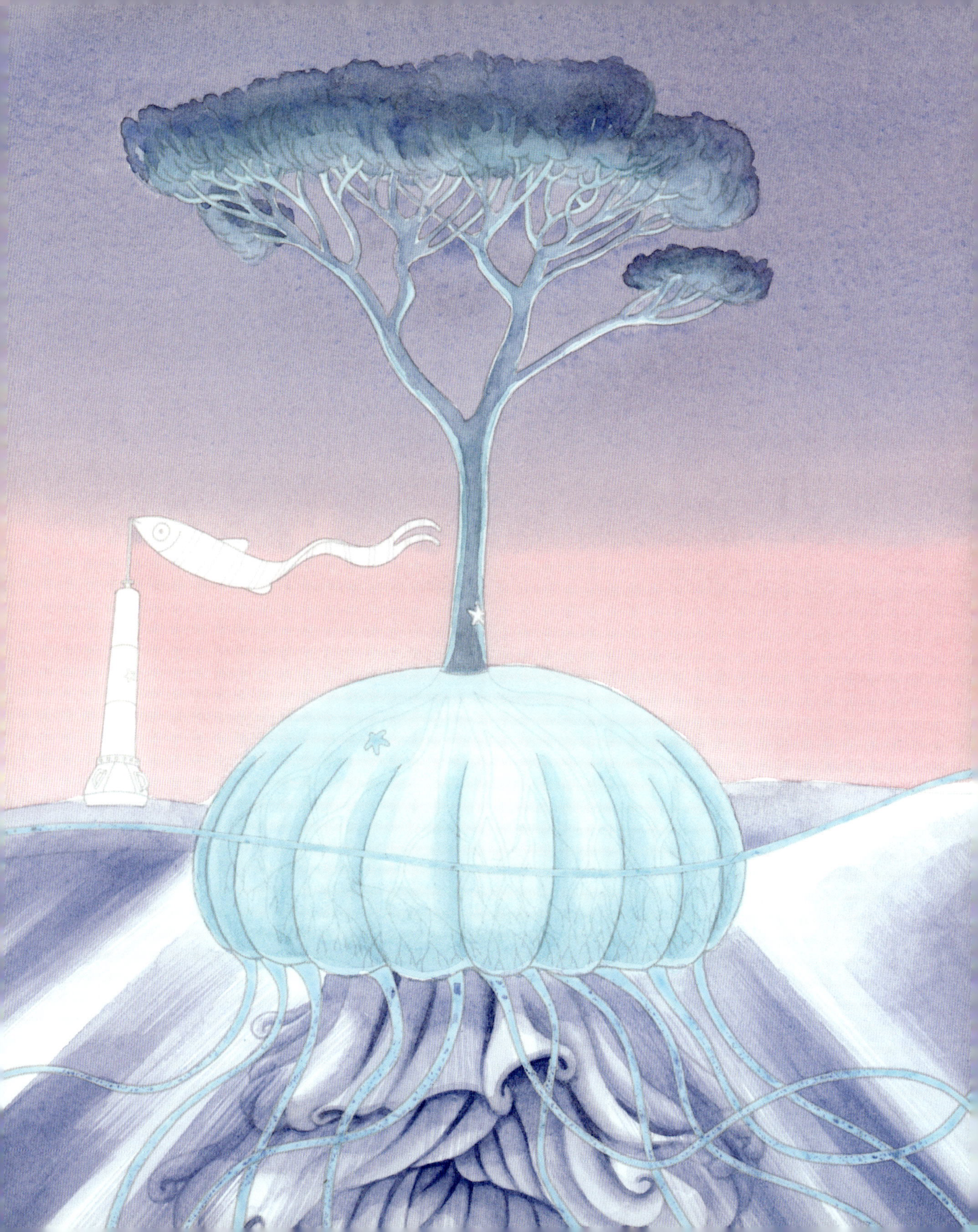

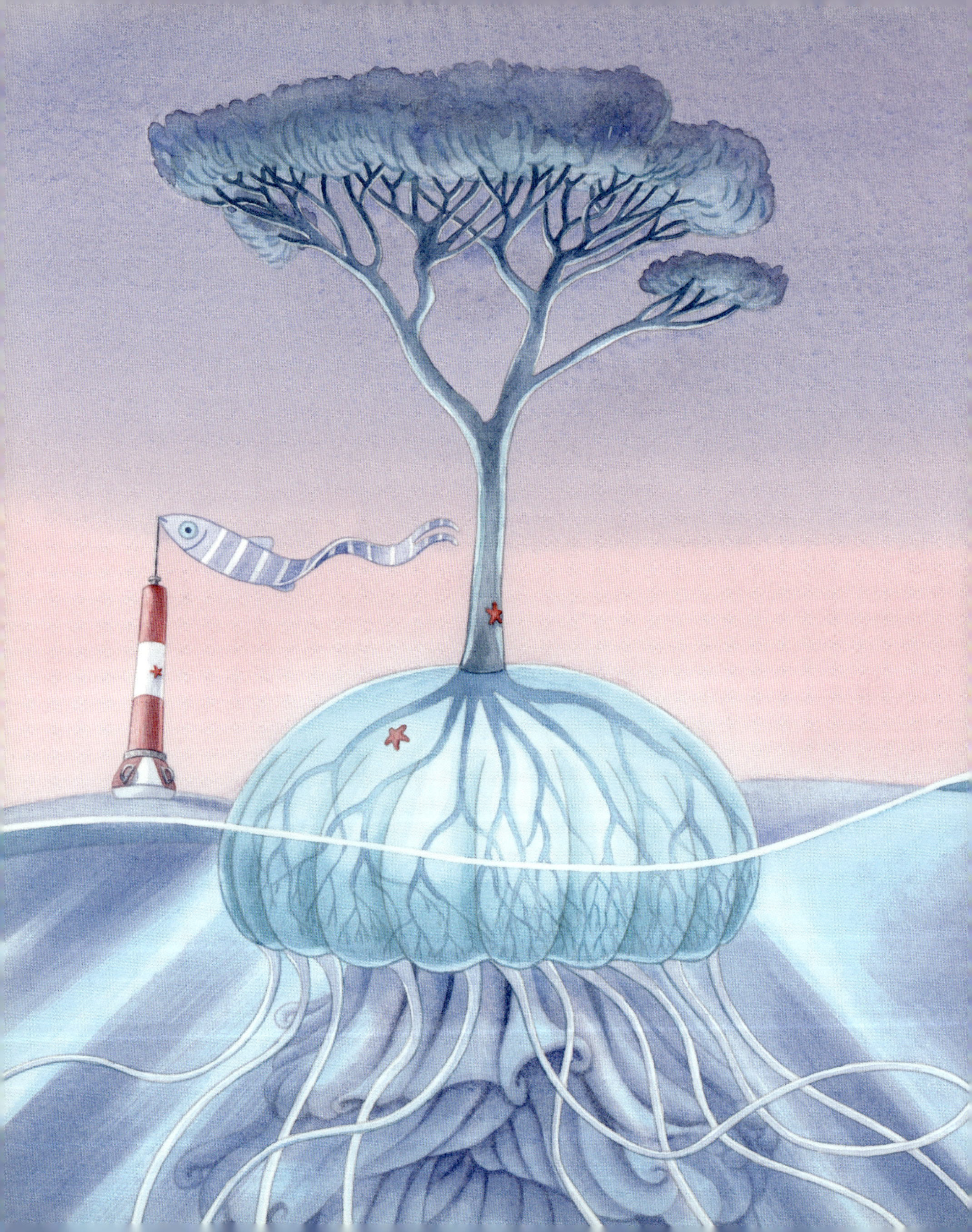

Step 5

Start by glazing the **Winsor Blue** and **Permanent Sap Green** mixture from Step 3 over all the water viewed below the surface. Once that has dried, add some **French Ultramarine** to the mix and paint in all the tree roots, keeping any roots around the middle of the jellyfish lighter than the rest. This will help create the sense that light is passing through the jellyfish. Once this is dry, you can remove all the remaining masking fluid.

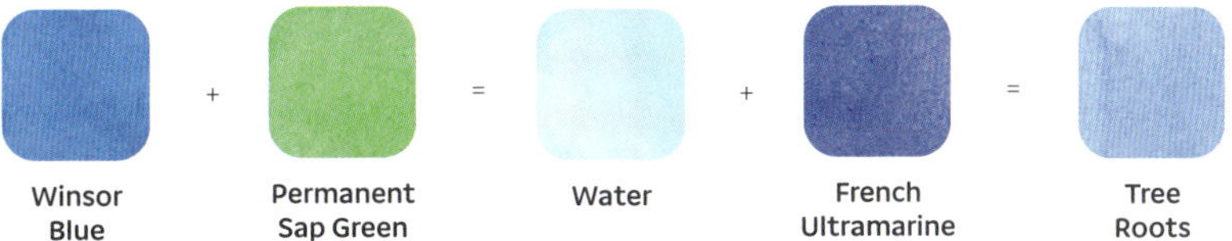

| Winsor Blue | + | Permanent Sap Green | = | Water | + | French Ultramarine | = | Tree Roots |

For the jellyfish tentacles, mix **French Ultramarine** with a small amount of **Burnt Sienna** to create some shadows just below the body; use it sparingly, as the tentacles are mostly left white.

| French Ultramarine | + | Burnt Sienna | = | Tentacle Shadows |

While you have some French Ultramarine and Burnt Sienna available on your palette, you can mix them with any of the other blue/greens you've previously made. Focus these darker tones on the tree and its branches below the canopy. The only thing left to do now is fill in the starfish and the flag on the buoy.

French Ultramarine – for the fish flag

Winsor Red + **French Ultramarine** – for the buoy and starfish

French Ultramarine + **Permanent Sap Green** – for the fish's eye

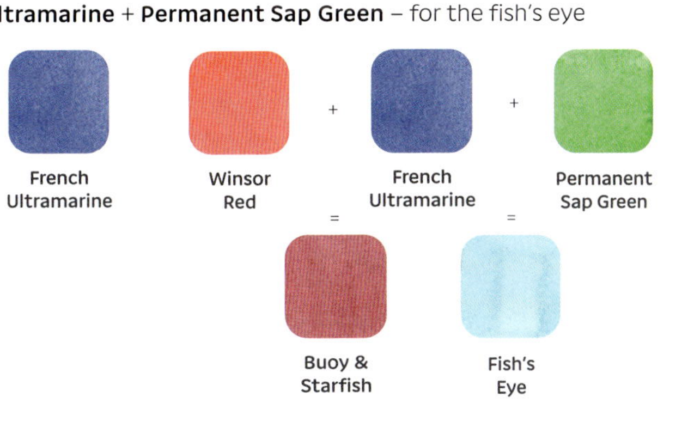

| French Ultramarine | Winsor Red | + | French Ultramarine | + | Permanent Sap Green |
| Buoy & Starfish | | = | Fish's Eye | = | |

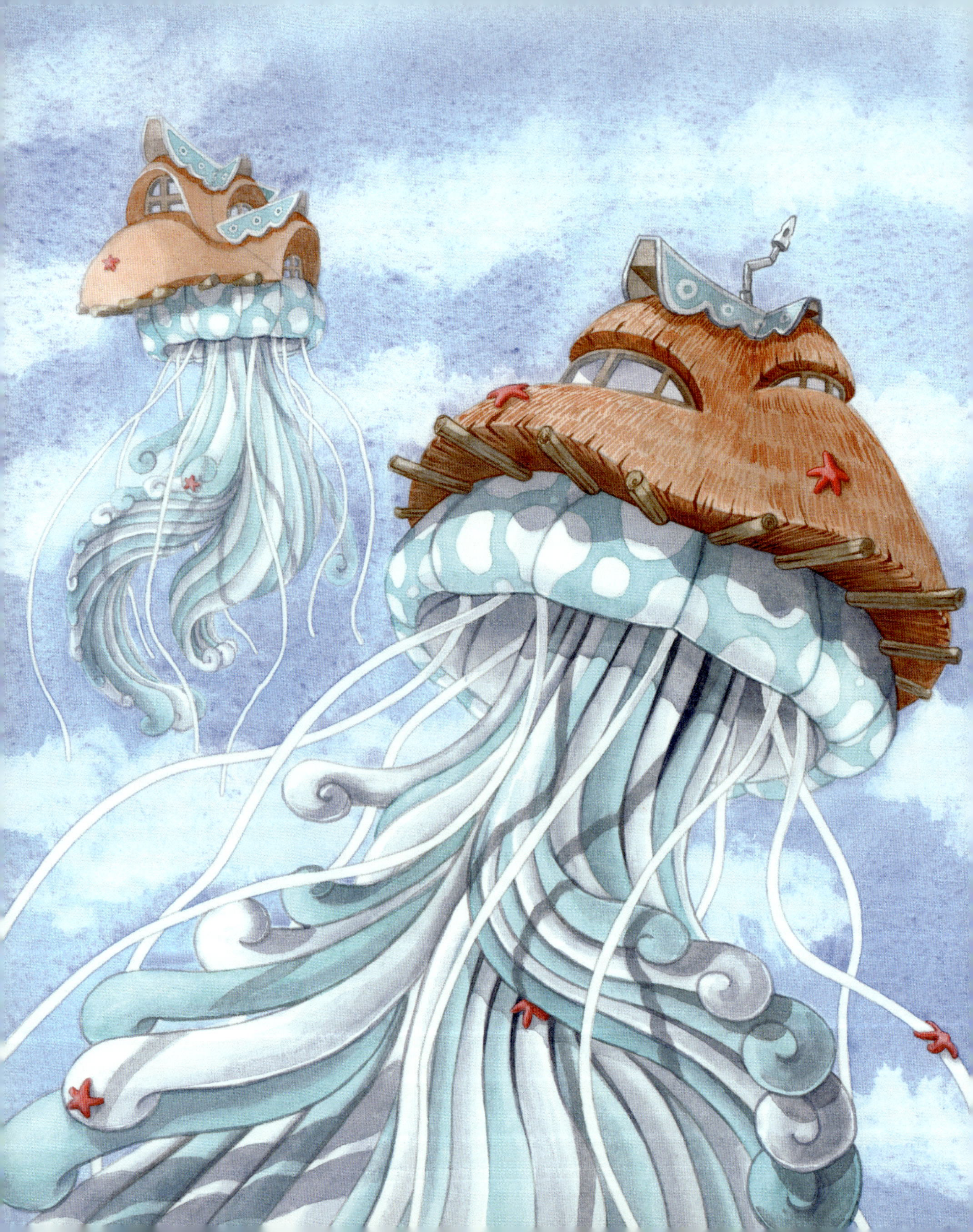

SOARING JELLY DWELLING

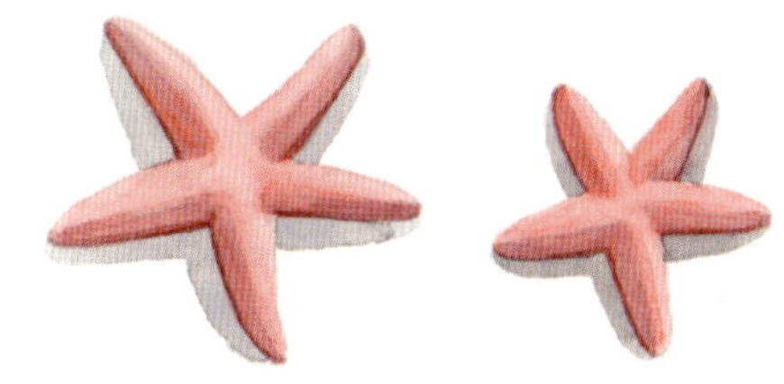

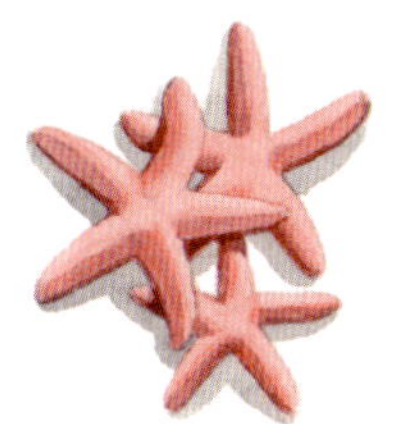

Jellyfish are excellent subjects for exploring various watercolor techniques due to their captivating shapes, delicate curves, and intricate folds. In this project, you will deepen your understanding of the jellyfish form by focusing on the relationship of shadows and light.

As you work, you'll experiment with how light influences the appearance of the jellyfish, revealing its textures and depth. You will also use a limited color palette, allowing you to highlight specific areas of your painting. This approach not only creates a sense of focus within the artwork but also encourages you to appreciate the beauty of simplicity.

Sketch

Draw the jelly dwellings freehand or trace the sketch template on page 211.

Step 1

In this project, there isn't much you'll need to mask. Apply masking fluid to the jellyfish tentacles and all of the starfish. Once you begin painting the background, you'll understand why this was an important step.

Step 2

Start by mixing **French Ultramarine** with some **Winsor Blue** on a palette, adding plenty of
water. You'll use this color to create a bright, sunny sky for the flying jellyfish. It's always helpful
to mix more paint than you think you'll need for areas like the sky, as you won't have much
time to prepare new paint if you run out before finishing. Use the wet-on-wet technique
(page 12) by wetting the paper first, then applying the paint mixture to the entire sky. Before
the paint dries, take a clean tissue and dab any areas where you'd like to create soft clouds.
You can also use a brush to absorb any excess paint pooling on the paper—this may occur in
small areas surrounded by masking fluid.

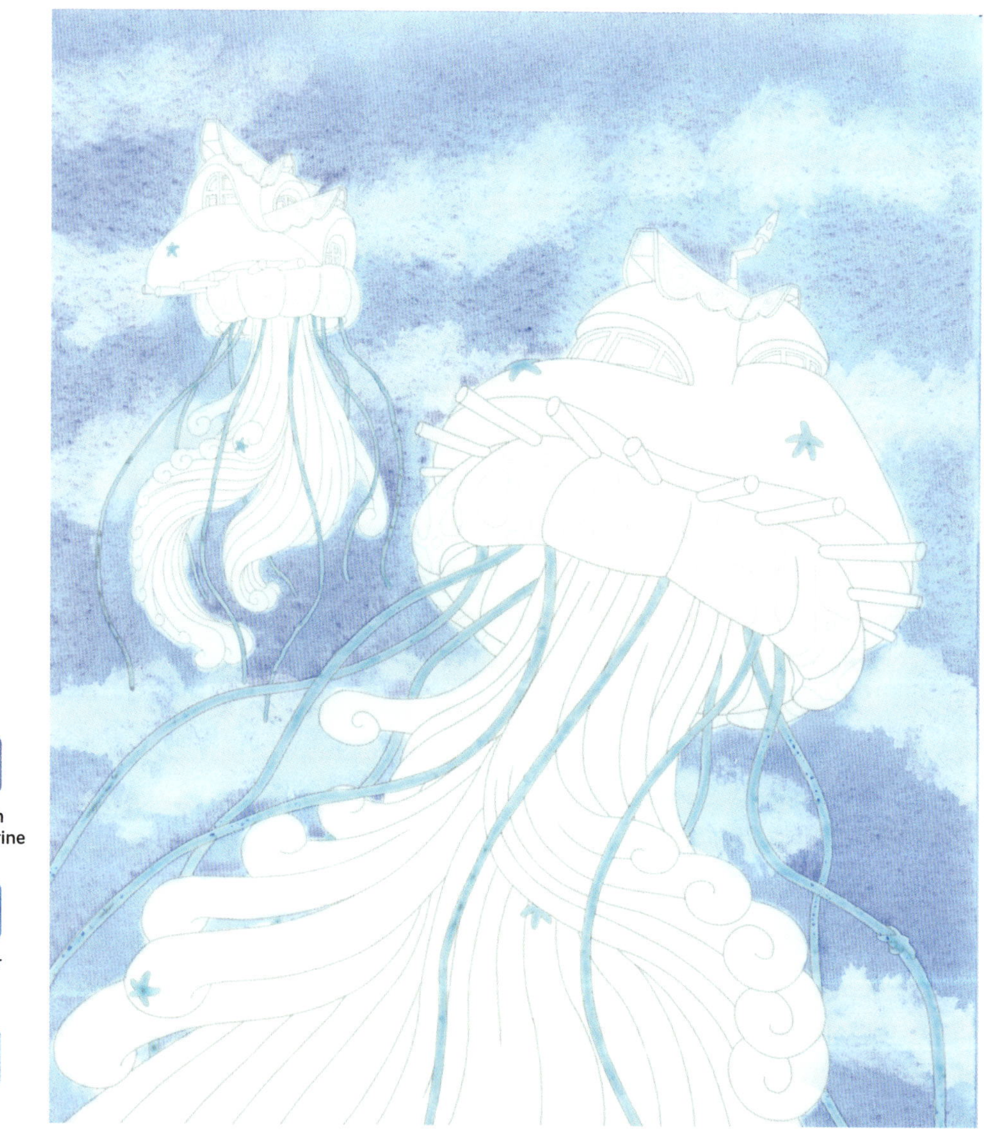

**French
Ultramarine**

+

**Winsor
Blue**

=

Sky

Step 3

Mix some **French Ultramarine** with **Burnt Sienna** to create a gray-blue shade for painting the shadows on the jellyfish and the houses. Imagine the light source shining down from above as you work. When painting shadows, don't worry about being too precise—an unrealistic shadow is always better than no shadow at all. Use my reference image as a guide. You may need to apply multiple layers to darken certain areas as needed.

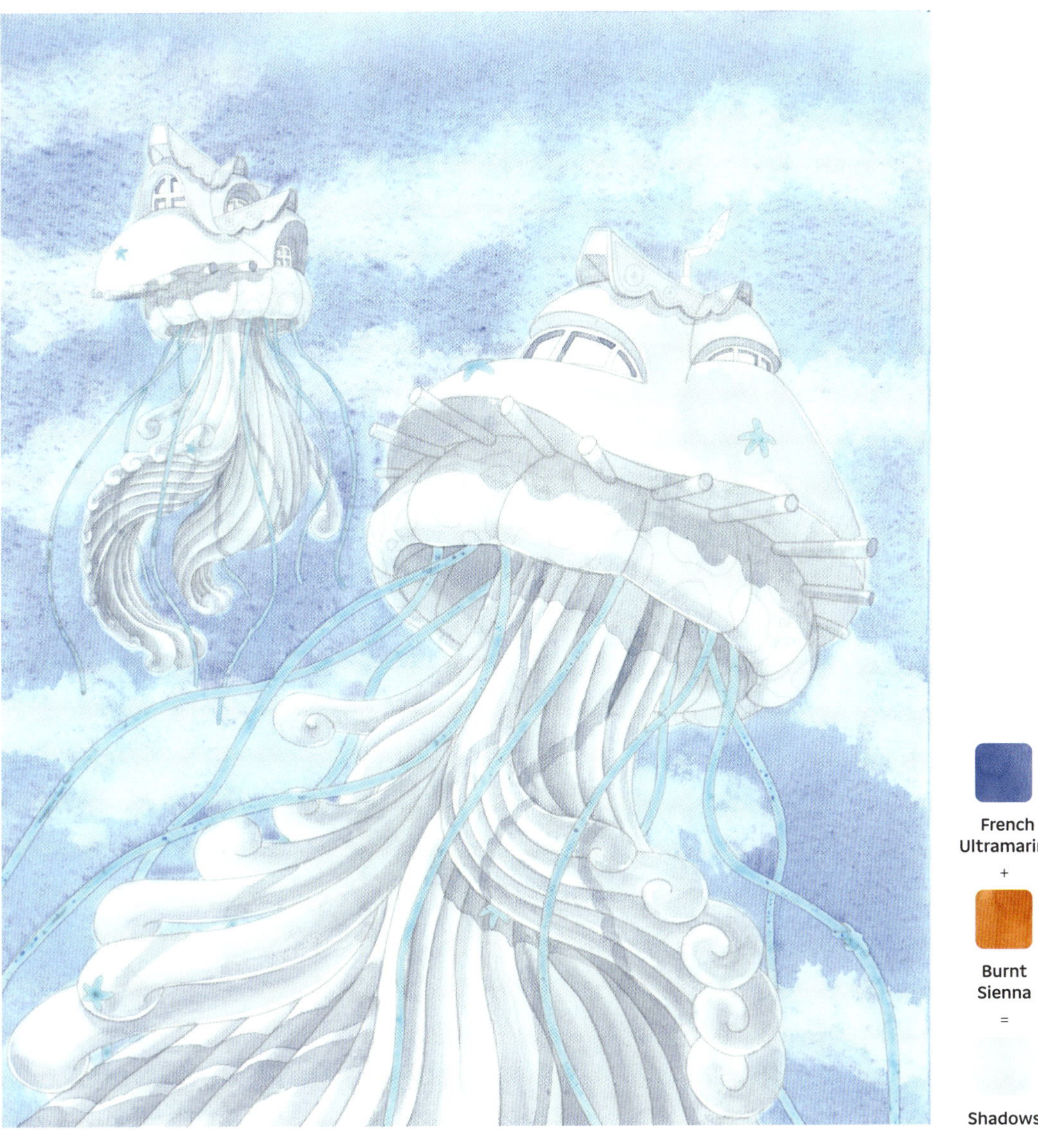

French
Ultramarine

+

Burnt
Sienna

=

Shadows

Step 4

Mix some **Burnt Sienna**, a small amount of **Permanent Sap Green**, and **Winsor Red** to create a brown-orange for the thatched roofs on the jellyfish houses. Glaze this color over each entire roof, including the areas where you previously painted shadows. Use a larger brush to create a more even finish. Since there isn't much pigment on the paper, you shouldn't encounter any issues.

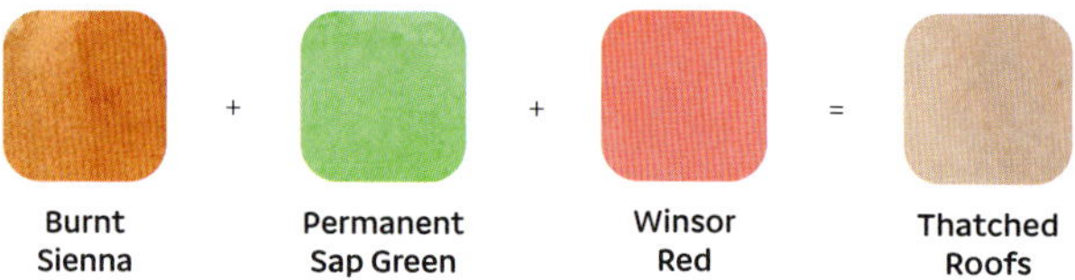

Mix **Winsor Red** and **Permanent Sap Green** to make a brown for the wooden support posts, window frames, and roof beams. You'll only need one color for the jellyfish, as half of the body will remain the white of the paper. It's not necessary to always cover every part of an illustration—negative space can be highly effective. To create the jellyfish color, mix **Winsor Blue** and **Permanent Sap Green**. Glaze this color over the jellyfish bells and tentacles, leaving the spots and every other oral arm white. Also, paint the decorative details on the roofs. All of these glazes should be applied lightly, without too much pigment.

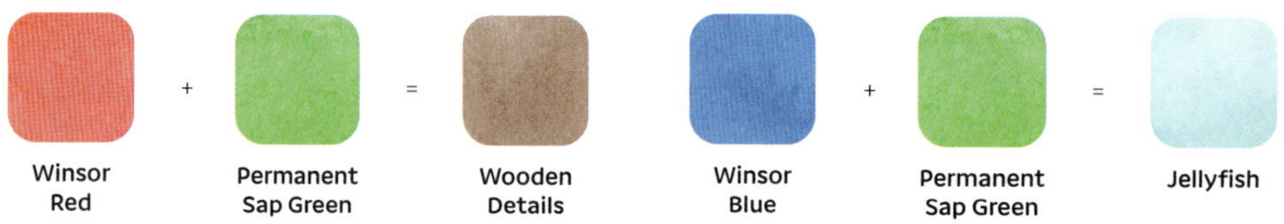

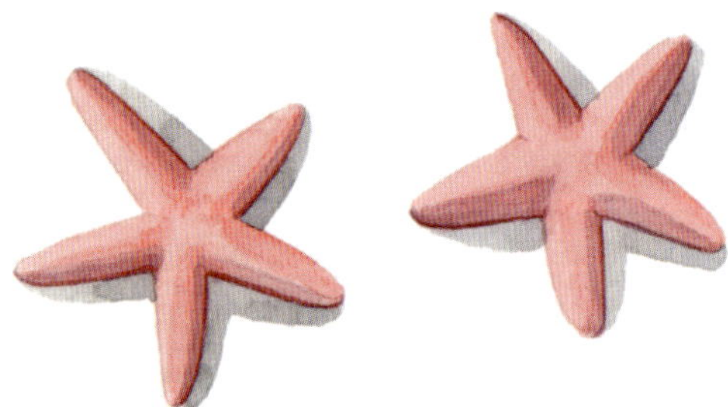

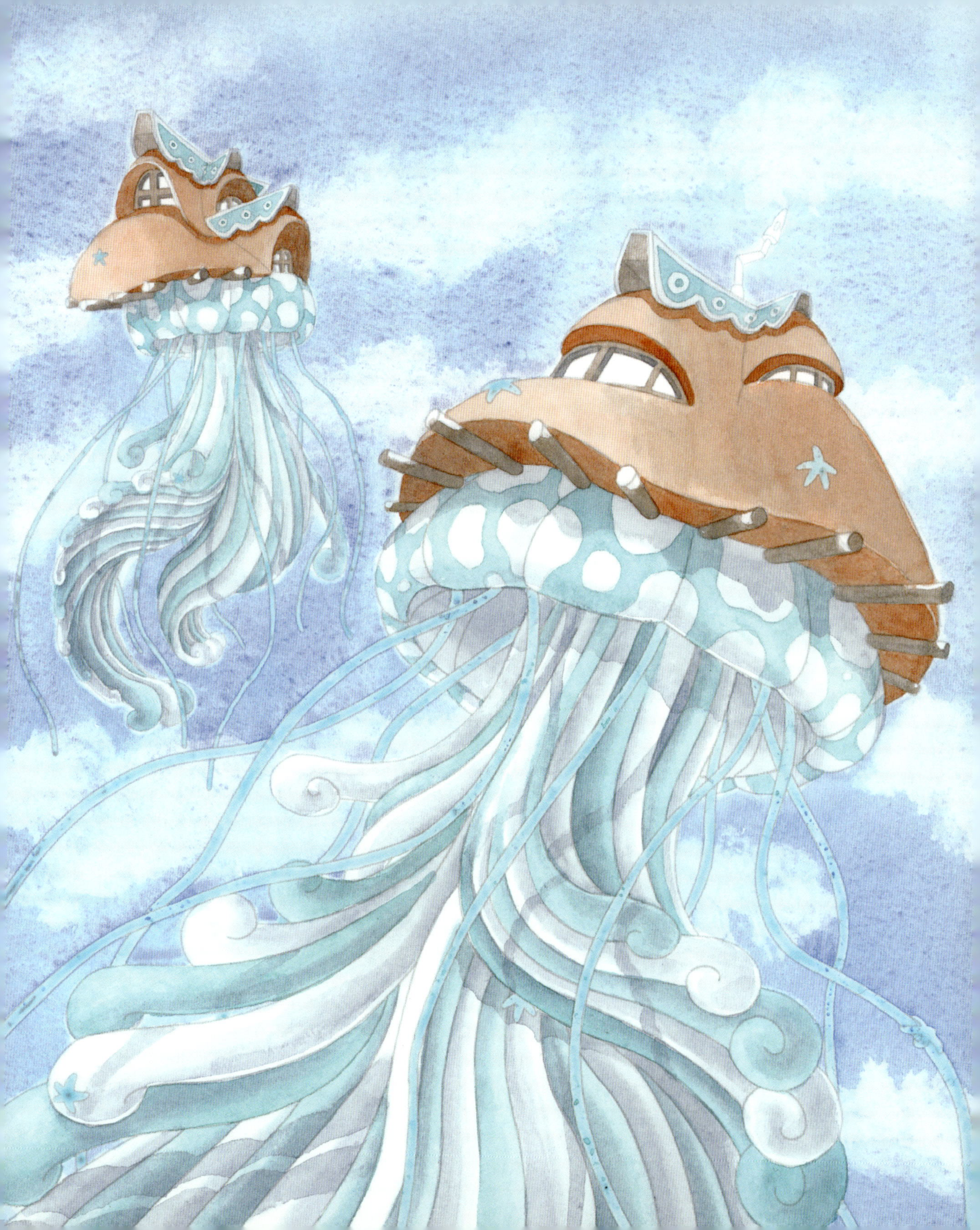

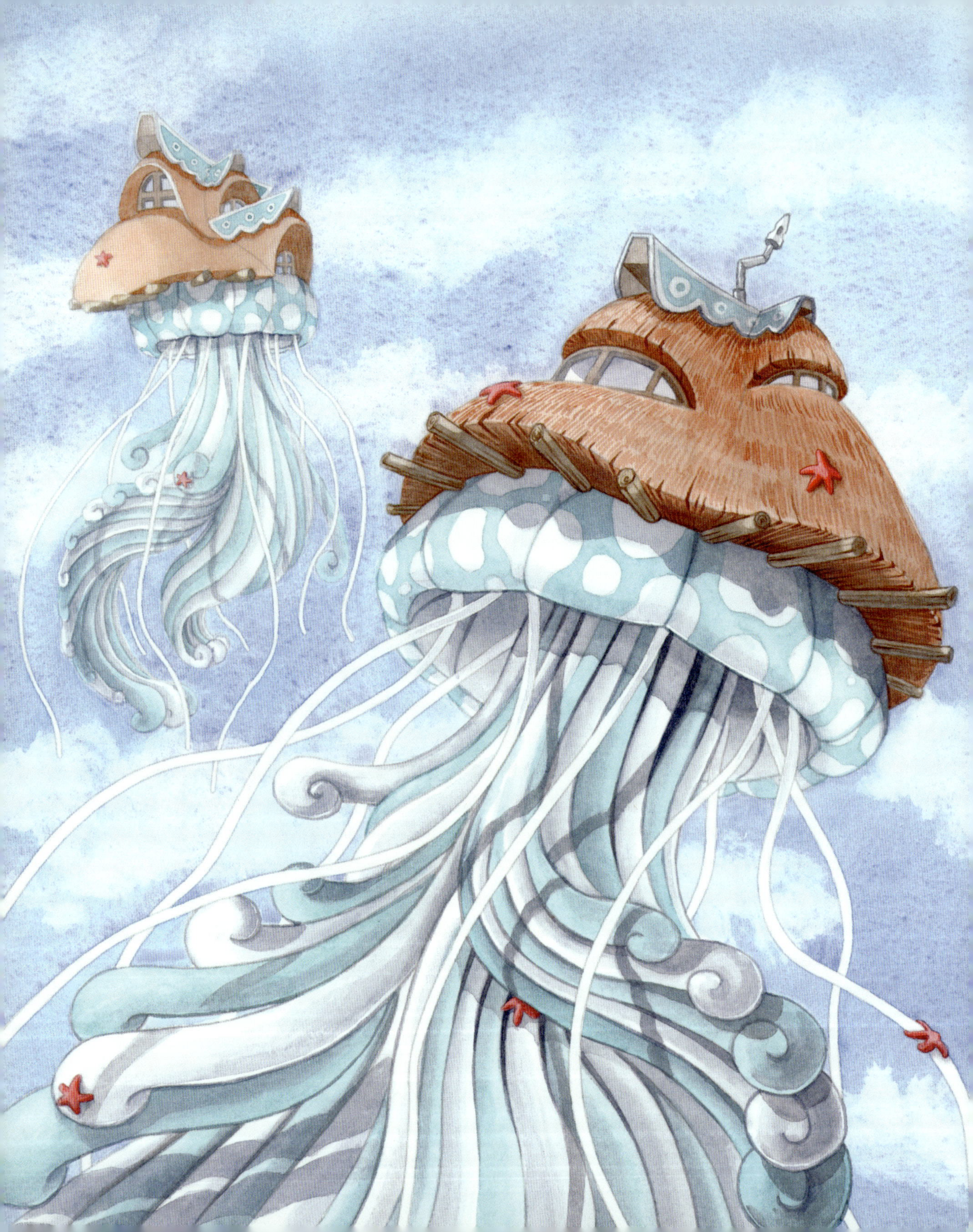

Step 5

For this final step, start by removing the masking fluid from the jellyfish tentacles and starfish. You can now use all the colors you've mixed on your palette to further darken and enhance the details throughout the picture, focusing more on the jellyfish house in the foreground. For the details on the thatched roof, mix in a little more **Winsor Red** to the brown-orange mixture you created in Step 4. This will create a more vibrant orange-brown that will draw the viewer's eye to the area.

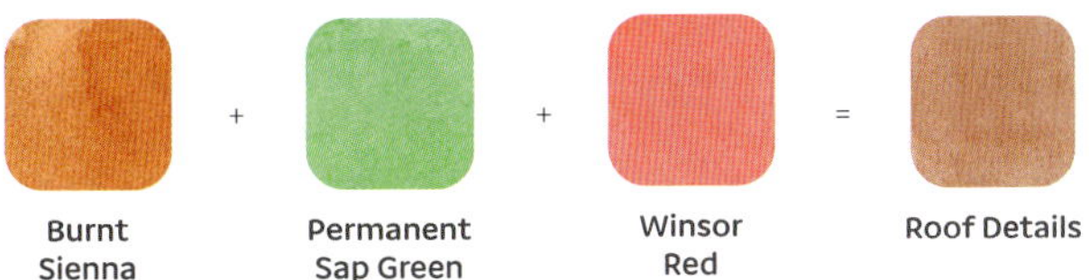

By also adding the **French Ultramarine** and **Burnt Sienna** mix from Step 3 to your thatched roofs color (from Step 4), you can create a darker tone to paint in all the deepest recesses of the thatched roofs. Refer to the example image for guidance.

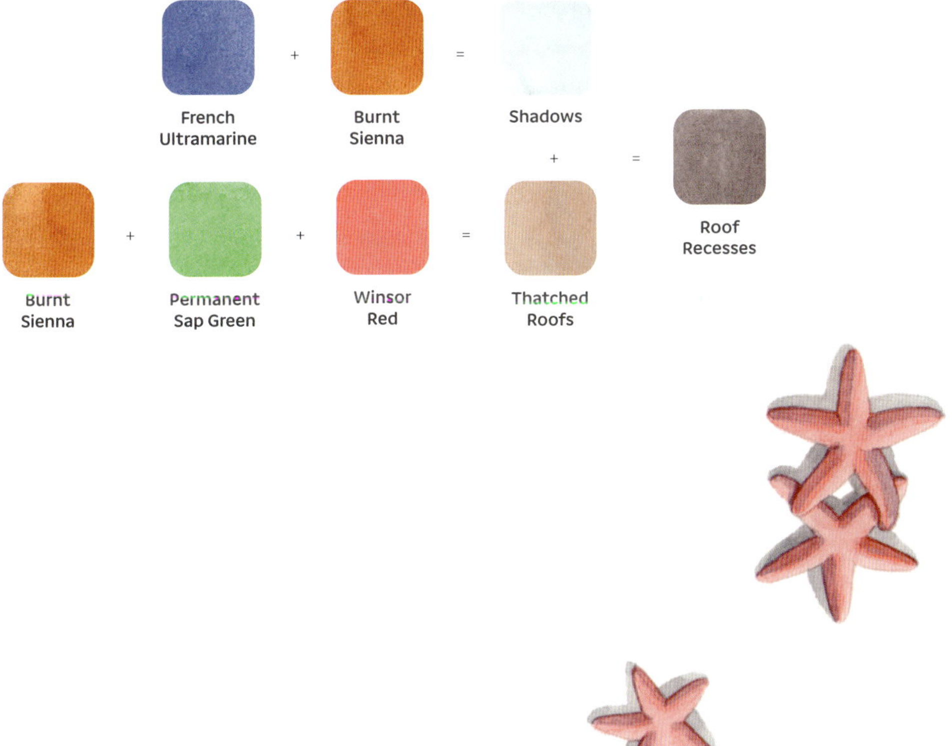

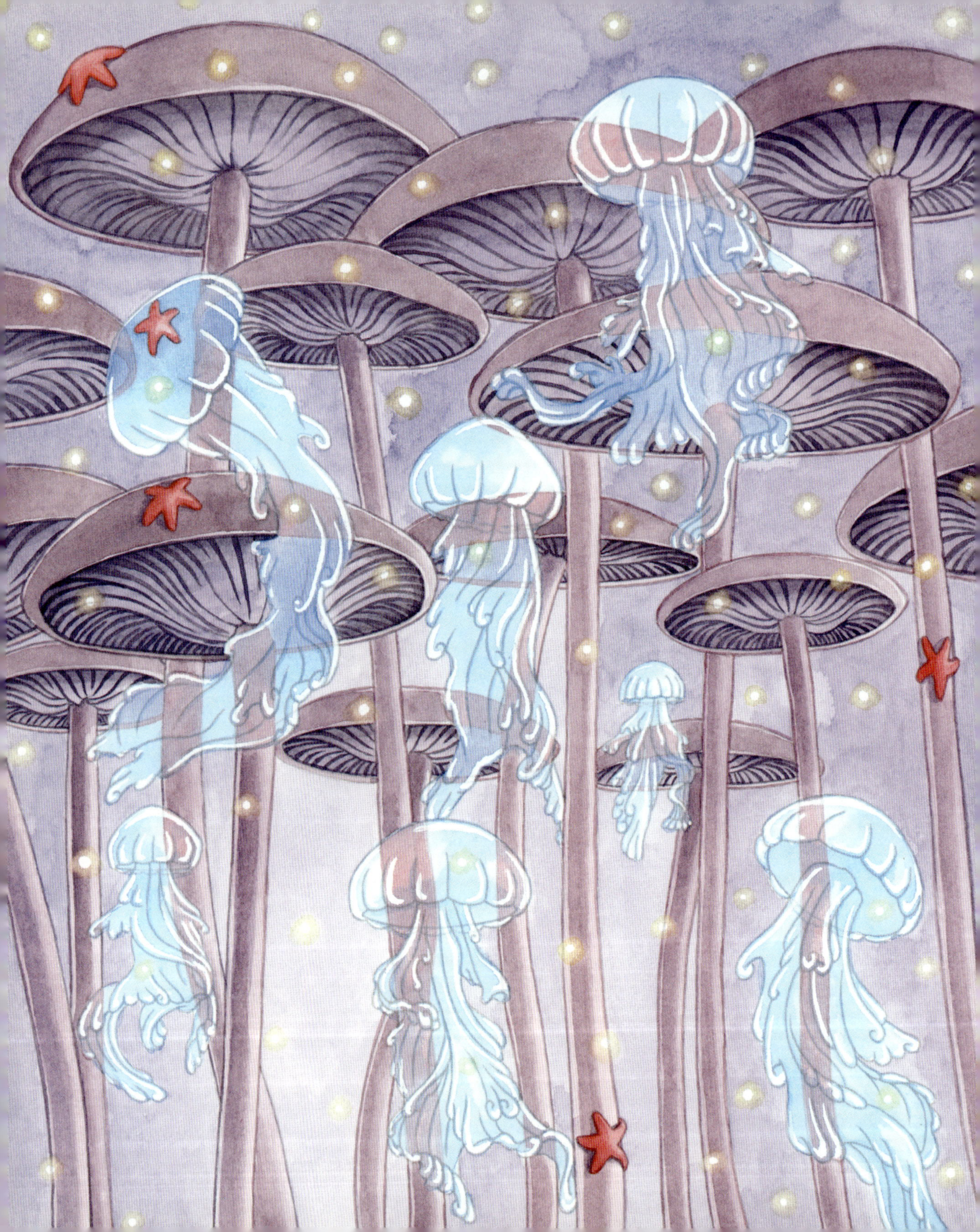

MUSHROOM TIDE

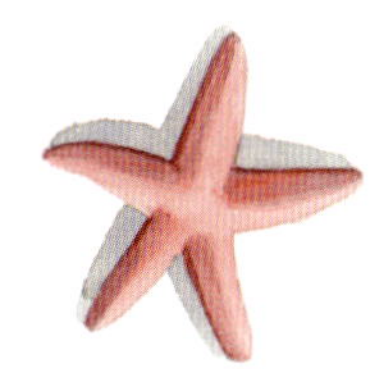

The translucent body of a jellyfish is a captivating sight, especially when light passes through, creating a beautiful glowing effect. This quality aligns perfectly with watercolor's transparency, making it an ideal medium for painting transparent subjects.

In this project, you will learn how to depict the jellyfish's transparent appearance by exploring the process of layering various colors to build depth and dimension while thoughtfully selecting background colors that enhance the jellyfish's luminosity.

Sketch

Draw the scene freehand or trace the sketch template on page 213.

Step 1

You may find applying the masking fluid in this painting challenging since you'll need to create small reflection lines on the jellyfish. But don't be intimidated—simply embrace the challenge without overthinking it. When applying the mask, place the reflections just inside your pencil lines. This process will certainly test your hand control but will provide valuable practice for intricate work in the future. Also, fill in all the starfish, and randomly add some dots across the picture, which you'll later transform into glowing orbs. Whenever applying the masking fluid, start on one side and work your way across to avoid resting your hand on any wet areas.

Step 2

Mix **French Ultramarine** and **Winsor Red** on your palette to create a purple for the background. Using the wet-on-dry technique (page 12), apply the color directly to the background, starting from the outside and working your way toward the center of the picture, filling in each section between the mushrooms. Since you're using the wet-on-dry technique, you should see some beautiful blooming and staining textures from the paint drying at different rates. Water down the paint more as you approach the center of the background. The goal is to create a glowing effect in the middle of the picture.

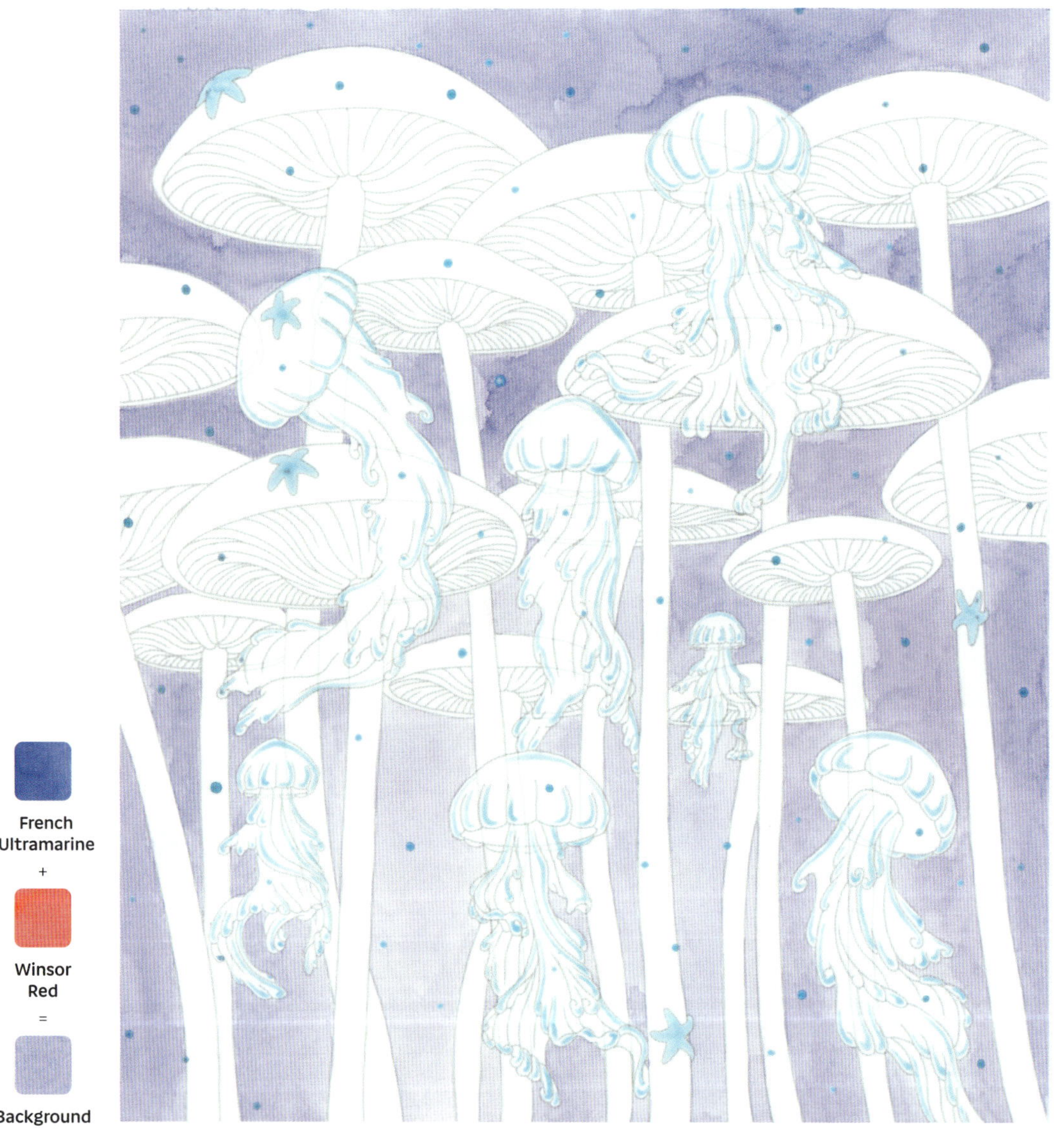

Step 3

You will need to mix a couple of colors on your palette before starting this step. First, mix **Alizarin Crimson** and **Winsor Blue** to create a pink-purple for the tops of the mushrooms and their stems. Next, mix **French Ultramarine** with **Alizarin Crimson** to create a darker purple for the underside of the mushrooms. After painting the first color, allow it to dry before moving on to the next to prevent them from bleeding into each other. Now, it's time to start creating the translucent effect on the jellyfish. Transfer two new colors to your palette: **Alizarin Crimson** and **French Ultramarine**. Not much pigment is needed for either.

Since the jellyfish are somewhat transparent, you want these two new colors to correspond with the colors already painted on the mushrooms. Use **Alizarin Crimson** to go with the tops of the mushrooms and their stems and **French Ultramarine** to go with the underside of the mushrooms. Don't worry if the colors seem a bit out of place at this stage—the magic of glazing will bring everything together in the next step.

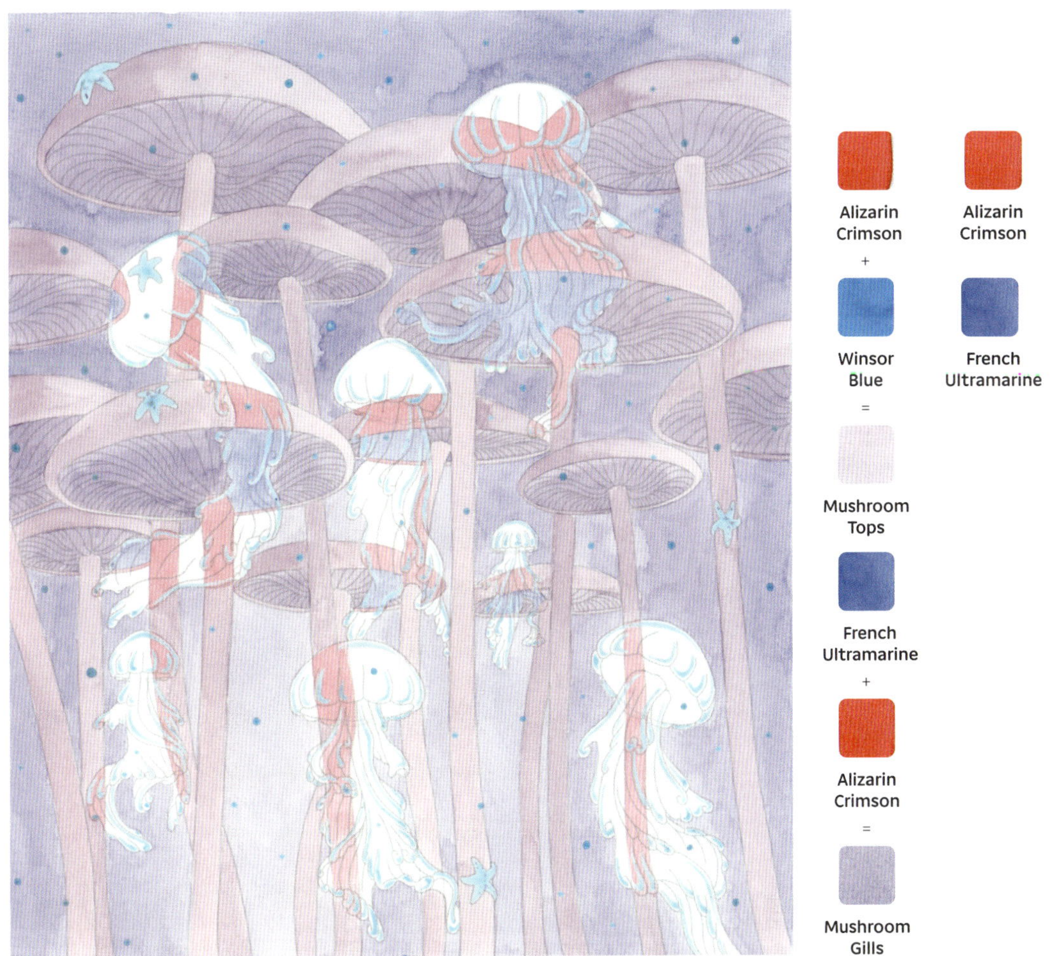

Step 4

Water down some **Winsor Blue** on a palette and glaze the color over each entire jellyfish, including the areas you previously painted. While the glaze is still wet, absorb some of the paint on one side with a tissue. This step is important for creating a glossy look on the surface of the jellyfish, as it also shows that light is passing through. I recommend doing one jellyfish at a time. Mix **Winsor Red** with **French Ultramarine** and paint a shadow around the underside of the mushroom. Finally, mix **French Ultramarine**, **Alizarin Crimson**, and a small amount of **Burnt Sienna** to further darken the tops of the mushrooms and their stems, making sure to stop at the edges of any jellyfish.

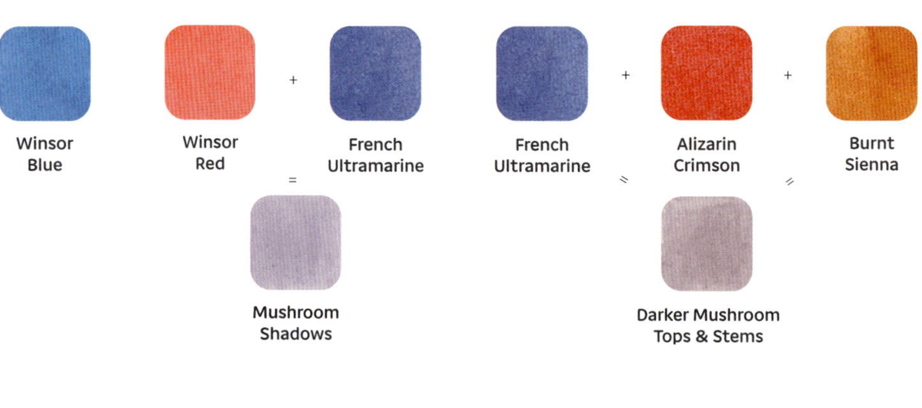

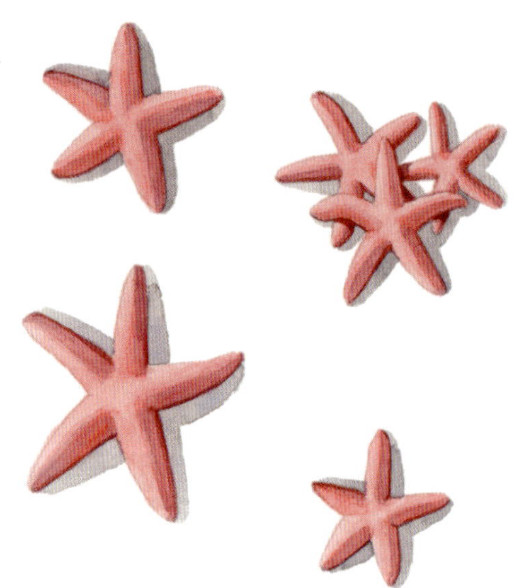

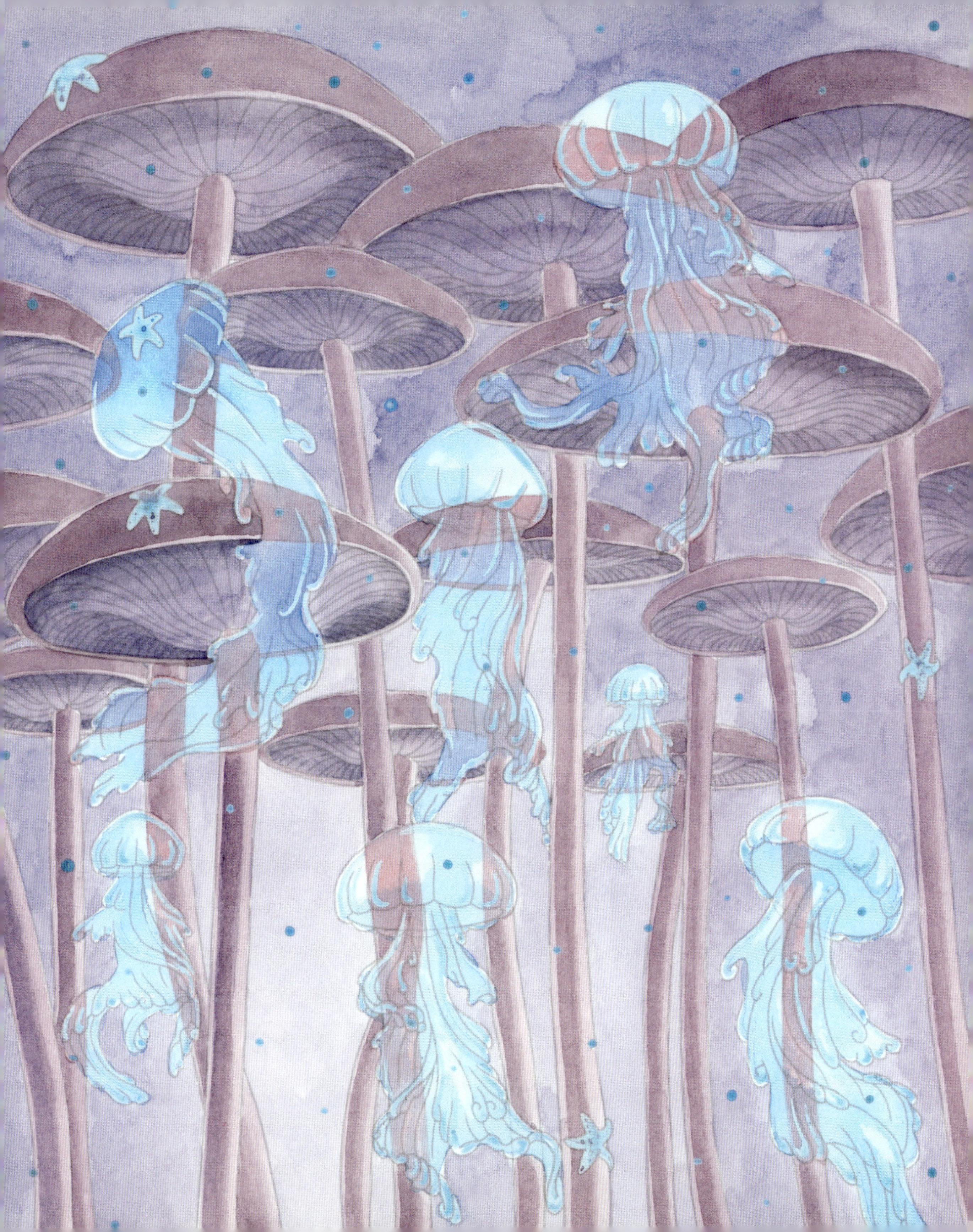

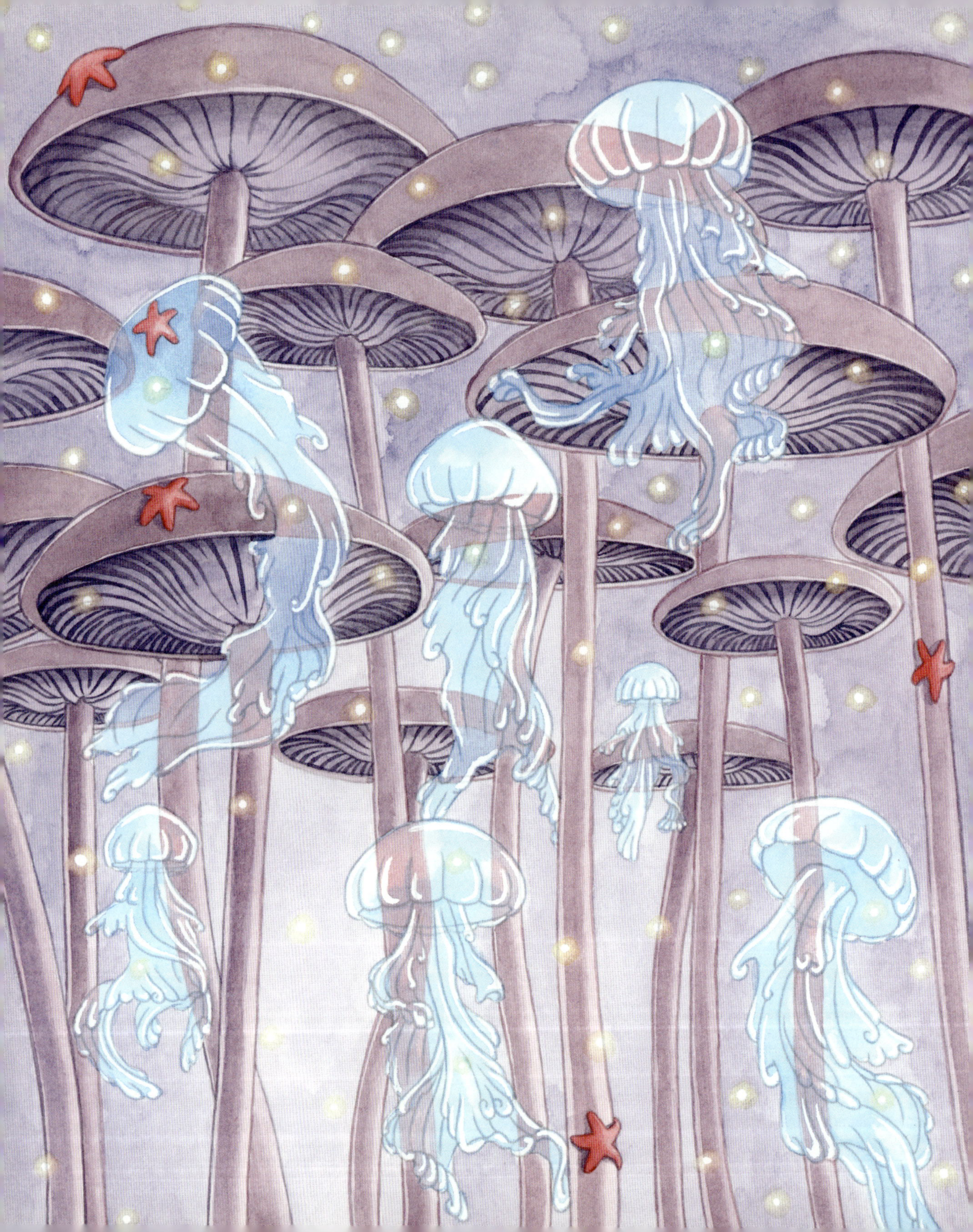

Step 5

Start by using the lifting technique (page 13) to soften the areas around all the light orbs. Then, paint around them with some heavily diluted **Winsor Yellow**. Once everything has dried, remove all the masking fluid. This last step mainly requires you to paint over your sketch lines with color to help differentiate the various areas. Use the appropriate colors already on your palette for the different areas, but apply them more concentratedly. More pigment is always needed for sharper details. Finally, paint the starfish with **Winsor Red** and mix in **French Ultramarine** for their shadows.

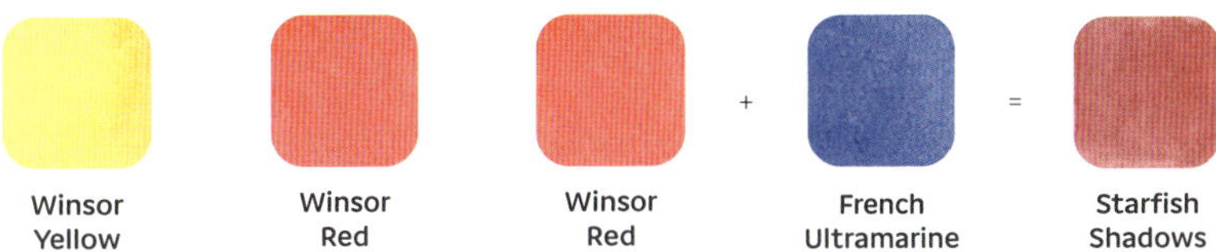

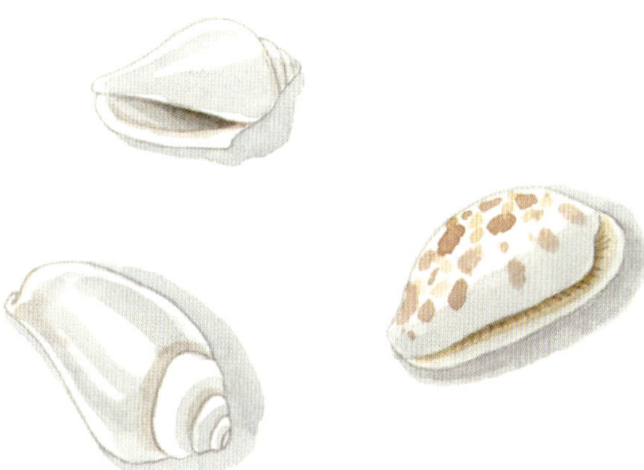

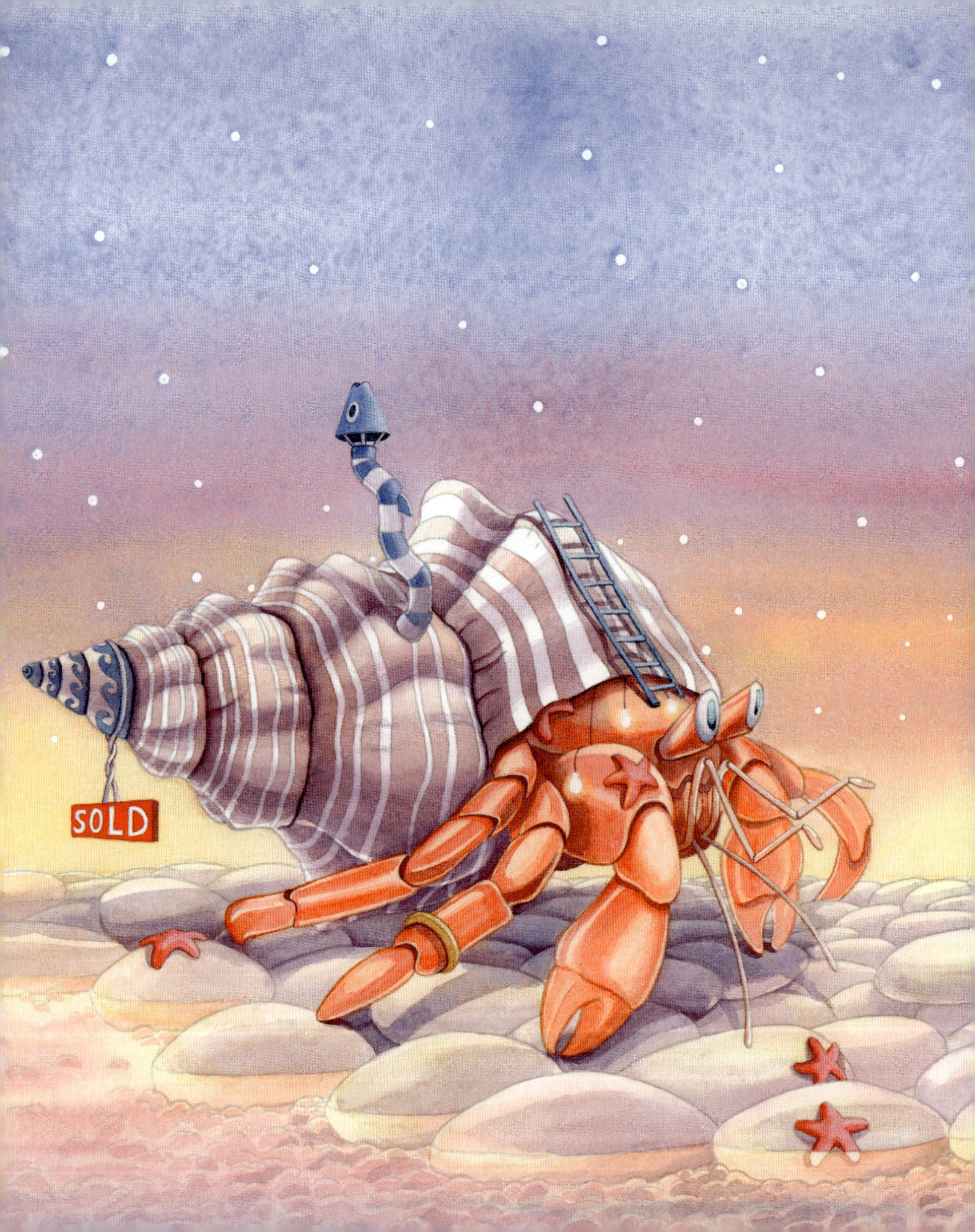
SOLD

Chorus of Shells

Have you ever imagined what it would be like to live inside a shell? I've often found myself fascinated by this idea, envisioning a world where you're shrunk down to fit within the intricate, natural architecture of a shell. There's something magical about these naturally occurring structures, which combine beauty, complexity, and strength in such a small space. This whimsical concept continues to inspire my work and serves as the foundation for this chapter.

I frequently discuss the importance of negative space and how it can elevate your painting. Many people think of negative space as merely empty, untouched areas, but it's far more than that. Negative space isn't just the absence of color; it's an essential tool used to define your subject's form, create depth, and enhance the vibrancy of your work. By thoughtfully leaving portions of the paper untouched, you can highlight details and guide the viewer's eye.

In this chapter, you'll explore negative space through three shell-inspired projects. These exercises will help you incorporate negative space from the start, using it to suggest light, form, and mood while enhancing the overall impact of your artwork.

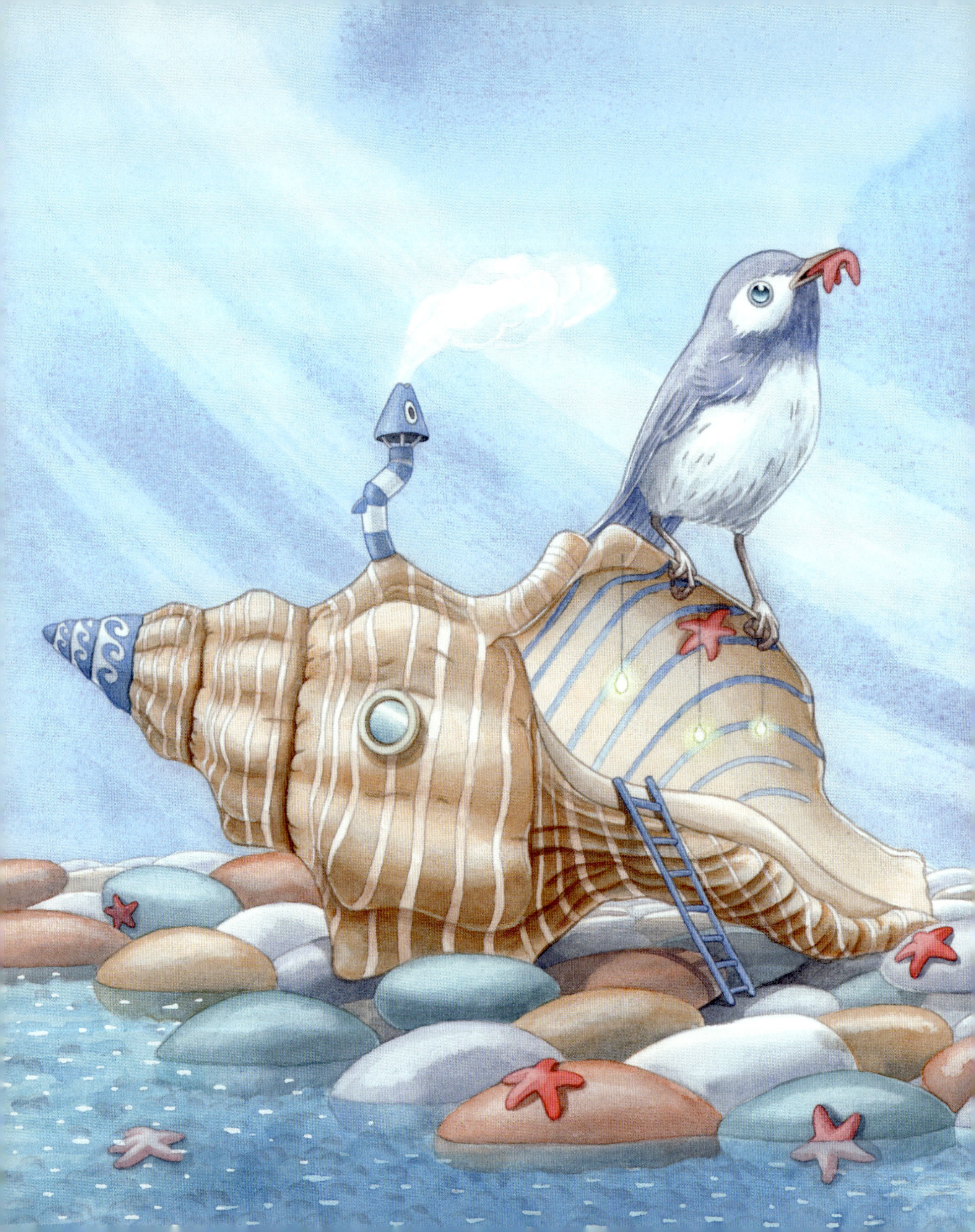

DISENCHANTED COASTAL WISH

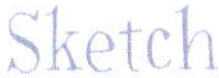

The unknown character in this story has always dreamed of living on the coast in a beautiful house surrounded by the gentle sea breeze. That distant dream became a reality, but it quickly transformed into a realization: The coast was not what he had expected. His fear of becoming someone's next meal diminished the once-appealing allure of the coastal lifestyle. He spends much of his time within his shell home, cautiously peering out from time to time.

In this project, you will gain a better understanding of how to use negative space and pattern to help emphasize the interesting shape of the shell house.

Sketch

Draw the scene freehand or trace the sketch template on page 215.

Step 1

To make painting the background easier, apply masking fluid to the chimney, the bird's legs, and the starfish in its mouth. Other areas to mask include the ladder, stripes on the shell, the light bulbs inside, and the remaining starfish. Finish off by adding some masking fluid marks on the water to the left; these will create reflections later on.

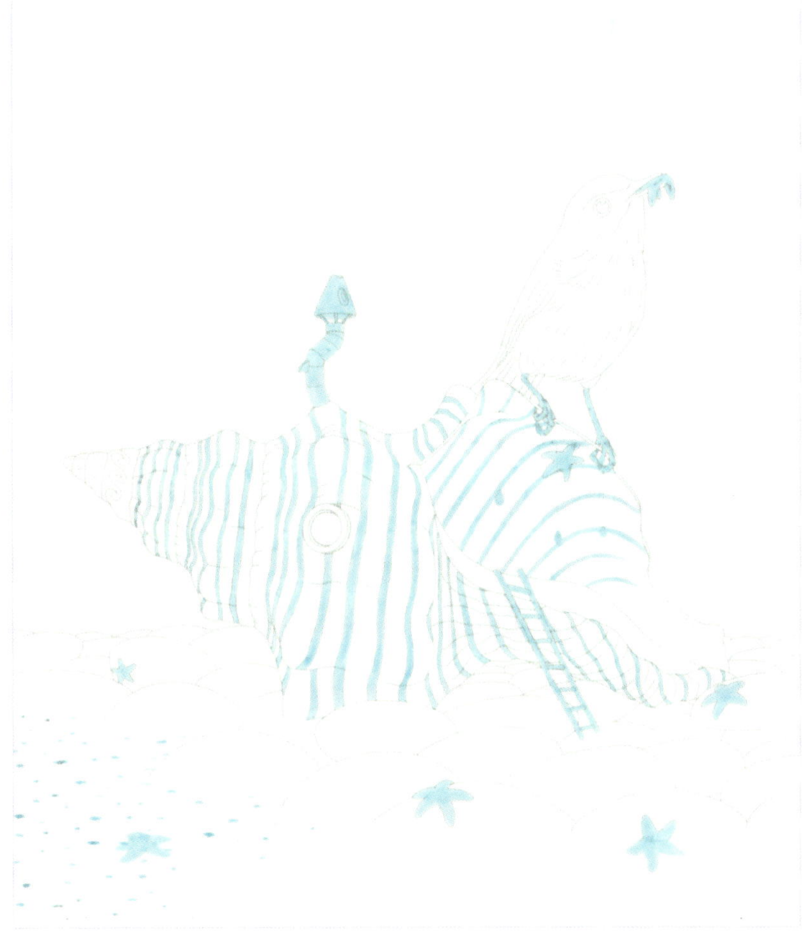

Step 4

Mix **Yellow Ochre** with **Burnt Sienna** and paint over the whole shell, keeping the top-facing surfaces lighter. Once the paint has dried, add some **French Ultramarine** to your shell mix and glaze over the underside of the shell to create a darker shadow. You can also apply this to the underside of the shell opening and beneath the porthole window. Use the reference image for guidance.

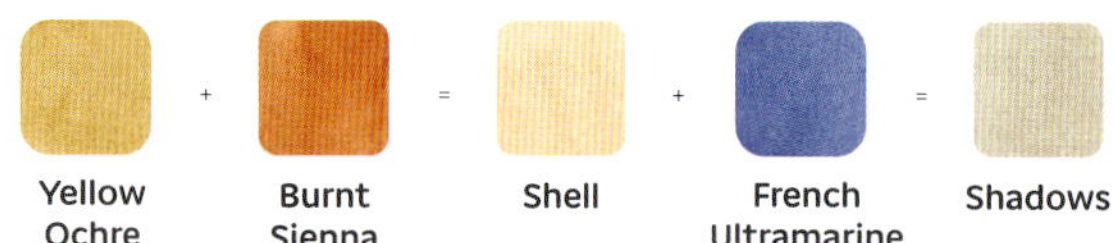

Now use the mix you made in Step 2 to paint the wave design on the tip of the shell and the chimney. For the porthole, mix **Yellow Ochre** and **Burnt Sienna** with a hint of **Permanent Sap Green**. For the glass and bird's eye, mix **Permanent Sap Green** with **Winsor Blue**.

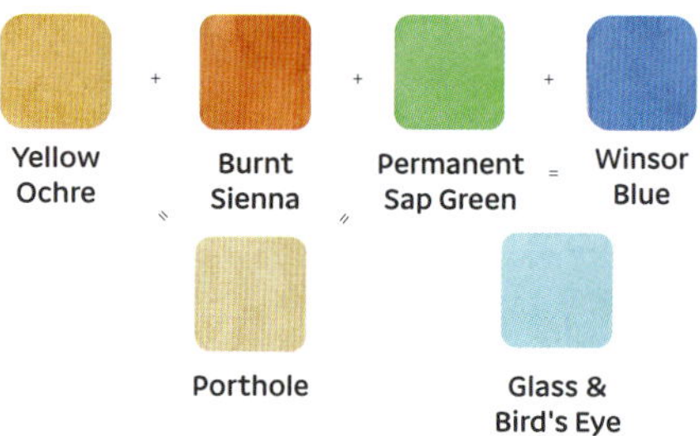

Next, shift your attention to the pebbles. Begin by premixing all the pebble colors on your palette. This will make the process much quicker:

Winsor Blue + **Burnt Sienna** + a hint of **French Ultramarine** – for the green pebbles

Burnt Sienna – for the yellow pebbles

Winsor Red + **Burnt Sienna** – for the terra-cotta pebbles

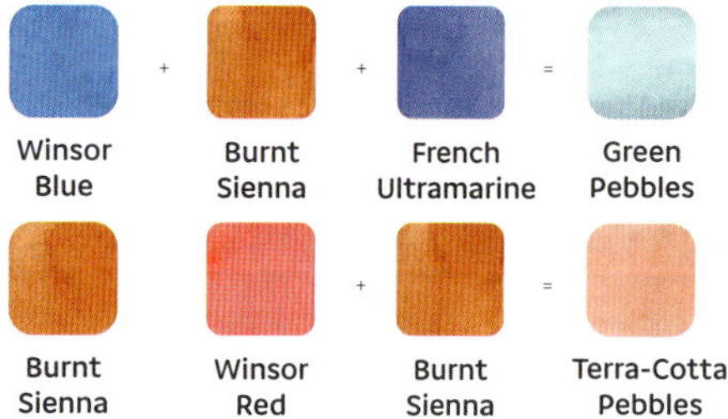

With each color, you can paint multiple pebbles at once. Apply a light layer of color to each pebble, as you will apply another coat once the water has been painted in. For this first coat, paint the whole pebble, including the ones in the foreground that are below the water level.

To finish the pebbles, start mixing **Permanent Sap Green** and **Winsor Blue** to paint all the water. Once it has dried, you can finish off the pebbles by glazing another coat of color on each. For any of the pebbles that are partly underwater, only paint the second coat on the area above the waterline.

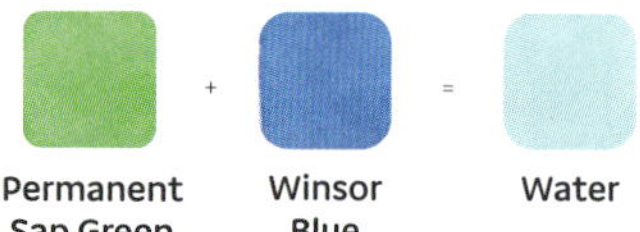

Lastly, mix some **French Ultramarine** and **Burnt Sienna** to paint a shadow under the shell and ladder. You can now remove the masking fluid from the bird and paint its feathers with **French Ultramarine**, using a mixture of **Winsor Red** and **Permanent Sap Green** for the legs and feet.

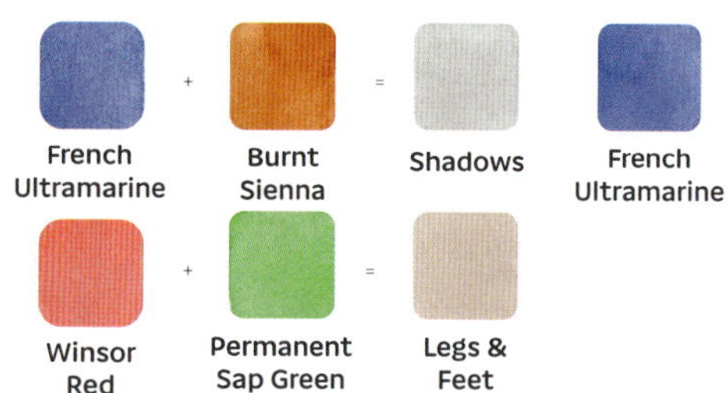

It's now time to remove the masking fluid from the shell, ladder, and starfish above the water. All the starfish need to be painted with **Winsor Red**. Now that the mask has been removed, you can also paint the ladder and lines inside the shell with your mix of **French Ultramarine** and a little **Winsor Blue** you made in Step 2.

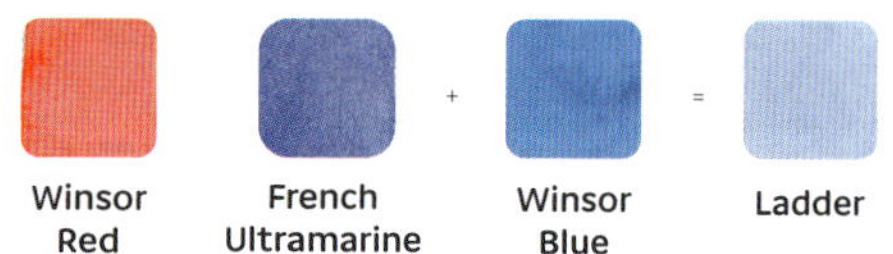

Lastly, before you go on to the next step, apply some random marks of masking fluid over the right side of the water.

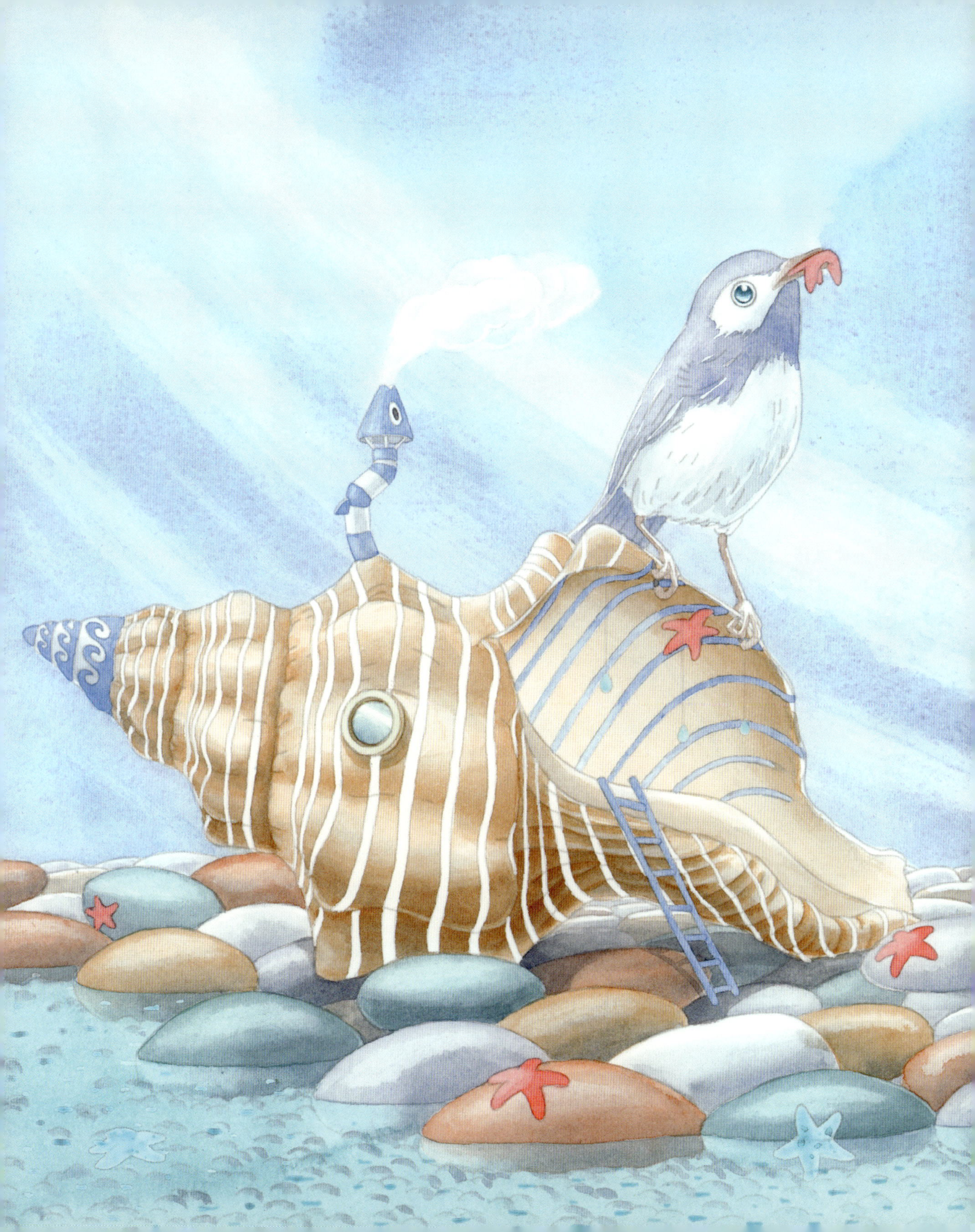

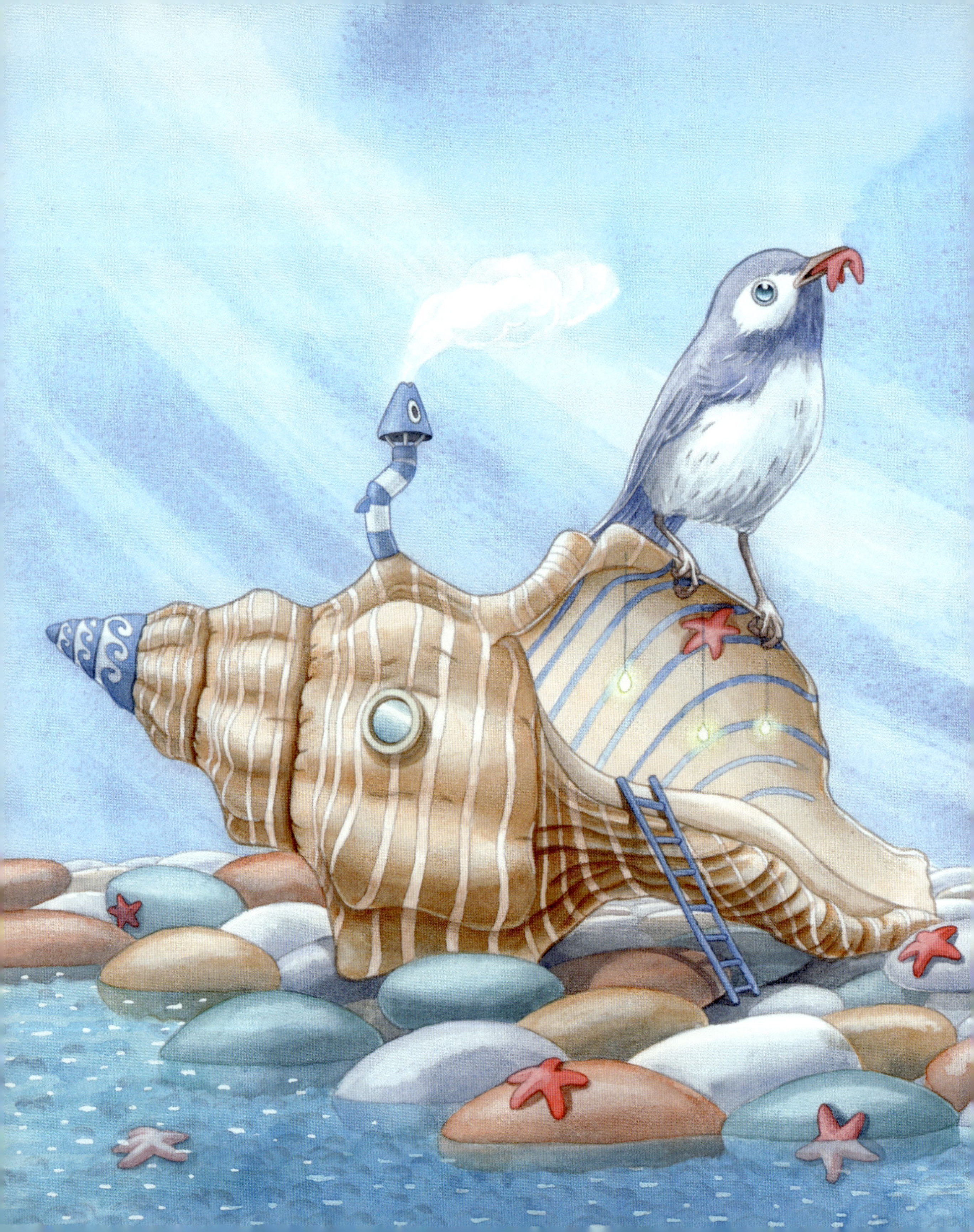

Step 5

Start by mixing some **Winsor Blue** with a hint of **French Ultramarine** to glaze a shadow over the water vertically aligned with the shell. Also, apply some broken rippling lines to the water on the left. Once the paint is dry, remove the masking fluid from the water and the two remaining starfish. They will need a faint layer of **Winsor Red**. Once dry, darken the shaded areas on the last two starfish with more **Winsor Red**. Next, darken the areas just below each starfish with the water shadow mix (**Winsor Blue** and **French Ultramarine**). Finally, glaze **Winsor Blue** over the entire starfish that is completely underwater, and over the submerged portion of the other starfish resting on the green pebble.

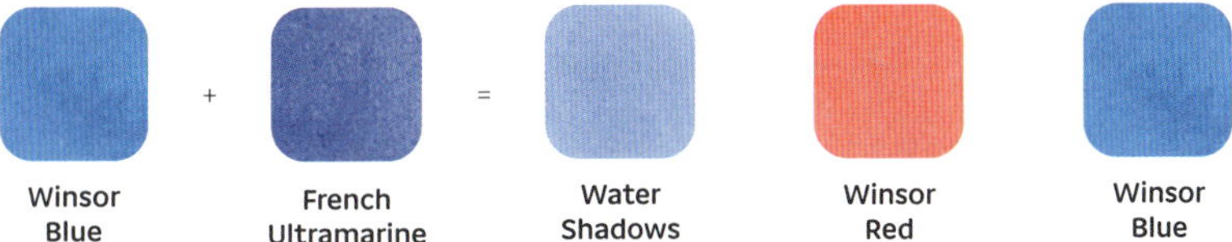

Now mix **Yellow Ochre**, **Burnt Sienna**, and a small amount of **Alizarin Crimson**. Your mixture should be light in pigment. Paint this color over the shadows that are already on the shell; this will deposit paint into the previously masked stripes, helping them appear to follow the contours of the shell rather than floating.

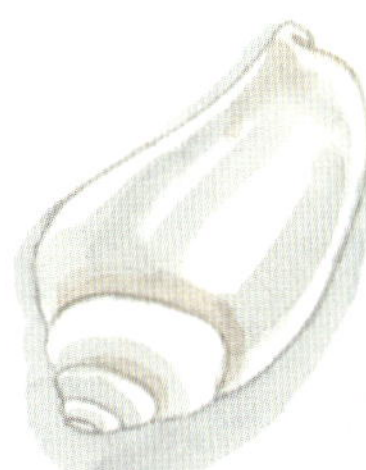

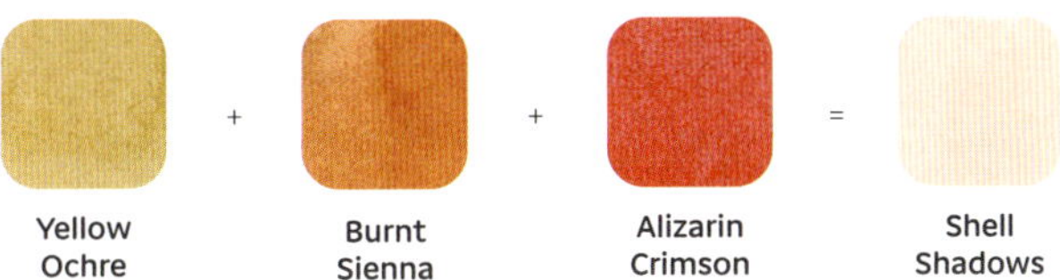

To detail and further darken all the deepest recesses in the shell, mix **Yellow Ochre**, **Burnt Sienna**, a little **Alizarin Crimson**, and **French Ultramarine**. For all the blue details, such as the ladder, chimney, wave design, and stripes, you can further darken them with a mixture of **French Ultramarine** and **Burnt Sienna**. This color can also be used for the bird's blue feathers, and by mixing in more Burnt Sienna, you can create a blue-gray shadow for the bird's belly. Proceed to use this color to create more depth among the pebbles under the shell. Lastly, using an old brush and clean water, lift the paint around the masking fluid light bulbs and add some **Winsor Yellow** before removing the mask.

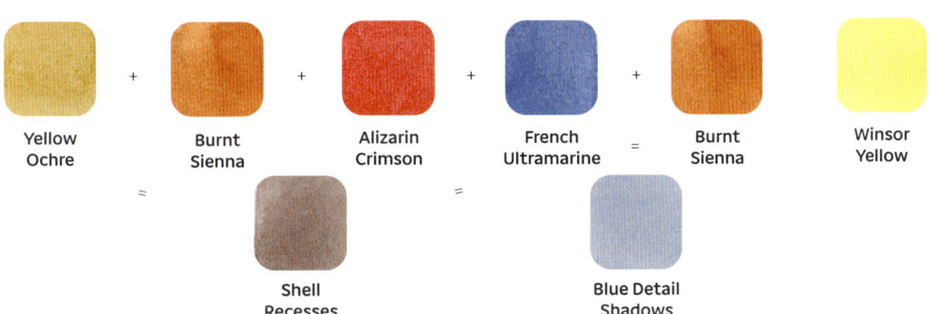

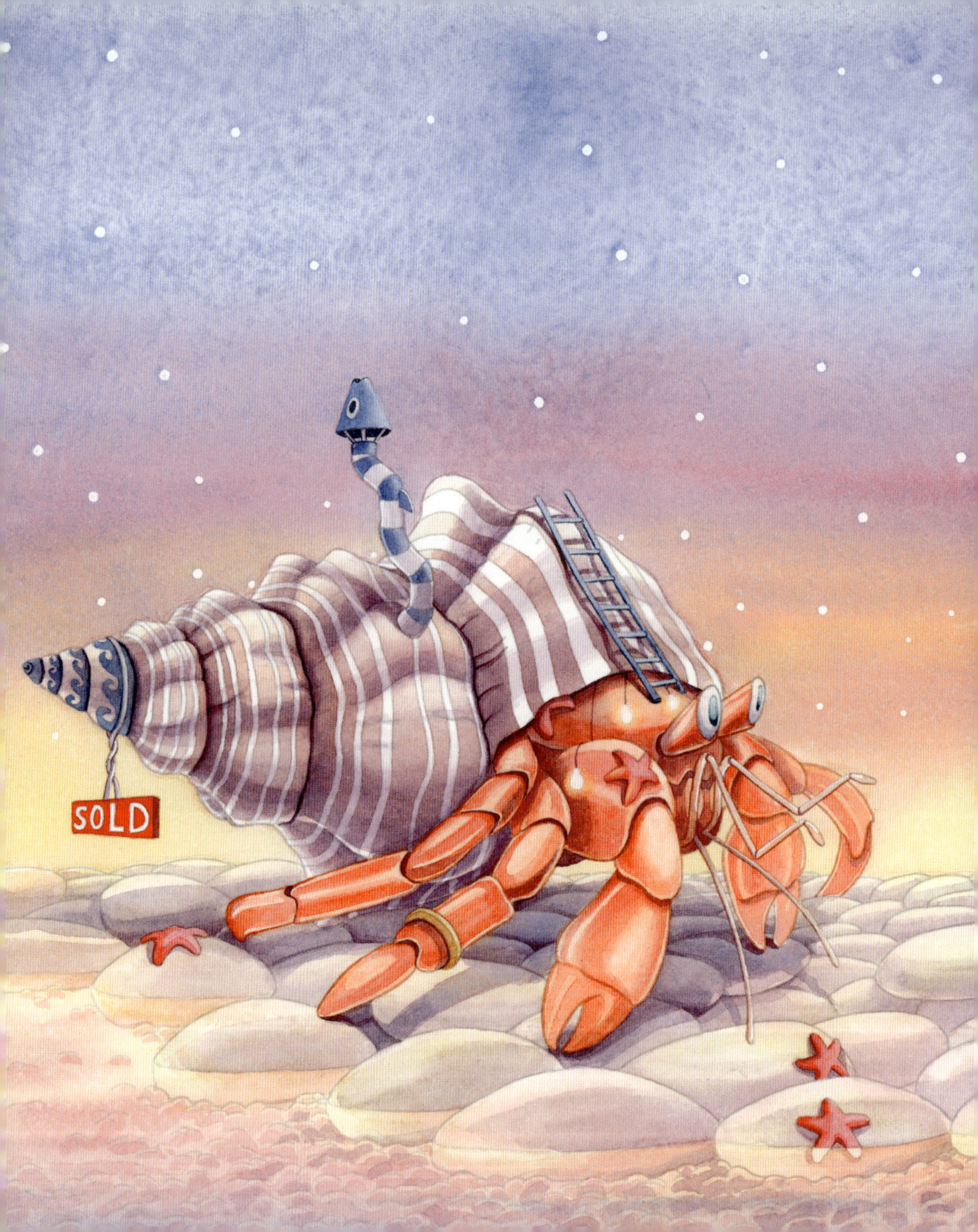

SOLD

SHELLTASTIC NEW HOME

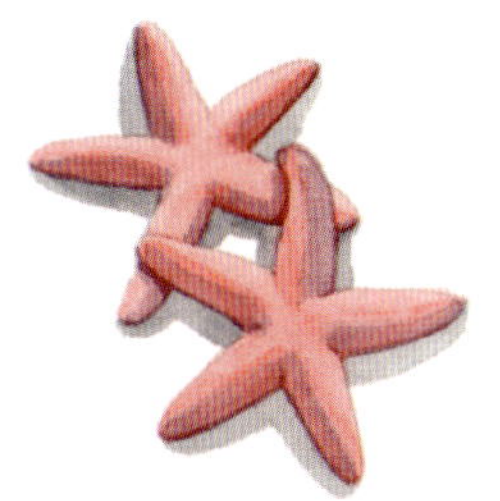

This scene is a continuation of the story from the previous project. The unknown character quickly parted ways with his dream and listed his house for sale. Large shell homes on the coast don't last long, and later that same day, his home was sold, with the excited new owner moving in.

As in the previous project, you will use negative space to build depth in the painting. This time, you will adapt the color scheme to represent an evening sunset.

Sketch

Draw the scene freehand or trace the sketch template on page 217.

Step 1

Apply masking fluid to create dots in the sky and use it to fill in the "Sold" sign, the stripes on the shell, chimney, ladder, light bulbs, starfish, the port-hole ring on the hermit crab's leg, and finally, its pupils and feelers.

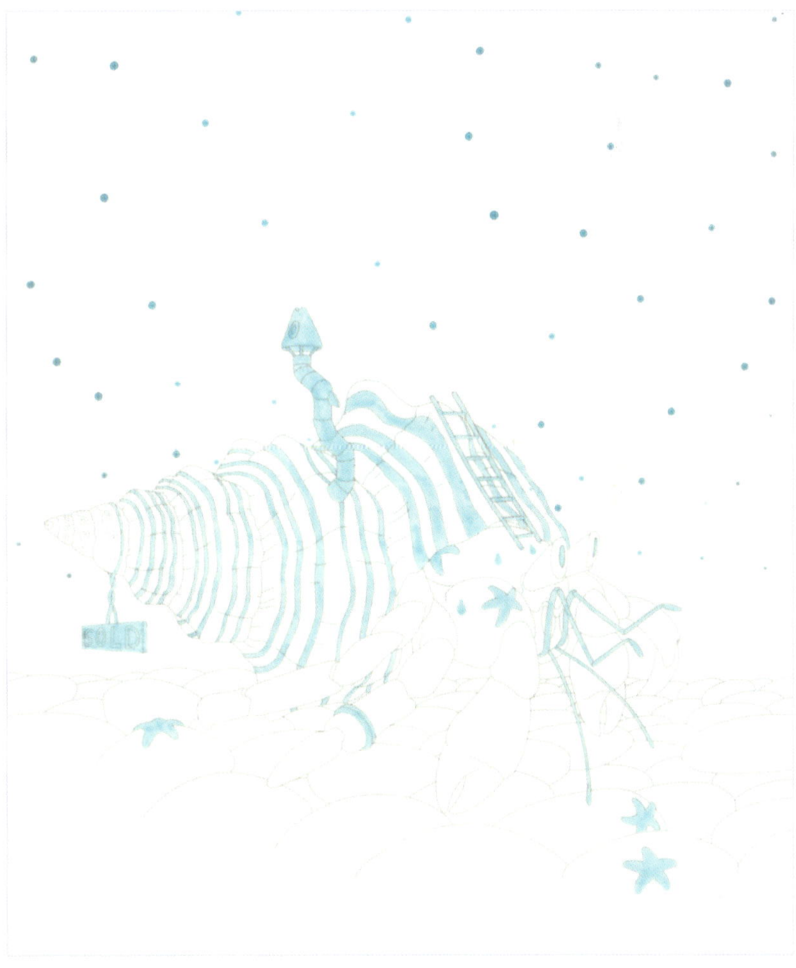

Step 2

To create the sunset background, mix three separate batches of paint on your palette. Make sure to prepare enough paint, as you'll also use these colors in the next step: **Winsor Blue**, **Alizarin Crimson**, and **Winsor Yellow**.

Using the wet-on-wet technique (page 12), wet the entire background with clean water. Start at the top with **Winsor Blue**, filling the upper third with horizontal brushstrokes. Clean your brush, and then use **Alizarin Crimson** to continue downward, finishing with **Winsor Yellow**. A few gentle strokes will help blend the colors, but don't overwork it. The colors will naturally blend as they dry.

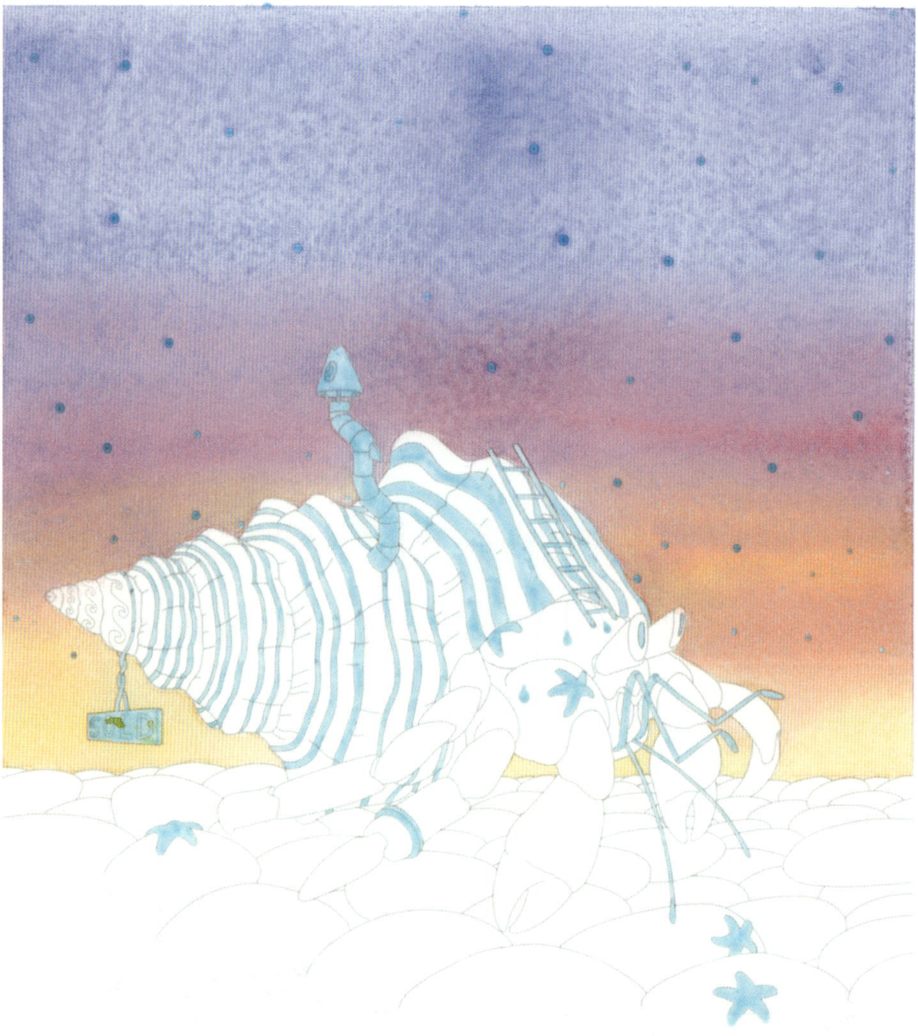

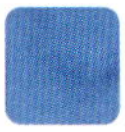

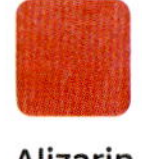

Winsor Blue

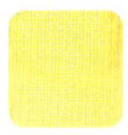

Alizarin Crimson

Winsor Yellow

Step 3

Using the leftover colors on your palette, start by applying **Winsor Yellow** to the shell, pebbles, and water. Before the yellow dries, use **Alizarin Crimson** to paint some of the shadows on the shell, among the pebbles, and over the water. Lastly, while everything is still damp, take a very small amount of **Winsor Blue** and drag it through the water. Before all these colors dry, use a tissue to lightly dab away some of the paint from the underside of the shell to create reflected highlights. Continue doing this for the most prominent points on the shell and over some pebbles. Once everything has dried, mix **Winsor Yellow** with **Alizarin Crimson** on your palette to paint the hermit crab. Before the orange paint dries, use a medium-sized brush to lift some of the paint from the hermit crab's limbs and eyes to create subtle highlights.

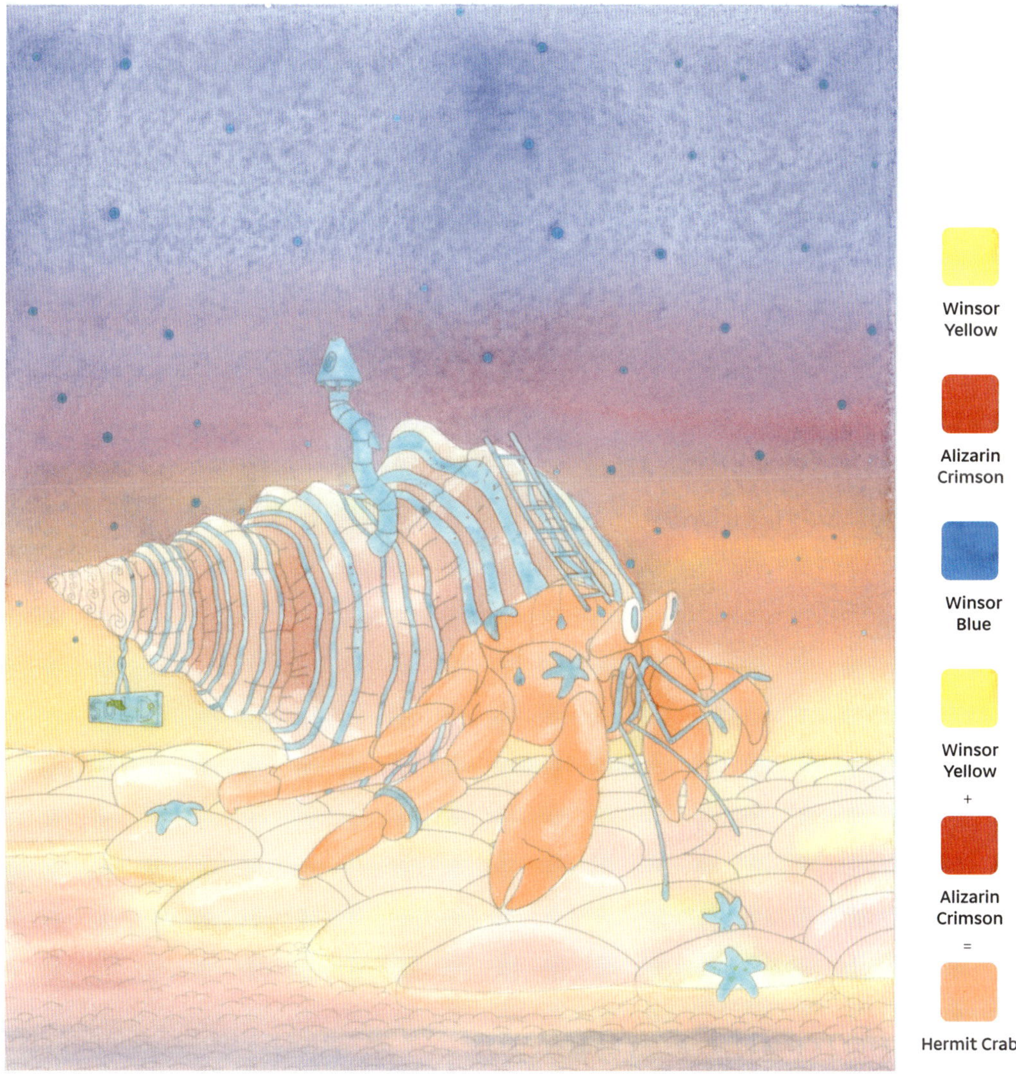

Winsor
Yellow

Alizarin
Crimson

Winsor
Blue

Winsor
Yellow

+

Alizarin
Crimson

=

Hermit Crab

Step 4

Before you can remove the masking fluid, you will need to create three new mixtures of paint to glaze over areas you have previously painted. The goal is to further enhance the shadows, creating more depth and contrast. Building this up with multiple light layers will be the best approach. Create these mixes:

Winsor Blue + **Alizarin Crimson** – for the shadows on the shell and eyes

Winsor Red + **Winsor Yellow** – for the shadows on the hermit crab

Alizarin Crimson + a touch of **French Ultramarine** – for the big and small pebbles, including the large shadow under the hermit crab's house

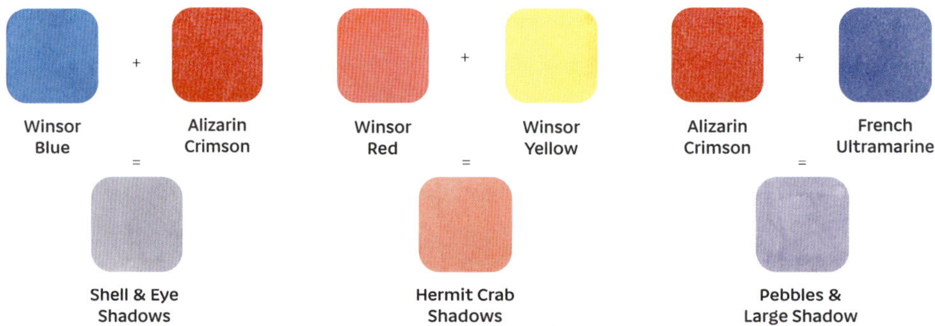

Using these color mixes and the reference image as your guide, proceed to paint in all the shadows. To create the illusion of smaller pebbles below the water, use the mixture of **Alizarin Crimson** with a touch of **French Ultramarine**. Starting on the right side, paint a little blob to represent the middle of each small pebble, leaving the top edge clear to create a highlight for each one. As you make your way to the left of the painting, gradually reduce the concentration of pigment in your mixture. Once everything is dry, mix some **French Ultramarine** with **Winsor Red** to further darken the large shadow under the hermit crab's house. When all the paint is completely dry, remove all the masking fluid from your painting.

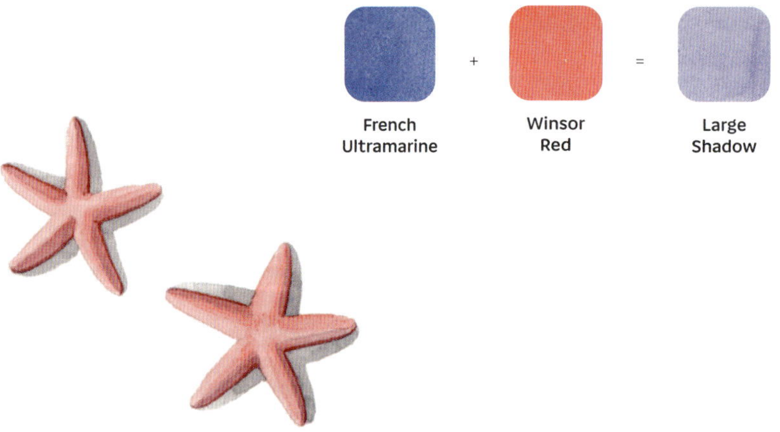

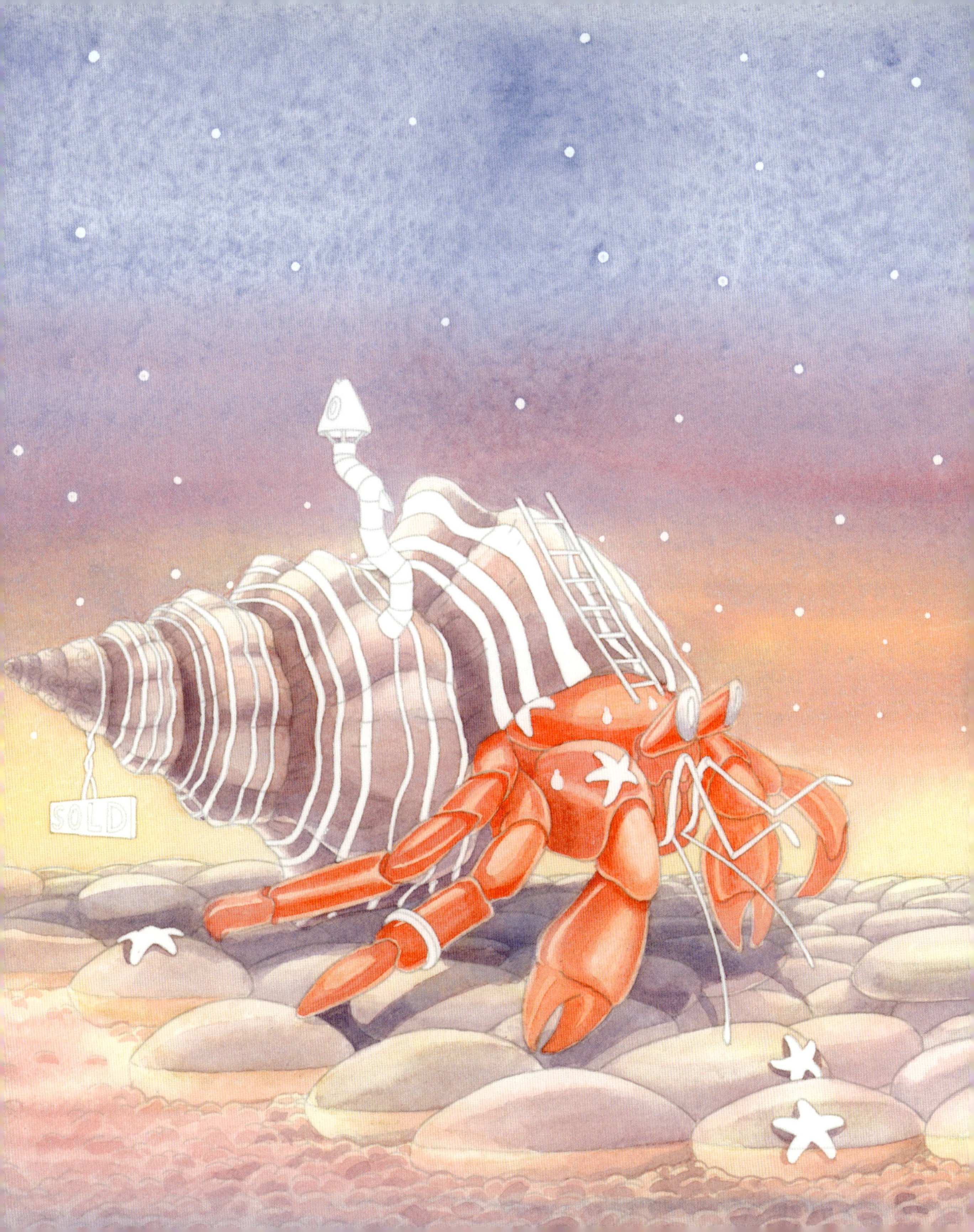

SOLD

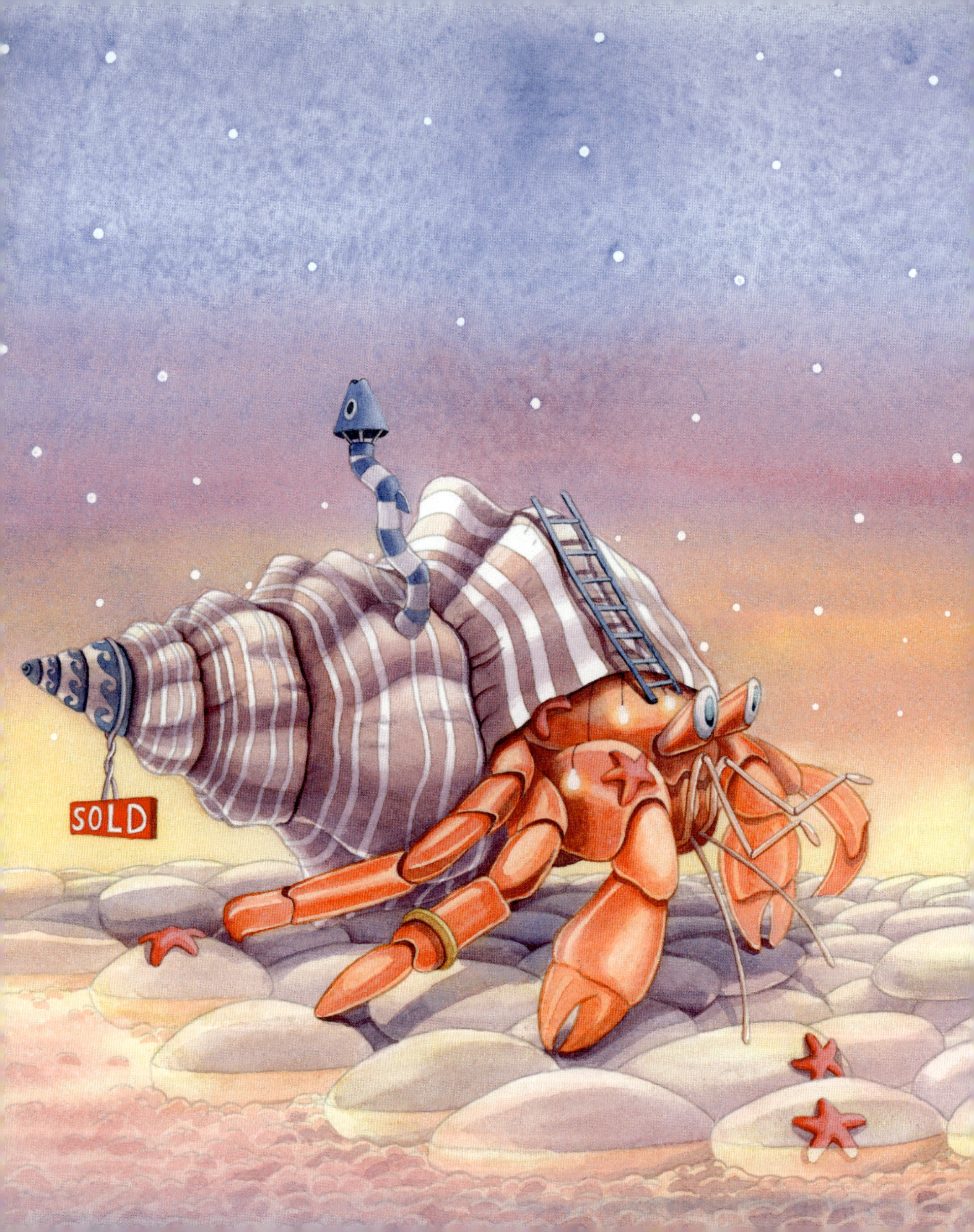

SOLD

Step 5

Create a new mixture of **French Ultramarine** and **Winsor Red**, with a bit more red than blue, to glaze darker shadows over what you previously painted. Your glaze will deposit color into the blank stripes that were previously masked. This will dramatically enhance the depth, making its bumps and grooves more prominent. Also, use this color to paint a shadow on the chimney.

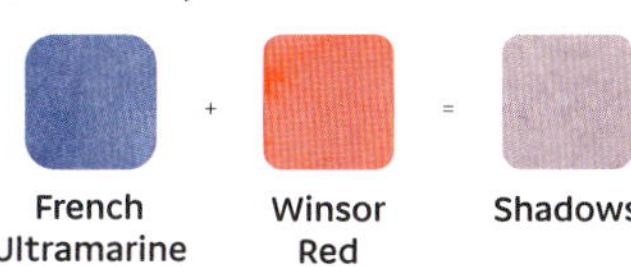

To create a blue for the decorative waves on the shell apex, chimney, and ladder, mix **French Ultramarine** with a small amount of **Winsor Blue** and **Alizarin Crimson**.

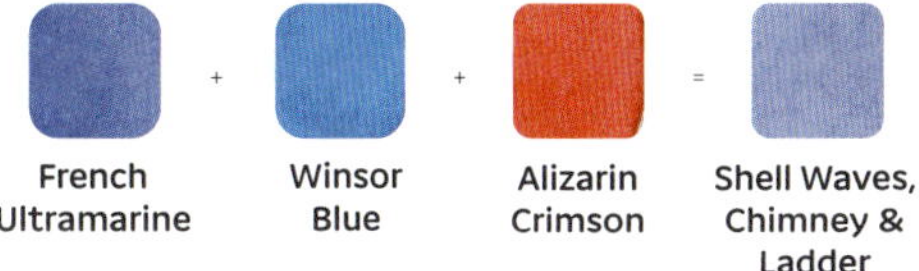

Now, focus your attention on the deepest recesses in both the shell and the joints of the hermit crab. Use concentrated pigment for both of these color mixes. Create these mixes:

French Ultramarine + Burnt Sienna + Alizarin Crimson – for the shell details

Winsor Red + Winsor Yellow + a small amount of French Ultramarine – for the hermit crab details

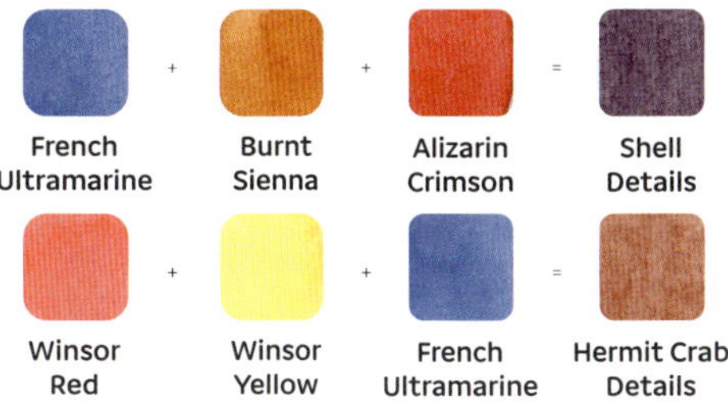

Once everything has dried, use some more of the French Ultramarine, Burnt Sienna, and Alizarin Crimson mix used for the shell details to further deepen:

* some of the leg joints

* beneath the lip of the shell opening

* under the ladder

* between the pebbles that are shaded by the hermit crab's house

To paint any of the blue details, simply use **French Ultramarine** mixed with **Burnt Sienna**. **Yellow Ochre** mixed with **Burnt Sienna** and a small amount of **Permanent Sap Green** can be combined for the porthole ring. It's always important to help draw attention to the character's eyes. Some contrast in color will achieve this. Mix **Winsor Blue** with **Permanent Sap Green** and paint the eyes. Now, paint the starfish and the "Sold" sign with **Winsor Red**, and by mixing in **French Ultramarine**, you can create their shadows. Lastly, lift the paint around the light bulbs and paint in some **Winsor Yellow**.

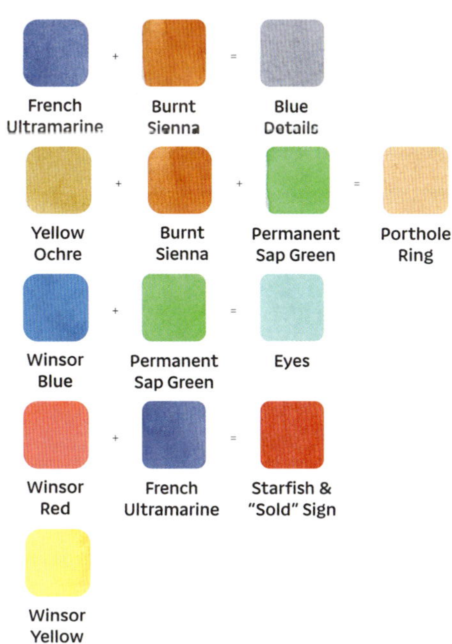

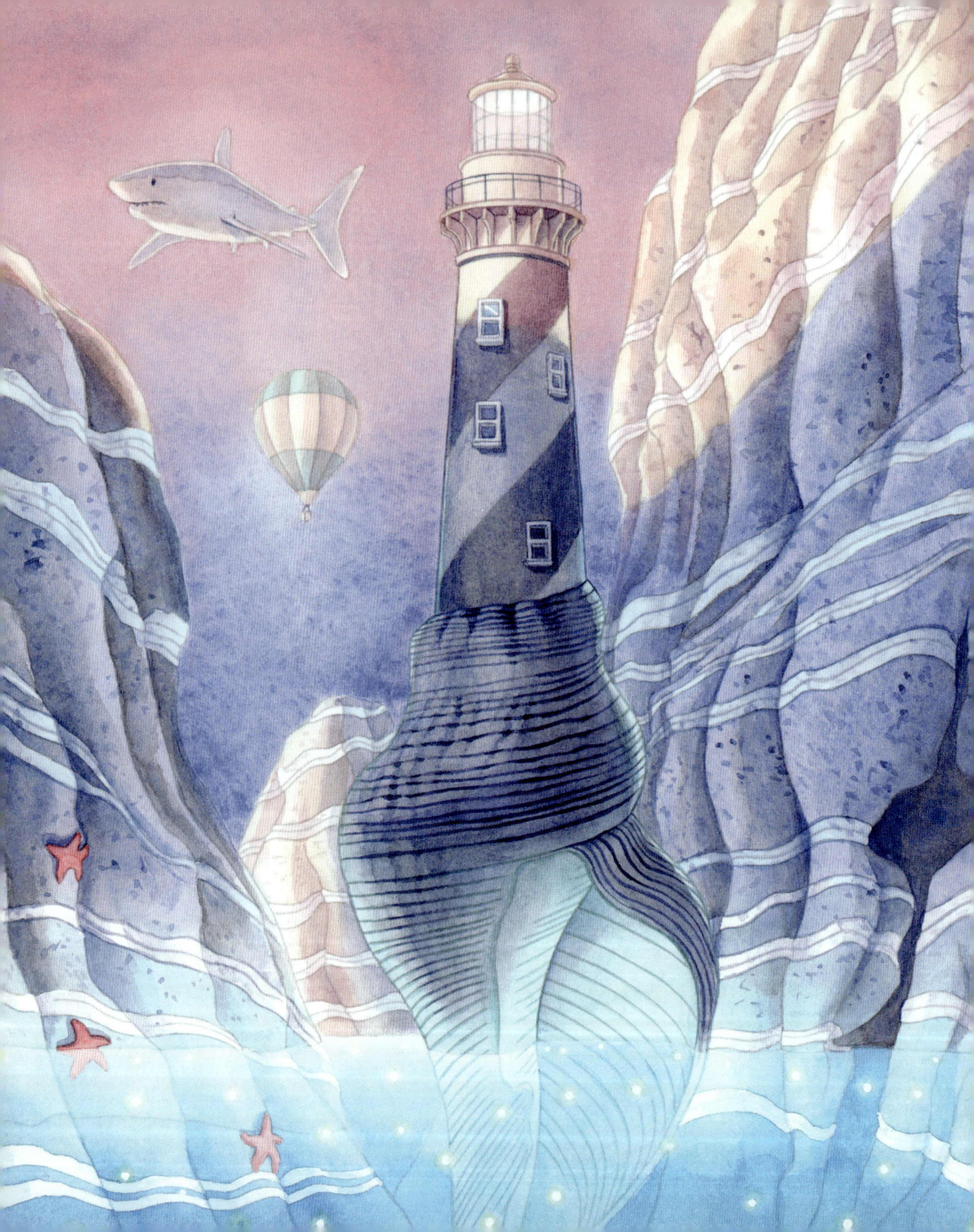

LUMINOUS SHELL BEACON

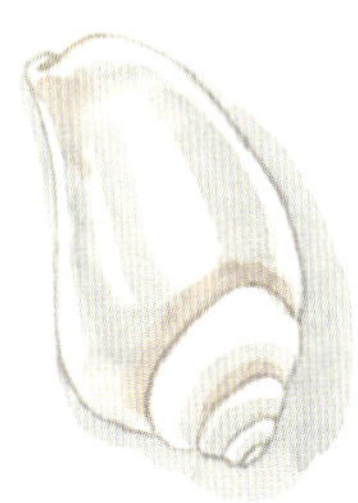

In this project, you will use negative space to bring form, movement, and texture to the cliffs and establish a glowing reflection from the water. You will also explore light direction to create a dramatic scene.

The lighthouse and the spiral shell complement each other with a balance of qualities. The lighthouse symbolizes guidance and stability, while the spiral shell signifies mystery and the cycles of nature. Additionally, their architectural similarities enhance this harmony, creating a seamless blend between man-made and natural. Well, at least that's my take on why I thought it would be interesting to combine the two. It is a concept I have played around with in my art before, and I know you will find a lot of enjoyment in painting this scene.

Sketch

Draw the scene freehand or trace the sketch template on page 219.

Step 1

Apply masking fluid to the stripes on the rock face, the window frames on the lighthouse, the starfish, and some random dots in the water. To make painting the background easier, mask all the fins on the shark and the hot-air balloon basket.

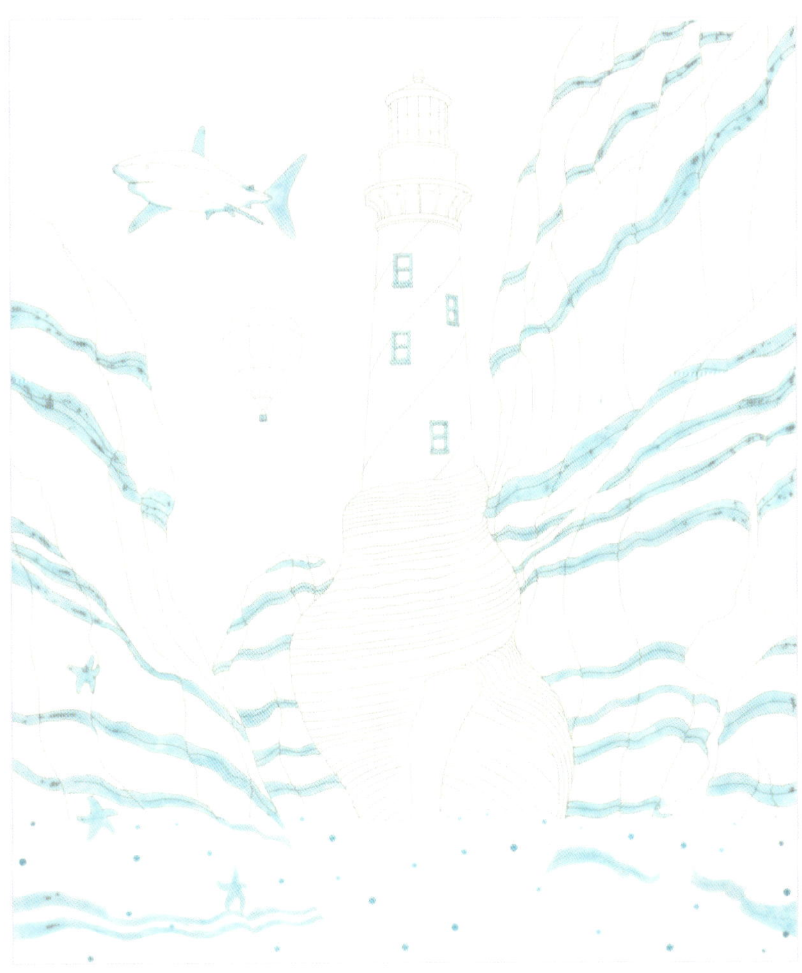

Step 4

For this step, you'll need to premix three different colors on your palette. They should be watered down enough to easily glaze over large areas but still have enough pigment so that one pass of the brush is sufficient. Create these mixes:

Winsor Yellow + a small amount of **Alizarin Crimson** – for all the areas the sun is hitting

French Ultramarine + a small amount of **Burnt Sienna** – for all the shaded areas

Winsor Blue + **Permanent Sap Green** – for the water, reflections, and the shell

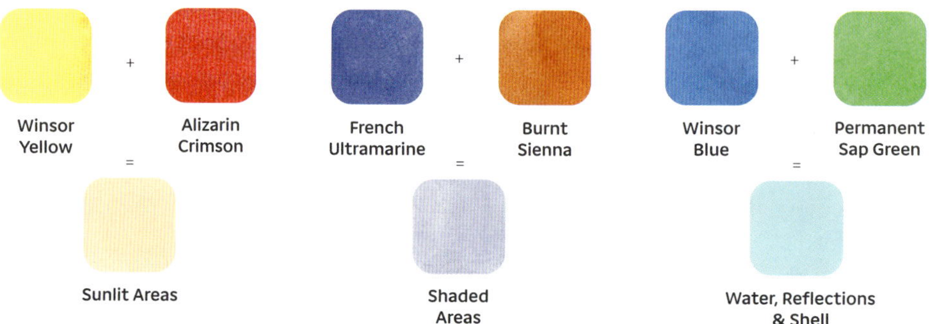

Start with the first mixture and glaze over any pink or purple areas, except for the sky. Once this has dried, use the second mixture to glaze over any areas where you painted a gray-blue. Lastly, use the third mixture for the water and shell, gently fading this color up into the rocks. It can also be used to paint the bands on the hot-air balloon.

Now that these colors have been applied, you should be able to see how leaving negative space in the previous step provided areas for the new colors to settle into, helping them maintain their vibrancy.

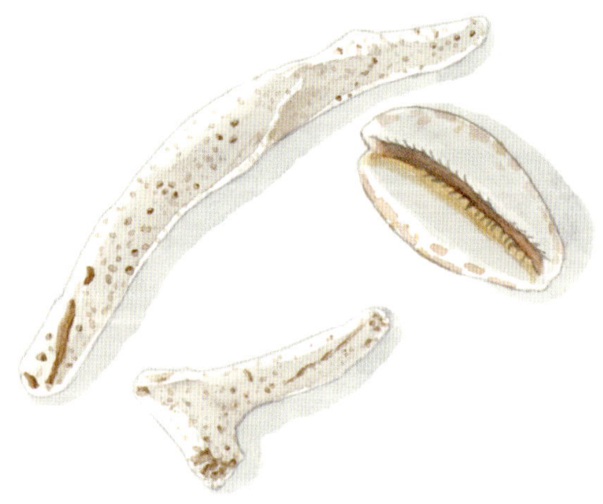

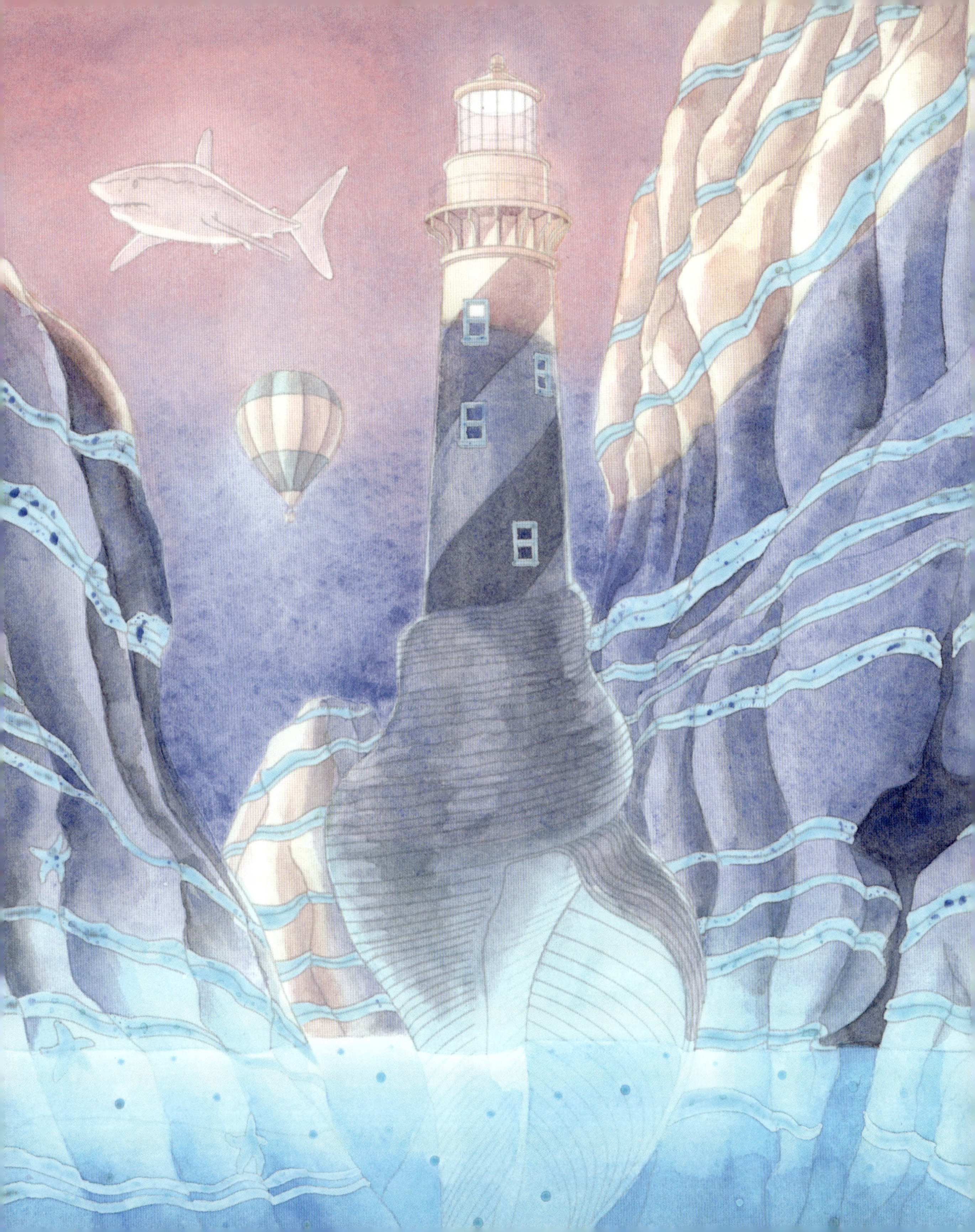

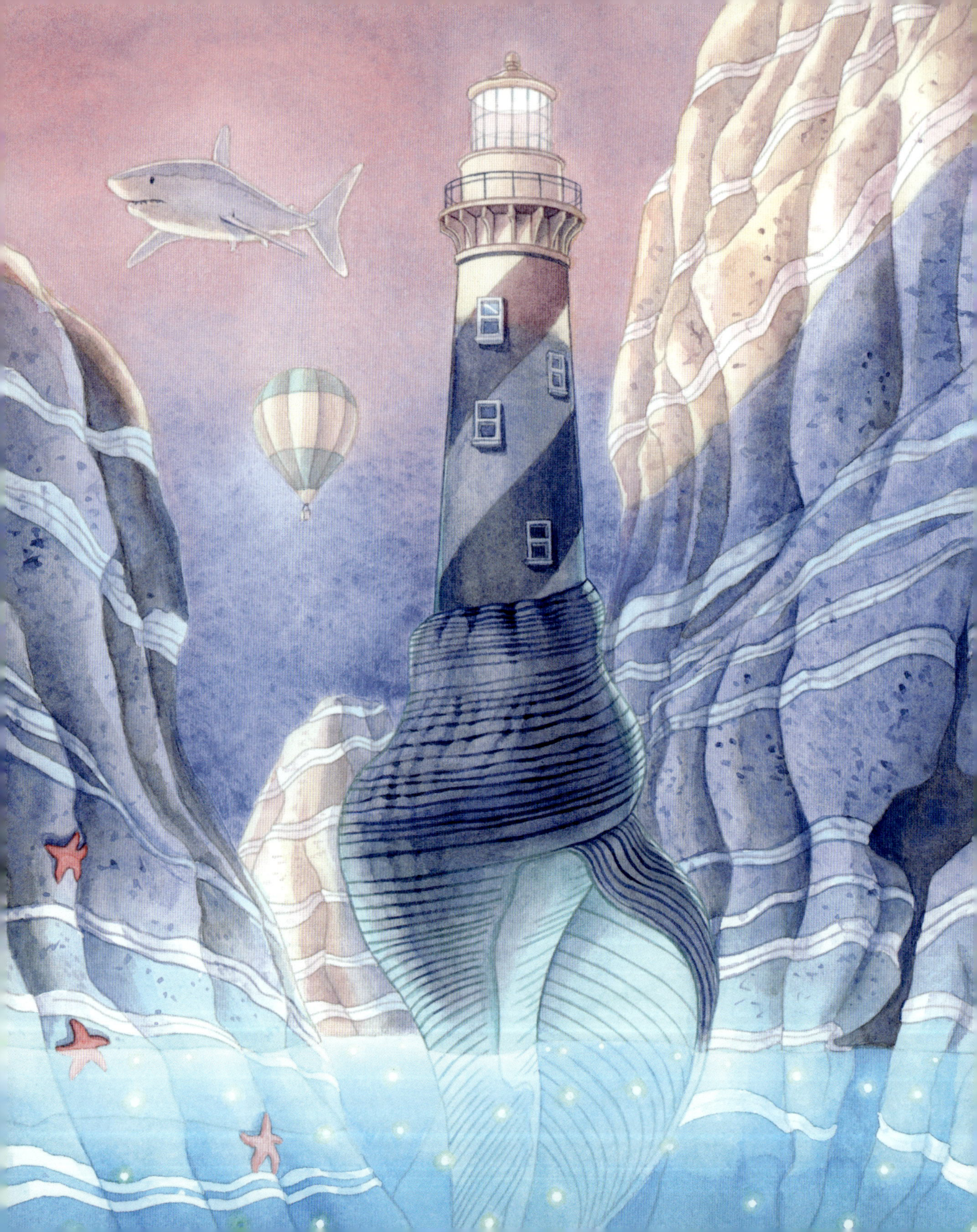

Step 5

Use an old brush and some clean water to lift and soften the paint around each light orb in the water. Once everything is dry, glaze some **Winsor Yellow** around each orb. The masking fluid can be removed once the paint dries. Continue removing the masking fluid from the rest of the picture.

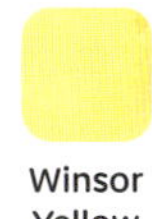

Winsor
Yellow

It's now time to paint shadows over all the white stripes on the rocks. Here are the colors for each section:

Alizarin Crimson + a small amount of **French Ultramarine** – for the warm sunlit stripes

Winsor Blue + **Permanent Sap Green** – for the first glaze over the stripes in the cool shaded areas and around the folds and deepest recesses underwater

a darker value mix of **French Ultramarine** + **Burnt Sienna** – for the second glaze to darken the folds, the deepest recesses on the stripes, and the deepest areas in previously established shadows

a lighter value mix of **French Ultramarine** + **Burnt Sienna** – for darkening the stripes just above the waterline

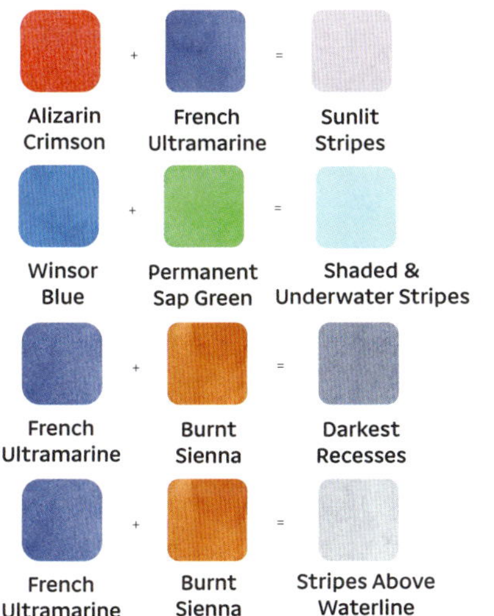

Alizarin Crimson	+	French Ultramarine	=	Sunlit Stripes
Winsor Blue	+	Permanent Sap Green	=	Shaded & Underwater Stripes
French Ultramarine	+	Burnt Sienna	=	Darkest Recesses
French Ultramarine	+	Burnt Sienna	=	Stripes Above Waterline

While these colors are still on your palette, use them to stipple (page 13) texture over the rocks.

The painting can now be completed by outlining all the details with more pigmented mixes and a fine detail brush:

French Ultramarine + **Burnt Sienna** – for any shaded areas

Winsor Blue + **Burnt Sienna** – for any areas on the shell with green reflected light

Alizarin Crimson + **French Ultramarine** – for areas that the sun is hitting

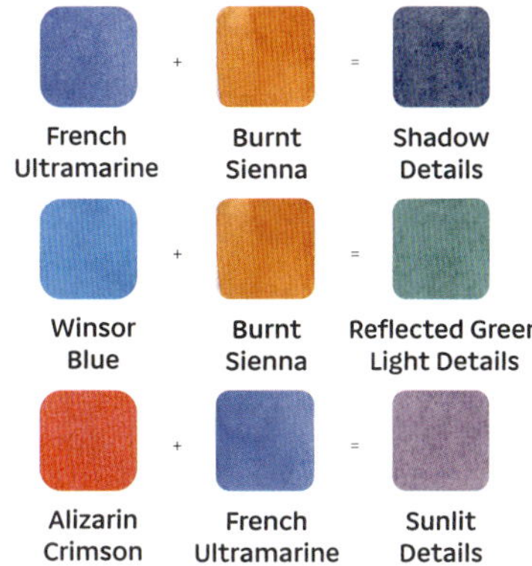

French Ultramarine	+	Burnt Sienna	=	Shadow Details
Winsor Blue	+	Burnt Sienna	=	Reflected Green Light Details
Alizarin Crimson	+	French Ultramarine	=	Sunlit Details

Finally, add some **Winsor Red** for the starfish. Add shadows below the starfish using the same colors you used to shade that area in the first half of this step.

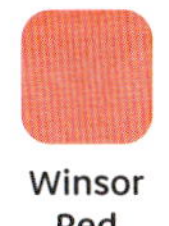

Winsor
Red

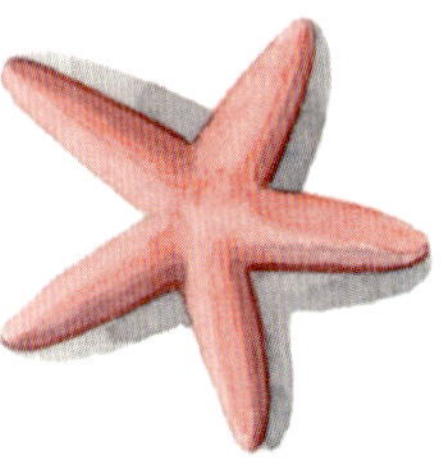

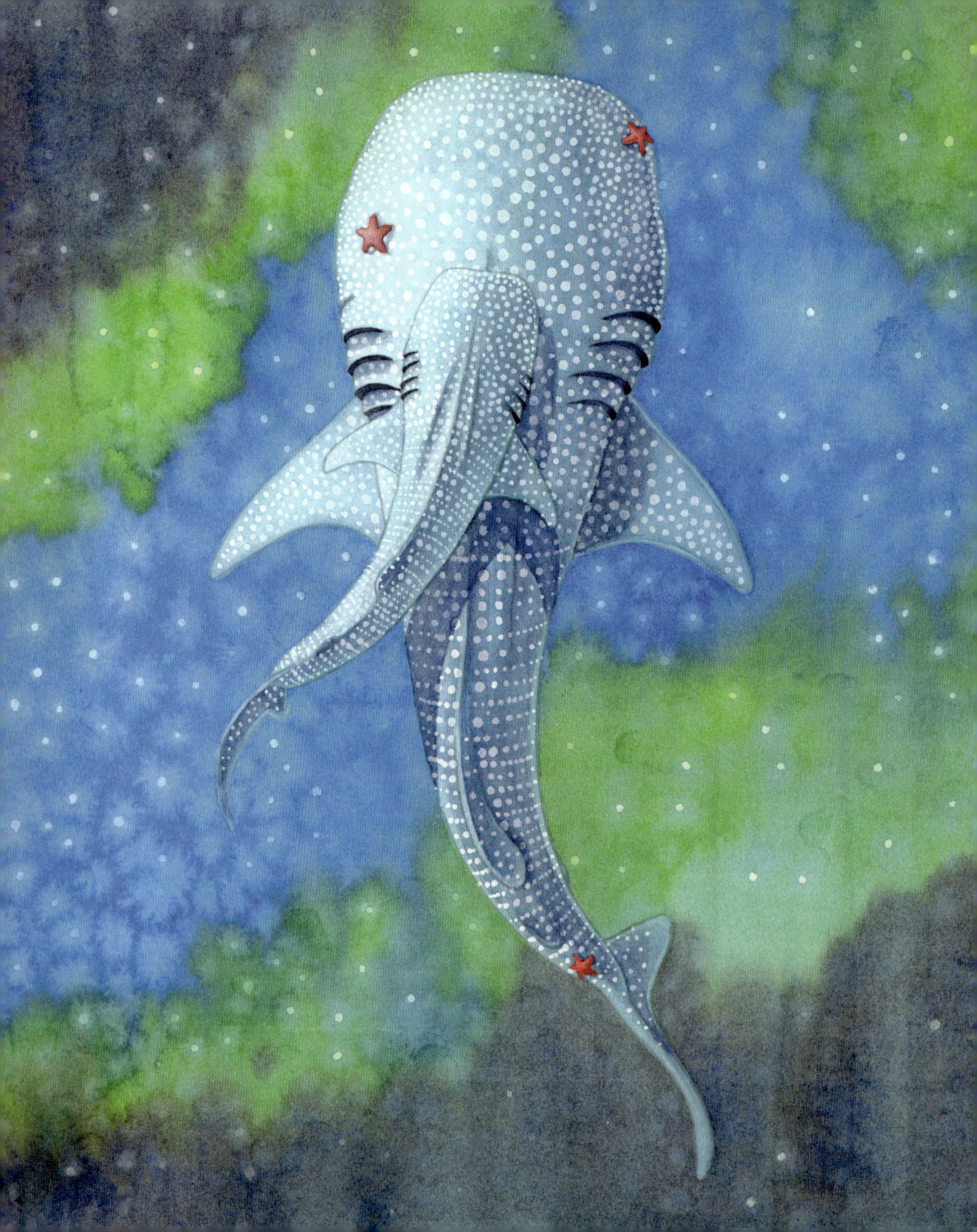

Cosmic Gliders

This chapter draws inspiration from my highly popular *Cosmic Gliders* series, which captures the essence of the underwater world's beauty and the limitless possibilities of outer space by blending them into a delightful fusion. The creation video of my first piece of art, *Shark & Turtle*, from the *Cosmic Gliders* series has been viewed more than 11 million times and continues to spark the imaginations of viewers around the world.

My *Cosmic Gliders* paintings are frequently requested as tutorials by my followers, so I couldn't create this book without including some simplified projects inspired by the original series. These projects allow you to explore this captivating theme while providing plenty of space for personal expression, especially in the backgrounds.

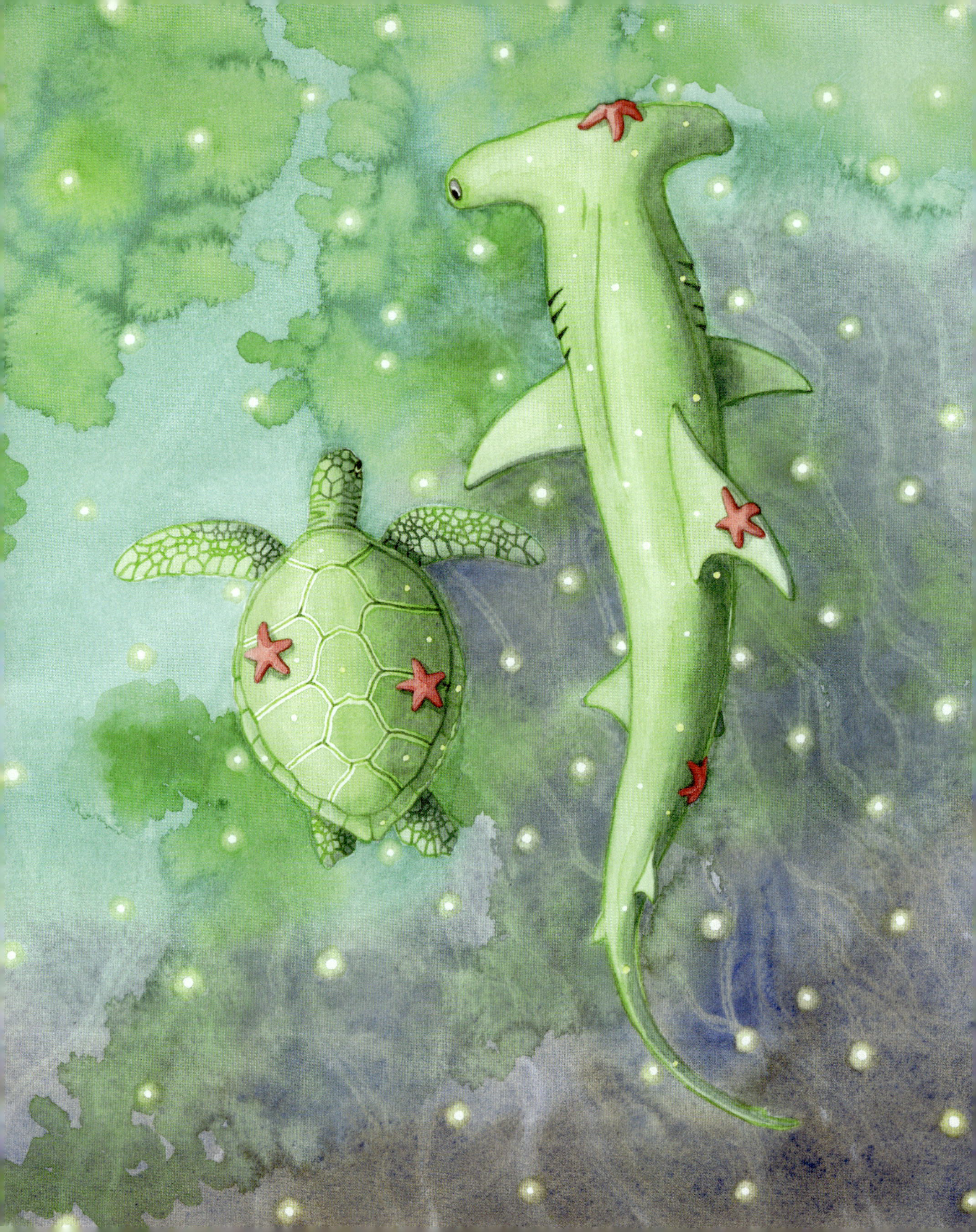

NEBULA NAVIGATORS

In the vast expanse of the cosmos, the celestial turtles glide with an aura of grace, embodying purity itself. Yet, within the uncharted realms of space, not all entities share their generous spirit. The turtles' inherent trustfulness makes them vulnerable to attacks, but they are never alone; a reliable guardian accompanies their cosmic journeys.

This symbiotic connection holds immense significance for the galaxy. Much like the bees of the universe, the turtles and guardians play a significant role in the cosmic ecosystem. As they traverse space, their presence serves as a cosmic pollinator, giving life to the celestial bodies they encounter. Their path through space mirrors the rhythmic flow of ocean waves, leaving in their wake a flourishing trail of abundance.

Sketch

Draw the turtle and the hammerhead freehand or trace the sketch template on page 221.

Step 1

Apply masking fluid to all the starfish, over the linework pattern on the turtle's shell (make it thicker than your pencil lines), and the eyes of both creatures. Add random dots to the entire page.

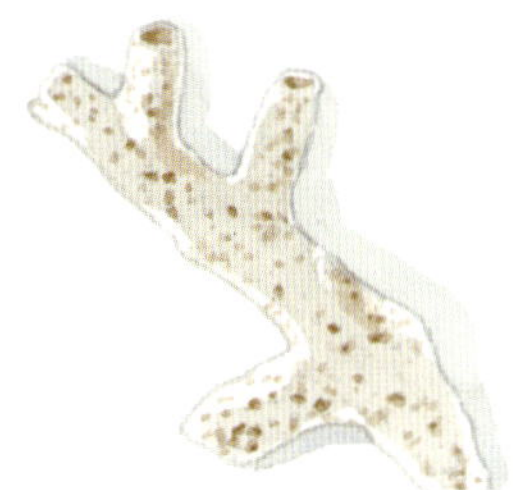

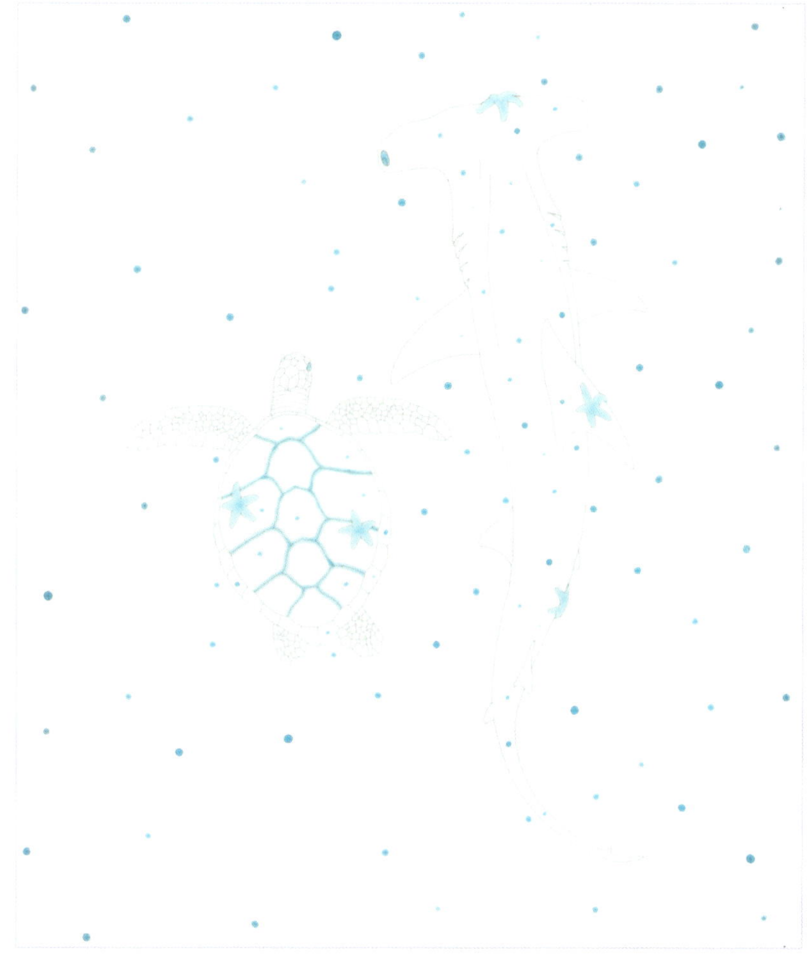

Step 2

Start by premixing two colors on your palette. You will need plenty of each:

Permanent Sap Green + **Winsor Blue** – for the green background

French Ultramarine + **Burnt Sienna** – for the blue background

It's important to perform the next steps consecutively, without much delay in between. Use a large quill brush to wet the entire background with clean water. While the paper is still damp, use the same brush to generously paint the first mixture in the top left and the second mixture in the bottom right. Let the two bodies of color blend together—you can also assist this process with your brush. While the paint is still damp, add some **Winsor Yellow** to the first mixture, transforming it into a bright green-yellow. Dab this color randomly in the top left to create texture blooms and sparingly into the color below. As the paint dries, use a small round brush to pull it through the wet puddles in the bottom right, creating movement and texture. Your brush will absorb the pigmented water as you pull it through the paint and you will notice the paint flowing back into the cleared area, so a few passes may be needed. Subtlety is key for these lines.

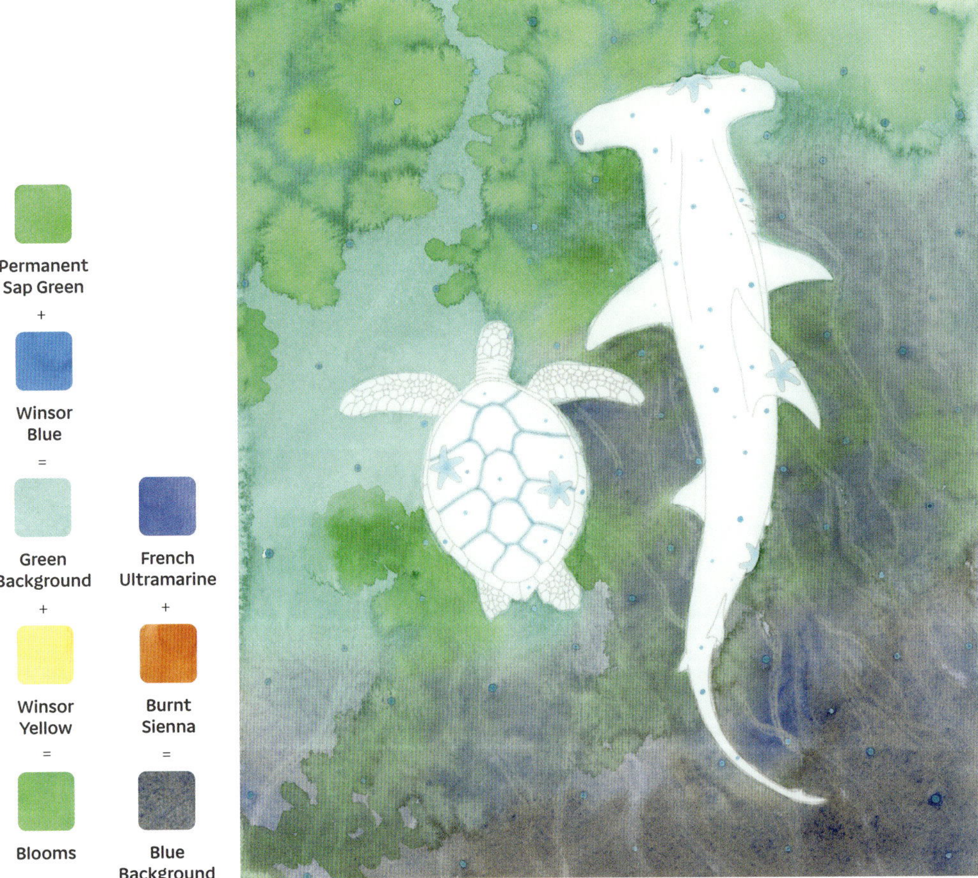

Permanent
Sap Green

+

Winsor
Blue

=

Green
Background

Winsor
Yellow

=

Blooms

French
Ultramarine

+

Burnt
Sienna

=

Blue
Background

Step 3

Once the background is completely dry, dilute some of the bright green-yellow mix from
Step 2 that you used for the blooms to cover both the turtle and the hammerhead shark.
A larger quill brush will make this quick and easy.

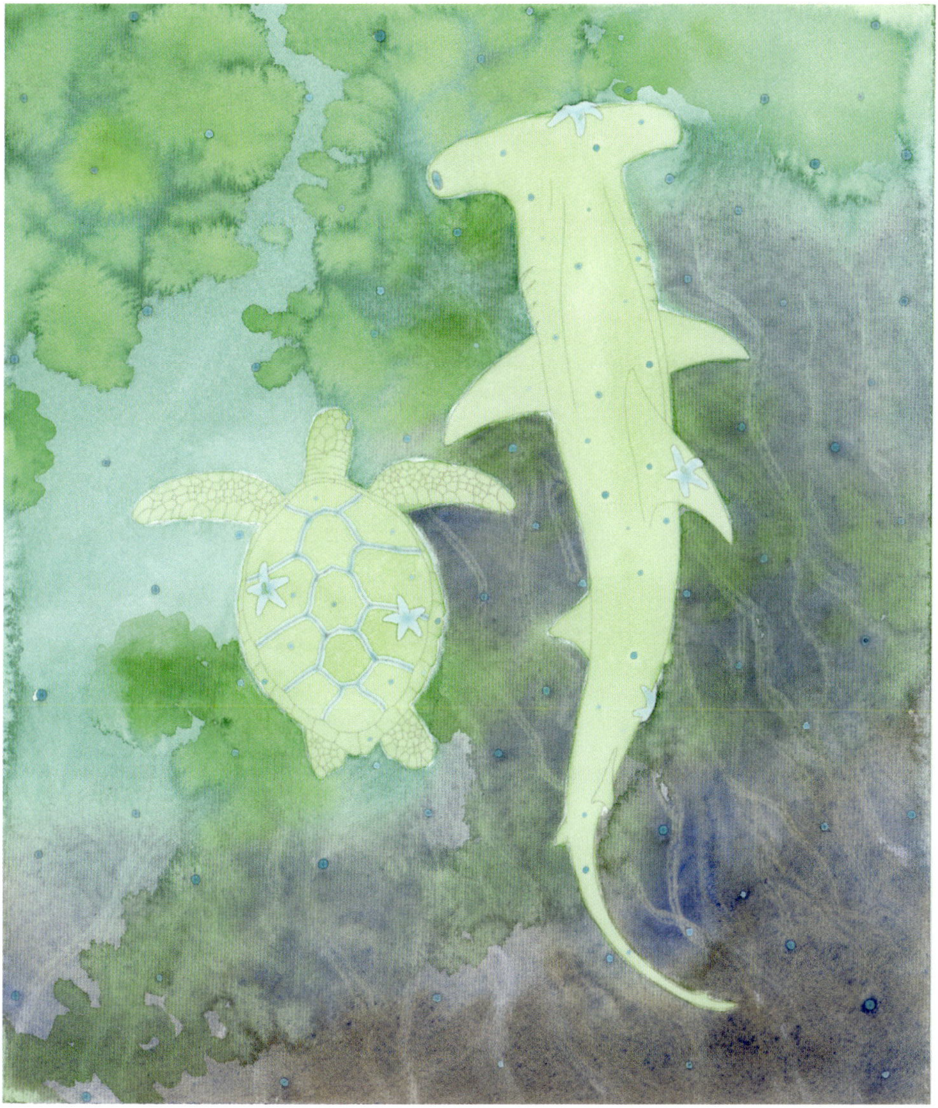

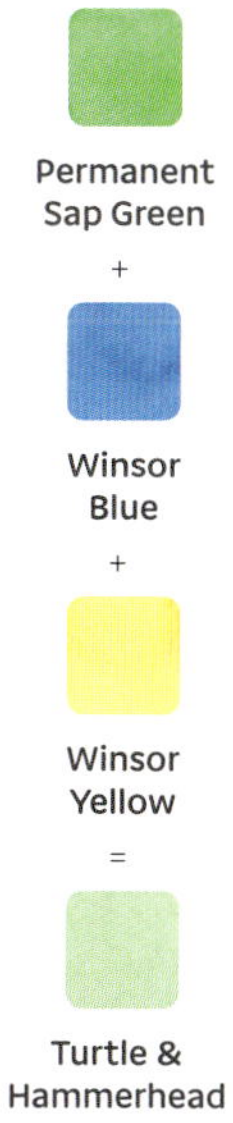

Permanent
Sap Green

+

Winsor
Blue

+

Winsor
Yellow

=

Turtle &
Hammerhead

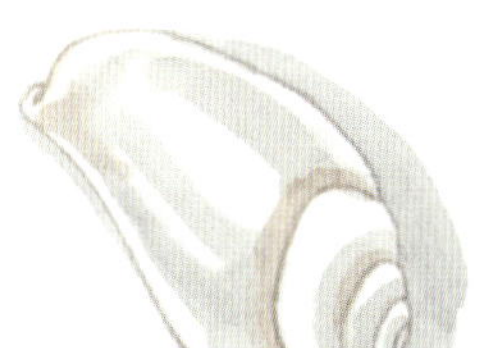

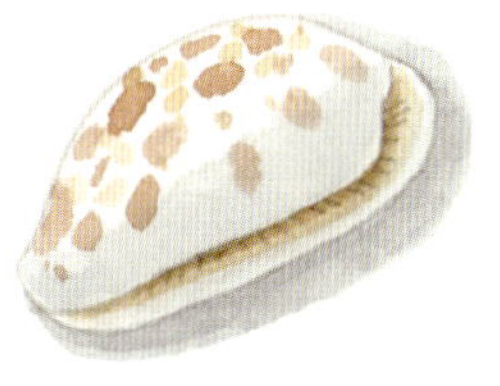

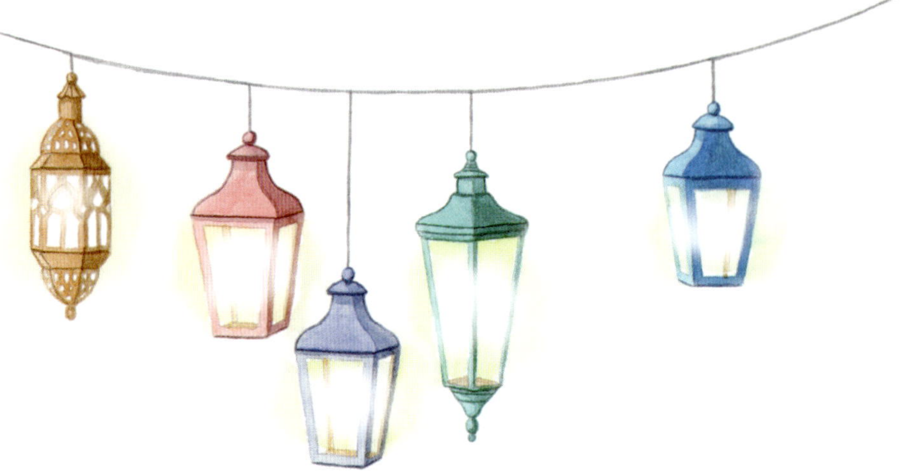

Step 4

Mix some **Permanent Sap Green** with **Winsor Yellow** to paint all the linework on the left side of the turtle and the hammerhead shark. Next, mix **Permanent Sap Green** with **French Ultramarine** and a small amount of **Burnt Sienna** to create a shadow color. This can be glazed over the right side of both creatures and used to add further details with a more concentrated version, targeting areas like the gills on the hammerhead shark and all the creases on the turtle's head and limbs.

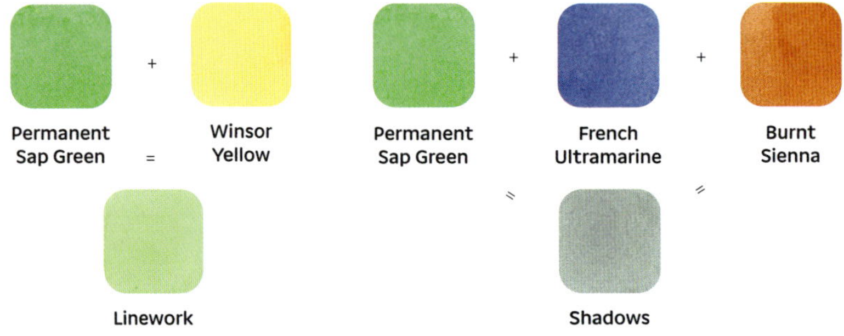

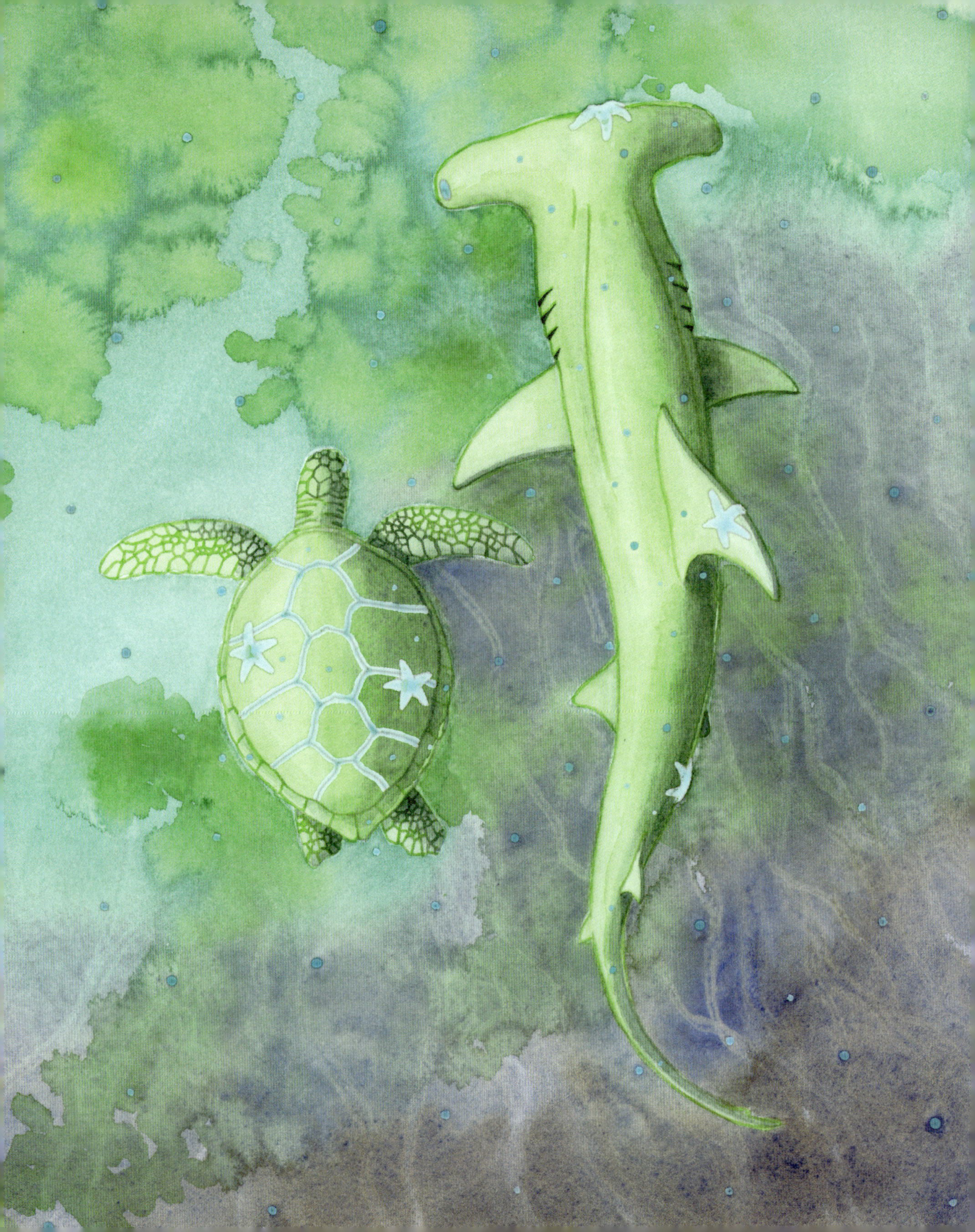

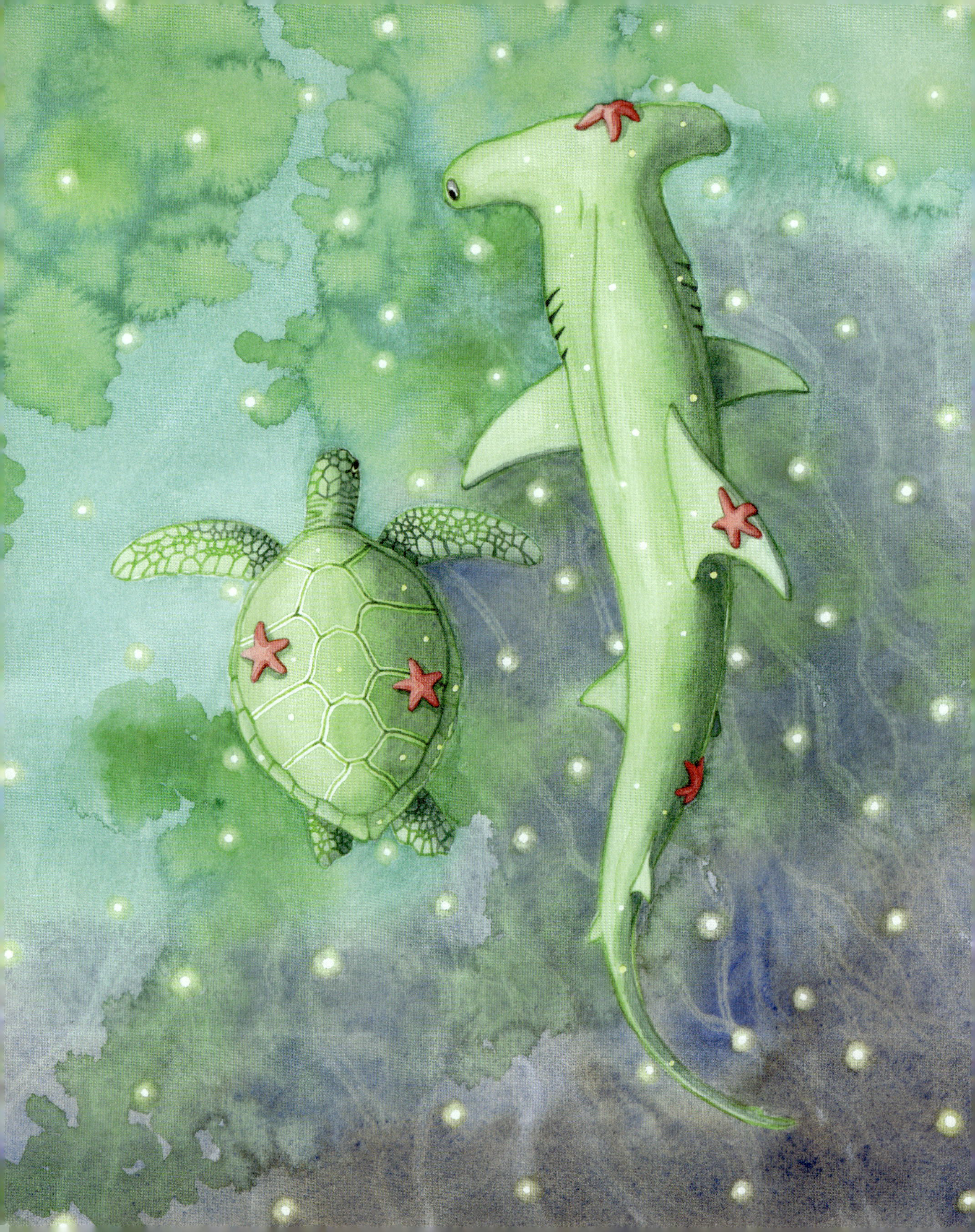

Step 5

Using an old brush and some water, lift some of the paint around the masking fluid dots. You can then add some diluted **Winsor Yellow** around each dot. Once they have dried, remove all the masking fluid.

Winsor
Yellow

Now, draw your attention to the turtle's shell pattern. Start by mixing **Winsor Yellow** with a small amount of **Permanent Sap Green**, and then carefully glaze over the areas that were previously masked. Focus on the right-hand side, fading into the white of the paper on the left. Take a concentrated version of the shadow color on your palette from Step 4 to paint in the details on the shell, defining each segment. Continue using this color for both of the creatures' eyes.

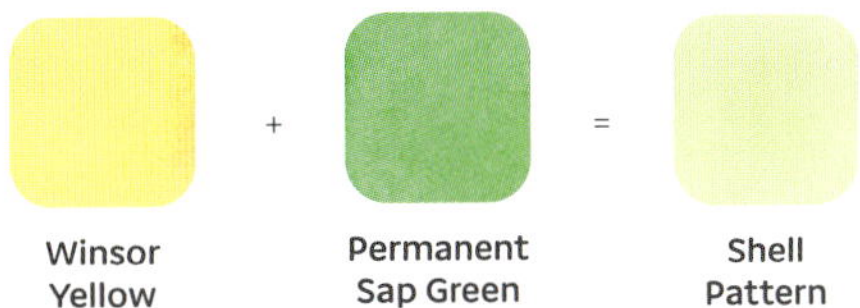

Winsor
Yellow

+

Permanent
Sap Green

=

Shell
Pattern

Lastly, use **Winsor Red** to paint all the starfish, and mix in some **French Ultramarine** to create contrast.

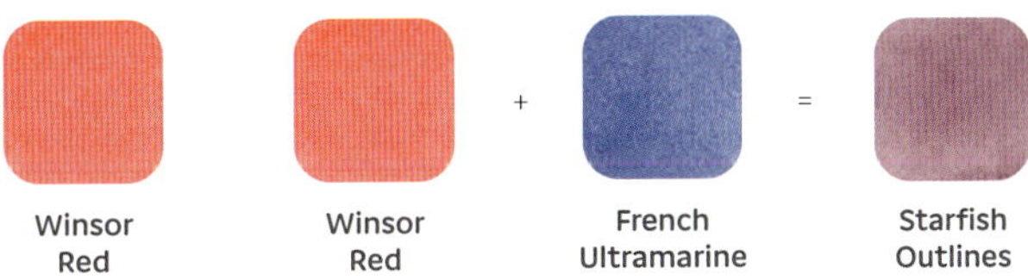

Winsor
Red

Winsor
Red

+

French
Ultramarine

=

Starfish
Outlines

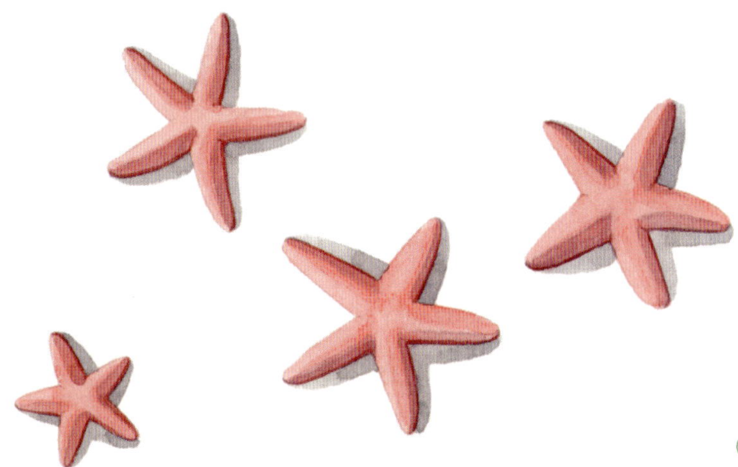

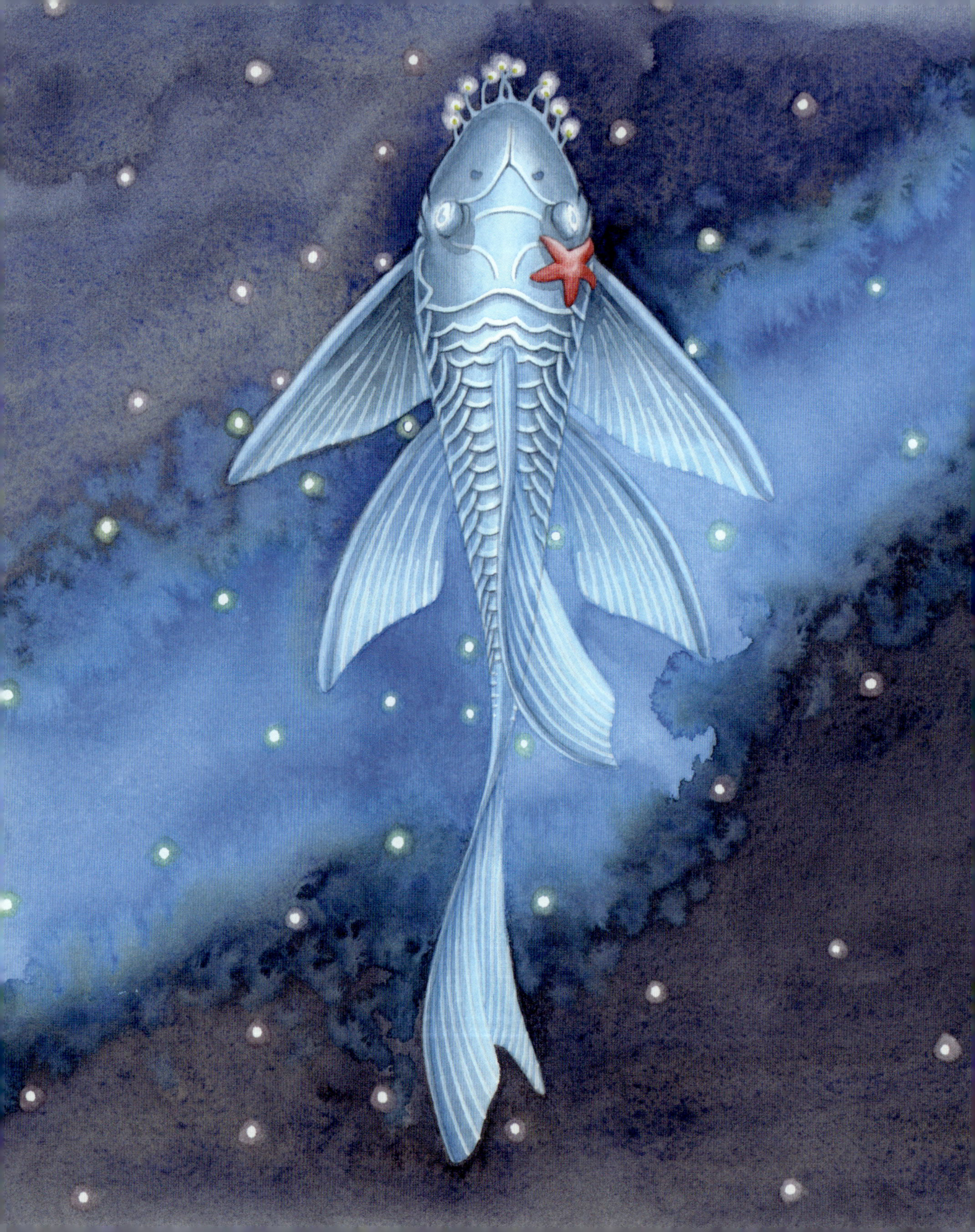

THE MOON SHAPER: A.K.A. HAROLD

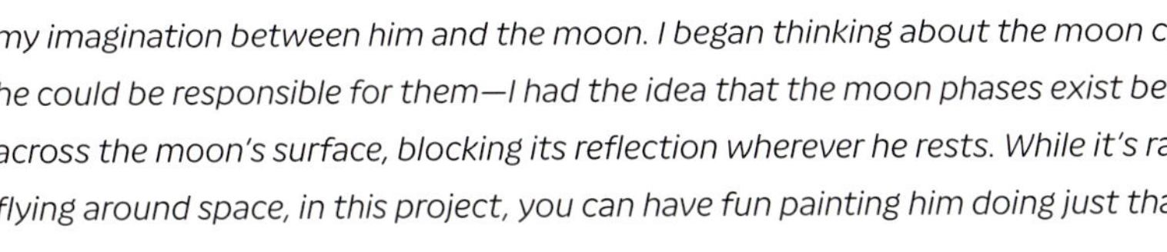

This project is based on one of my older artworks. The idea for my original piece came from my interest in aquariums and a beloved bristlenose catfish I had at the time. He was so beautiful, with an extremely solid black body covered in tiny white dots, resembling the night sky. I would often observe him on his favorite rock, which was smooth and rounded. The way his body molded around the curved rock, combined with his starry appearance, sparked a connection in my imagination between him and the moon. I began thinking about the moon cycles and how he could be responsible for them—I had the idea that the moon phases exist because he moves across the moon's surface, blocking its reflection wherever he rests. While it's rare to see Harold flying around space, in this project, you can have fun painting him doing just that!

Sketch

Draw Harold freehand or trace the sketch template on page 223.

Step 1

Since Harold's body and fins are simple shapes, you should have no trouble painting around them quickly and easily with a large brush. However, painting around his feelers might be a bit more challenging. Start by masking them, and also extend the masking slightly into the nose area so you can easily glide your brush over it when you begin the background. Next, fill in the eyes and the starfish. Lastly, mask neatly above your pencil lines on the fins and body scales. Don't forget to add some dots in the background that will later become stars.

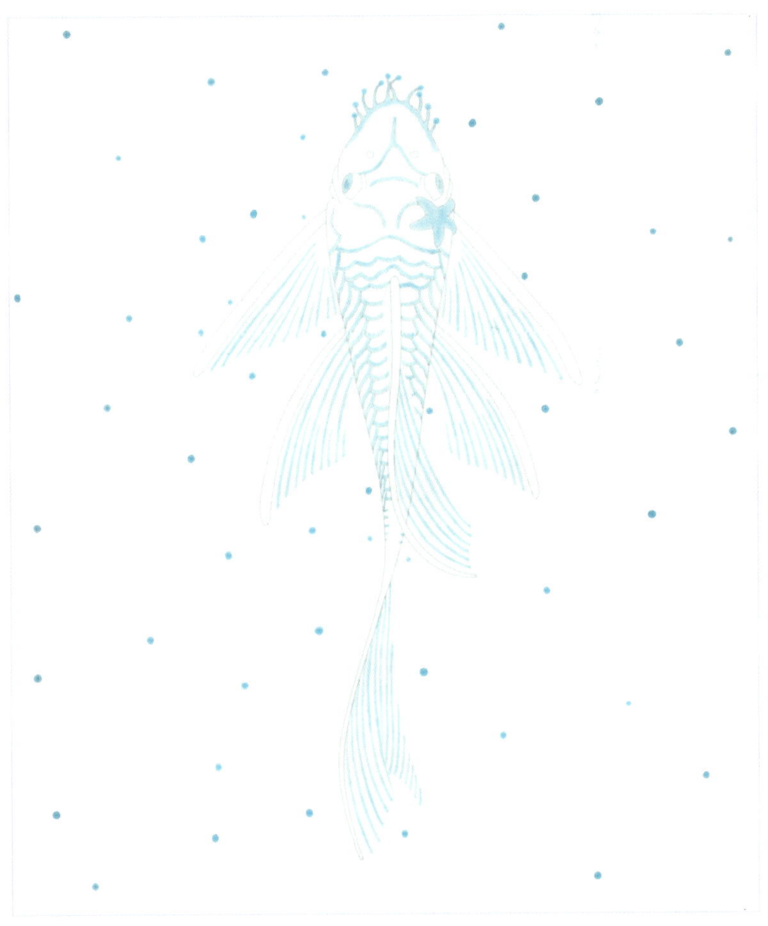

Step 2

As with Nebula Navigators (page 131), you will need to premix two colors, ensuring you have plenty of each:

> **Winsor Blue** – for the diagonal band of color in the background

> **French Ultramarine + Burnt Sienna** – for most of the deep space background

Use the wet-on-dry technique (page 12) to apply the first color in the middle of the background, creating a diagonal band of color. While the paint is still wet, use the second color to fill in the remaining background, allowing the two colors to naturally blend. While everything is still damp, use a small brush to dab the first color just beyond where the two colors meet. This will create small blooms of blue. Create as many as you feel are necessary.

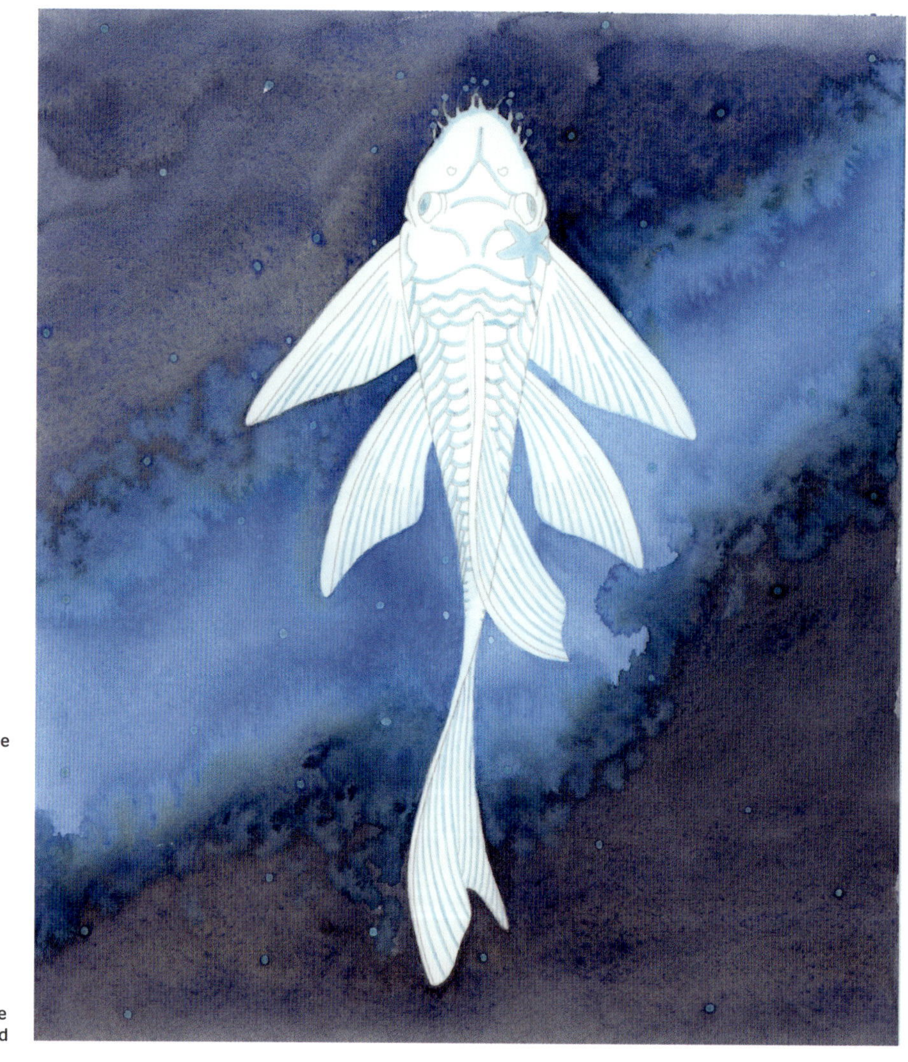

Step 3

Once everything has dried, use some diluted **Winsor Blue** to paint over Harold's fins and body, keeping the fins and the center of his body lighter than the rest.

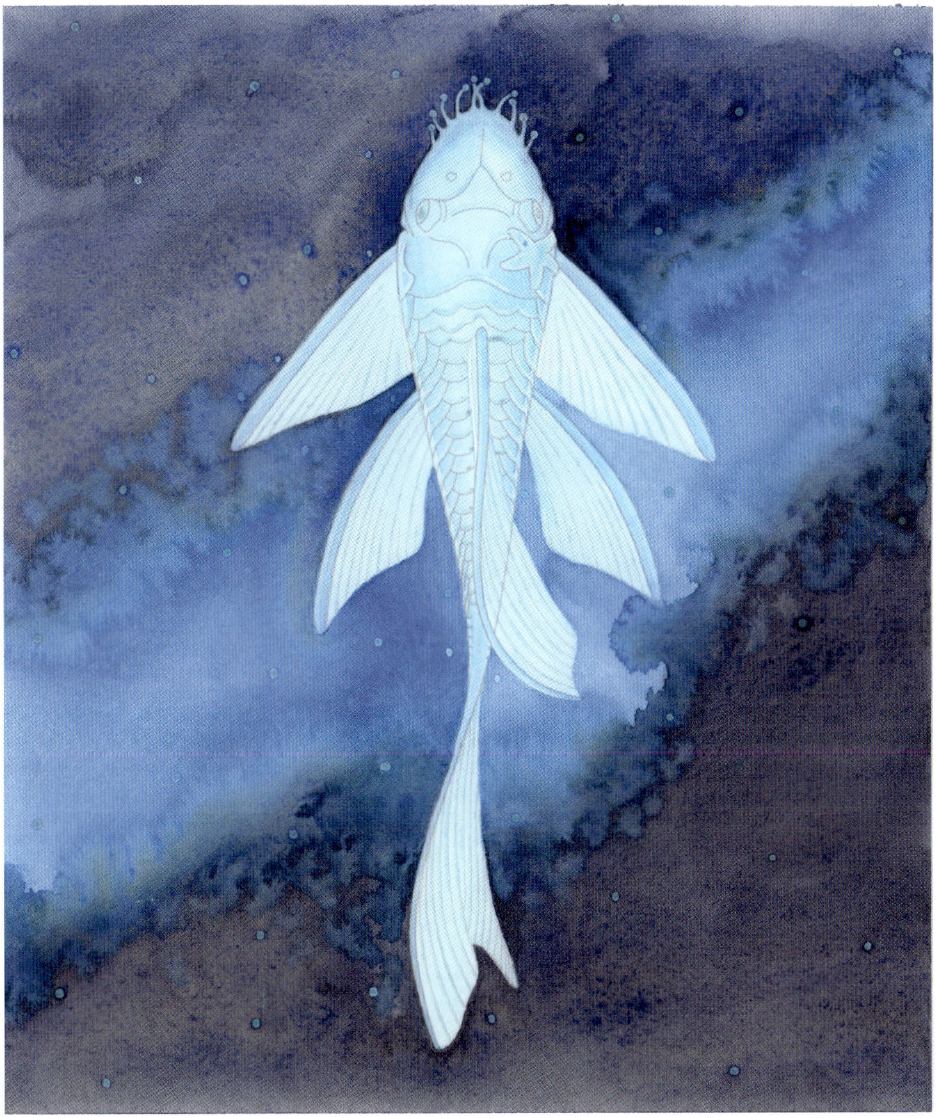

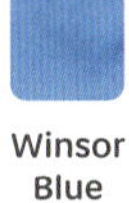

Winsor
Blue

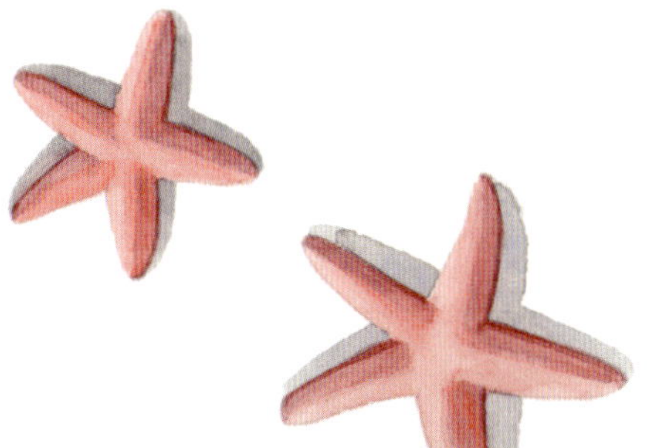

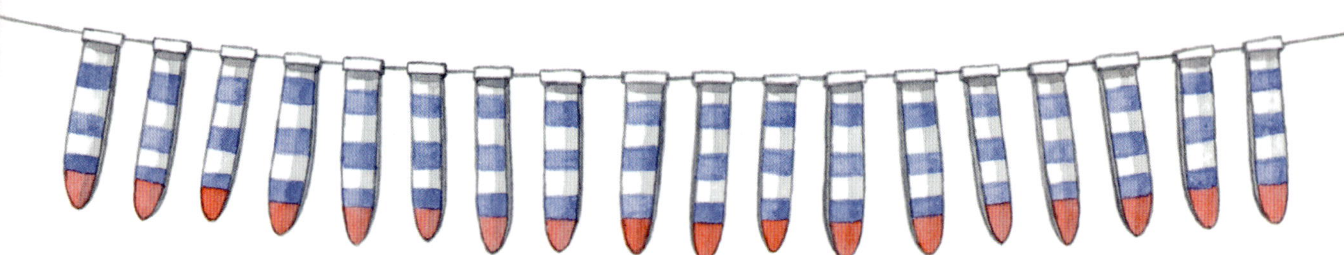

Step 4

Start by mixing the two colors from Step 2 together to create a shadow color for the fins and body. You should still have those two colors available on your palette. Darken further around the edges of Harold's body and where his fins attach. For any fins that are above the diagonal blue band, use more **Winsor Blue** in your mix. Once the paint has dried, remove all the masking fluid except for the stars in the background and the light orbs on the ends of Harold's feelers. Lastly, use some **Winsor Red** to paint the starfish.

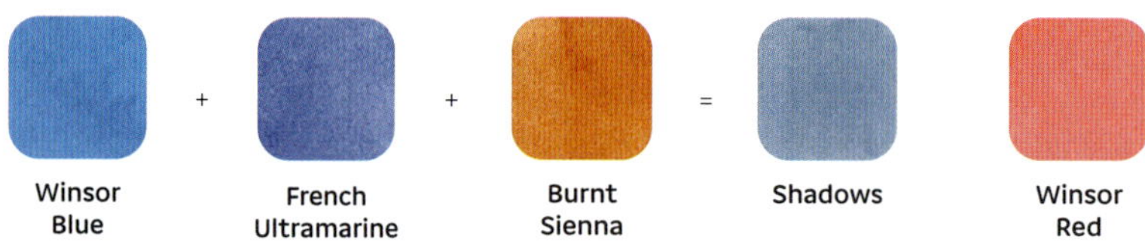

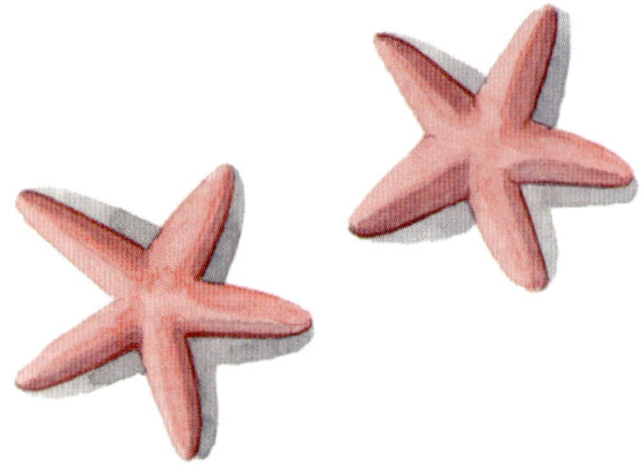

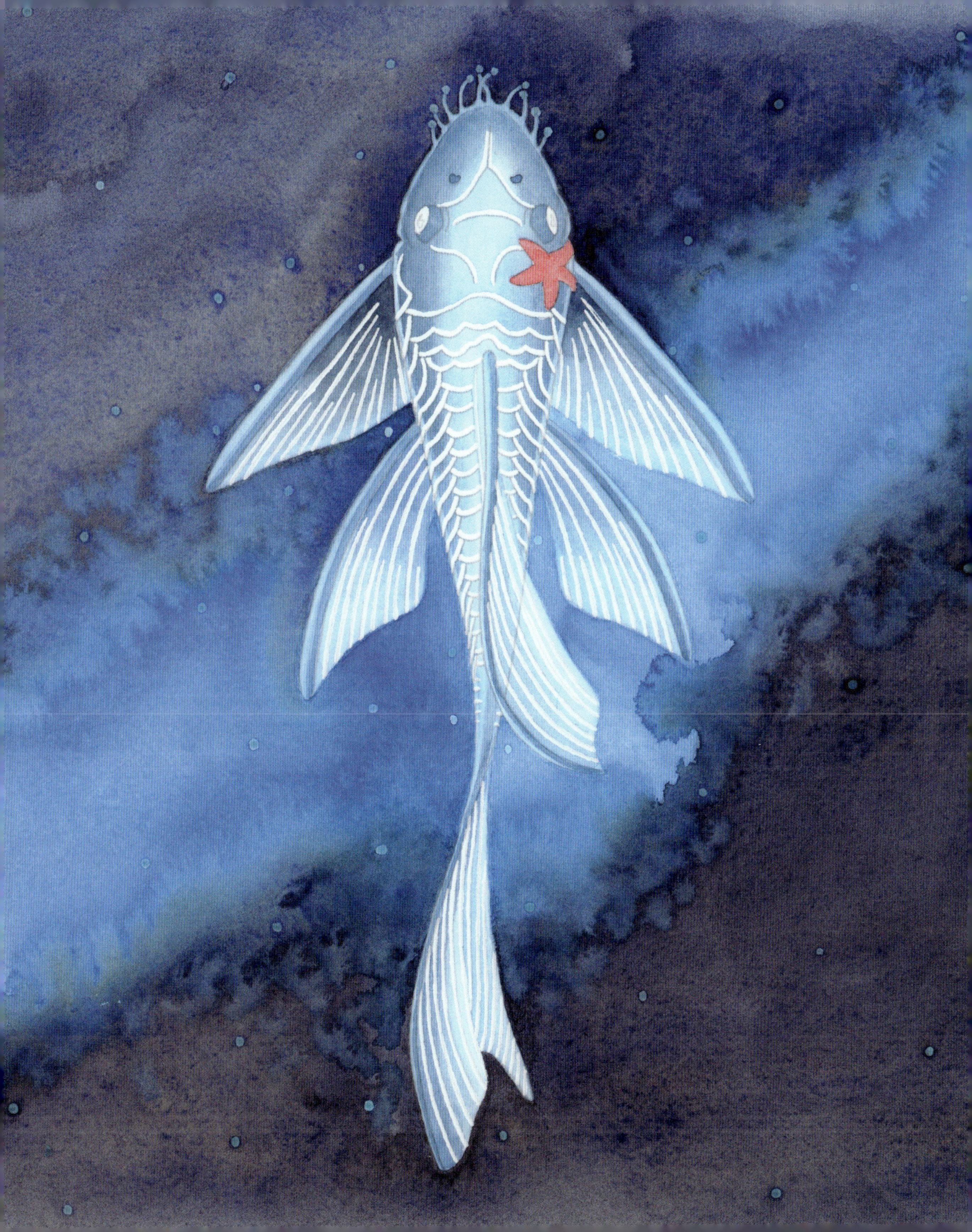

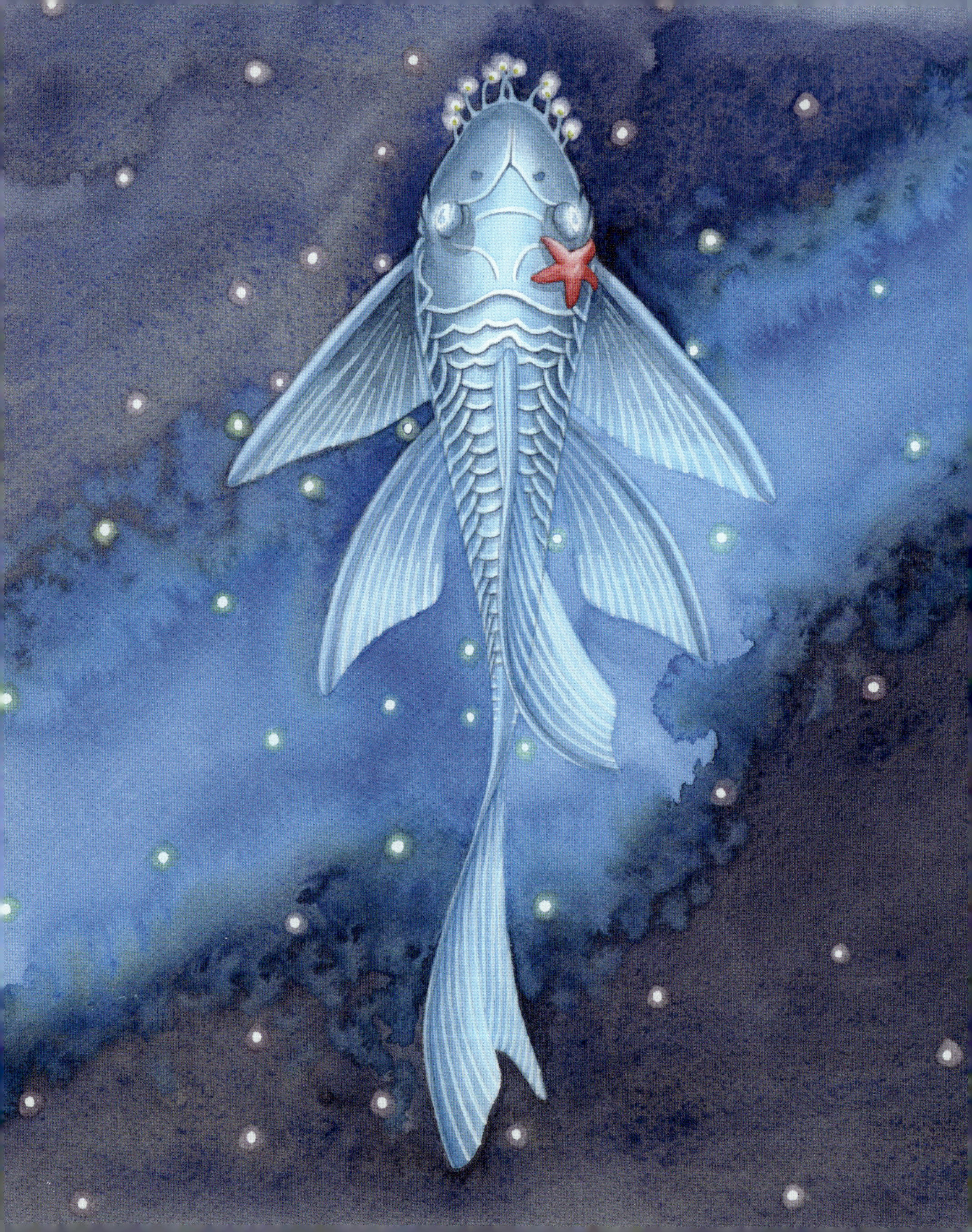

Step 5

Glaze the shadow color from Step 4 over the previously masked lines on the top fins where they meet the body. Do the same for all the other fins, but this time use **Winsor Blue**. Also, lightly glaze **Winsor Blue** on both sides of the body to add color to the blank areas that were masked. If you have any Winsor Blue left on your palette, mix it with a tiny amount of **Permanent Sap Green** and glaze it over the entire body and all the fins. Before everything dries, use a tissue to dab away some of the paint on the head and the first few layers of scales.

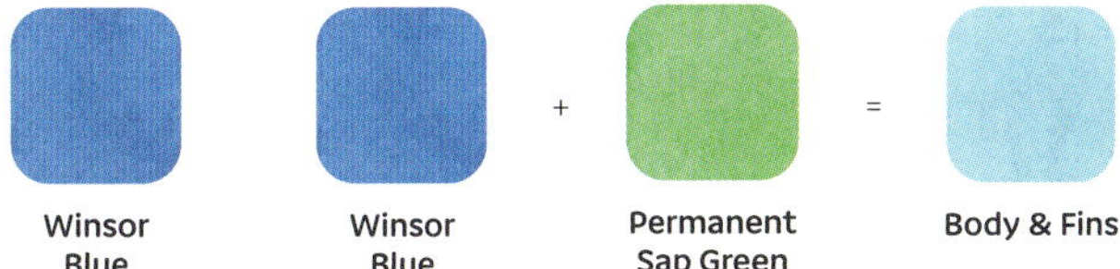

Now that everything is dry (and probably the colors on your palette are too), reactivate the shadow color from Step 4 on your palette with a small detail brush and use it to paint over your pencil lines on the scales. Take an old brush with clean water and lift some paint around each dot of masking fluid in the background, including Harold's eyes and the orbs on the ends of his feelers. Mix **Permanent Sap Green** with **Winsor Yellow** to lightly paint around all the stars above the diagonal blue band in the background. For the remaining stars, mix **Winsor Blue** with **Alizarin Crimson** to create a subtle purple.

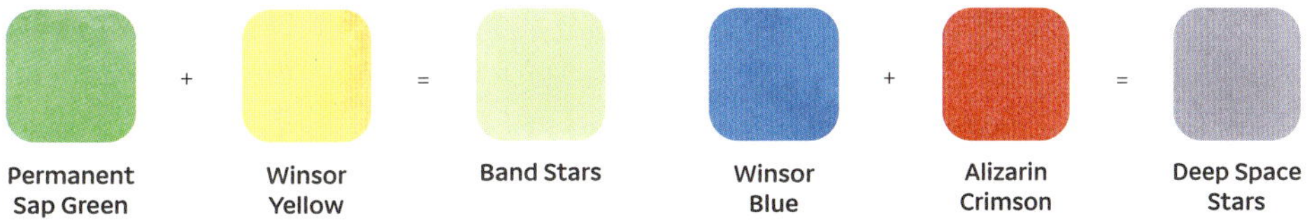

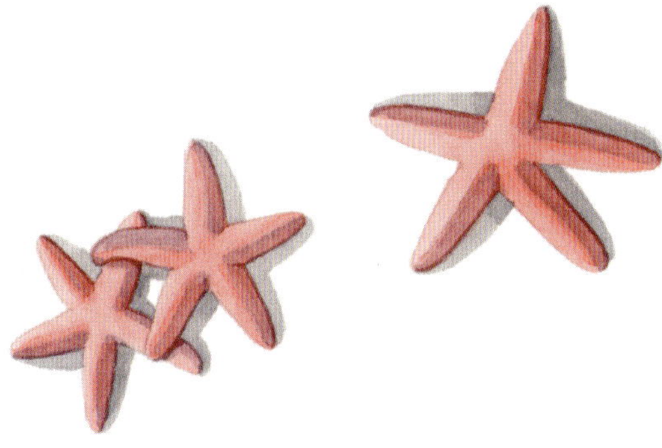

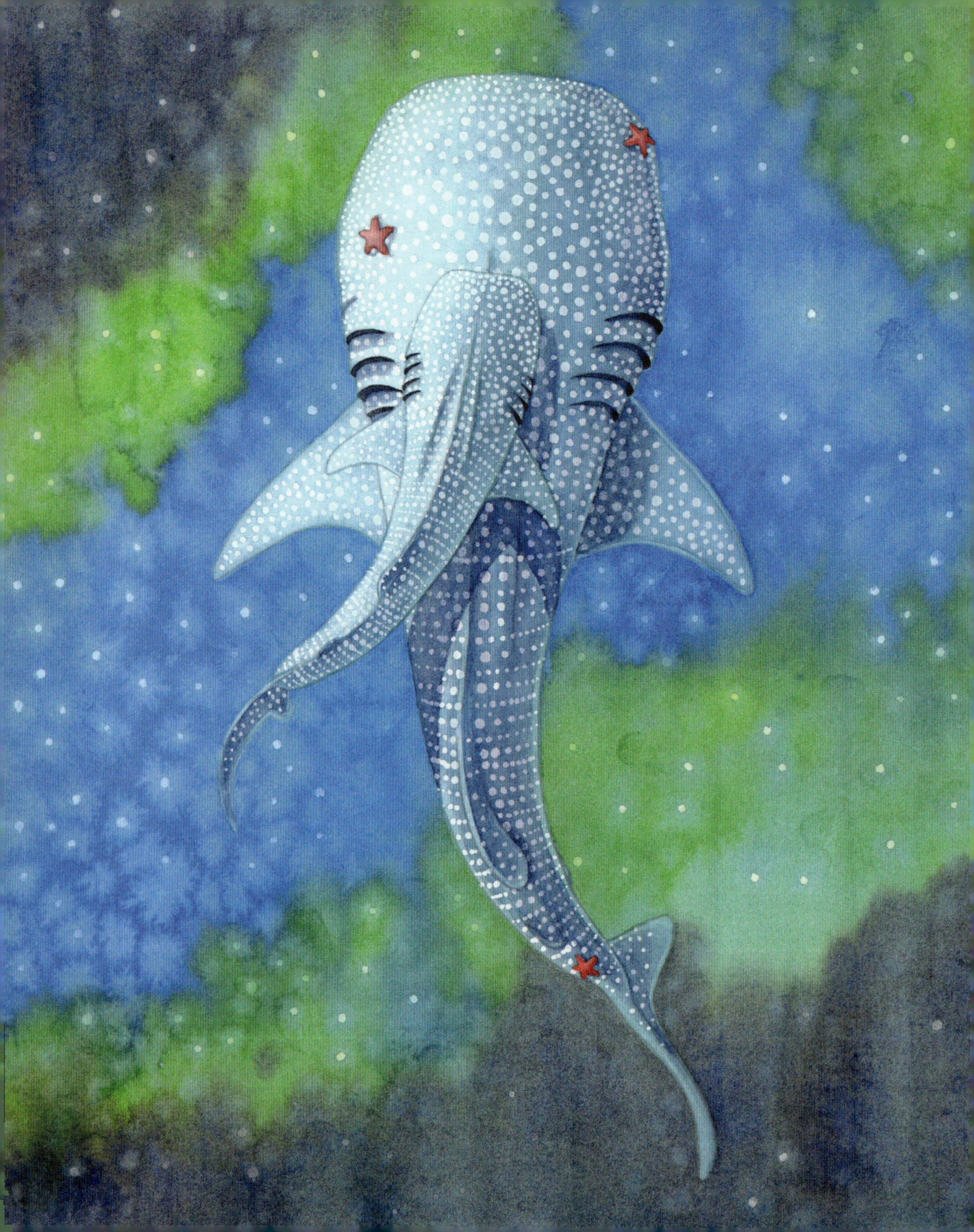

NURTURING STARLIT JOURNEY

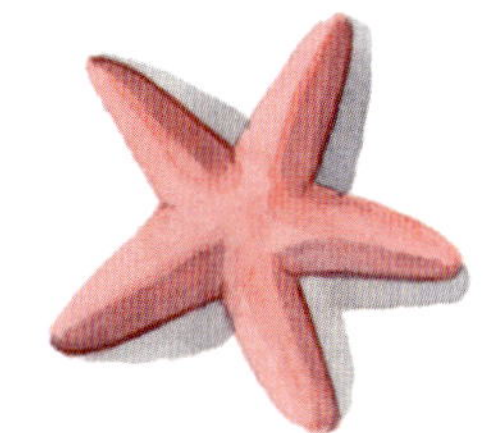

The cosmic whale shark is one of the largest creatures in the galaxy and among the gentlest and most nurturing. With shimmering, star-speckled bodies, these majestic beings glide silently through the galaxy's nebulae, their presence radiating calming energy. However, their rarity has become more pronounced in recent times, as they are targeted by dark forces that hunger for their immense life force. These predators drain the whale sharks' cosmic energy, causing their numbers to dwindle.

A baby whale shark is born only once every thousand years, making its appearance a rare event. The bond between mother and baby is strong, with the mother guiding her young through the stars. Seeing them together is considered a sign of hope and good fortune, with some spacefaring cultures even holding festivals to honor such sightings, believing these giants bring balance and peace to the cosmos.

Sketch

Draw the whale sharks freehand or trace the sketch template on page 225.

Step 1

Let's try something different for the masking fluid step on this project! Some of the mask will be applied now and some later after painting. Start by applying dots of masking fluid to the skin of the whale sharks. For the head, apply random dots in the center, gradually making them smaller as you move toward the edges. As you continue down the whale shark from the head, use varying dot sizes to create broken lines that emphasize the curved shape of the tail. Also, fill in the starfish as you go.

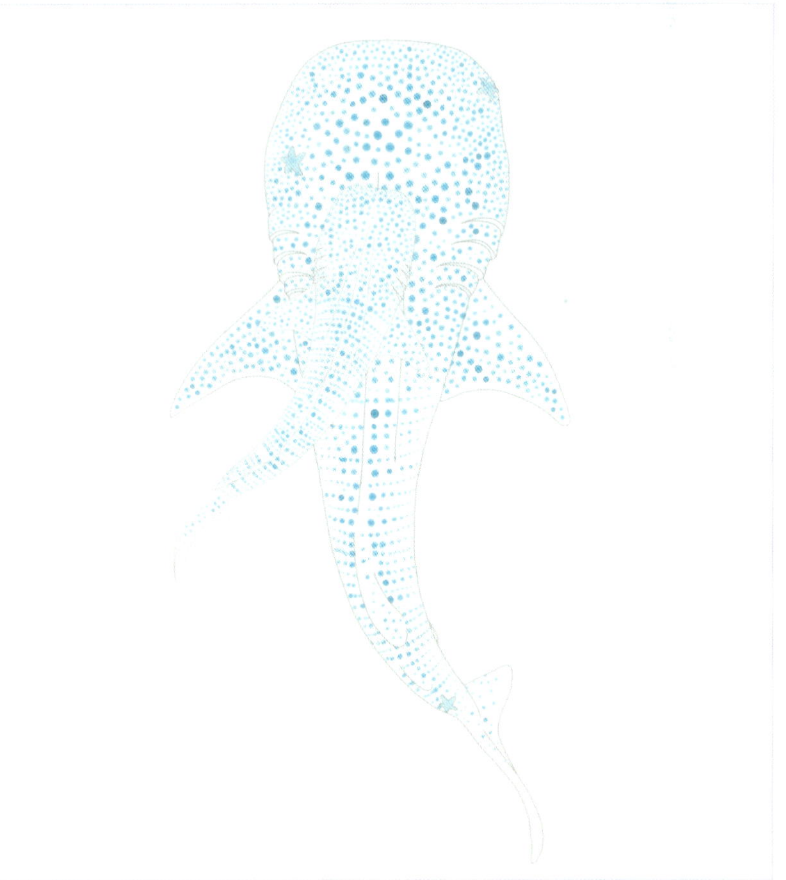

Step 2

You will be using masking fluid again in this step, but first, you'll need to paint the background colors. Prepare your palette with three mixtures:

Winsor Blue – for the diagonal blue band

Permanent Sap Green + **Winsor Yellow** – for the yellow-green background

French Ultramarine + **Burnt Sienna** – for the dark blue background

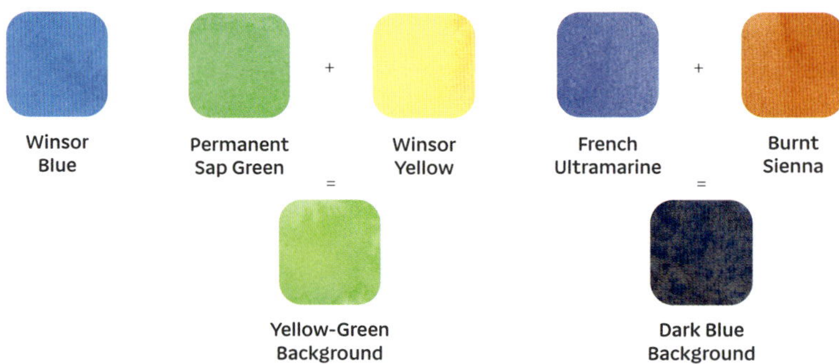

Using the wet-on-wet technique (page 12), first apply water to the entire background and allow it to absorb into the paper. Then, apply the first mixture to create a blue diagonal band of color in the middle. Next, use the second mixture to expand the width of the blue band with the yellow-green mix, allowing the two colors to blend together. Finally, while everything is still wet, add the third mixture to the remaining background areas, letting it blend into the green.

While the colors are still damp, use a small detail brush with clean water and evenly dab drops of water over the entire background. These mini blooms will later become stars. To further remove pigment from a few selected stars, use a tissue with a twisted end to absorb the color. You can be completely random with the stars you choose—this helps create variation and visual interest.

Once the background has fully dried, use masking fluid to put a dot inside any of the mini blooms you like. Try choosing some of the blooms that are still rich in color, especially in the yellow-green areas, as this will become more noticeable in future steps.

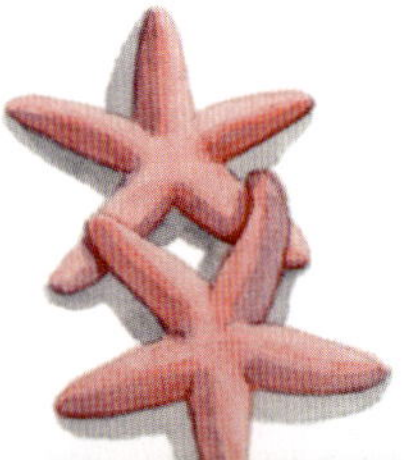

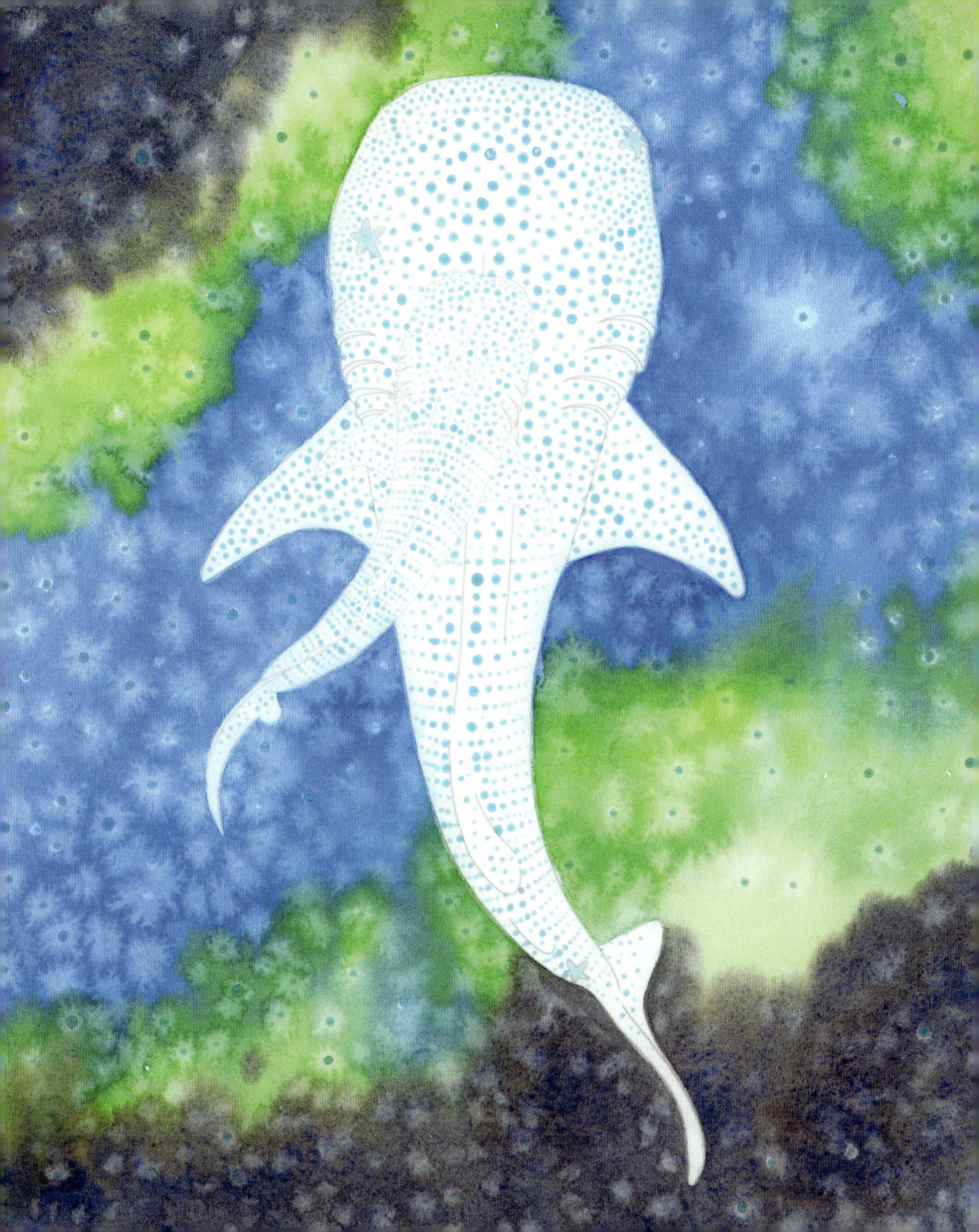

Step 3

Start by mixing **Winsor Blue** with **Permanent Sap Green**, gradually adding **French Ultramarine** to darken the color. Using the largest flat brush you have, glaze this color over the entire picture with vertical strokes, working your way across. If you prefer a smooth finish without streaks, a single pass with the brush will give the best results. However, if you'd like some subtle streaking to represent movement, lightly brush over the desired area a few times. While glazing, you're essentially reactivating the colors underneath, so avoid overworking any sections. Before the glaze dries, use a tissue to gently dab away some pigment from the left side of both whale sharks. Once everything is completely dry, remove the masking fluid to reveal the stars in the background. You'll notice that by applying masking fluid over some of the color, you've created subtle stars. Their brightness has been further enhanced by the glaze you just added.

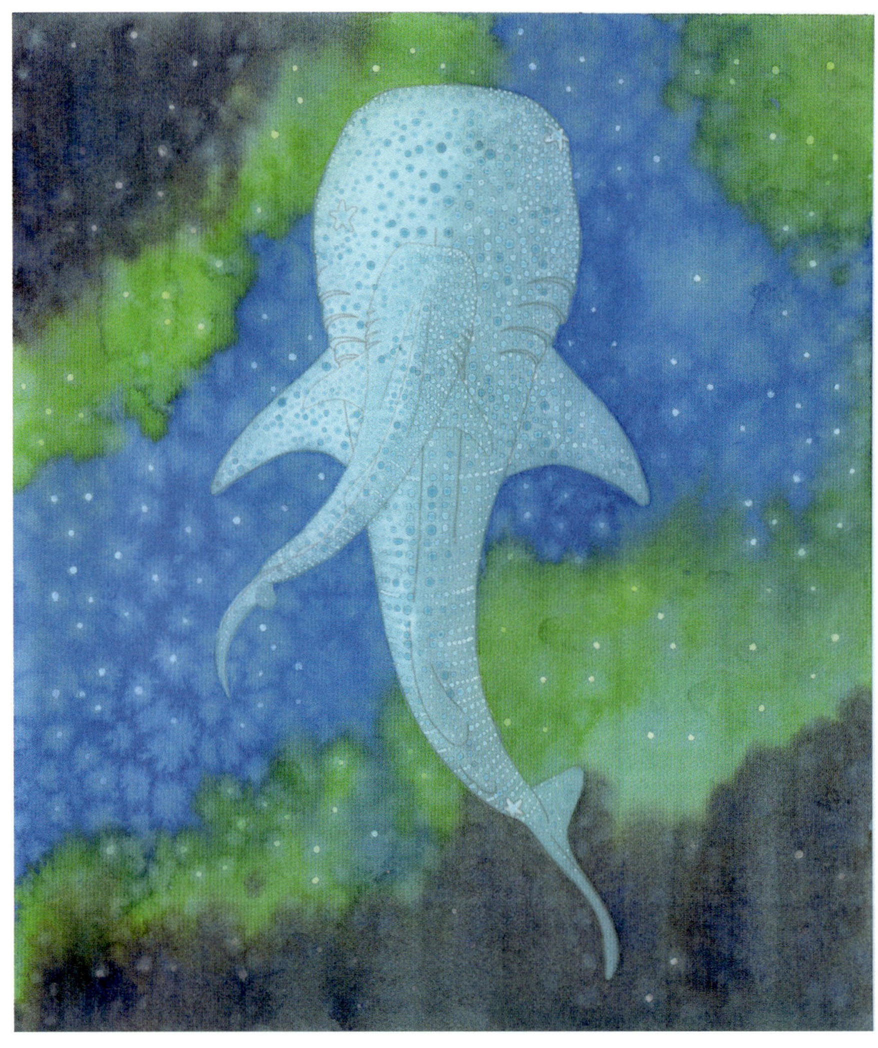

Winsor
Blue

+

Permanent
Sap Green

+

French
Ultramarine

=

Glaze

Step 4

Now that the background is complete, you can start focusing on creating the form of the whale sharks. To do this, you'll need to mix a shadow color. A blend of **French Ultramarine** with a hint of **Burnt Sienna** works well to tie the whale sharks to the background. Glaze a light value of this color over the right-hand side of both whale sharks, concentrating on areas like behind the dorsal fins, tails, and around the gills. Building these areas up with multiple layers will give you better results than applying a heavily pigmented mix all at once. Once the general shadows are dry, reactivate the **French Ultramarine** and **Burnt Sienna** mixture from Step 2, adding more pigment if necessary, to paint and define the gills. Then, return to your diluted shadow color to work on the shadows cast from the baby whale shark onto its mother and the shadows cast from the mother's body onto her pectoral fin. Finally, add small shadows under each starfish.

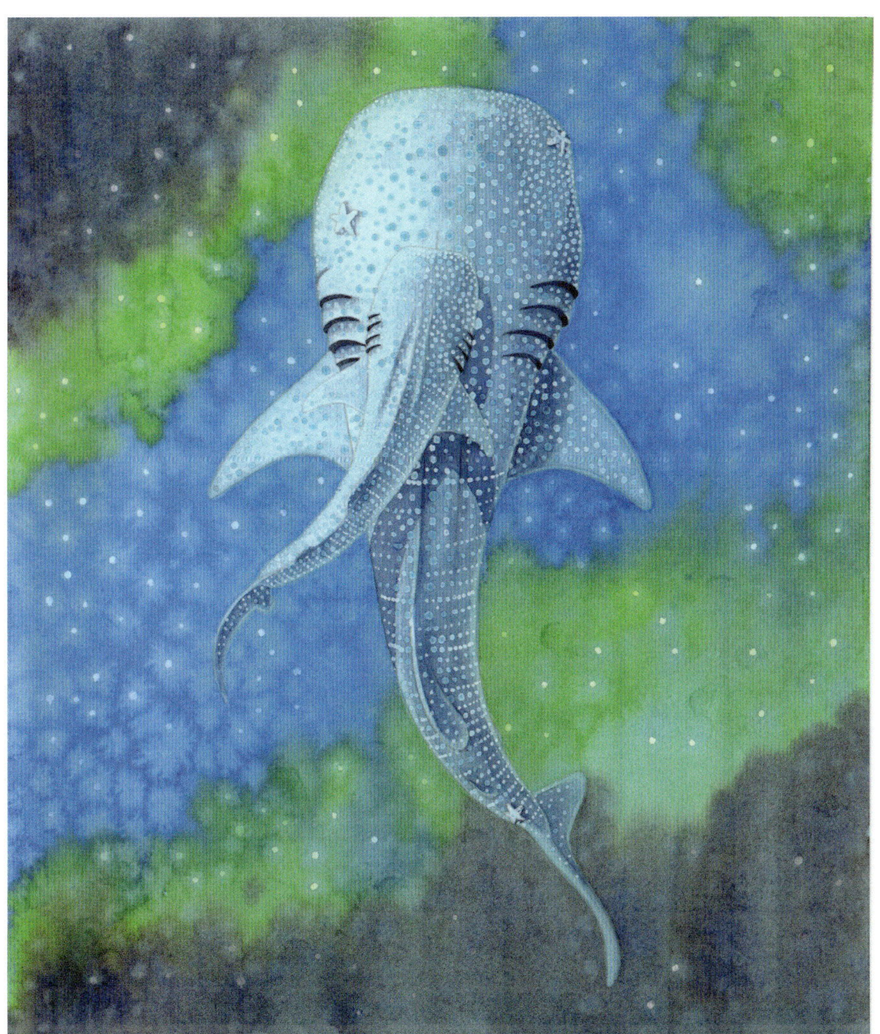

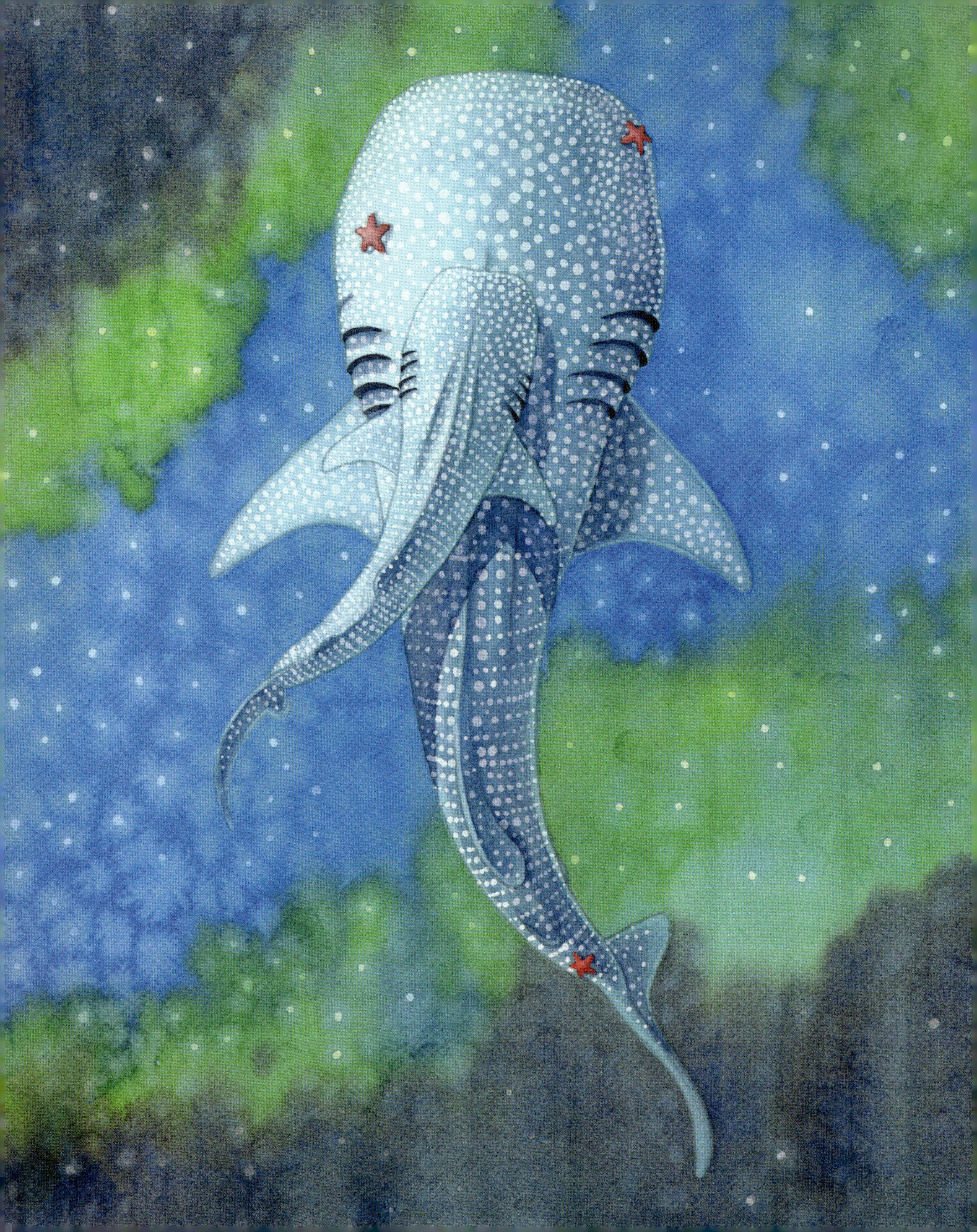

Step 5

This is the step you've been waiting for—the big reveal! Remove all the masking fluid from the whale sharks and the starfish. You should notice how much more contrast and brightness the whale sharks have now. To enhance this further and create a more three-dimensional look, dilute some of your diluted shadow color from Step 4 and lightly glaze it over any areas where you previously painted shadows. What you are doing is settling pigment into the blank areas that the masking fluid was covering. Be careful not to overwork this! One gentle pass with the right paint consistency will be enough. This single glaze should dramatically transform the appearance of the whale sharks, giving them a striking and eye-catching look.

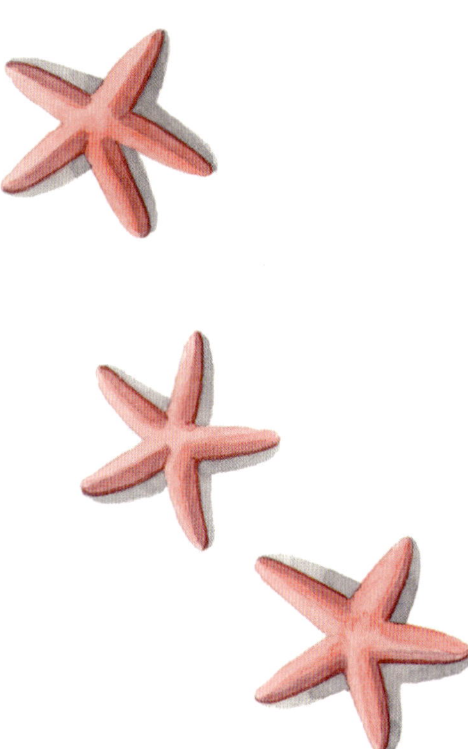

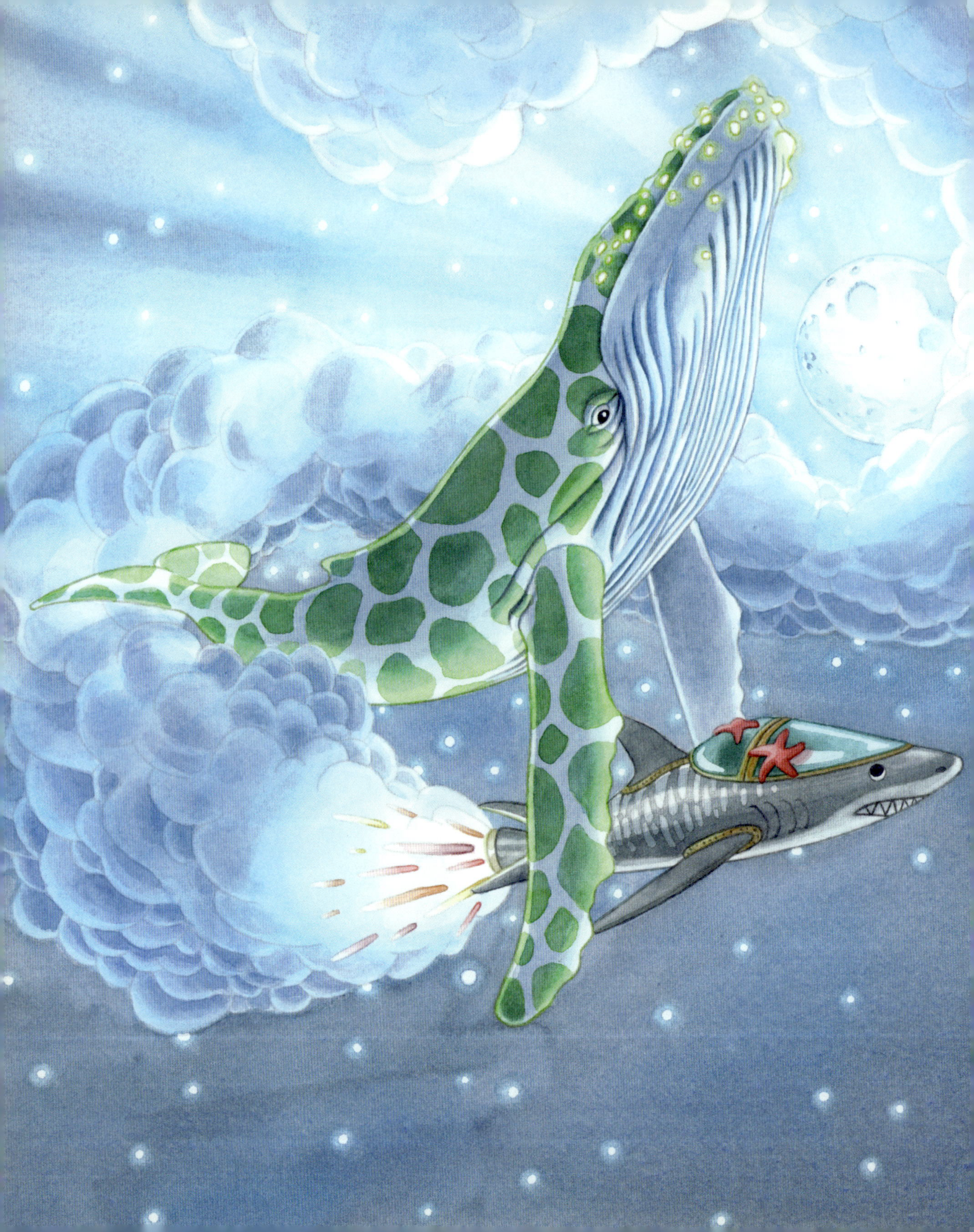

ASTRAL WHALESHIP

The celestial whale glides gracefully through the vastness of space, a rare sight that captivates all who are fortunate enough to witness it. Its beauty is unmatched by anything in the galaxy, with its unique bold green pattern and embedded glowing stars on its body. These majestic creatures travel in solitude, collecting wisdom and knowledge from the countless worlds they visit. Once every decade, they gather in a designated location, forming a breathtaking spectacle as they unite to exchange tales of their extraordinary journeys across the galaxy, sharing the lessons learned from the wonders and challenges encountered along the way.

Sketch

Draw the scene freehand or trace the sketch template on page 227.

Step 1

This project only requires you to use masking fluid for small details. Start by masking the bumps on the nose of the humpback whale and its eye. Move down to the spaceship, filling in the rear sparks, the back pattern, the reflection lines on the cockpit window, and the two starfish. You may need to let these areas dry before adding some masking fluid dots to the background.

Step 4

In this step, you'll be filling in some areas with new colors, followed by three challenging glazes. Start by mixing these four colors:

French Ultramarine + **Burnt Sienna** + **Winsor Blue** – for the spaceship

French Ultramarine + **Permanent Sap Green** – for the cockpit window

Burnt Sienna + **Yellow Ochre** + a hint of **Permanent Sap Green** – for all the brass trim on the spaceship

Winsor Red – for the starfish

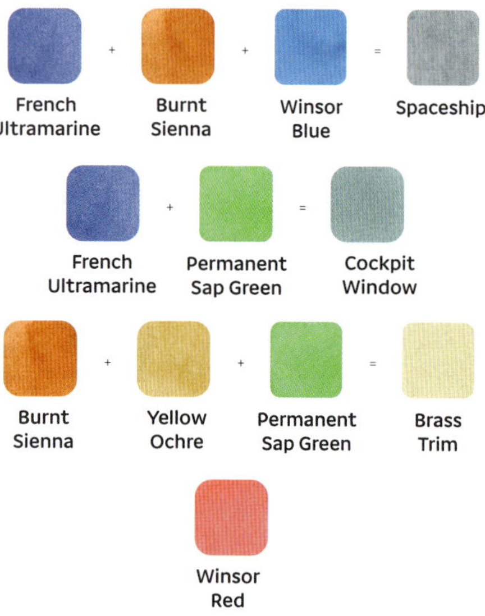

It's now time to apply the glazes. First, mix **Permanent Sap Green** with **Winsor Yellow** to glaze misshapen dots on the outer skin of the whale. You can use a pencil to lightly sketch these shapes if you're not confident painting them freehand; use the reference image for guidance. As mentioned before, you'll get better results with a less concentrated mixture, as the idea is to allow the color underneath to show through.

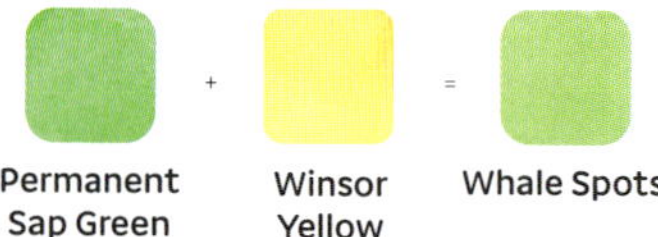

Now mix some **French Ultramarine** and **Burnt Sienna** together. Glaze this on the lower half of the background using the wet-on-wet technique (page 12), which is still possible on areas you've previously painted. This method is often a good choice for areas that require more time and for achieving an even finish. Use the same color to darken the background between the light rays, fading out toward the moon.

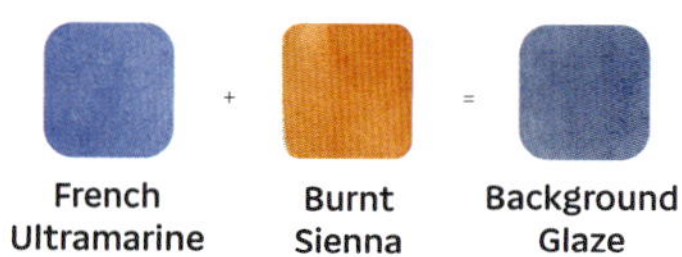

Lastly, create a diluted **Winsor Blue** glaze to apply over all the shaded areas on the smoke cloud, making sure to paint in a shadow cast by the whale that rolls over the cloud. Once everything has dried, you can remove the masking fluid from the spaceship.

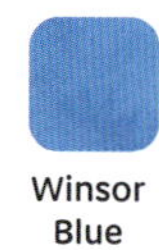

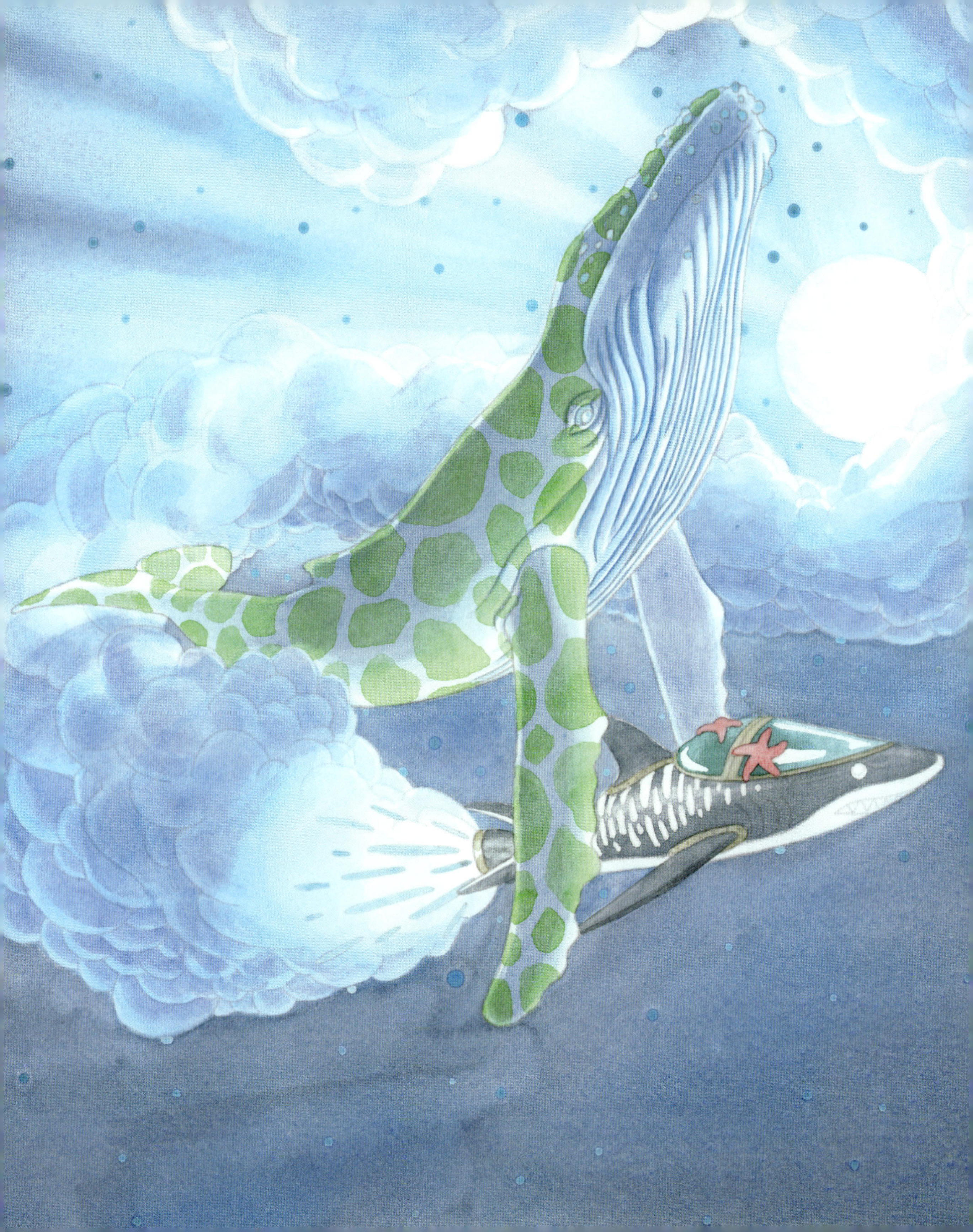

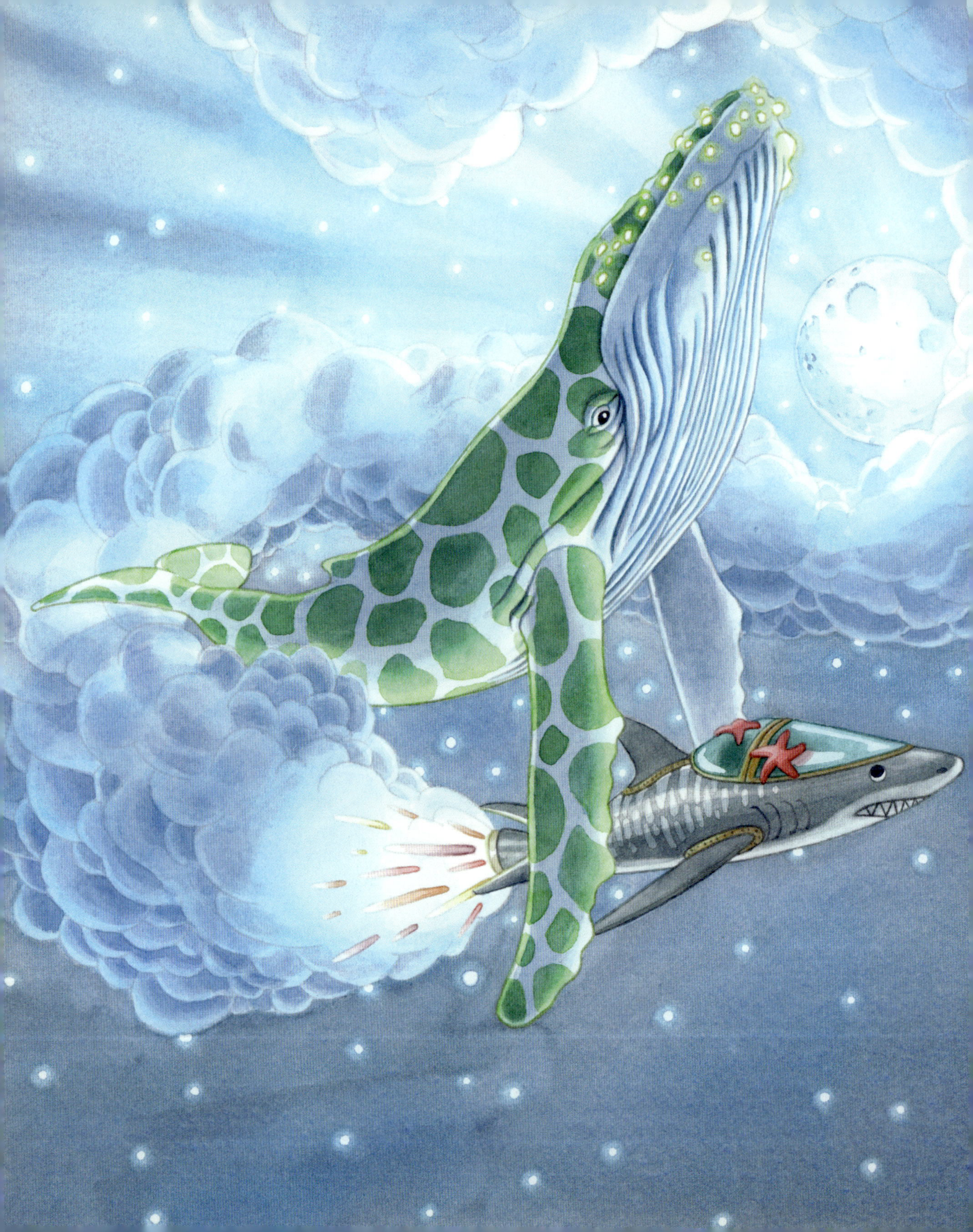

Step 5

As in previous projects, this step focuses on enhancing the shadowed areas with a series of additional layers. You can achieve this by using the colors you already have on your palette. However, to darken the green on the whale spots, you will need to mix **French Ultramarine** and **Permanent Sap Green** with a small amount of **Winsor Yellow**. Similar to the Puffed-Up Adventurer (page 27), use the shaded areas you previously painted as your guide for where to apply the dark green. For areas like the tail and the underside, where the misshapen dots are both shaded and illuminated, paint a gradual transition across the shape without covering any highlighted areas. Use the reference image to help you visualize this.

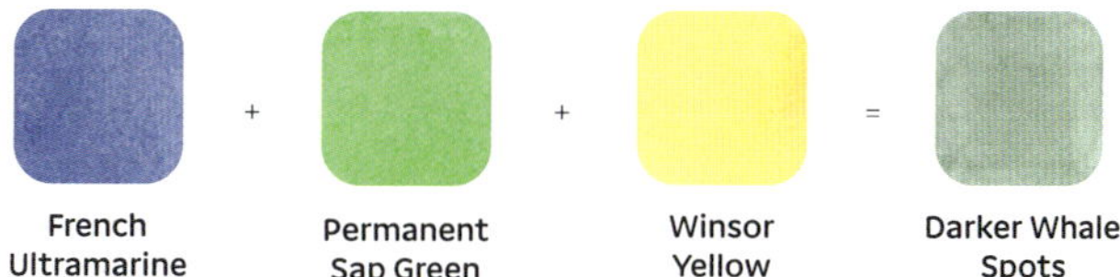

French Ultramarine + Permanent Sap Green + Winsor Yellow = Darker Whale Spots

Now is a good time to use a concentrated mix of **French Ultramarine** and **Burnt Sienna** for painting the eye and the deepest recesses around it. You can also use this color to define the details on the spaceship. Dilute the same color to paint the crevices on the moon. Wait for it to dry, and then glaze over it with some faint **Winsor Blue**. Now that your picture has more depth, you can create the glowing stars. Use the lifting technique (page 13) to soften the edges around each dot of masking fluid, including those on the nose of the whale. Mix some diluted **Winsor Blue** for the stars in the background and diluted **Winsor Yellow** for the stars on the whale. You can now remove the masking fluid from all the stars and the sparks from the back of the spaceship. To paint the sparks, use **Alizarin Crimson**, **Winsor Yellow**, and a combination of both to create an orange.

French Ultramarine + Burnt Sienna = Darkest Details

Winsor Blue

Winsor Yellow

Alizarin Crimson + Winsor Yellow = Sparks

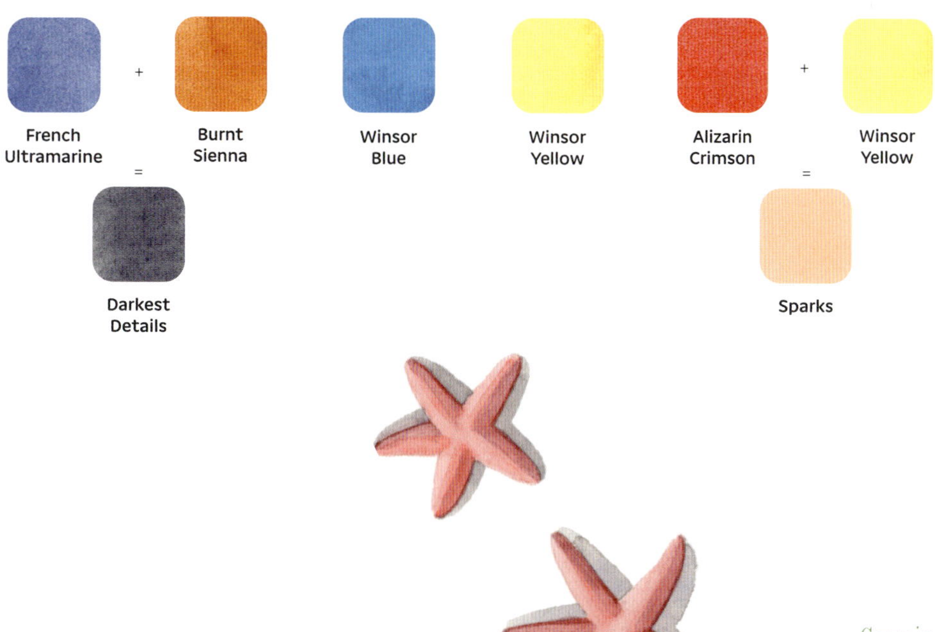

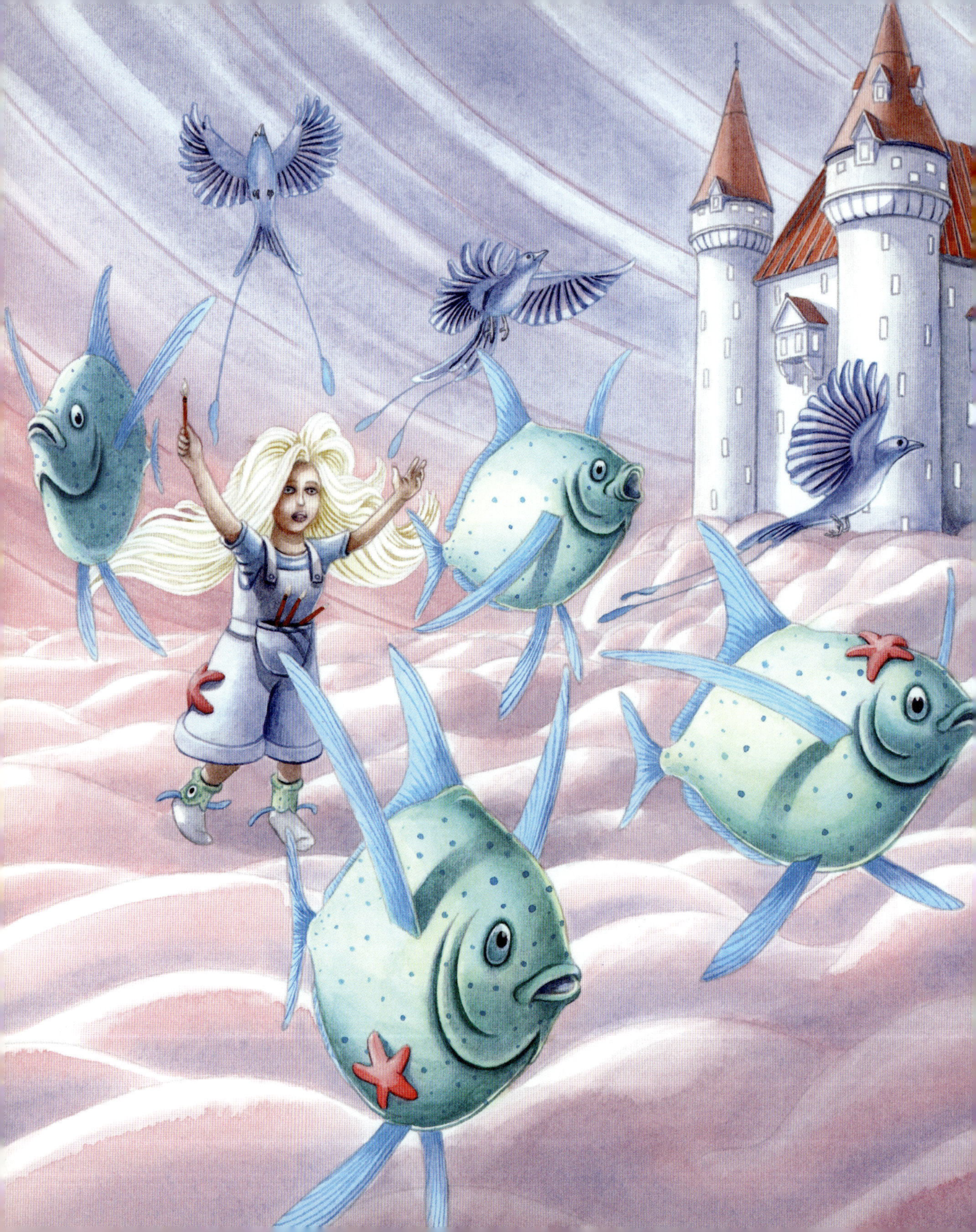

Floating Dreamscapes

Many of my artworks are inspired by my travels and all the incredible things I've seen. I'm very grateful to have experienced so many amazing places around the world, and I look forward to discovering even more in the future. When you think about it, it's quite remarkable how you can board a flight, soaring through the air above the clouds, to reach a foreign location previously unknown to you. When you strip it back, this experience is incredibly inspiring and almost dreamlike. I believe it's important to reflect on this, regardless of how many times you've done it before or how old you get.

In this chapter, you will explore those dreamlike qualities of travel and creatively expand upon them, focusing on painting scenes that exist above the clouds using a dominant color approach. By emphasizing color dominance, you will create a unique atmosphere and mood that transport viewers to that surreal environment, inviting them to experience the beauty and magic of flight and exploration.

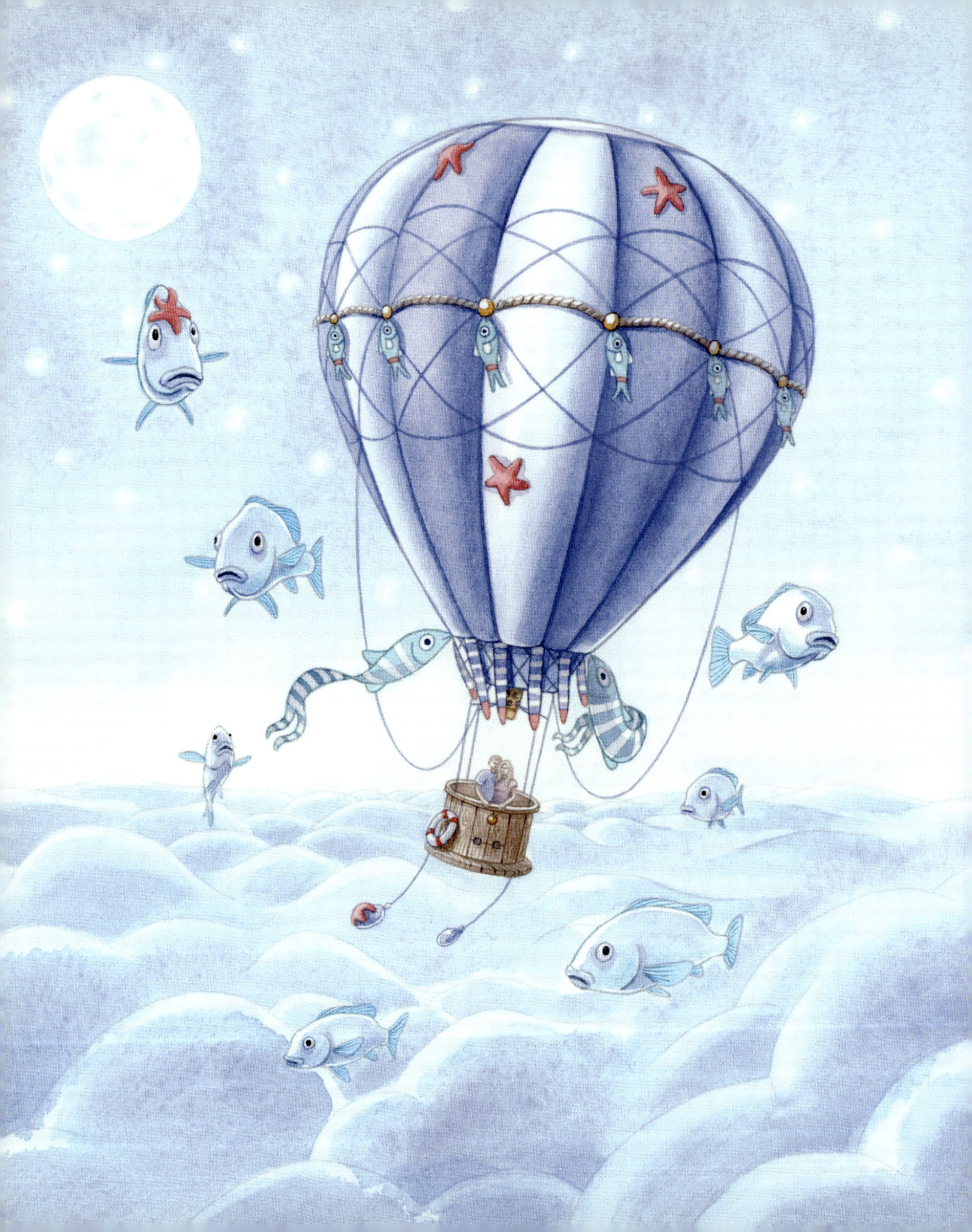

BALLOONING FISH PARADE

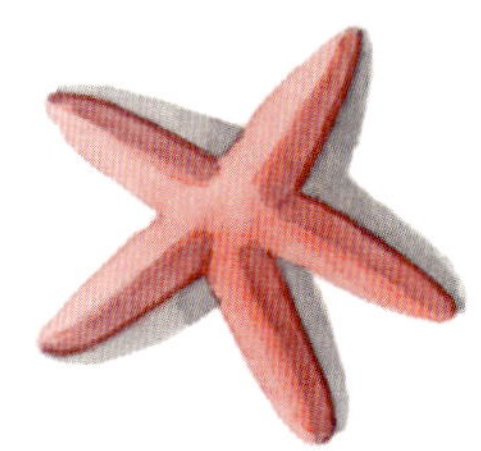

Having a dominant color in your painting is a powerful tool, as it promotes harmony and consistency, directs the viewer's attention, and sets a particular emotional tone. This approach streamlines the creative process, simplifies blending and layering techniques, and emphasizes focal points. Furthermore, it allows for impactful contrasts with accent colors, encouraging experimentation with various values and techniques within that color scheme. Ultimately, a dominant color enhances visual appeal and atmosphere. Using this approach, you will paint a simple hot-air ballon scene filled with fun and interesting nautical elements.

Sketch

Draw the scene freehand or trace the sketch template on page 229.

Step 1

As you've done before, use masking fluid to fill in any small areas that will make painting around them easier later. Also, add some dots in the sky. Use the reference image as your guide.

Step 2

Mix **French Ultramarine** with **Winsor Blue** and plenty of water on your palette. With a clean brush, apply water to the entire sky area. While it's still wet, start painting the color from the top and gradually fade it out toward the horizon line. Once the paint has dried, use an old brush and some water to lift the pigment around each masking fluid dot. Alternatively, you could lift the paint faster with a dry brush or tissue before the background dries; however, this option provides less control.

Now, apply some clean water to all of the clouds and proceed to paint them with the blue on your palette. Paint the color just below your sketch lines—this will create highlights on the cloud peaks. As your paper is damp, the paint may start to flow into the highlights. Simply remove this with a clean brush or tissue. The idea is to create a gradual transition within the clouds to give a smooth and soft appearance.

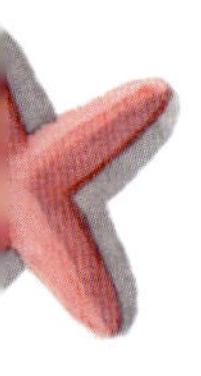

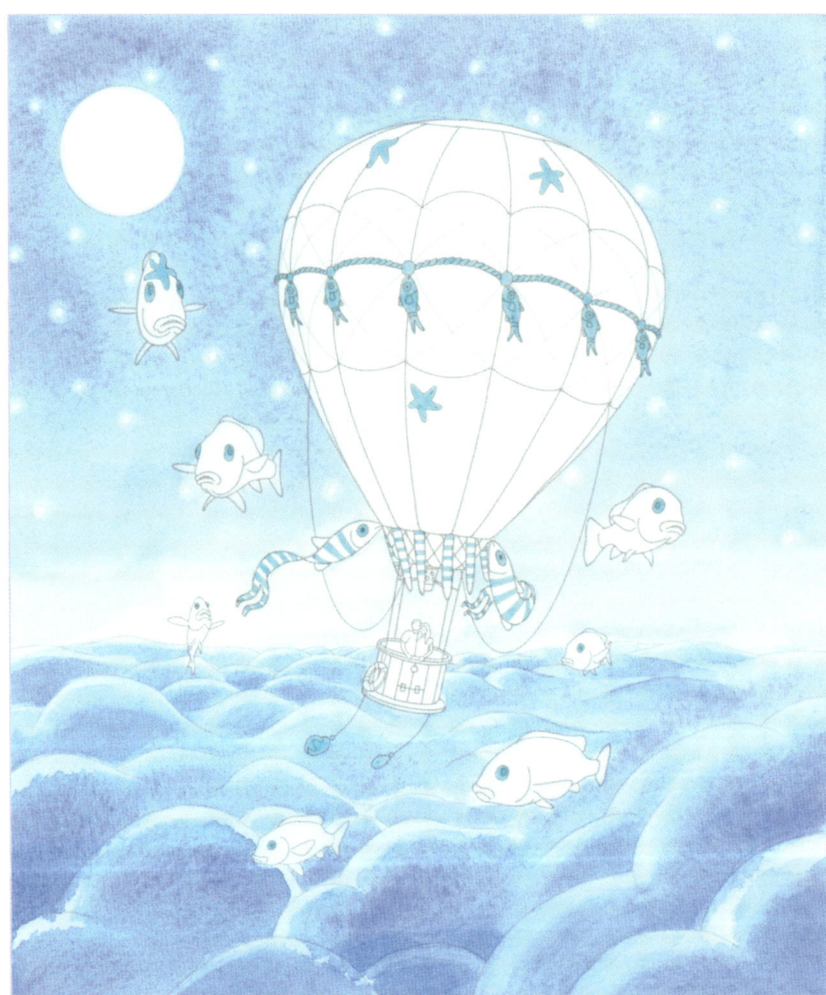

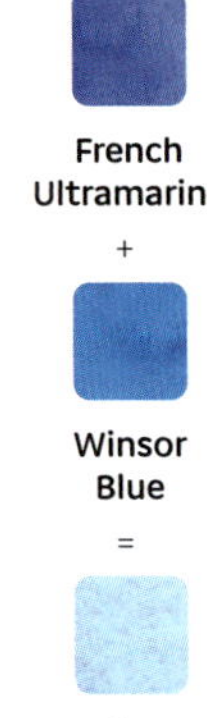

French Ultramarine

+

Winsor Blue

=

Sky

Step 3

Continue using the blue mixture from Step 2 on your palette to paint the shadows on the hot-air balloon. Loosely base your shadows around the moonlight in the sky. Start by applying shadows between each segment of the balloon, and once that has dried, glaze a larger shadow to cover one entire side. Next, add shadows to all of the fish, making sure to leave small highlights (negative space) along their edges. Use the reference image as a guide to help you with this detail.

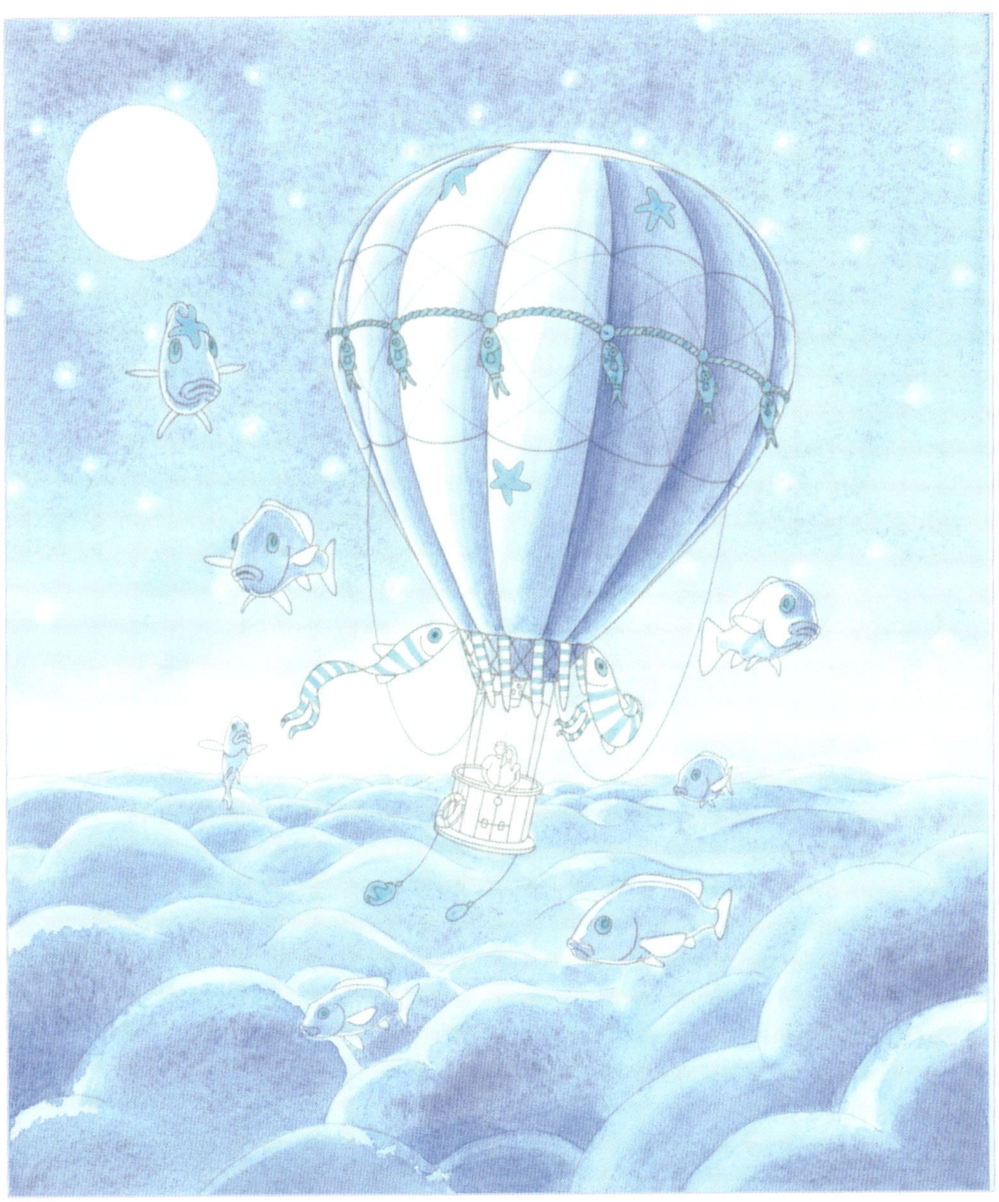

Step 4

The blue mixture on your palette may be running low at this stage, so mix a more concentrated combination of **French Ultramarine** and **Winsor Blue**. Use this color to further darken the area between each segment on the balloon and the ribbons. Once this has dried, mix **French Ultramarine** with a hint of **Burnt Sienna** to glaze every second balloon segment, creating a blue-and-white pattern.

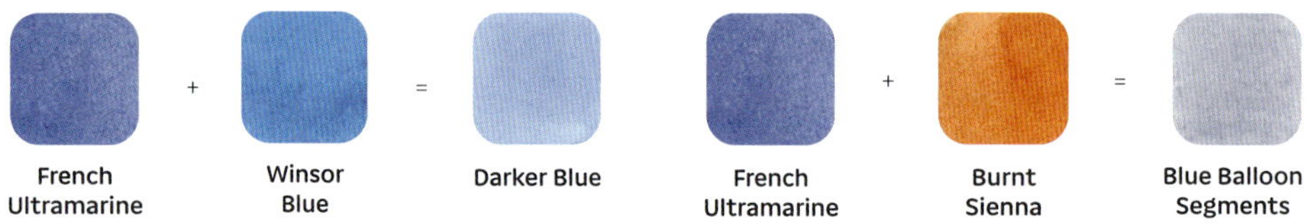

You can now paint the following colors:

Winsor Blue – for the fish fins

Winsor Red – for the tips of the ribbons and the stripes on the lifesaver float

Winsor Blue + **Permanent Sap Green** – for the fish flags

Alizarin Crimson + **Permanent Sap Green** – for the wooden basket

French Ultramarine and **Alizarin Crimson** on their own – for the T-shirts on the characters in the balloon

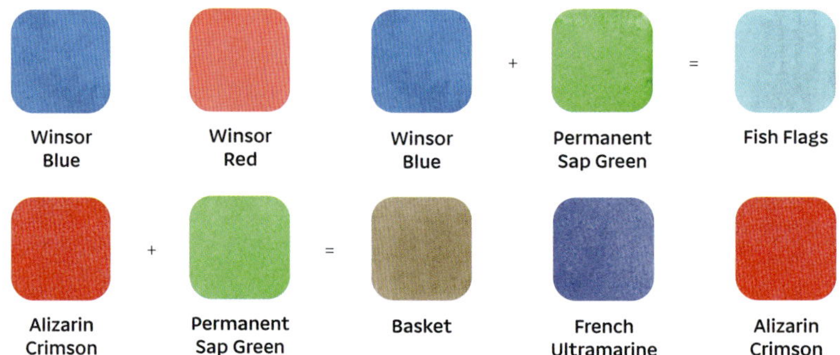

Once all the paint has dried, remove the masking fluid from the entire picture.

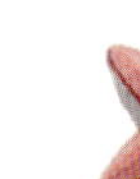

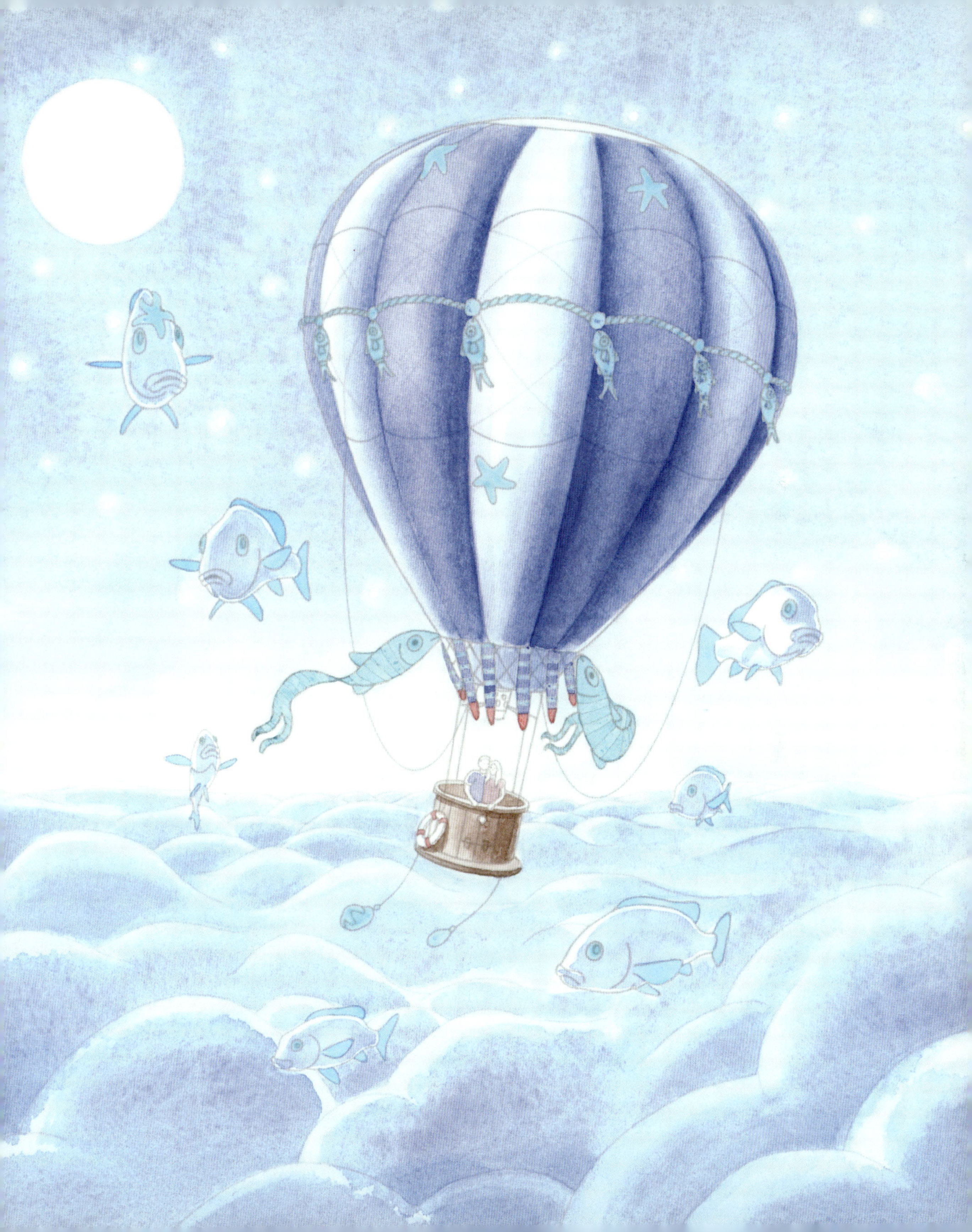

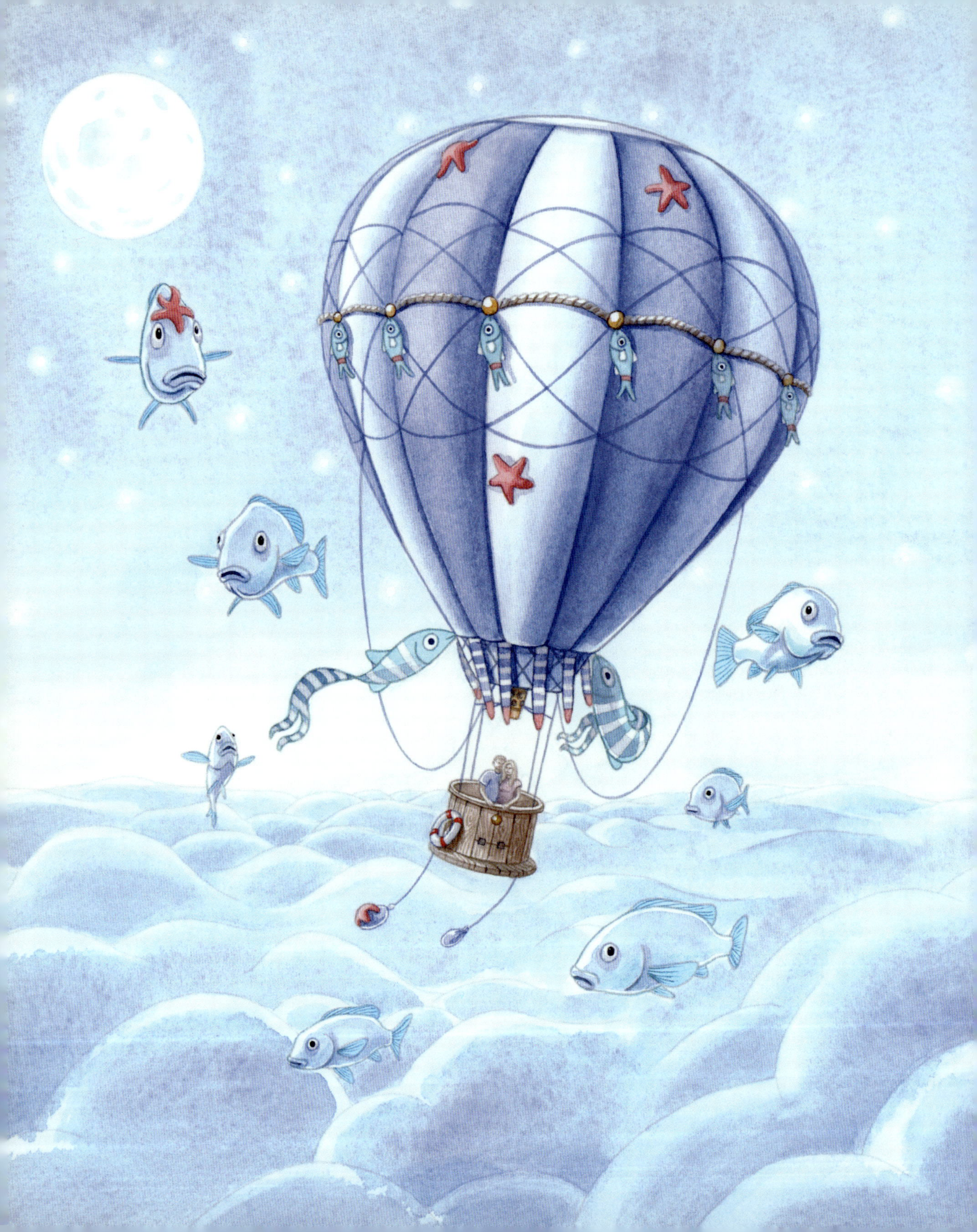

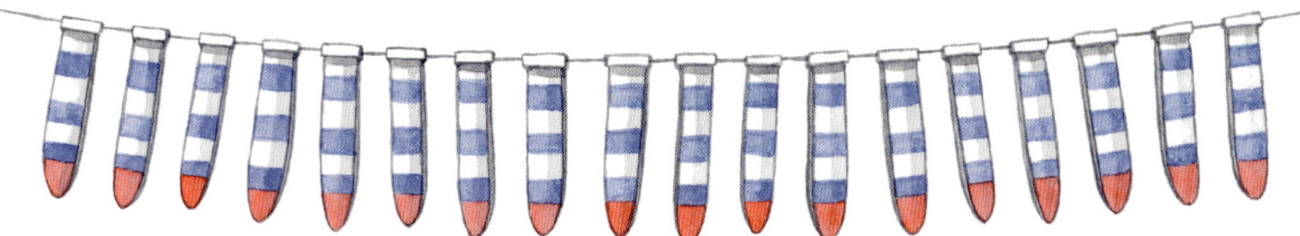

Step 5

This final step involves painting over your pencil lines with color. Since the focus is on creating a picture dominated by one color, reactivating the blues already on your palette will be helpful for outlining the details on the balloon and fish. Use varying ratios of **French Ultramarine** and **Burnt Sienna**. Add a bit more pigment to the darker blue mixture from Step 4 for the vibrant lines, like the crisscross pattern on the balloon. For the details on the fish fins and flags, mix **Winsor Blue** with **Burnt Sienna**. The starfish and tail stripes on the mini fish ribbons can be painted with **Winsor Red**. To create shadows for these areas, add some **French Ultramarine** into the **Winsor Red**. For any brass or gold areas, mix **Raw Sienna** with a little **Burnt Sienna** and **Permanent Sap Green**. It's always fun to bring the fish to life by painting in their eyes at the end, using a concentrated mixture of **French Ultramarine** and **Burnt Sienna**.

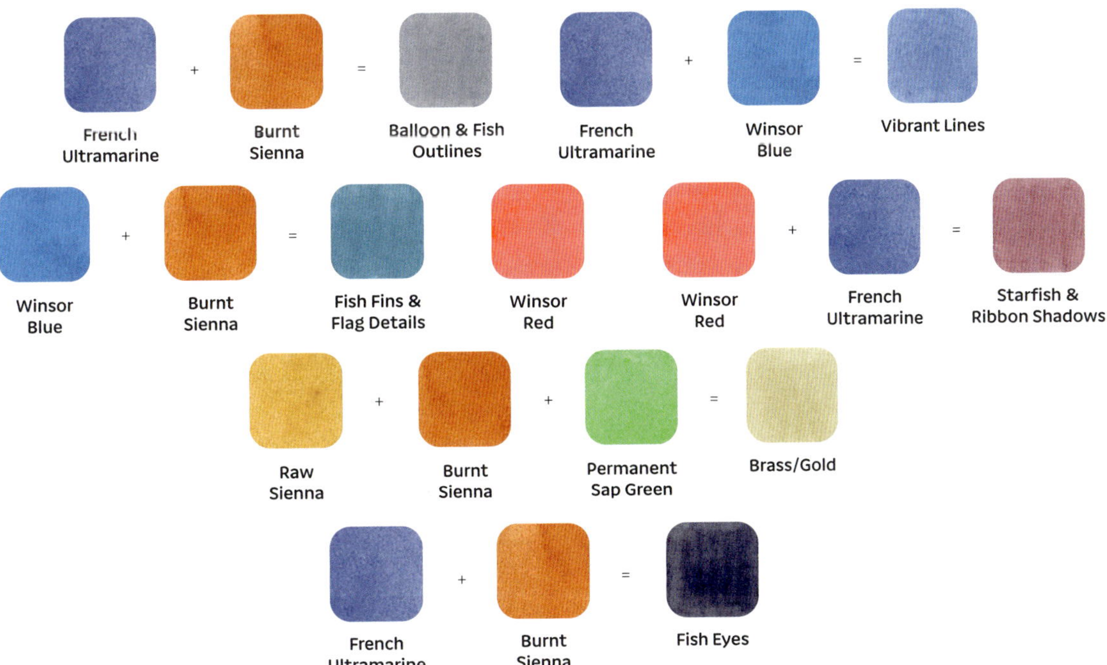

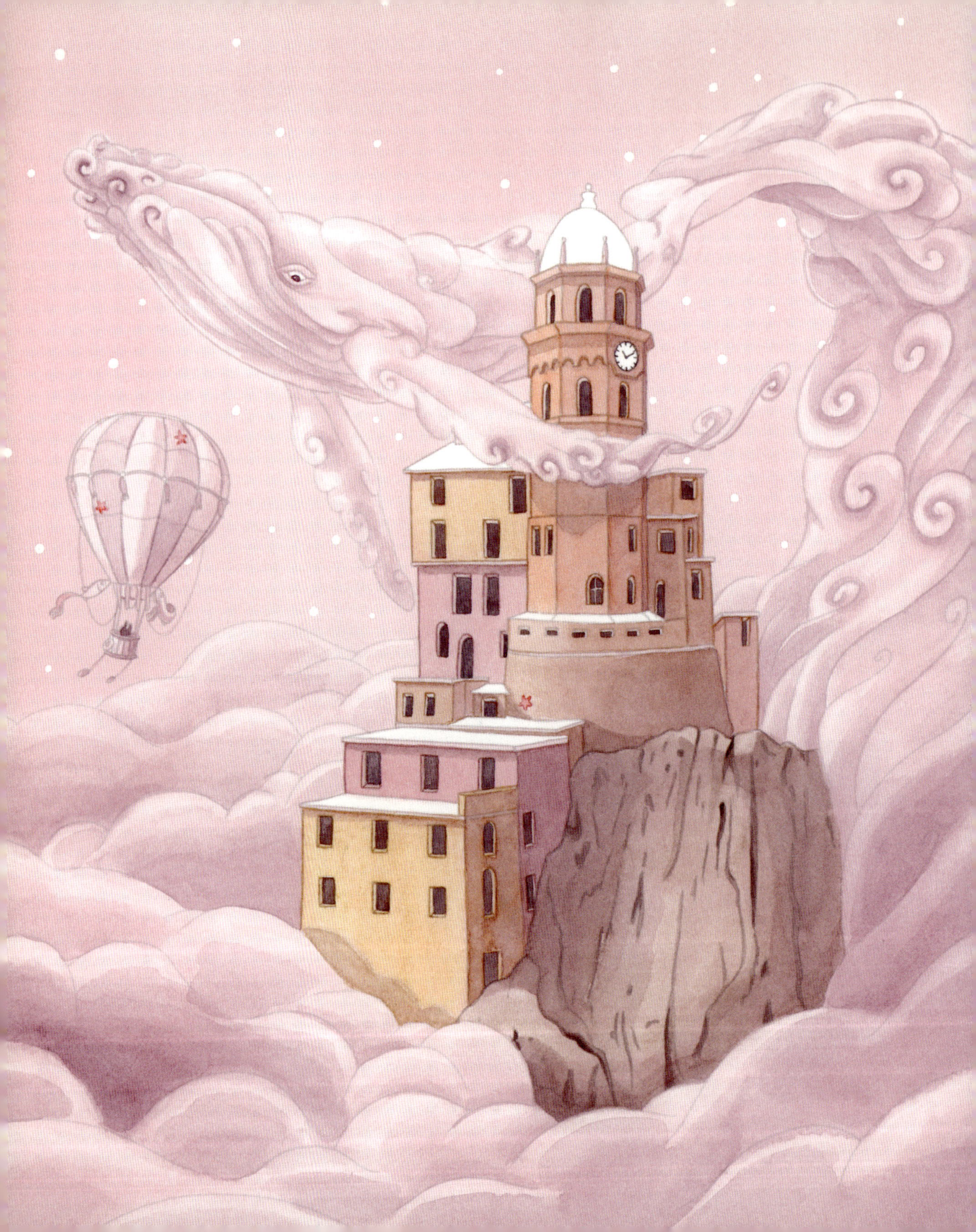

ETHEREAL WHALE TALE

This painting depicts the hot-air balloon's—from Ballooning Fish Parade (page 165)—destination. Every year, couples visit the castle in the clouds, drawn by the legend of a magical whale sculpted from clouds. According to the tale, at 11:11 a.m. on a single day each year, the cloud whale appears, transforming the sky into a stunning pink hue, symbolizing love and commitment.

The castle itself is inspired by a trip to Italy, where my partner and I explored the beautiful, colorful towns along the Cinque Terre coast. In this project, you will use a wash early in the process to cover the entire picture, establishing a foundation for a moody, one-color-dominant scheme.

Sketch

Draw the scene freehand or trace the sketch template on page 231.

Step 1

Since this picture will primarily feature one dominant color, not much masking fluid is needed. Apply masking fluid to the stars in the sky and cover all the roofs of the castle. To draw attention to the clock face and the cloud whale's eye, make sure to mask them as well.

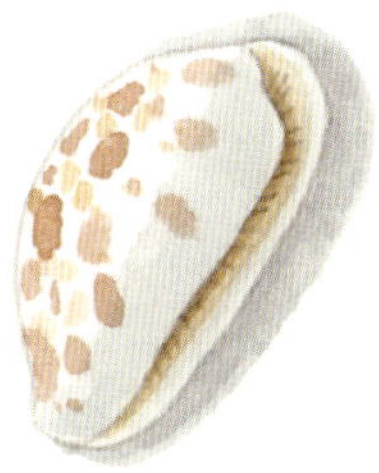

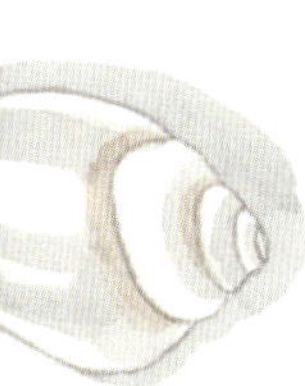

Step 2

Prepare some **Alizarin Crimson** on your palette, diluted with plenty of water. Using the wet-on-wet technique (page 12), apply clean water to the entire picture with the largest flat brush you have (such as a 1½-inch [4-cm] flat brush). Next, apply the Alizarin Crimson to the top of the page, working vertically from one side to the other. Let the paint settle briefly, and then use a tissue to lift some pigment from the areas where highlights should be. The main light source is coming from the left. Don't worry about being too precise at this stage, as you'll have limited time to lift the paint before it dries.

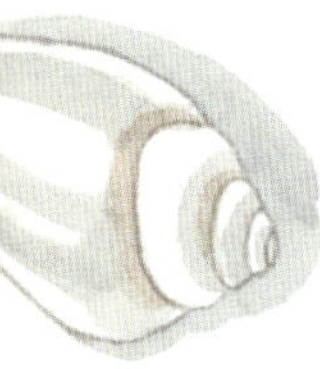

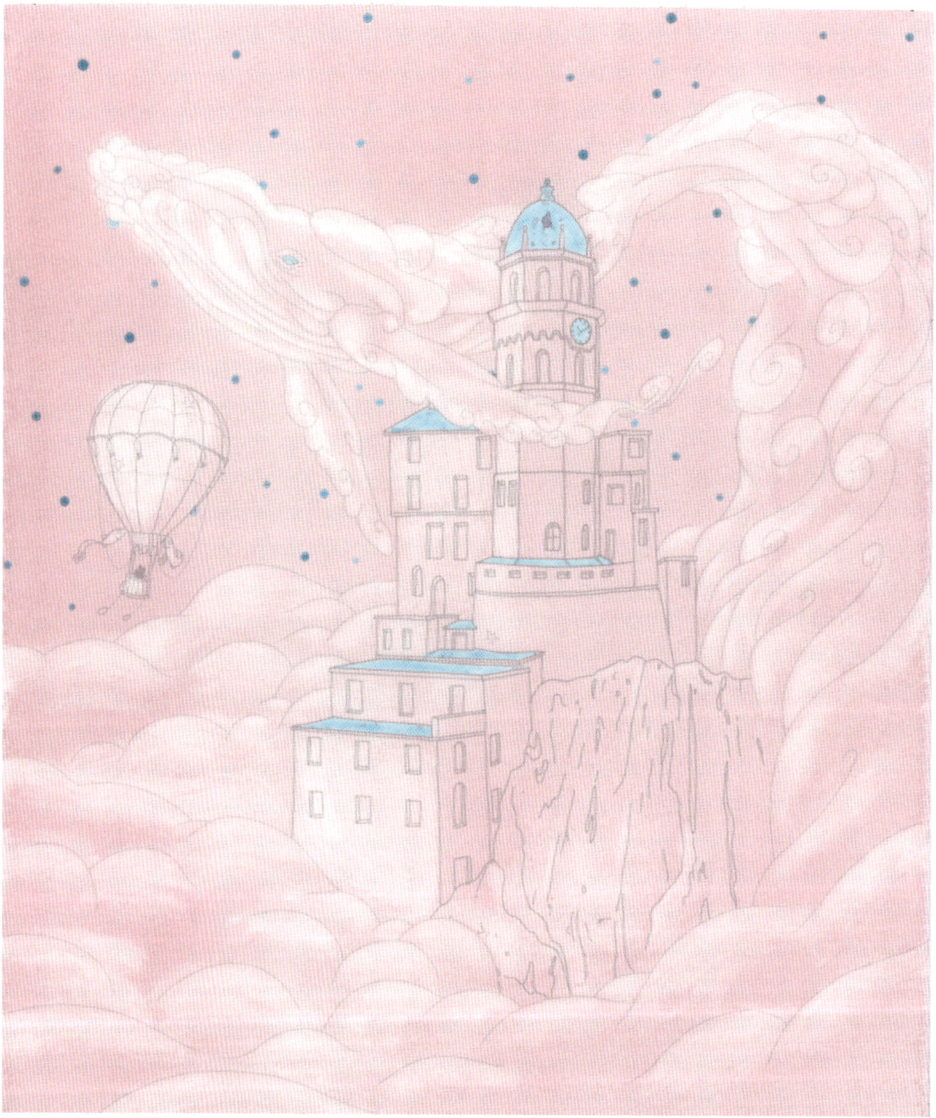

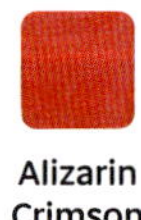

Alizarin Crimson

Step 3

Now that the picture has completely dried, you can begin building up shadowed areas on the rocks, castle, clouds, and hot-air balloon to create stronger contrast in the scene. To do this, mix **French Ultramarine** with the **Alizarin Crimson** already on your palette. Use varying ratios of this mixture to achieve different levels of shadow throughout the scene. Use the reference image for guidance.

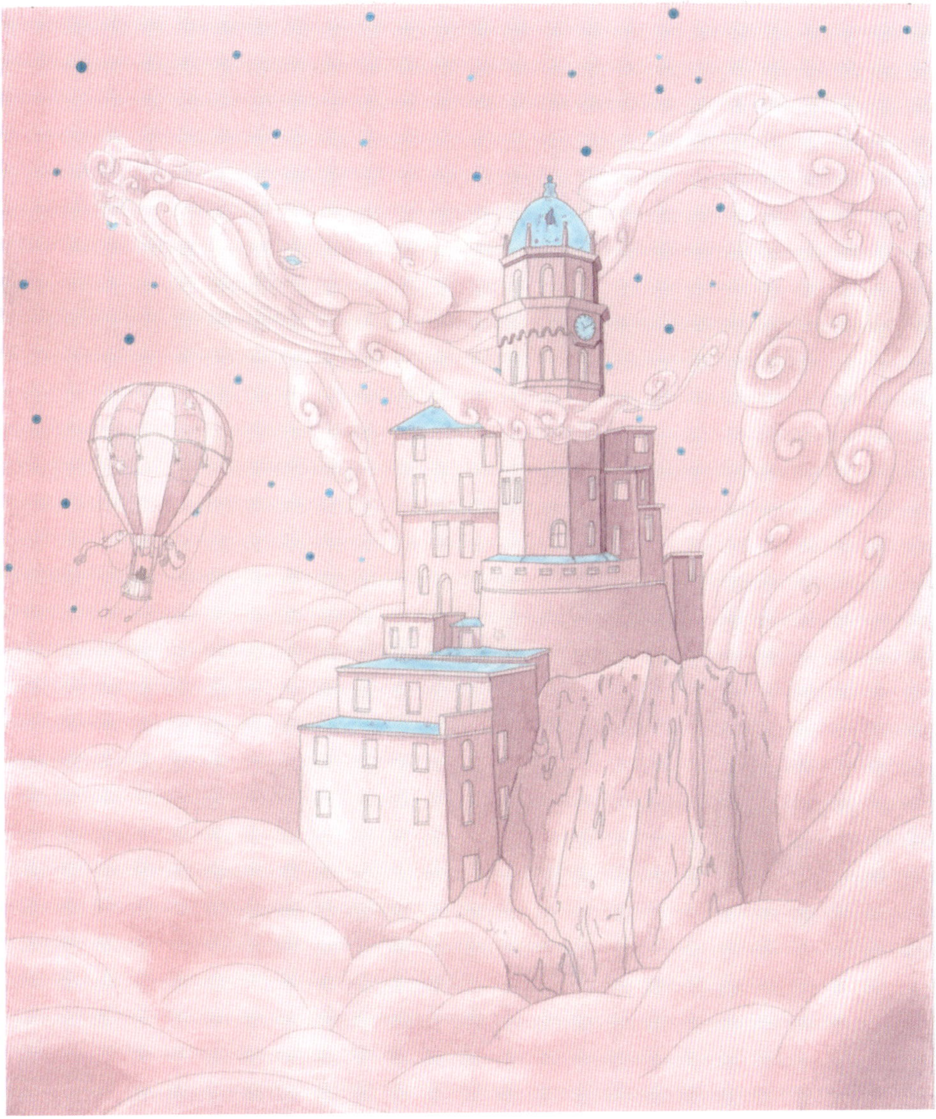

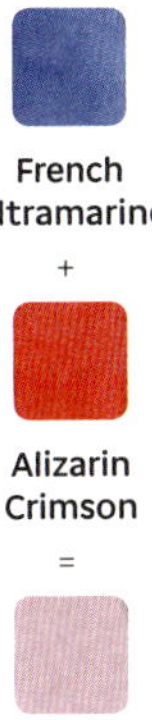

French
Ultramarine

+

Alizarin
Crimson

=

Shadows

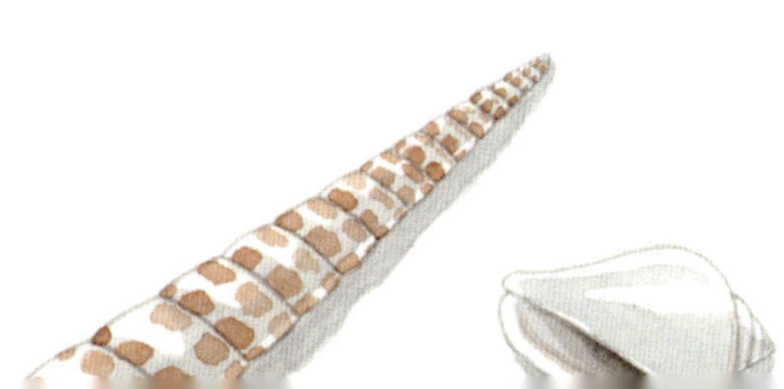

Step 4

Once everything is completely dry, remove the masking fluid dots in the sky and from the whale's eye. Next, you will need to prepare four colors to create some variation on the castle. All of these colors should be diluted with water to ensure they can be easily used for glazing. The purpose of the glaze here is to allow the Alizarin Crimson to show through the new colors. Create these mixes:

Winsor Yellow + Raw Sienna – for the yellow buildings

Alizarin Crimson + water – for the pink buildings

Winsor Red + Yellow Ochre + Burnt Sienna – for the terra-cotta buildings

Winsor Red + Permanent Sap Green – for the rocks (if you'd like to add more variation to the castle, you can mix this color with the terra-cotta mix to paint the curved building beneath the central terra-cotta turret)

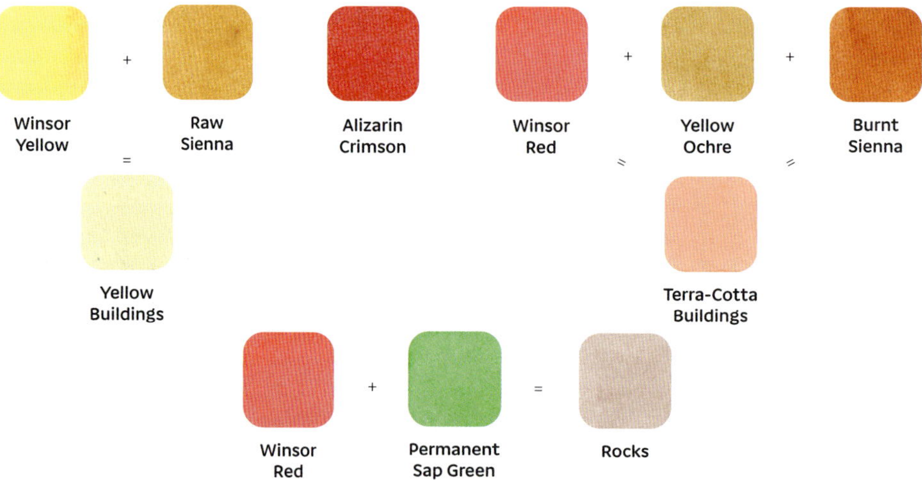

Lastly, you can paint the starfish with **Winsor Red** and the whale's eye with **Alizarin Crimson** and **French Ultramarine**. Once all the paint has dried, you can remove the remaining masking fluid.

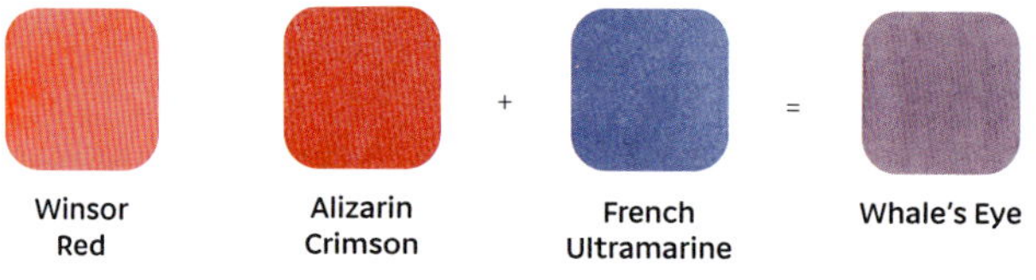

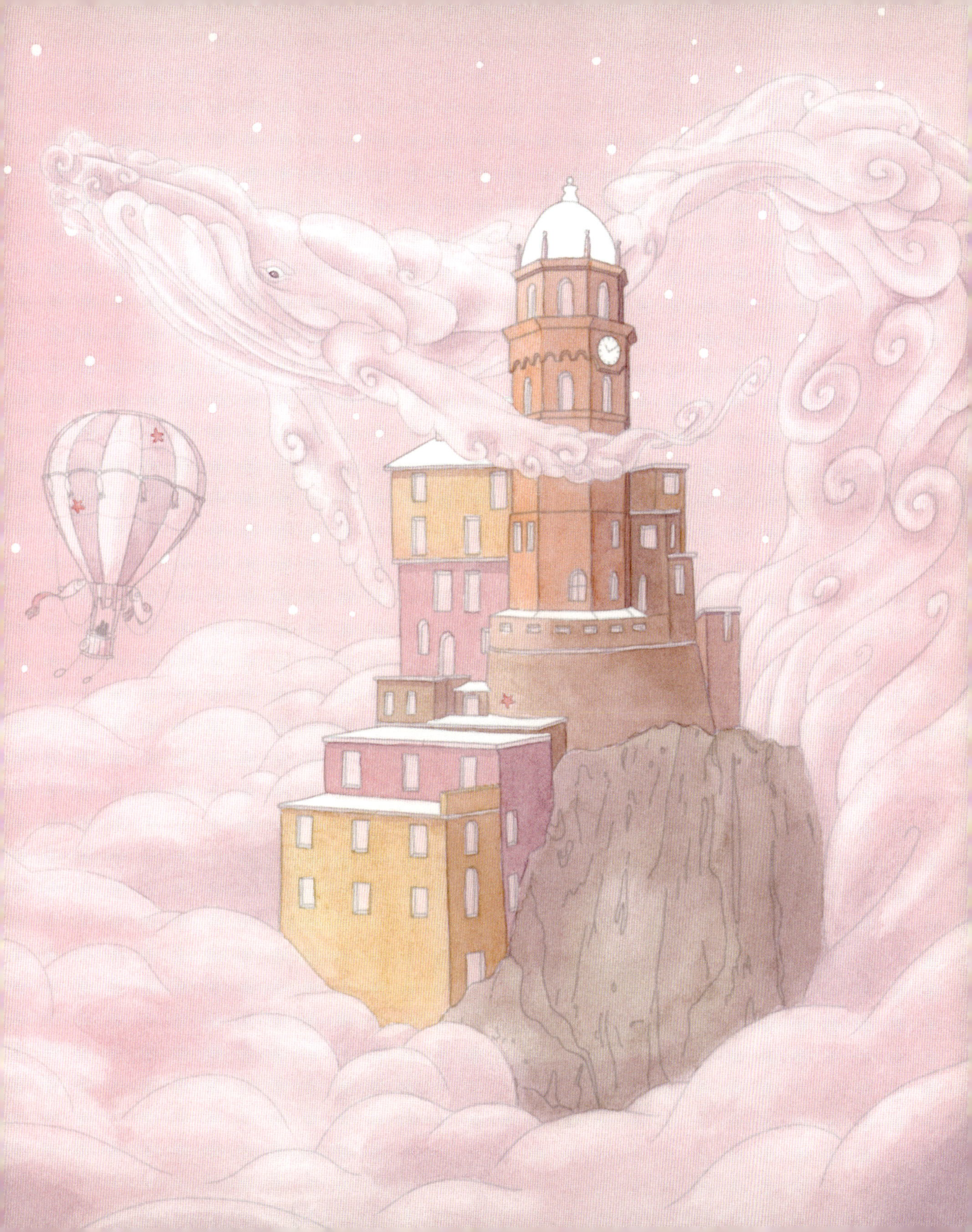

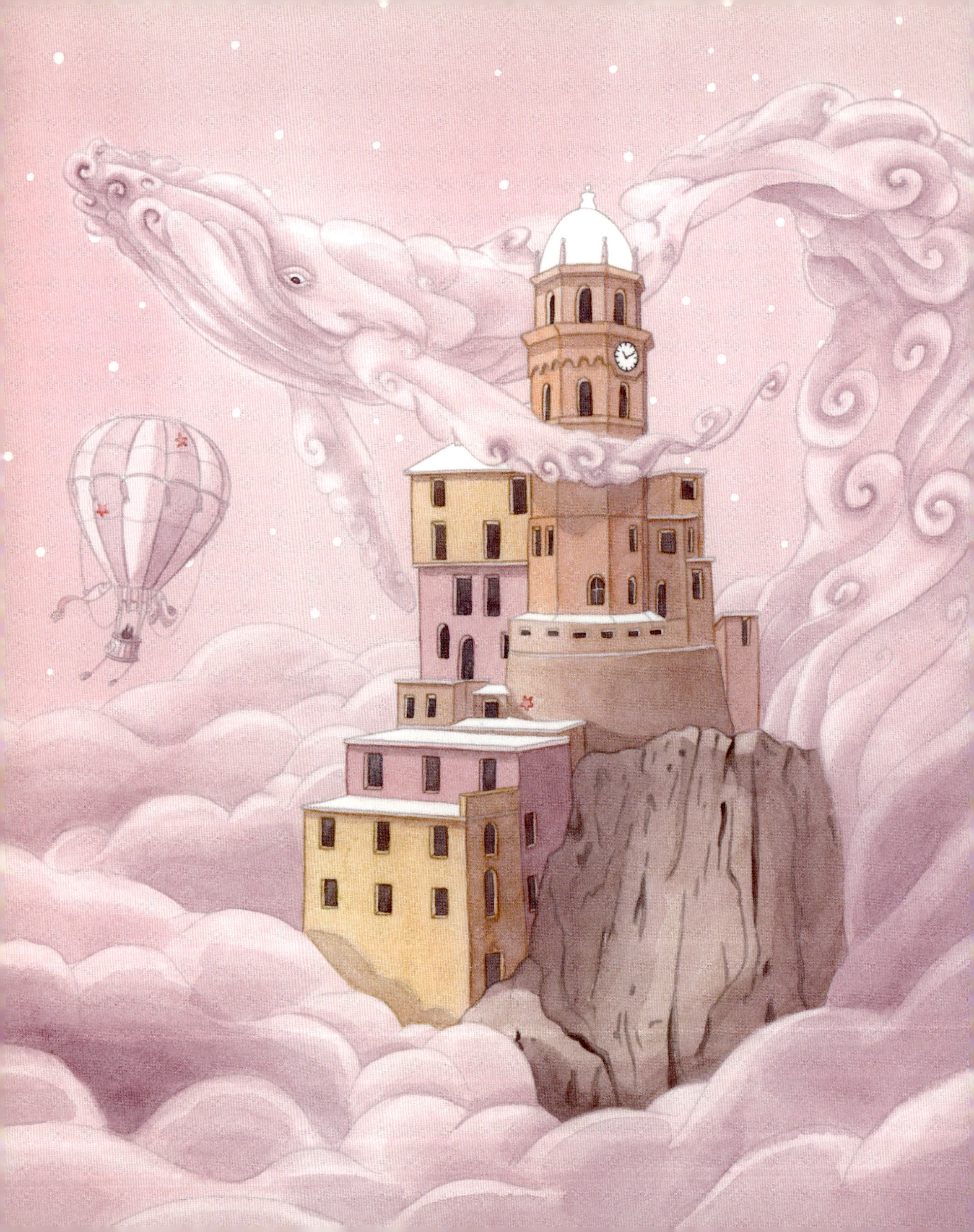

Step 5

First, you will need to mix two separate bodies of paint, which will then be gradually combined until you achieve the desired color:

Winsor Red + **Permanent Sap Green** – this is the same mix you created for the rocks in Step 4; use what's on your palette or mix up more if necessary

French Ultramarine + **Burnt Sienna** – for a light shadow color

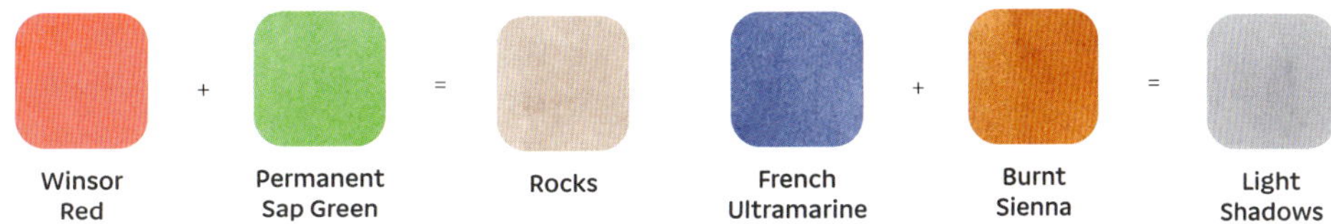

Once these two mixes are mixed, fill in all the windows on the castle and paint all the recesses on the cliff face. Next, add more water to dilute your color further, allowing you to glaze shadows cast by the clouds and buildings. By applying multiple thin layers to areas like the cliff face, you can gradually build up the shadows. Use the reference image as your guide.

After everything has dried, use a small amount of water to reactivate the four colors you previously mixed for the castle, as they should have dried on your palette by this stage. Using a small detail brush, paint the concentrated pigment over the sketch lines to define the borders of each building. Then, use your previously mixed light shadow color to add detail in the deepest recesses of the cliff face. For the clock face, mix **French Ultramarine** with **Burnt Sienna**.

Now that the castle is complete, shift your attention to creating more depth within the clouds and hot-air balloon by using darker shadows. Mix **Alizarin Crimson** with **French Ultramarine** and a small amount of **Burnt Sienna** to create the shadow color. Glaze a large shadow on the right side of the castle, and then focus on the spiral details of the cloud whale. By adding darker shadows to create deeper areas within the clouds on the left, you will enhance the composition, giving the impression that the clouds have settled around the mountain and castle. Lastly, use your **Alizarin Crimson** and **French Ultramarine** mix from Step 4 to further darken the whale's eye and the two travelers in the hot-air balloon basket. Leaving the castle roofs as negative spaces enhances the overall brightness and contrast of the color scheme.

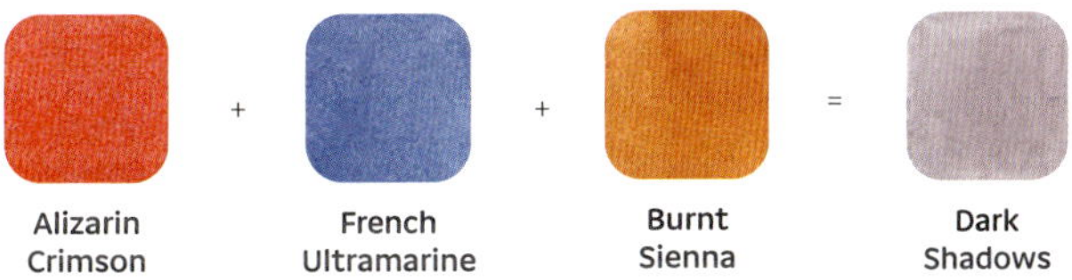

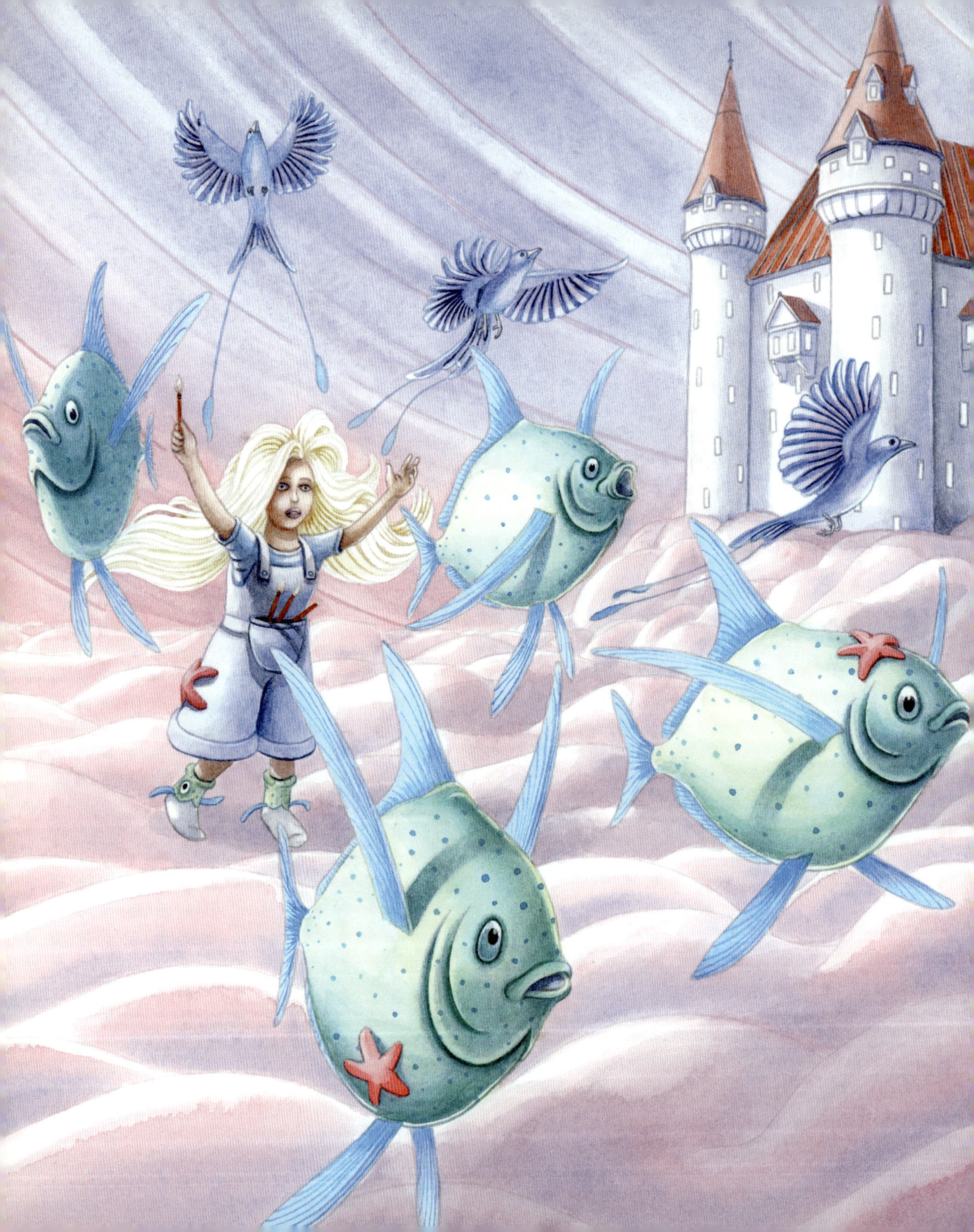

THE OPAH'S ARTISTIC UPLIFT

This project is a bit different from the others. Instead of providing step-by-step instructions, I will describe what I'm considering as if I were completing the five main steps. This approach will hopefully give you more insight into the process. Throughout this book, you've used only nine colors to mix everything, so I want to challenge you to re-create the colors in this picture using what you've learned about color mixing. However, feel free to create your own colors if you're inspired to do so.

The opah is a fascinating fish, being the only known fully warm-blooded fish. Its unique appearance, with vibrant colors and a distinct, rounded body shape, makes it an excellent subject to paint, encouraging your creativity to flow freely. When I designed this scene, I let the opah's striking features and fluid movements guide my choices in composition and color palette. I hope this fish sparks the same sense of wonder in you. Let the opah inspire you to approach this painting with curiosity and artistic freedom.

Sketch

Before painting, it can be helpful to have a sketch laying out the major parts of your composition. Focus on sketching out your key players, leaning into what inspires you. If you want to replicate my piece, draw the scene freehand or trace the sketch template on page 233.

Step 1

The first thing I consider before starting any painting is how I will use layers to achieve my desired result. Watercolor is transparent, and because of this, your first layer of paint will have an impact on the last. Once I have a rough idea, I decide which techniques will make the process as easy as possible. Every picture requires slightly different considerations, but I usually begin by masking certain parts of the image. However, I avoid masking if it's not absolutely necessary.

(continued)

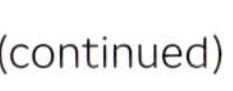

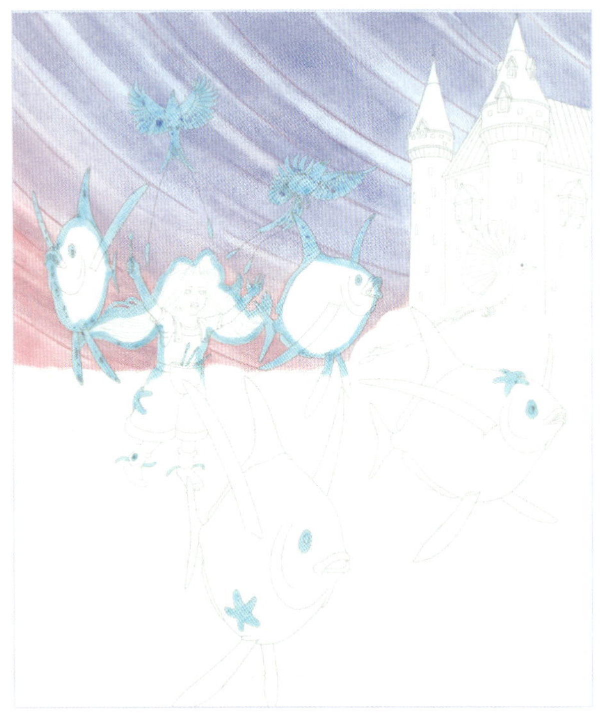

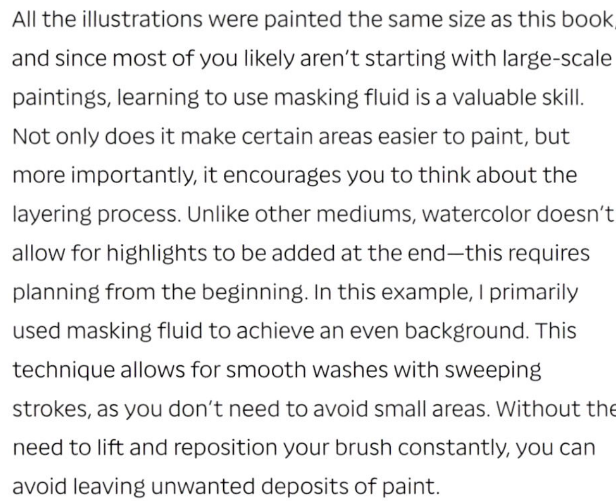

All the illustrations were painted the same size as this book, and since most of you likely aren't starting with large-scale paintings, learning to use masking fluid is a valuable skill. Not only does it make certain areas easier to paint, but more importantly, it encourages you to think about the layering process. Unlike other mediums, watercolor doesn't allow for highlights to be added at the end—this requires planning from the beginning. In this example, I primarily used masking fluid to achieve an even background. This technique allows for smooth washes with sweeping strokes, as you don't need to avoid small areas. Without the need to lift and reposition your brush constantly, you can avoid leaving unwanted deposits of paint.

Step 2

Once the masking fluid step is complete, I typically begin by determining the time of day in my scene, and then I paint the background. In this particular scene, I went with a sunset with a low casting light. This approach makes sense since everything else will be placed in front, and it helps establish the mood and atmosphere using the transparency of watercolor. The lighting and color choices for the background often guide further decisions for the foreground elements, even if those choices weren't pre-planned. Some of the best color schemes emerge naturally through this process.

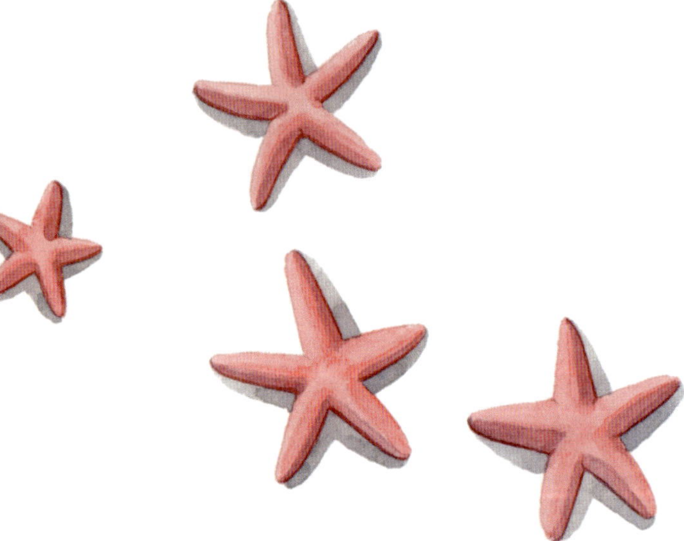

Step 3

Now that I have a direction for the color scheme, I begin to further plan the lighting and how each subject will be illuminated. There should never be a fixed way to do this, as there are endless lighting possibilities. When creating believable lighting, it's best to work on the painting as a whole rather than on each element individually. This approach helps maintain consistency across the entire picture. This is where an underpainting can be helpful. By mixing a shadow color, you can paint all areas where a shadow might fall, allowing you to begin building tonal value for the entire picture without worrying about different colors. These values will contribute to the overall complexity and mood of the painting later on. Additionally, filling in large areas at once can be exciting, helping to build your confidence in the direction you're heading. Any tonal work should be applied lightly, with minimal pigment, and you can gradually build it up over multiple layers.

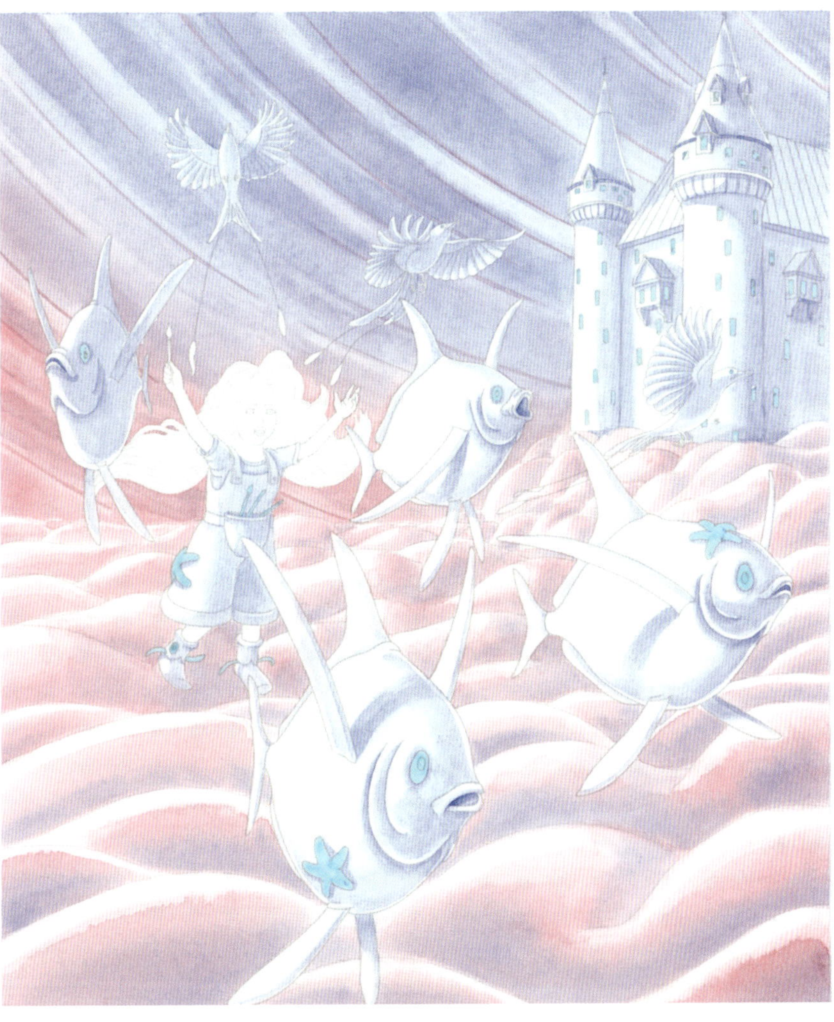

Step 4

At this point in the painting, I begin adding the main colors. While doing this, I keep the lighting in mind to ensure I use negative space effectively, allowing certain areas to remain vibrant later on. Preserving the brightness of the paper is crucial to avoid a dull or flat appearance, which can result from covering the entire surface with color. I apply watery paint with minimal pigment to wash or glaze most areas. Often, I choose colors for my subjects that contrast with the background to help separate them and draw focus. Once the colors are in place, they serve as a starting point for building depth by glazing over previously painted shadows with darker colors.

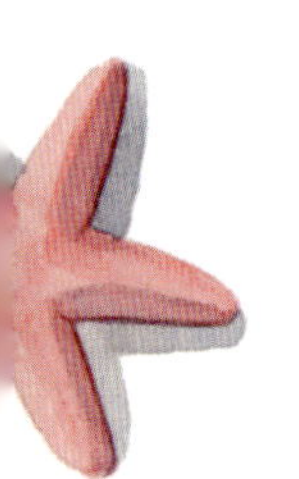

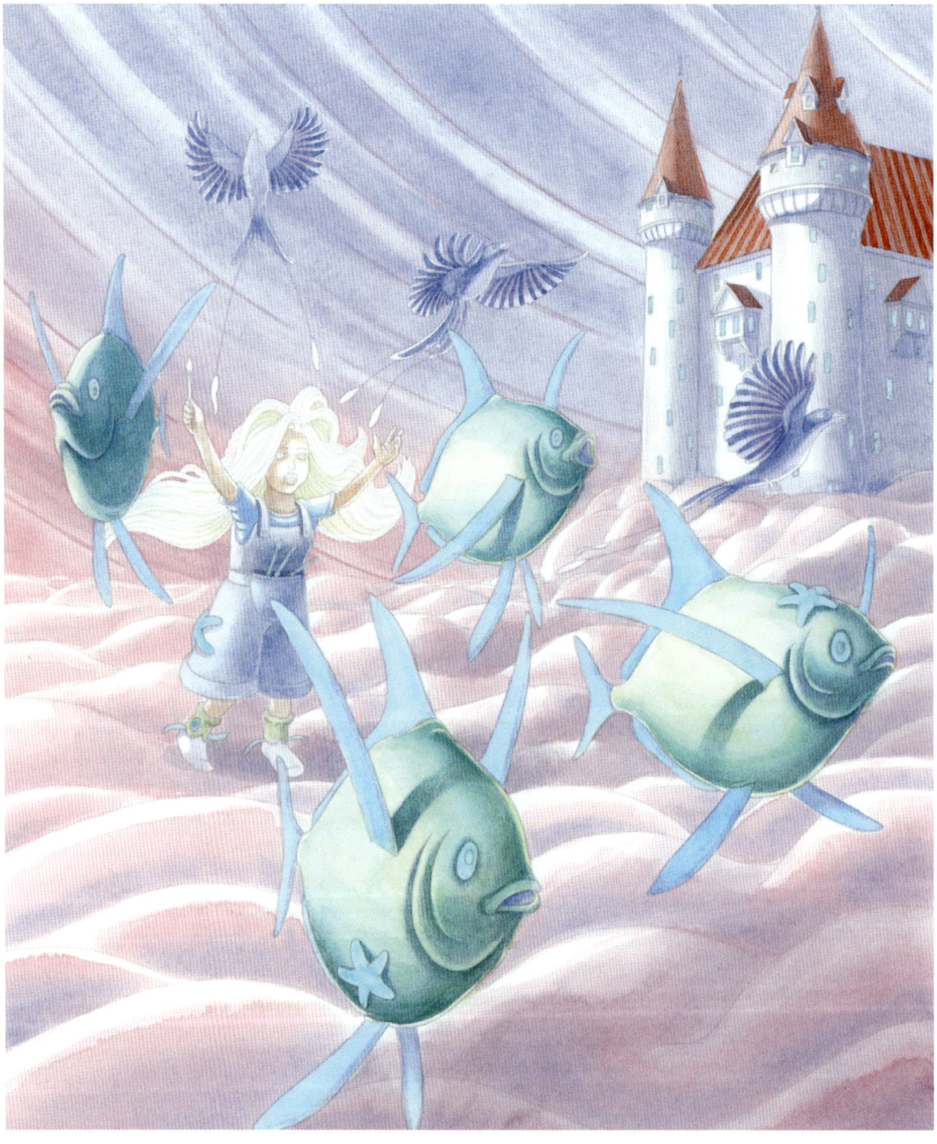

Step 5

At this stage of the painting, you can clearly see everything coming together and determine whether the picture is balanced. Colors achieve balance when light and dark hues, warm and cool tones, and contrasts work harmoniously without overwhelming any part of the composition. This phase is also the most enjoyable, as you can create focal points by emphasizing specific details. Fine details enhance depth and texture, giving the painting a more three-dimensional feel. These elements add complexity to the composition, help tell a story, and contribute to the overall mood.

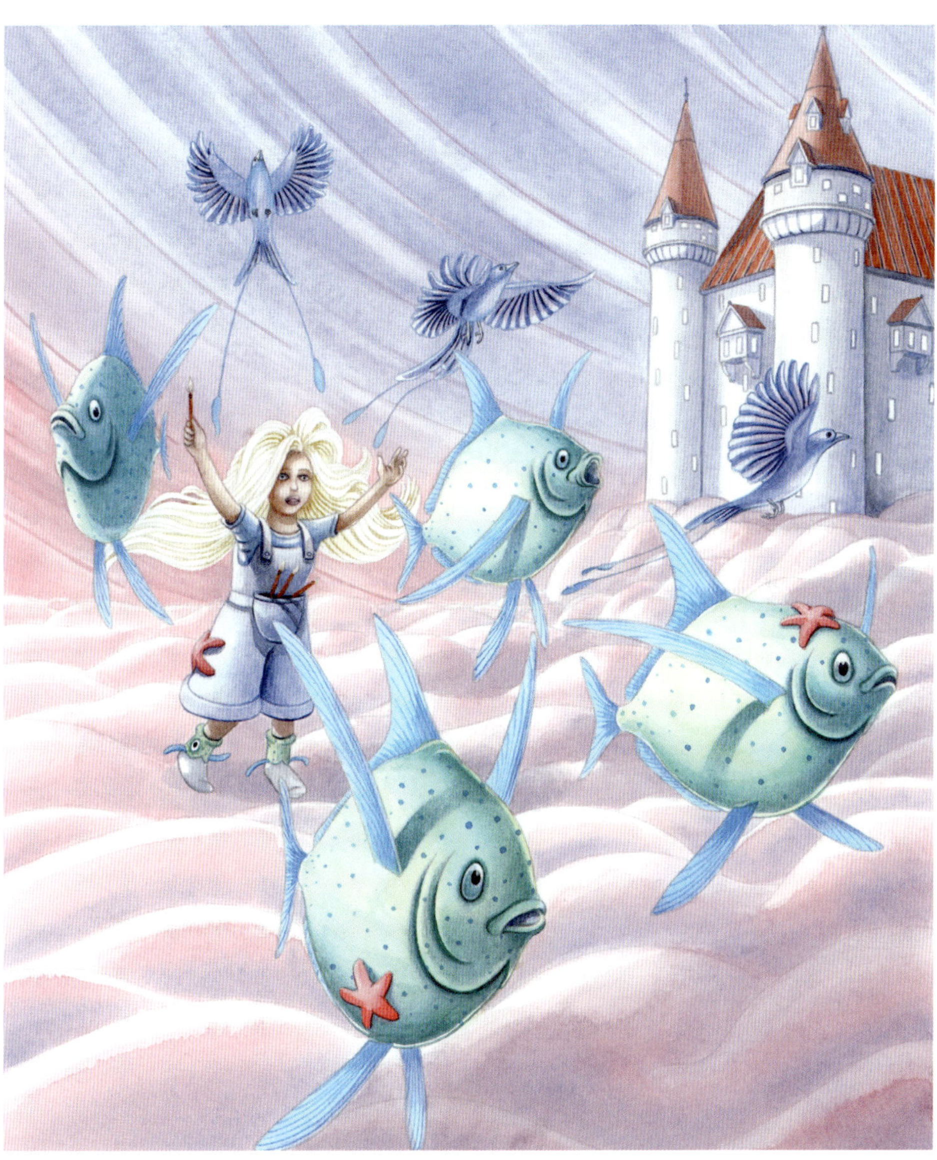

FINDING INSPIRATION

Exploring the world with childlike curiosity and openness holds the key to endless inspiration. The best place to start is by exploring your personal passions and hobbies. You could also incorporate personal experiences or dreams; it's about experimenting with themes that interest you.

Developing a personal style and voice will be very difficult if you're not exploring something you find incredibly interesting and fascinating. Many people struggle to find inspiration—and may even consider it the hardest part of creating—and I'm often asked how I find mine. In many cases, individuals actively try too hard to search for something interesting instead of being themselves and looking within to discover what truly excites them.

Don't get the impression that you can't seek out a beautiful landscape or paint a single orchid if that excites you. In fact, that's exactly what you should do! Personally, I've found that creating worlds helps me bring together all my interests and the things I love in a more focused and manageable way.

I encourage you all to be yourselves and celebrate your individuality because that is what will stand out the most in your work. If you believe that your current painting ability restricts your creativity, you will close yourself off to making real improvements and creating work that truly represents you as a person.

I hope my work can inspire you to embark on or continue your creative journey.

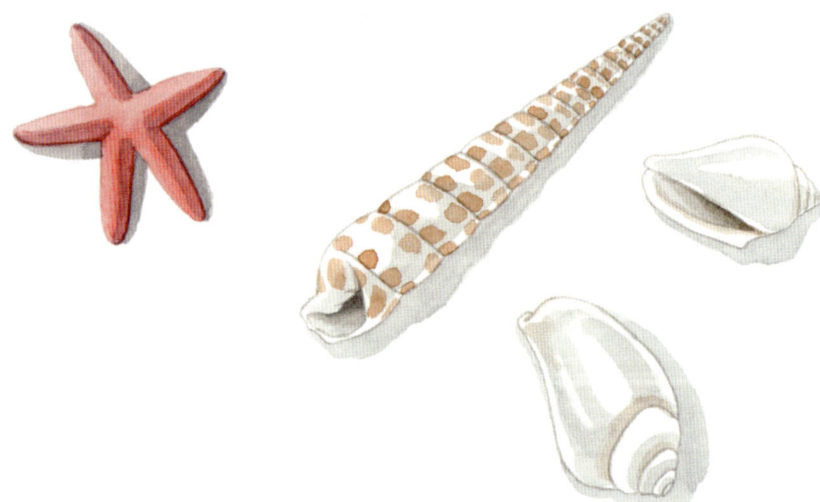

CONCLUSION

Watercolor painting can be challenging due to its unpredictability, transparency, and difficulty in controlling water and pigment, along with the need for advanced techniques, the reliance on quality paper, and the complex color mixing—all of which require practice and patience. Should this deter you from using watercolor? Absolutely not! Like anything, it takes time and practice to see improvements, but it's also extremely rewarding to complete something you are happy with and proud of.

I think it's important to reflect on my quote from the start of the book: "There are no mistakes when you are having fun." What I mean by this is that when you enjoy an activity, any perceived errors or imperfections become less significant, allowing you to be creative without the fear of making mistakes. At the end of the day, this is art—not something like mathematics, which has one correct answer for specific problems. There is no single way or rule to create art, which is why it should be a fun and creative process.

Everything in this book serves as a guideline rather than the sole approach to creating art; it reflects my perspective and experience. The five steps outlined for each project provide the foundational techniques and processes I use to create my own illustrations. These steps lay the perfect framework to make all kinds of artwork, from beginner-friendly pieces to advanced creations.

I hope you enjoyed my first art book and found joy in re-creating the artworks within it. My goal was for you to gain insights into how you can use or adapt these techniques in your own work. It's always an honor to inspire others through my art, and I hope you feel excited to create imaginative scenes that truly represent who you are.

I would love to see your completed projects from this book or any you are working on, so feel free to share them with me on Instagram @christophermaxwellart using the hashtag #watercolordreamscapes.

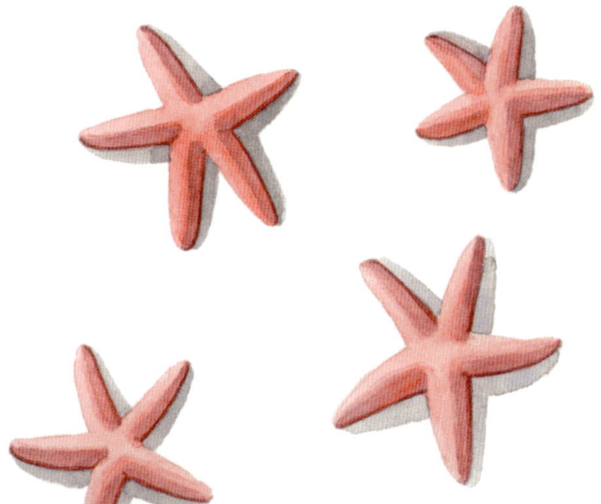

ACKNOWLEDGMENTS

Thank you to my loving mum and dad, who have invested so much time into shaping me into who I am today. No achievement would be possible without their nurturing influence from birth.

To my beautiful partner, Jess, who truly understands what it means to follow your dreams and do what makes you happy—you are an inspiration to me.

A special thank you to the incredibly organized and professional Sadie Hofmeester and the rest of the Page Street Publishing team for making this book possible.

To all my online supporters who have purchased something from me—whether it be this book, a course, or artwork—I cannot express my appreciation enough. Even for those who have simply liked or commented on my posts, your support truly means a lot to me.

ABOUT THE AUTHOR

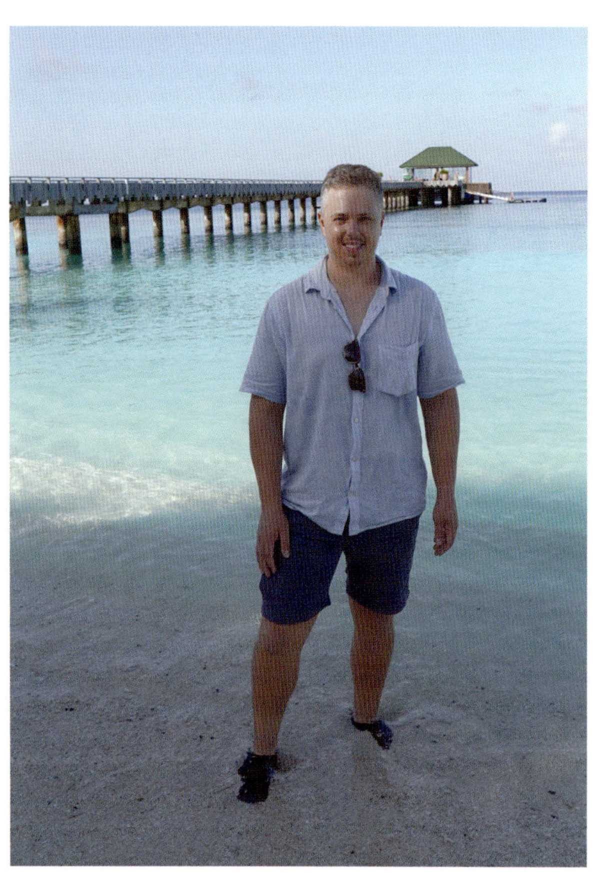

Christopher John Maxwell is a professional illustrator with a passion for watercolors, residing in Perth, Australia. His love for art began at a young age while looking at illustrations in picture books and has only grown stronger since. After exploring various art mediums in his younger years, he now dedicates most of his time to watercolor.

Christopher loves how watercolor's soft, translucent layers create a dreamy, atmospheric effect that feels both timeless and calming. He believes its unpredictability and delicate blending of colors evoke a deep sense of nostalgia and emotional resonance—qualities that continually draw him back to this captivating medium.

Inspired by his love for nature and personal experiences, Christopher's unique style and approach to watercolor have ignited the imagination of many around the world. He has gained a large following online, where he teaches watercolor through online courses and shares his knowledge to inspire others to start or continue their creative journeys.

Christopher can be found at christophermaxwellart.com and on Instagram, YouTube, and TikTok @christophermaxwellart.

INDEX

Sketch Templates

I encourage you to try freehand copying the project sketches. This practice can enhance your observational skills and hand control. You're also welcome to add or subtract details to create your own interpretation.

If you prefer to dive straight into painting, you can use the sketch templates provided for all 20 projects. These templates are printed on perforated pages, making them easy to tear out and trace onto your watercolor paper of choice.

The simplest tracing method, which requires no additional tools, is to tape both the tear-out and your watercolor paper to a bright window. This will allow you to see through both layers and trace easily. Alternatively, you can use a lightbox (LED tracing board) or graphite transfer paper for a more convenient tracing experience.

If you've purchased this book as an e-book, please feel free to download and print the templates using the QR code below or by going to: christophermaxwellart.com/pages/free-download.

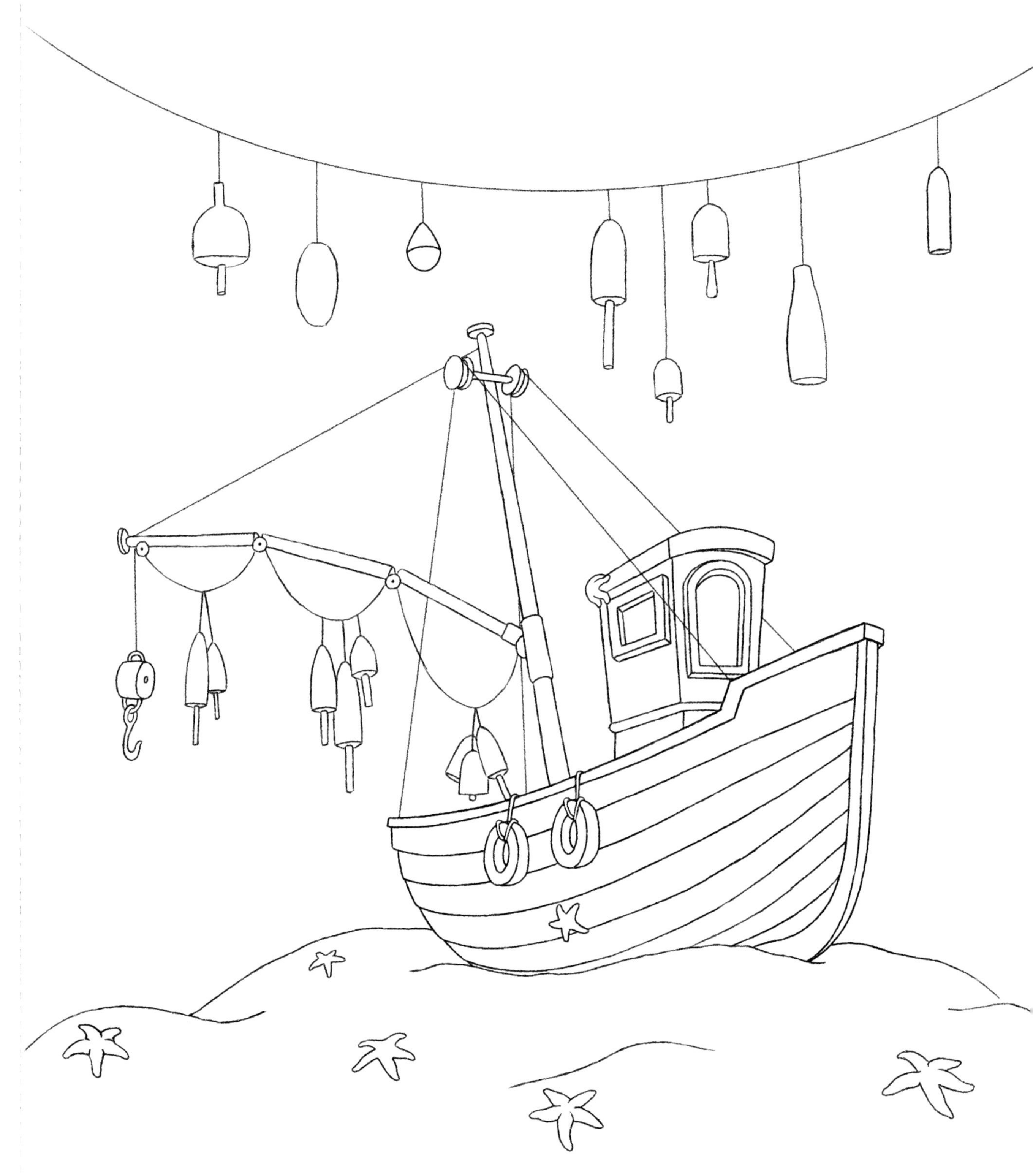

Enchanted Trawler (page 19)

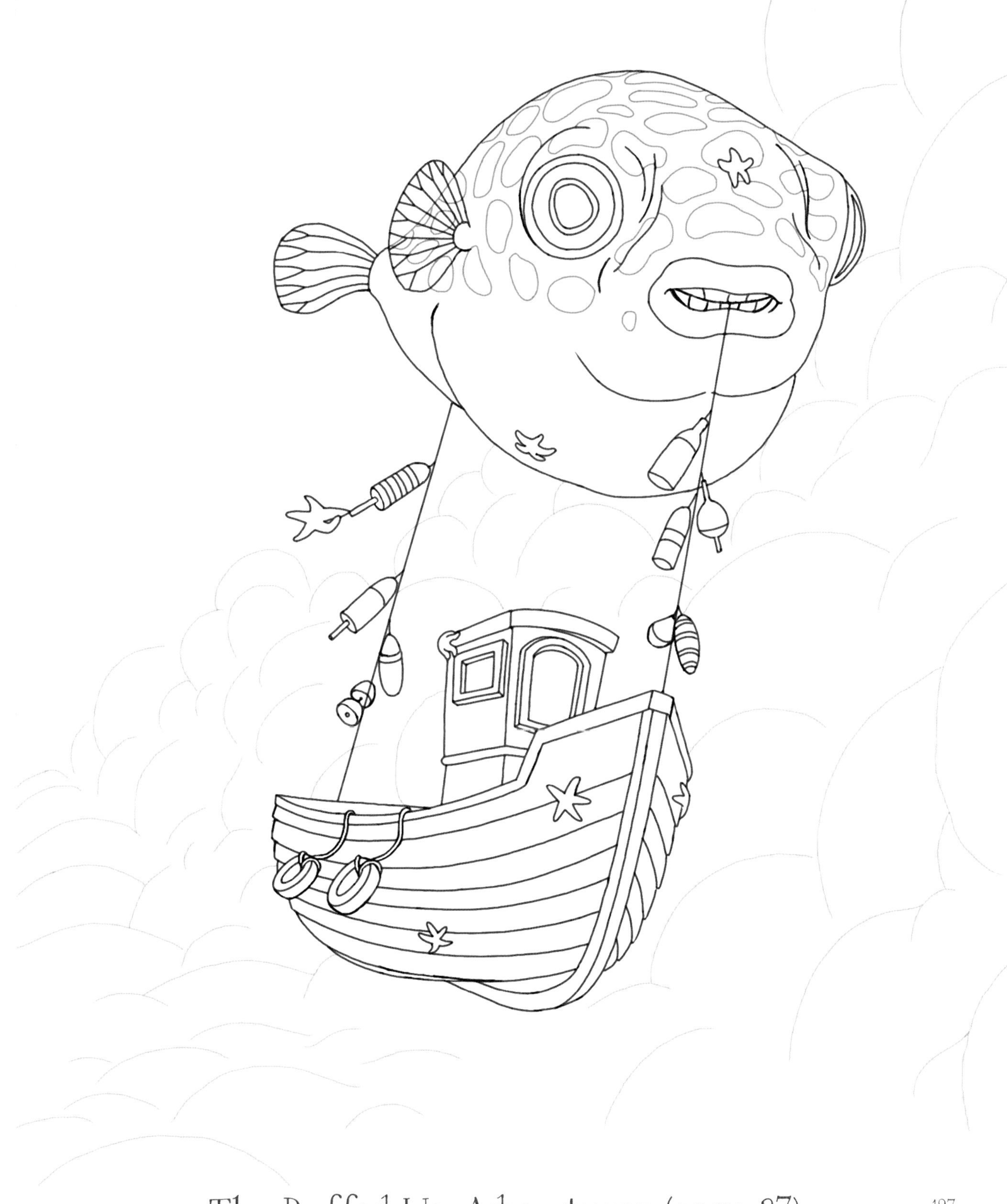

The Puffed-Up Adventurer (page 27)

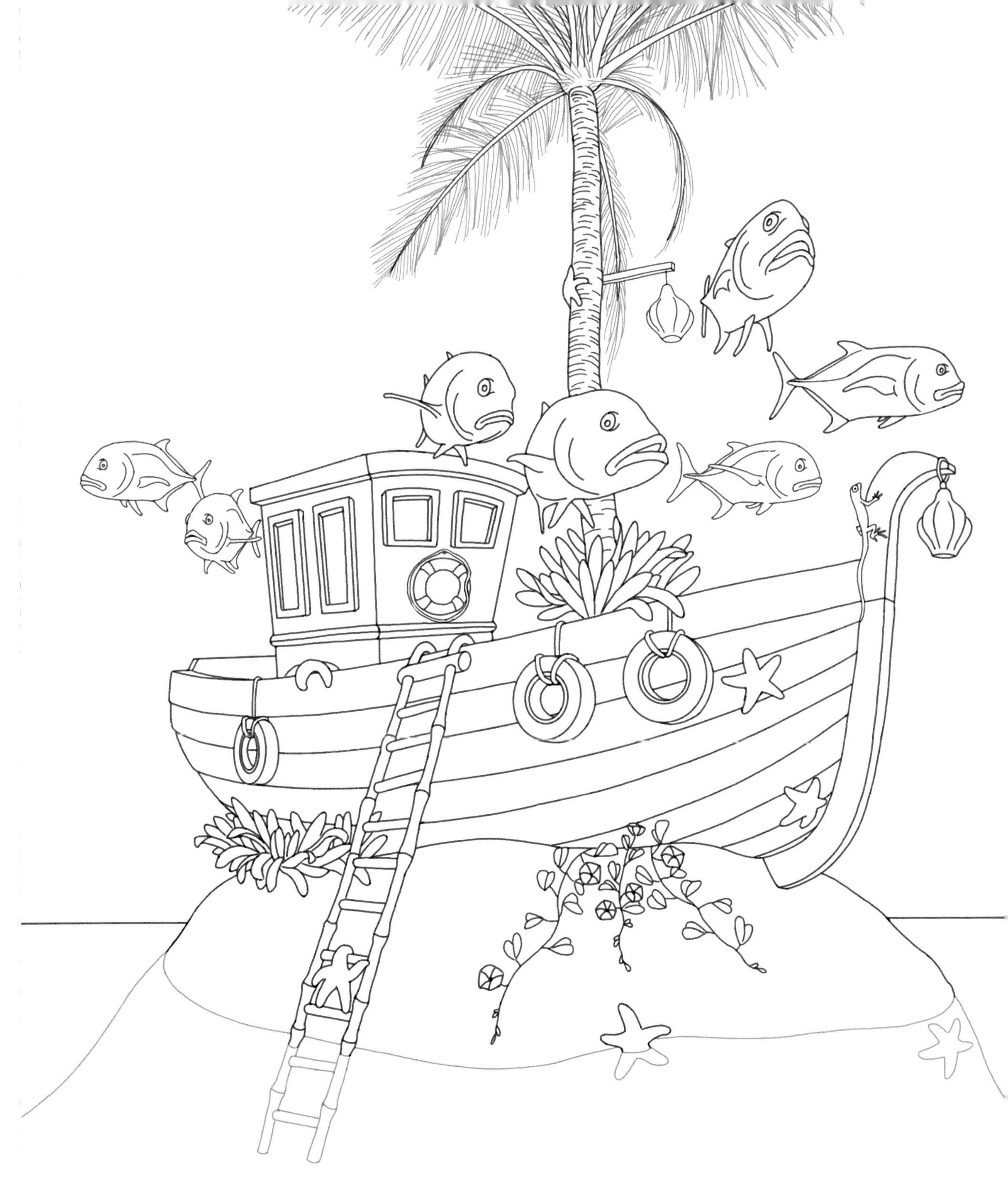

Aquatic Dream (page 43)

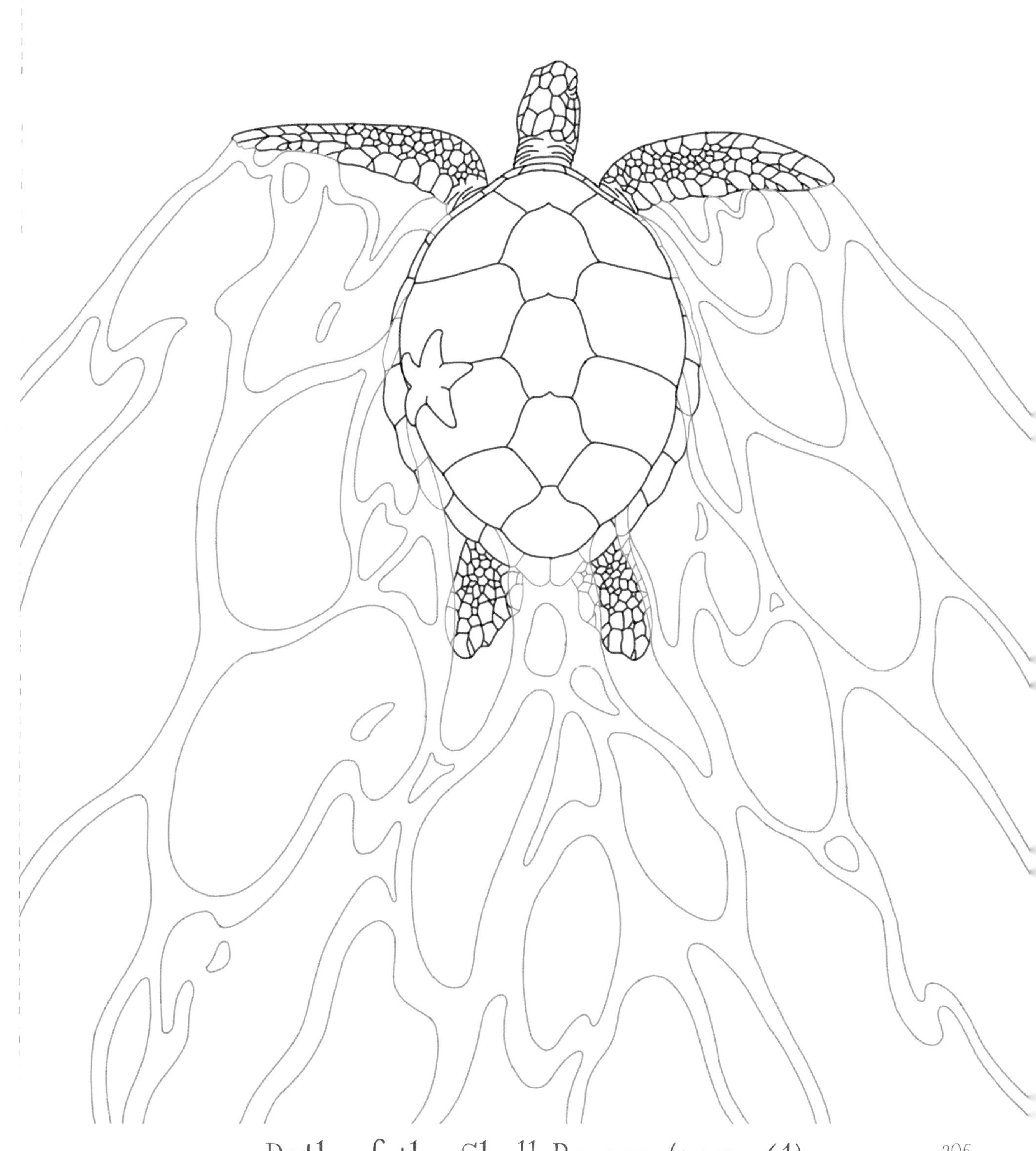

Path of the Shell-Bearer (page 61)

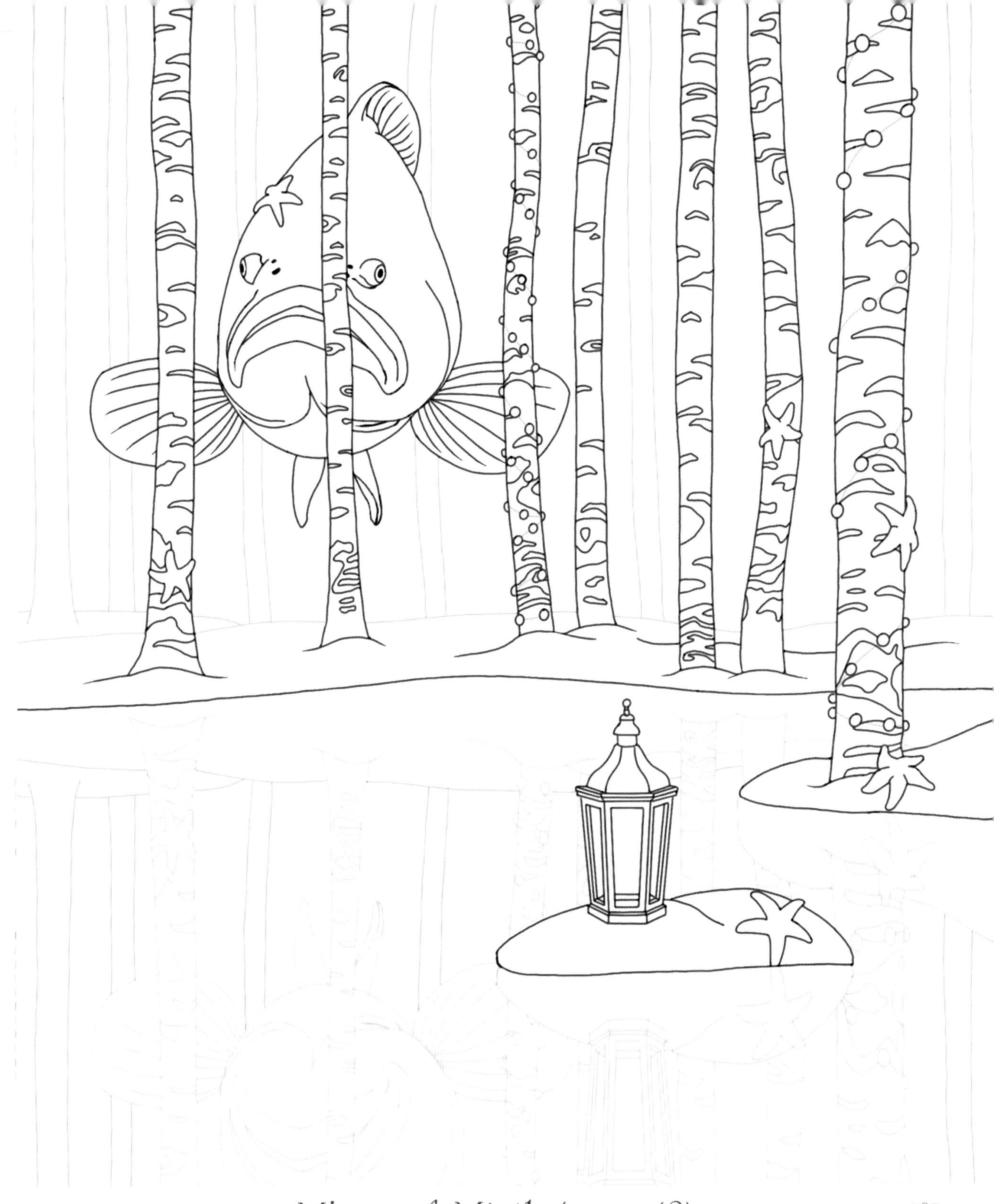

Mirrored Mirth (page 69)

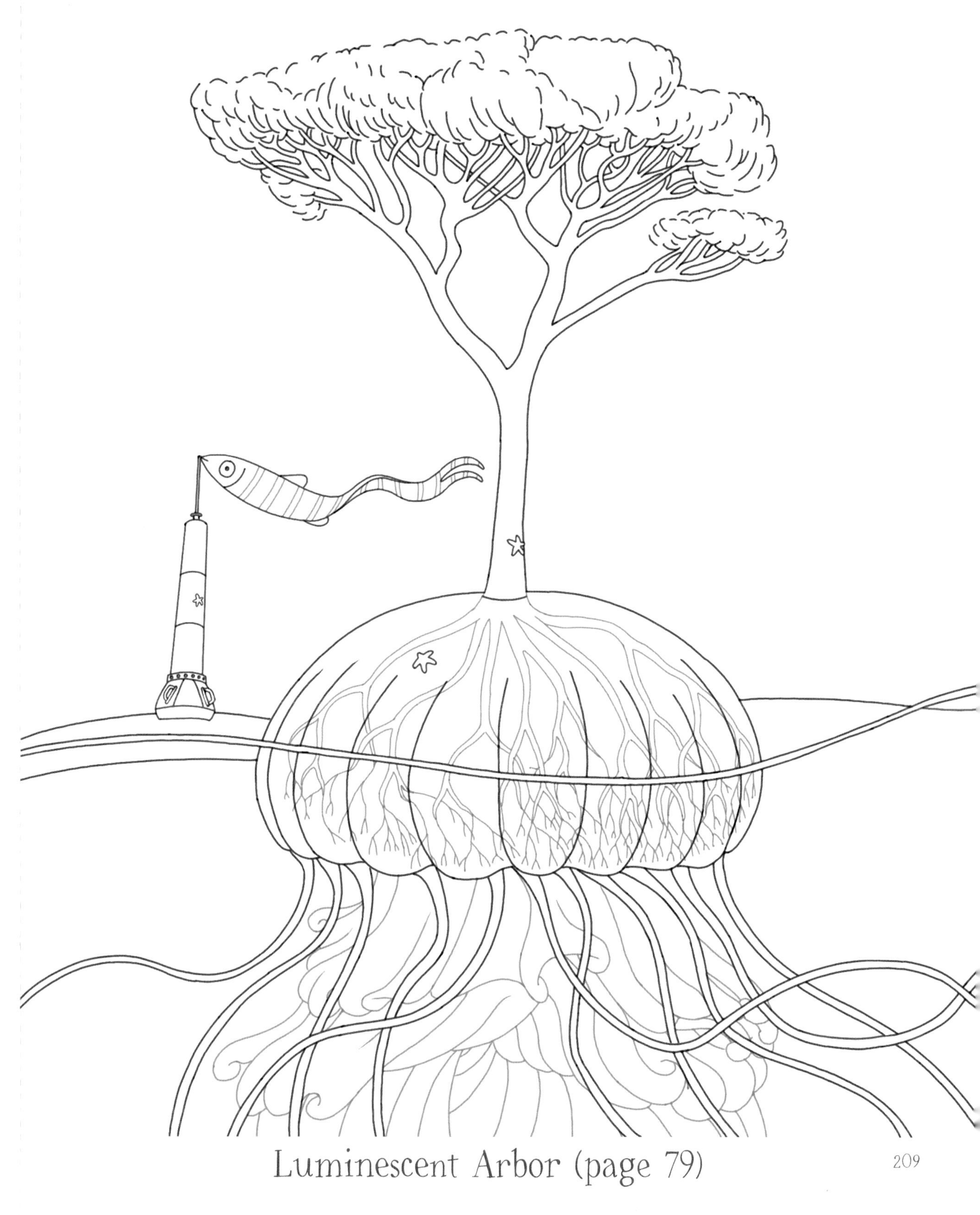

Luminescent Arbor (page 79)

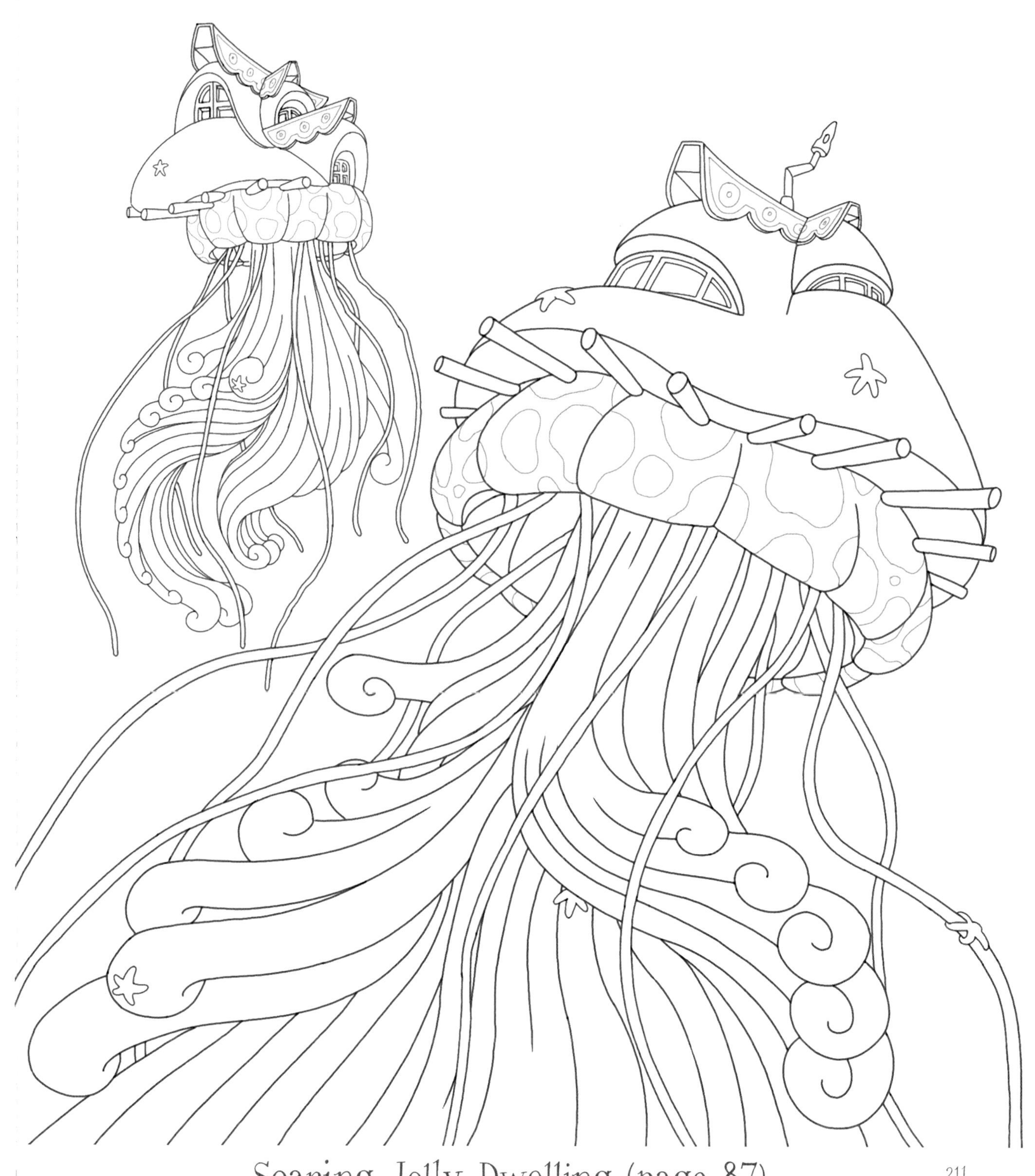

Soaring Jelly Dwelling (page 87)

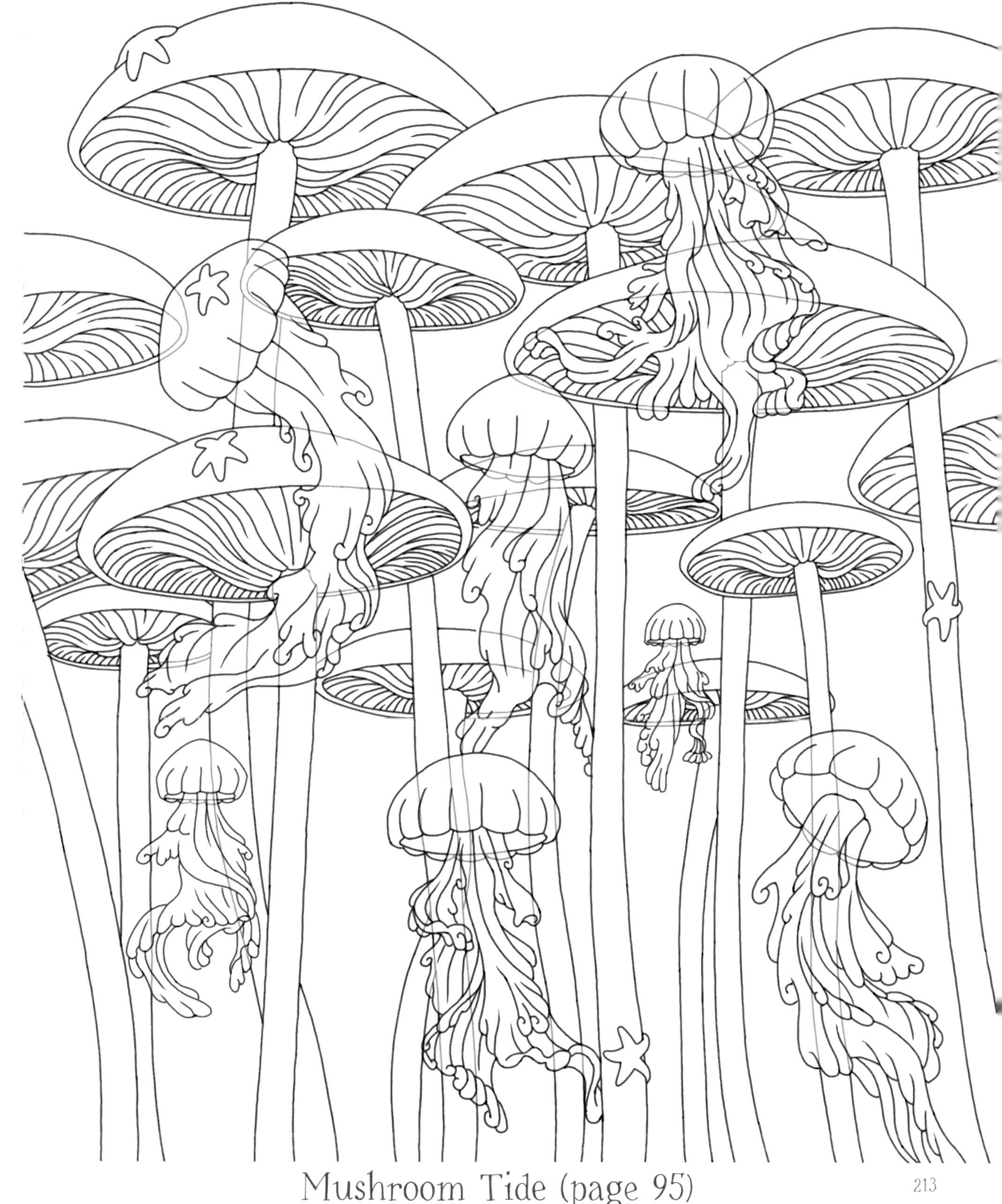

Mushroom Tide (page 95)

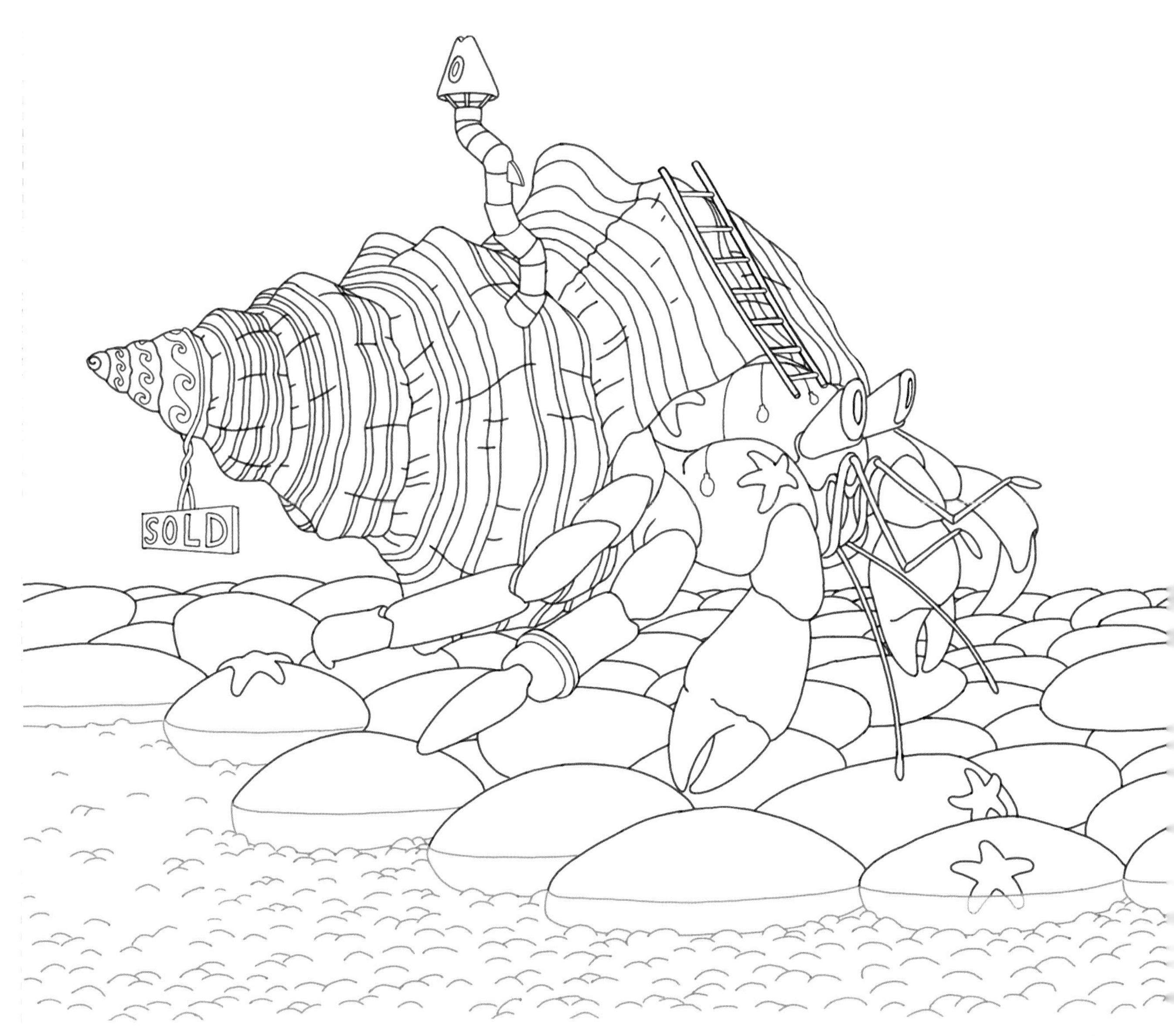

Shelltastic New Home (page 113)

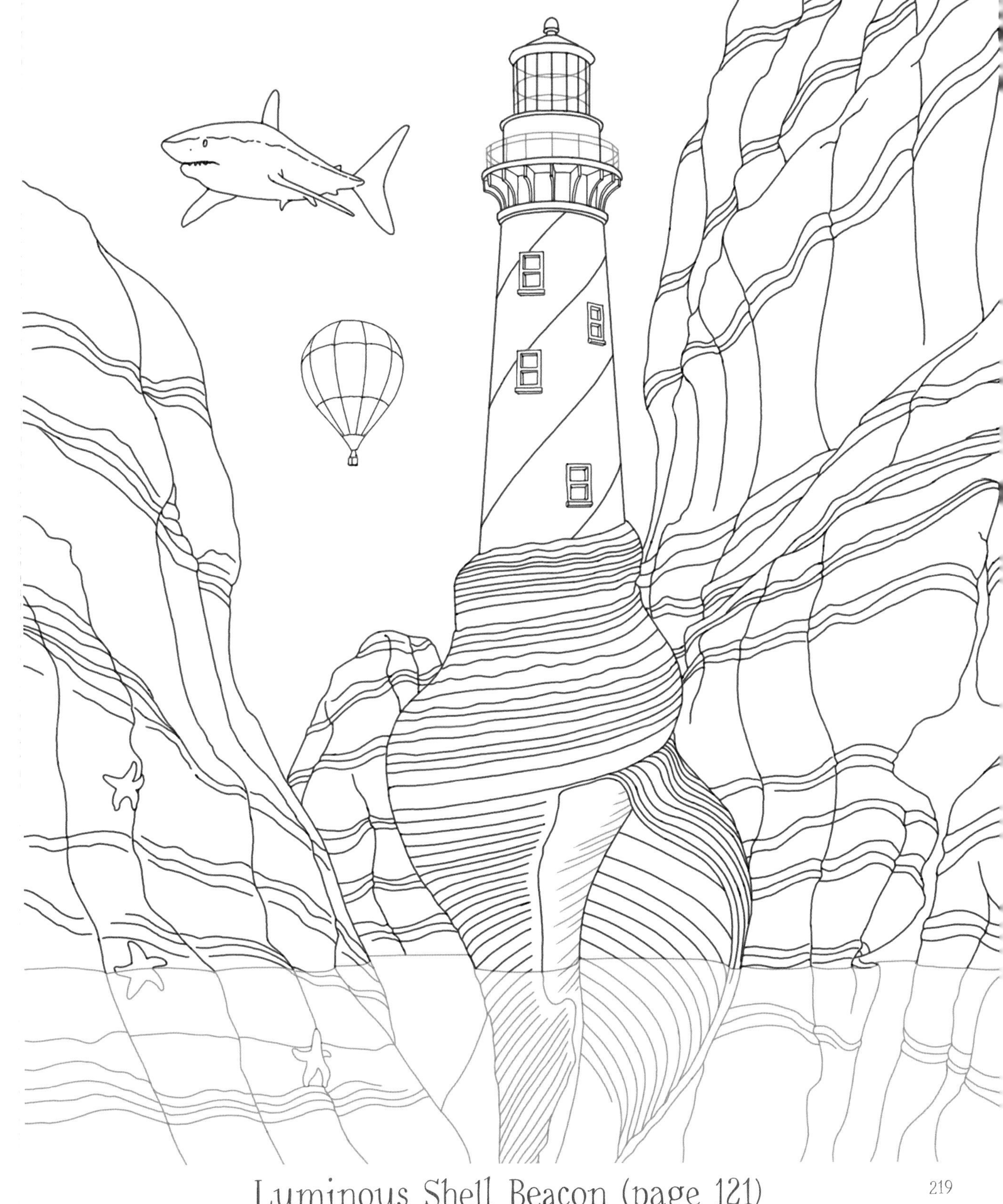

Luminous Shell Beacon (page 121)

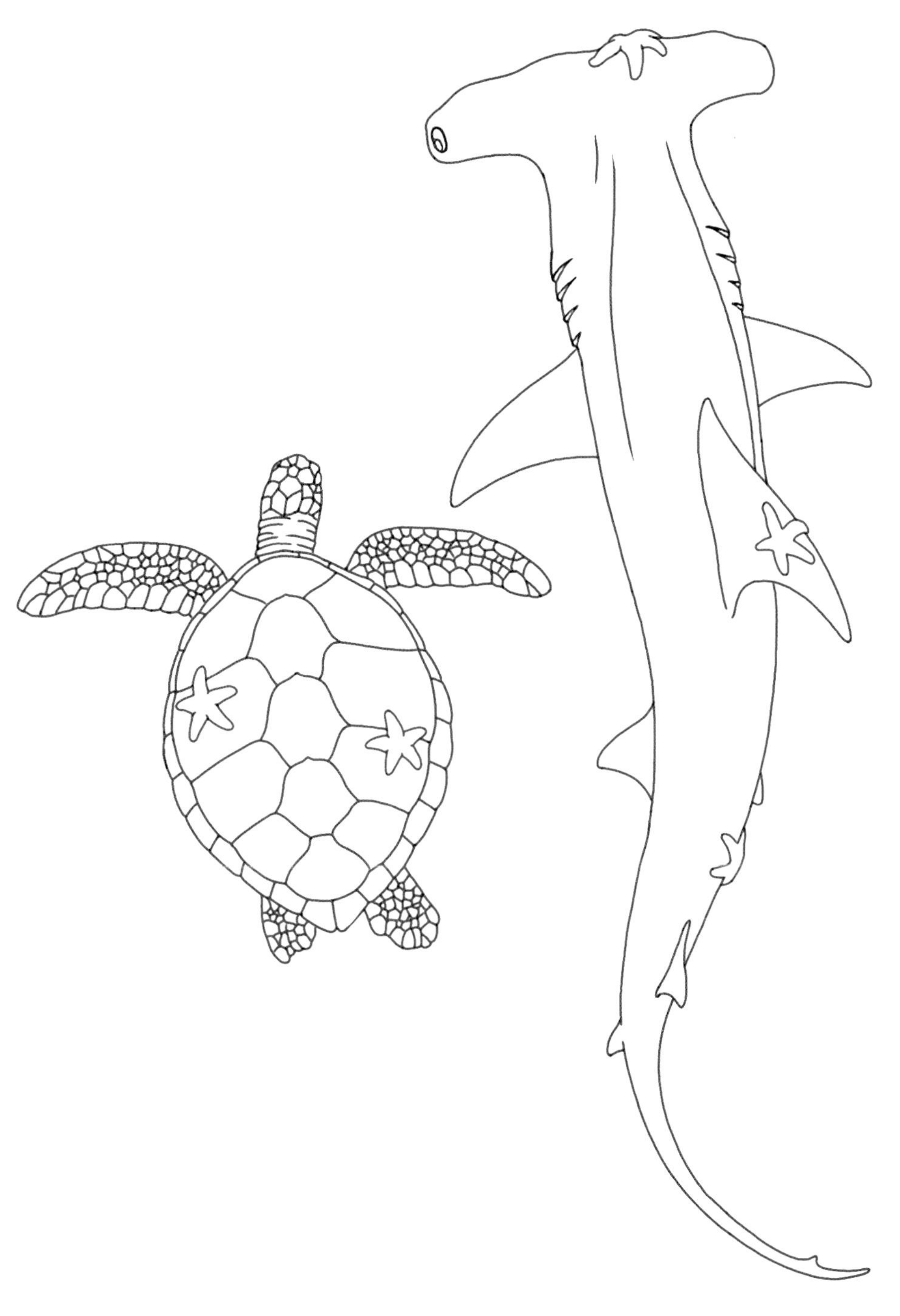

Nebula Navigators (page 131)

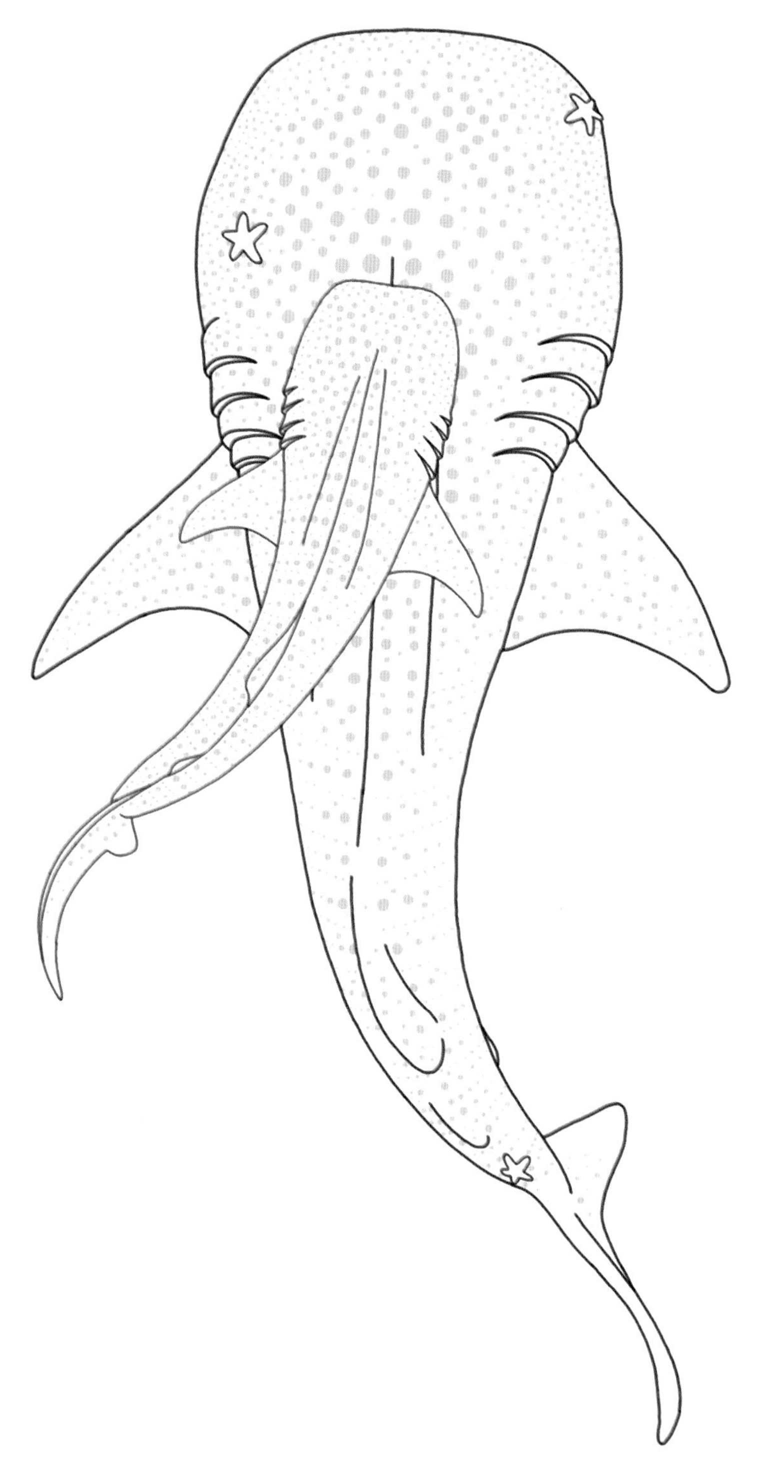

Nurturing Starlit Journey (page 147)

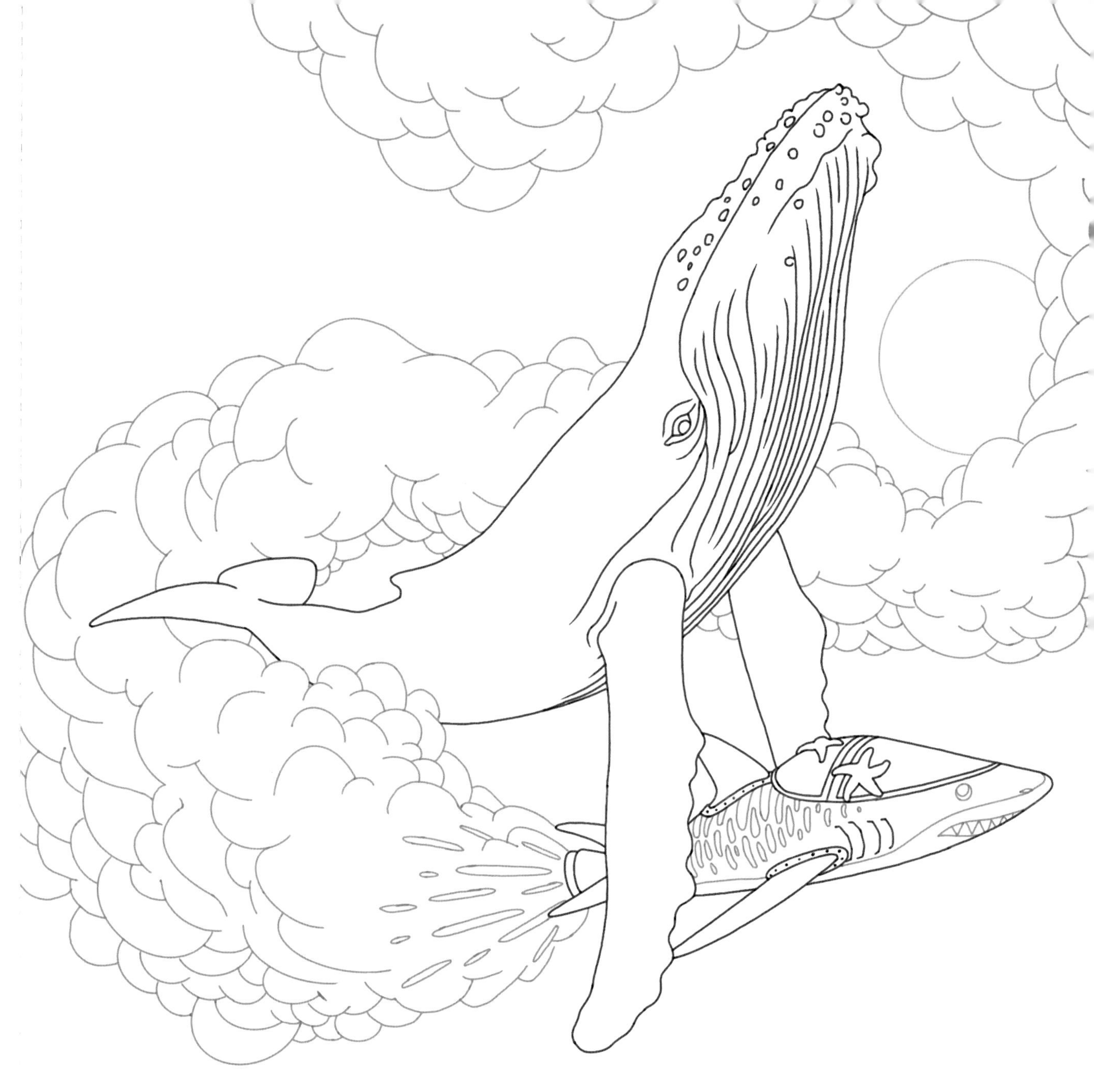

Astral Whaleship (page 155)

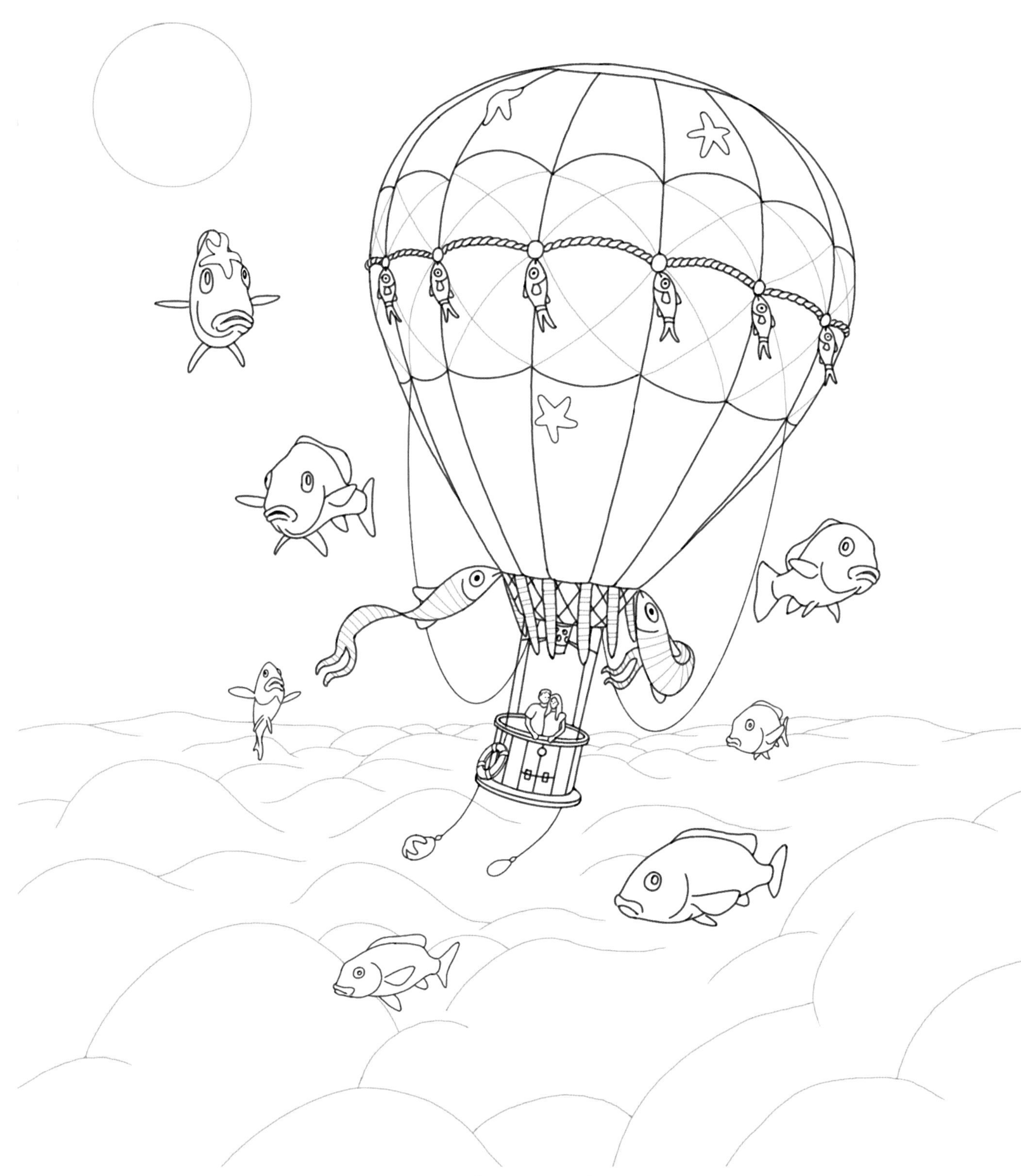

Ballooning Fish Parade (page 165)   229

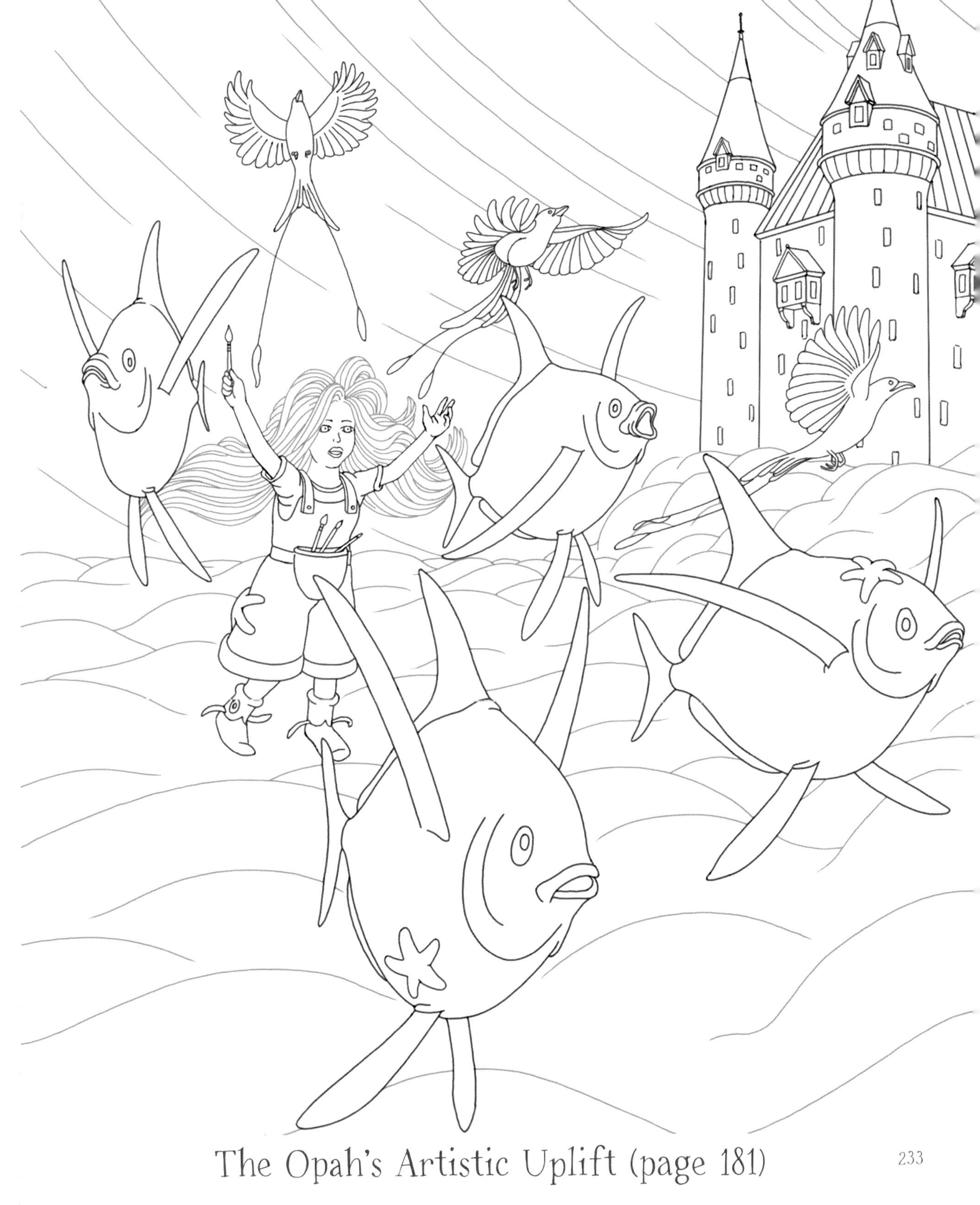

The Opah's Artistic Uplift (page 181)

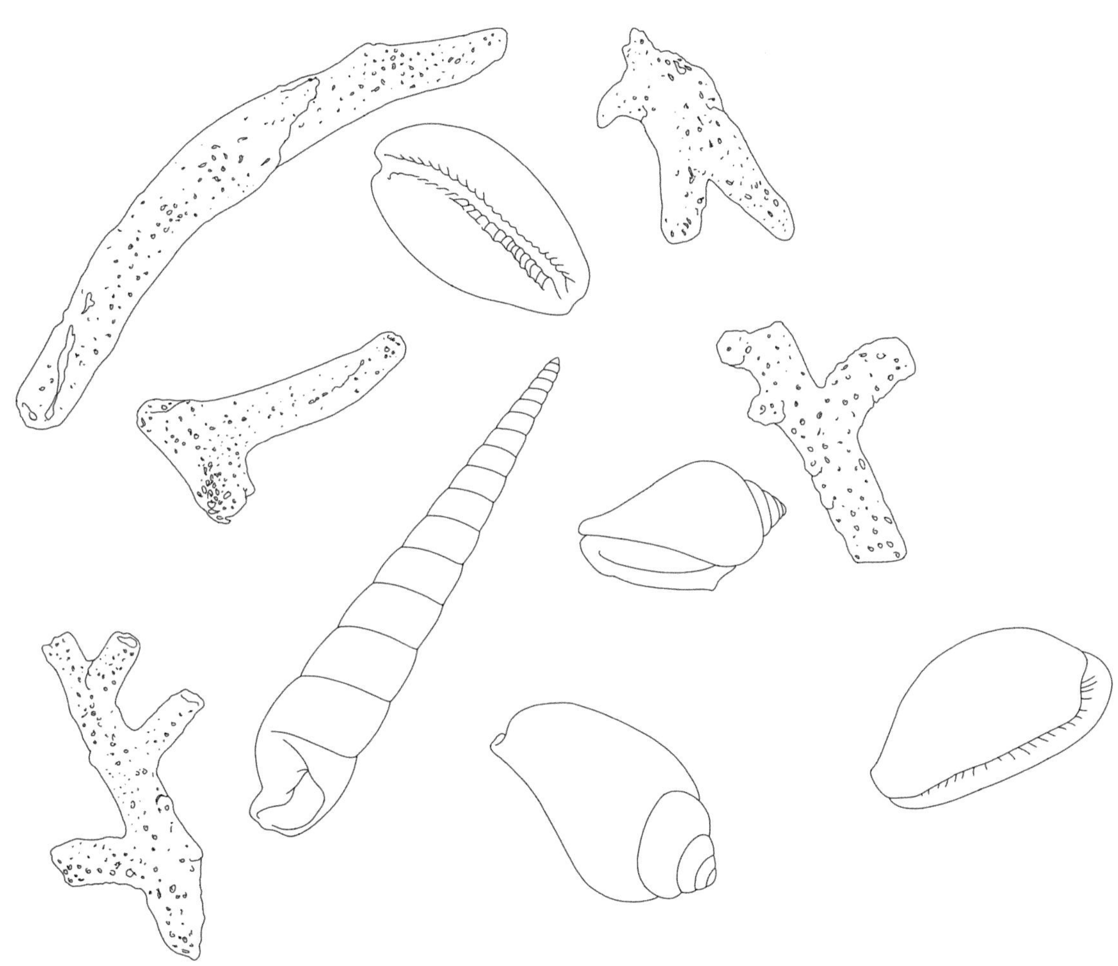

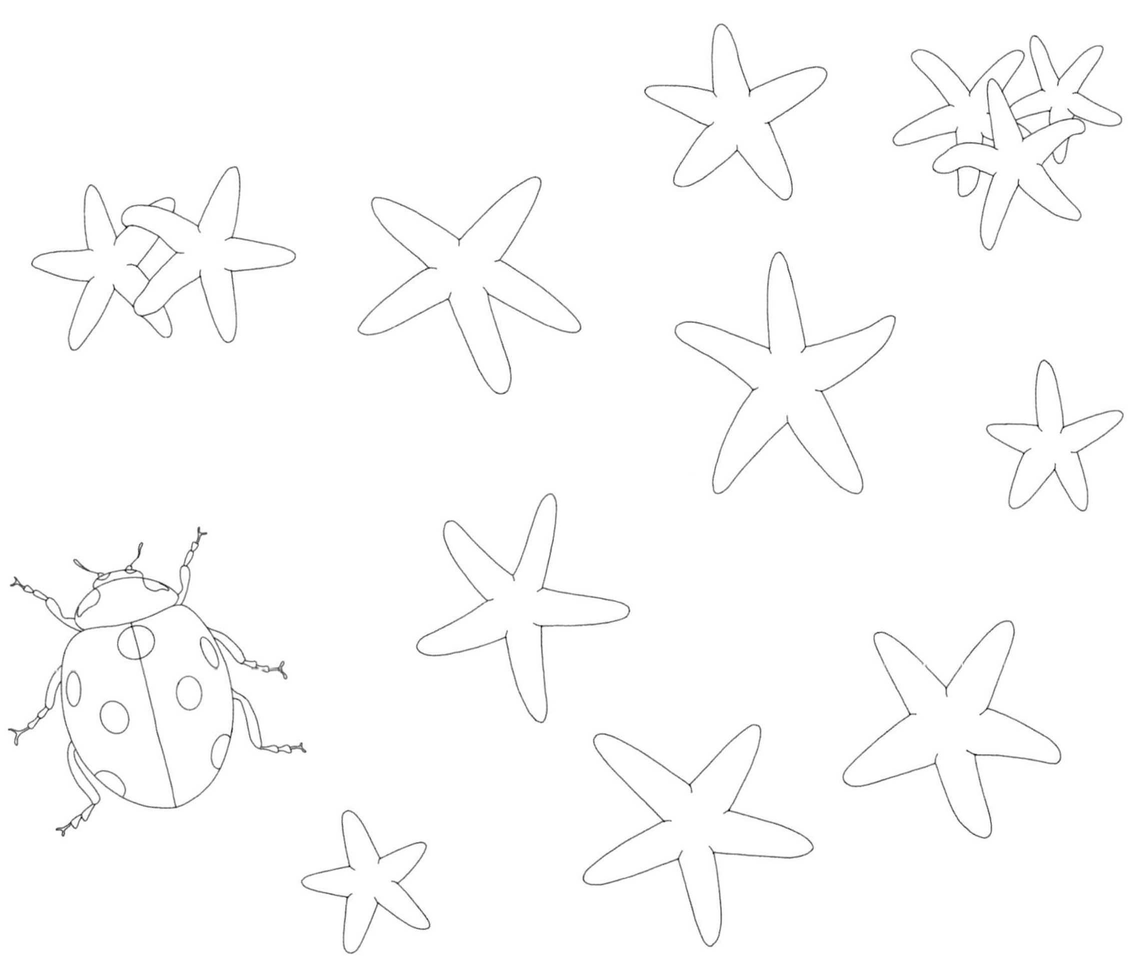

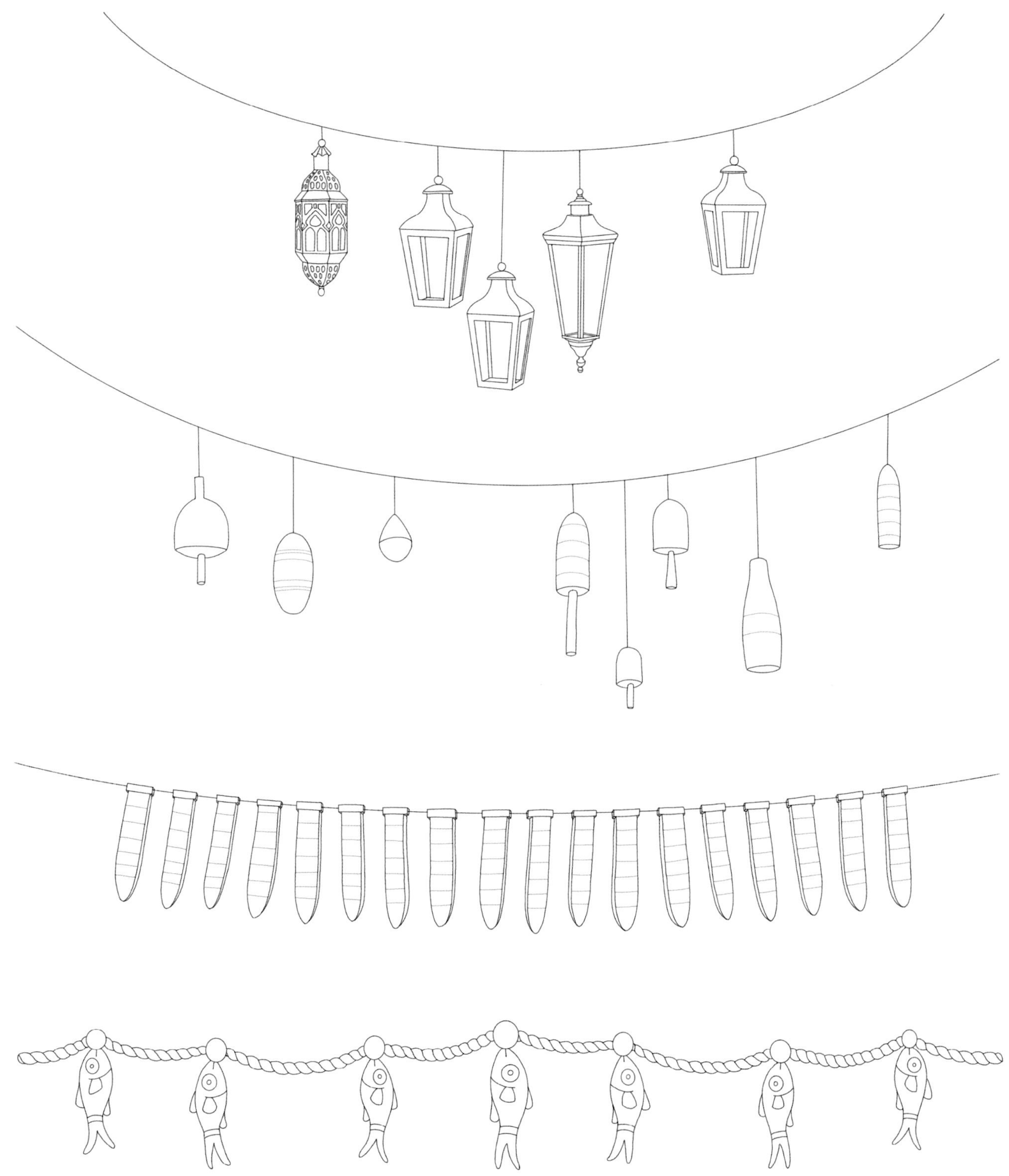